A-Level Year 1 & AS

Economics

Revising for Economics exams is stressful, that's for sure — even just getting your notes sorted out can be seriously taxing. But help is at hand...

This brilliant CGP book covers AQA, OCR and Edexcel Economics A. It explains **everything you'll need to learn** — and of course, it's all written in a straightforward style that's easy to get your head around.

We've also included **exam-style questions** for every topic, along with a section of advice on how to pick up as many marks as possible in the final tests!

A-Level revision? It has to be CGP!

Contents

Section One — The Economic Problem

Section Two — Competitive Markets

Section Three — Business Economics

Section Four — Market Failure

Section Five — Government Intervention

Section Six — Measuring Economic Performance

Section Seven — Aggregate Demand and Aggregate Supply

Section Eight — Government Economic Policy Objectives

Section Nine — Macroeconomic Policy Instruments

Do Well in Your Exam

This book is suitable for:

AQA, OCR, Edexcel Economics A.

There are notes on the pages that tell you which bits you need for your specification:

- Notes at the top of pages in **bold** tell you which exam boards the **page** is for (or **pages** if the topic covers more than one page).
- Notes in the margins point out if **part** of a page is only for some boards.

Published by CGP

Editors:
Chris Lindle, Kirstie McHale, Sarah Oxley

Contributors:
John Grant, Alison Hazell, Samantha Uppal

Proofreaders:
Andy Park, Glenn Rogers, Victoria Skelton

With thanks to Laura Jakubowski for the copyright research.

This book contains data adapted from the Office for National Statistics, licensed under the Open Government Licence v.3.0.
https://www.nationalarchives.gov.uk/doc/open-government-licence/version/3/

Inflation (Consumer Price Index) data on page 133 from databank.worldbank.org
World Development Indicators Source: Integrated Household Survey (IHS) 2012.

Every effort has been made to locate copyright holders and obtain permission to reproduce sources. For those sources where it has been difficult to trace the originator of the work, we would be grateful for information. If any copyright holder would like us to make an amendment to the acknowledgements, please notify us and we will gladly update the book at the next reprint.

ISBN: 978 1 78294 357 0

Printed by Elanders Ltd, Newcastle upon Tyne.
Clipart from Corel®

Based on the classic CGP style created by Richard Parsons.

An Introduction to Economics

So, here it is — your shiny new Economics book. Ready to get down to business... or economics? Good. Let's get cracking.
This page is for AQA, Edexcel and OCR.

Economics is a Social Science

1) Economics is considered to be a **social science** because it looks at the **behaviour** of **humans**, either as individuals or as part of organisations (such as firms and governments), and their use of **scarce resources** (see p.6 for more).
2) The **methodology** that economists use to tackle Economics is **similar** to the methodology used by scientists in **natural** and **other sciences** (e.g. Biology). Economists will:
   - Develop **theories** and create economic **models** to explain phenomena (e.g. how exchange rates are determined).
   - Use **simplifying assumptions** to limit the number of variables in an investigation.
   - **Test** theories and models against relevant known facts, making use of observation, deduction, graphs, statistics and other tools.
   - Use **empirical data** to improve and revise their economic models.
   - Use economic models to make **predictions**.

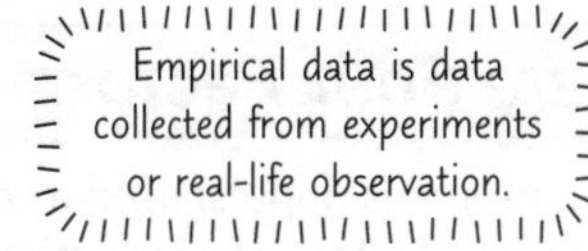
Empirical data is data collected from experiments or real-life observation.

3) However, **unlike** in natural sciences, economists **can't** conduct **controlled laboratory experiments** where only one variable is changed at a time. For example, if an economist examines the impact of price on the demand for cheese, they can't keep consumers' income constant — in the **real world**, income won't remain constant.
4) To get around the problem of the existence of multiple variables in an economy, economists use the **assumption** known as ***ceteris paribus***, which is Latin for '**all other things remaining equal**'.
5) Economists use *ceteris paribus* when they're looking at the **relationship** between **two factors** (e.g. price and demand). They'll **assume** that **only** these two factors change and **all other factors** (e.g. income, changes in taste) that would have an effect on any other variable being considered **remain the same**.
6) Using *ceteris paribus* enables economists to **develop theories** and **models**, and **make predictions**.

Economic Decisions might not always make the most Economic Sense

Because Economics deals with real people, you have to keep in mind that the **decisions** made by **individuals**, **firms** or **governments** will often be based on **opinions** and **judgements**. For example, decisions might be based on:

- **Normative statements** (see below), which are people's **opinions**.
- **Moral views** and **value judgements** (e.g. the view that people shouldn't live in poverty, so wealth should be shared).
- **Political judgements** (e.g. lowering taxes may win votes for a government).
- **Short-term positive consequences** of a decision, regardless of long-term consequences (e.g. reducing taxes may win an election, but it will reduce the government's income and may lead to public spending cuts).

There are Two Kinds of economic statement

Before moving on to more specific things, you need to know about the **two** kinds of **statements** you can make in economics.

POSITIVE statements

Positive statements are **objective** statements that can be **tested** by referring to the available **evidence**.

- For example:
  "A reduction in income will increase the amount of people shopping in pound shops."
- With suitable data collected over a period of time, you should be able to tell if the above claim is true or false.

Positive statements are important because they can be **tested** to see whether **economic ideas** are **correct**.

NORMATIVE statements

Normative statements are **subjective** statements which contain a **value judgement** — they're **opinions**.

- For example:
  "The use of fossil fuels should be taxed more highly than the use of renewable fuels."
- It's not possible to say whether the above statement is true or not — only whether you agree or disagree with it.

Normative statements are also important because **value judgements** influence **decision-making** and **government policy**, e.g. a political party in government may wish to increase taxes for the rich to redistribute income to the poor.

The Economic Problem

If you condensed Economics down to one statement it'd be something like: Economics is all about satisfying infinite wants and needs with limited resources. "What does that mean?", I hear you ask. Well, read on and find out... ***For all boards.***

*Economics — how best to satisfy **Infinite Desires** using **Limited Resources***

1) Everyone has certain basic **needs** in life — e.g. food, water, a place to live, and so on. Everyone also has an infinite list of things they **want** — e.g. designer clothes, smartphones, holidays, houses.
2) However, there's a **limited** amount of **resources** available to satisfy these needs and wants (i.e. resources are **scarce**).
3) These facts lead to the **basic economic problem**:

How can the available **scarce resources** be used to satisfy **people's infinite needs and wants** as effectively as possible?

*There are **Four Factors of Production***

The scarce resources (inputs) used to make the things people want and need (outputs) can be divided into four **factors of production**. These factors are: **Land**, **Labour**, **Capital** and **Enterprise**.

Individuals and firms are rewarded for providing these factors, e.g. with wages or rent.

***Land**: including all the **Natural Resources** in and on it*

As well as actual 'territory', **land** includes all the Earth's **natural resources**:

- **non-renewable** resources, such as natural gas, oil and coal
- **renewable** resources like wind or tidal power, or wood from trees
- **materials** extracted by mining (e.g. diamonds and gold)
- **water**
- **animals** found in an area

Non-renewable resources will eventually run out if we carry on using them.

Renewable resources can regrow or regenerate. But some renewable resources have to be used carefully if they're not to run out — e.g. to be sustainable, enough trees need to be planted to replace those that are used.

1) Nearly all things that fall under the category of 'land' are **scarce** — there **aren't enough** natural resources to satisfy the demands of everyone.
2) One exception is **air**, but even this isn't as simple as it first looks...
   - Air is **not** usually considered a scarce resource — there's enough for **everyone** to have as much as they want.
   - But this **doesn't** mean all air is equally good — air can be **polluted**, as can be seen in a lot of big cities.
   - In fact, the **environment** is considered by some people to be a **scarce resource**.

Because there's enough air for everyone to have as much as they want, in theory it's **impossible** to **sell** it. (*Why would you **buy** it when you can get it **for free**?*) Economists call things like this **free goods**. Things that are **scarce** and which can therefore be traded are known as **economic goods**.

Labour**: the **Work** done by **People

In the UK, the number of people of working age with a job is around 30 million.

1) Labour is the **work done** by those **people** who contribute to the production process. The population who are available to do work is called the **labour force**.
2) There's usually also a number of people who are **capable** of working and who are **old enough** to work, but who **don't** have a job. Economists refer to these people as **unemployed**.
3) There are also people who **aren't** in **paid employment** but still provide things people need or want, e.g. homemakers.
4) Different people have different levels of education, experience or training. These factors can make some people more 'valuable' or productive in the workplace than others — they have a greater amount of **human capital**.

***Capital**: **Equipment** used in producing goods and services*

1) **Capital** is the equipment, factories and schools that help to produce goods or services.
2) **Capital** is different from **land** because capital has to be **made** first.
3) Much of an economy's capital is **paid for** by the **government** — e.g. a country's road network is a form of capital.

Enterprise**: willingness to take a **Risk** to make a **Profit

Enterprise refers to the people (**entrepreneurs**) who take **risks** and create things from the other three factors of production.

1) They set up and run **businesses** using any of the factors of production available to them.
2) If the business **fails**, they can **lose** a lot of money. But if the business **succeeds**, the **reward** for their risk-taking is **profit**.

The Economic Problem

Scarcity requires the Careful Allocation of Resources

1) **Economic activity** involves **combining** the factors of production to create **outputs** that people can **consume**. The **purpose** of any economic activity is to **increase** people's **economic welfare** by creating outputs that **satisfy** their various **needs** and **wants**.
2) In Economics a wide range of things count as **economic activity**.
3) One form of economic activity is the making of **goods** and the provision of **services** (i.e. creating outputs).
   - GOODS: '**Physical**' products you can **touch** — such as washing machines, books or a new factory.
   - SERVICES: '**Intangible**' things — such as medical check-ups, teaching, or train journeys.
4) **Consumption** (i.e. buying or using) is also a form of **economic activity**. When you consume something, you're trying to satisfy a **need** or a **want**. You can consume both goods and services.

Lots of other things are also classified as economic activity, such as doing housework, DIY and bringing up children (even though you might not get paid for doing it).

5) Since there's an **endless** array of things that could be produced and consumed, but only **limited resources**, this leads to three fundamental questions:
   - **What** to produce?
   - **How** to produce it?
   - **Who** to produce it **for**?

Economic Agents react to Incentives

1) The **agents** ('participants') in an economy can usually be thought of as:

   Producers — firms or people that make goods or provide services.
   Consumers — people or firms who buy the goods and services.
   Governments — a government sets the rules that other participants in the economy have to follow, but also produces and consumes goods and services.

2) Each of these **economic agents** has to make **decisions** that affect how resources are allocated. For example:
   - **Producers** decide what to make, and how much they're willing to sell it for.
   - **Consumers** have to decide what they want to buy, and how much they're willing to pay for it.
   - **Governments** have to decide how much to intervene in the way producers and consumers act.
3) In a **market economy** (see page 10), all economic agents are assumed to be **rational** (see page 13), which means they'll make the decisions that are best for **themselves**. These decisions will be based on economic **incentives**, such as making profit or paying as little as possible for a product.
4) Considering people's incentives helps to answer those fundamental questions above.
   - **What to produce?** This will be those goods that firms can make a profit from.
   - **How to produce it?** Firms will want to produce the good in the most efficient way they can, in order to maximise their profits.
   - **Who to produce it for?** Firms will produce goods for consumers who are willing to pay for those goods.

So in effect consumers decide what is to be produced. Producers won't want to produce things that nobody wants to buy.

Practice Questions

Q1 What is the basic economic problem?

Q2 What are the four factors of production? Give an example of each.

Q3 Give three different types of economic agent.

Exam Question

Q1 State and explain three factors of production which would be necessary for opening a new restaurant. [6 marks]

Learn the facts about factors of production...

Economics is a funny one... you might think it's going to be all about banks and money and stuff. But there's a bit of groundwork to do before you get to all of that. It's interesting though, and getting your head around all of this will definitely help you later on. Those four factors of production are at the heart of everything in economics, by the way... so learn them well.

Production Possibility Frontiers

Production possibility frontiers (PPFs) — also known as production possibility curves (PPCs) or production possibility boundaries (PPBs) — show the maximum amount of two goods or services an economy can produce. ***For all boards.***

Production Possibility Frontiers show the Maximum possible output

The basic problem in Economics is how best to allocate scarce resources. A **production possibility frontier** (PPF) shows the options that are available when you consider the production of just **two types** of goods or services.

1) The PPF below shows the **maximum** number of **houses** (on the horizontal axis) and **vehicles** (on the vertical axis) that can be made, using the **existing** level of resources in an economy.

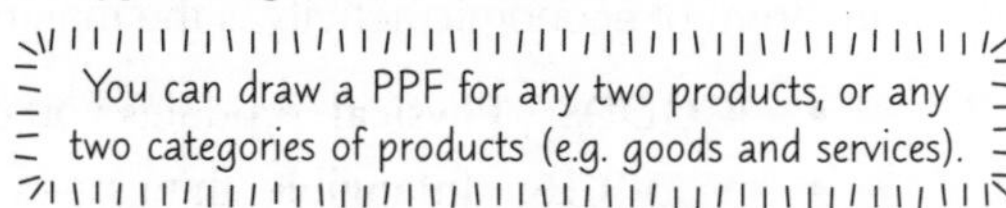

You can draw a PPF for any two products, or any two categories of products (e.g. goods and services).

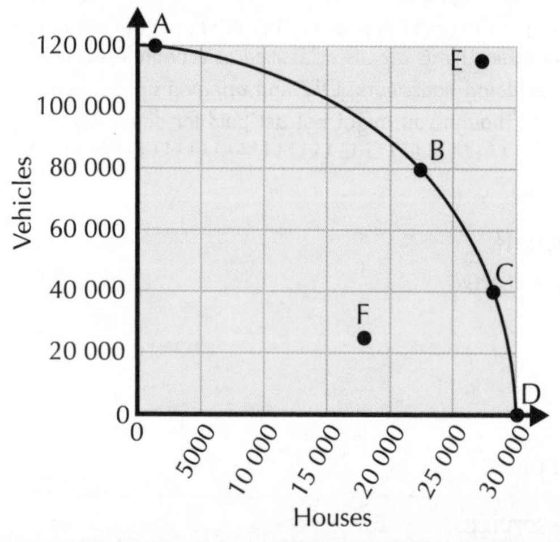

2) Points A, B, C and D (and every other point on the PPF) are all achievable **without** using any **extra** resources. However, they are **only** achievable when **all** the available resources are used as **efficiently** as is actually possible.
   - Notice how, as you move along the curve from A to B, you're building **more houses** (about 22 500 instead of 1000) but **fewer vehicles** (80 000 instead of 120 000).
   - Moving along the curve from A to B like this corresponds to allocating **more resources** to the production of houses, and **fewer resources** to the production of vehicles.
   - In other words, there's a **trade-off** between 'building more houses' and 'making more vehicles' — to do **more** of one, you have to do **less** of the other.

A **trade-off** is when you have to choose between conflicting objectives because you **can't** achieve all your objectives at the **same time**. It involves **compromising**, and aiming to achieve **each** of your objectives **a bit**.

3) All points **on** the PPF are **productively efficient** (see p.59) because all resources are used as efficiently as possible to produce the **maximum possible output**. **Not** all points on the PPF are **allocatively efficient**. This is because not all points will reflect the allocation of resources that lead to the production of goods which **maximise consumer satisfaction** (fulfil people's wants or needs). E.g. if all resources are used to produce vehicles, this might not match society's need for houses.

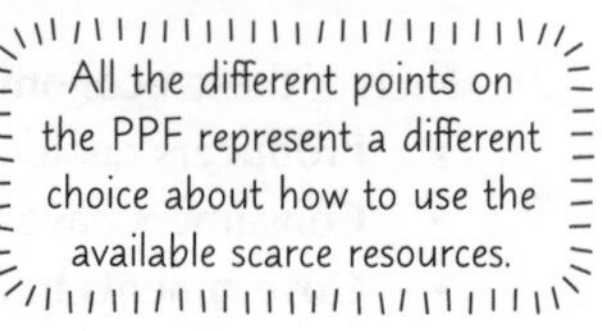

All the different points on the PPF represent a different choice about how to use the available scarce resources.

4) Point E lies **outside** the PPF, so it **isn't achievable** using the **current level** of resources in the economy. To build that many houses and vehicles at the same time, **extra** (or **better**) **resources** would need to be found.
5) Point F lies **inside** the PPF (rather than **on** it) — this means making this mix of goods is **productively inefficient**. With the current level of resources, you could build more houses **without** making fewer vehicles (or more vehicles **without** making fewer houses).

Opportunity Cost is the next best thing that you're forced to give up

1) The trade-off described above involves an **opportunity cost**.
2) An opportunity cost is what you **give up** in order to do something else — i.e. it's the cost of any choice that's made.
3) So moving from A to B on the PPF above means you have the opportunity to build 21 500 extra houses as long as you **give up** the opportunity to make 40 000 vehicles. In other words, the **opportunity cost** of building 21 500 extra houses is the lost production of 40 000 vehicles.

The **opportunity cost** of a decision is the **next best alternative** that you **give up** in making that decision.

4) Opportunity cost is a key concept in Economics which is used to ensure a more **efficient allocation** of **resources**. For example, **consumers** use the concept to **choose** what to **spend** their **income** on; **producers** use it to look at the **profit forgone** by not making an **alternative product**; and **governments** use it to look at the **lost value** to **society** from the policies they choose **not** to implement.
5) However, there are some **problems** with using the concept of opportunity cost:
   - Often, not all alternatives are known.
   - Some factors don't have alternative uses.
   - There may be a lack of information on alternatives and their costs.
   - Some factors (e.g. land) can be hard to switch to an alternative use.

Production Possibility Frontiers

Economic Growth shifts the PPF

1) A PPF shows what's possible using a **particular level** of resources (e.g. a particular number of people, a particular amount of capital and raw materials, and so on).
2) If this level of resources is **fixed**, then movements **along** the PPF just show a **reallocation** of those resources.
3) However, if the total amount of resources **changes**, then the PPF itself **moves**.
   - For example, **increased resources** (e.g. an increase in the total number of workers) would mean that the total possible **output** of that economy would also **increase** — so the PPF **shifts outward.**
   - For the economy shown by this PPF, the extra output could be **either** more houses **or** more vehicles **or** a combination of both.

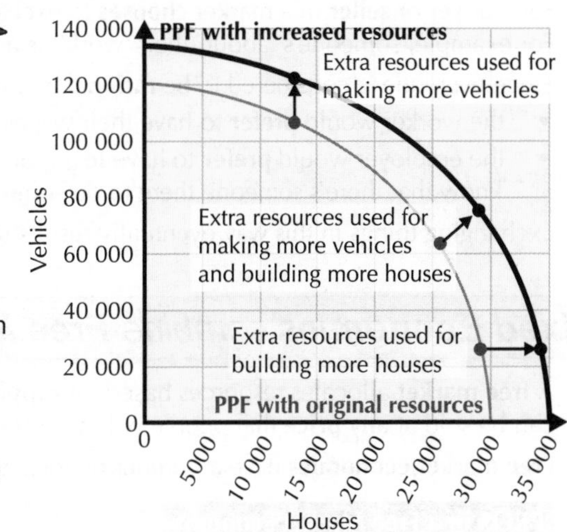

4) **Improved technology** or **improvements** to **labour** (e.g. through training) can also shift the PPF outwards, because it allows **more output** to be produced using the **same resources**.
5) An **outward shift** of the PPF shows **economic growth**.
6) When **fewer** total resources are available (e.g. after some kind of **natural disaster**), the opposite happens — the PPF **shifts inwards**, showing that the total possible output has **shrunk**. This shows **negative economic growth**.

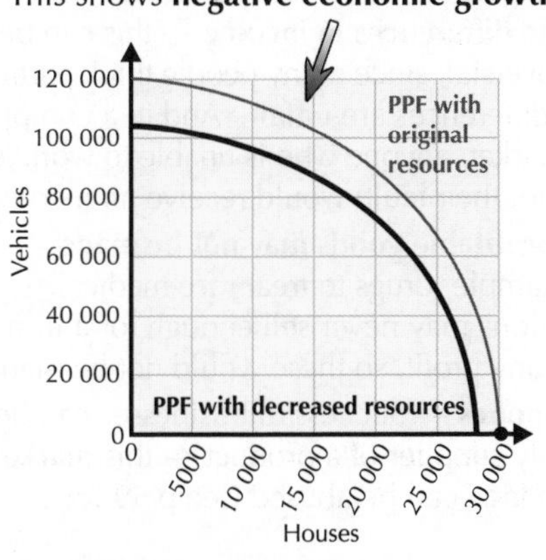

7) In this example, the possible output has **grown** because of improved technology. However, this particular technology can only help with **house-building** — this means the PPF has been stretched in only the **horizontal direction**.

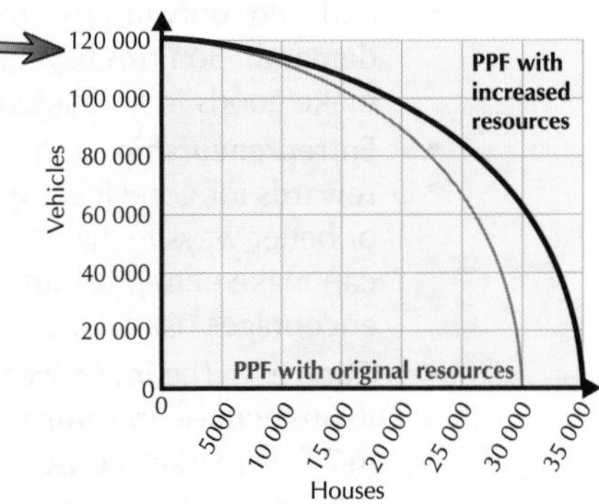

Practice Questions

Q1 Explain what a production possibility frontier (PPF) shows.

Q2 What is meant by a trade-off?

Q3 Describe why a PPF might move outwards. What does it mean if it moves inwards?

Exam Questions

Q1 Look at the diagram on the right. Which of the following combinations of cars and butter cannot currently be produced in this economy using the existing resources?

A) Only W
B) Only X
C) Only W, Y and Z
D) Only Y and Z

[1 mark]

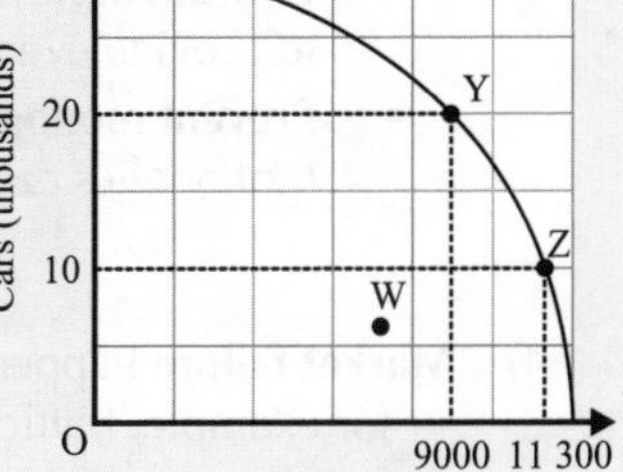

Q2 Use the diagram on the right to explain the term opportunity cost. [5 marks]

Decisions, decisions, decisions...

It's important to get your head round these PPFs. Think of different points on a PPF as representing different decisions you could make about how you want to allocate your all-too-scarce resources. Then they don't seem (quite) as bad.

Markets and Economies

Markets are a way to allocate resources to different economic activities. But sometimes governments decide that things would work out better if things weren't left entirely up to the market. ***These pages are for all boards.***

Markets are a method for Allocating Scarce Resources

1) **Markets** are a way of **allocating resources**. They **don't** have to be a place, or involve the exchange of physical objects.
2) Each **buyer** or **seller** in a market **chooses** to exchange something they have for something they'd prefer to have instead. For example, someone's labour (their 'work') is a resource. If they have a job, they exchange their labour for a salary.
3) Since everyone is considered to be **rational** in a free market (see p.13), an economist would assume that:
   - the worker would **prefer** to have their wages, but less free time,
   - the employer would **prefer** to have less money, and to know that there's someone there to do some work.

Any exchange can only happen because different people or organisations value things differently.

4) Exchanging things in this way eventually results in a particular **allocation of resources**.

Mixed Economies combine Free Markets and Government Intervention

1) A **free market** allocates resources based on **supply and demand** and the **price mechanism**. In other words, **anything** can be sold at **any price** that people will pay for it. (See Section 2 for more about the free market.)
2) **Free market economies** have a number of advantages... but there are also some downsides.

PROS of a Free Market Economy

- **Efficiency** — As **any** product can be bought and sold, only those of the **best value** will be **in demand**. So firms have an **incentive** to try to make goods in as efficient a way as possible.
- **Entrepreneurship** — In a market economy, the **rewards** for good ideas (e.g. new, better products, or better ways to make existing products) can make entrepreneurs a lot of money. This encourages risk-taking and innovation.
- **Choice** — The **incentives** for innovation can lead to an increase in **choice** for consumers. (And in a free market, consumers aren't restricted to buying only what the government recommends.)

CONS of a Free Market Economy

- **Inequalities** — Market economies can lead to huge **differences in income** — this can be controversial, since many people think particularly large differences are **unfair**. And in a completely free market, anyone who is unable to work (even if it's not their fault) would receive no income.
- **Non-profitable goods may not be made** — For example, drugs to treat **rare** medical conditions may never sell enough for a firm to make any profit, so these would not be made.
- **Monopolies** — Successful businesses can become the only supplier of a product — this **market dominance** can be abused (see p.59).

3) In a **command** (or **planned**) economy, it's the **government** (not markets) that decides how resources should be allocated. **Communist countries** (e.g. the former USSR) have command economies, but they're **much rarer** since the **collapse** of **communism** in the **late 20th century**. However, some countries **still** have command economies, such as **North Korea**.

PROS of a Command Economy

- **Maximise welfare** — Governments have more control over the economy, so they can **prevent inequality** and **redistribute income fairly**. They can also ensure the production of goods that people **need** and are **beneficial** to **society**.
- **Low unemployment** — The government can try to provide everyone with a **job** and a **salary**.
- **Prevent monopolies** — The market dominance of monopolies can be **prevented** by the government.

CONS of a Command Economy

- **Poor decision-making** — A **lack of information** means that governments may make **poor** (and **slow**) **decisions** about what needs to be produced.
- **Restricted choice** — Consumers have a **limited choice** in what they can **consume**, and firms will make what they're **told** to make.
- **Lack of risk-taking and efficiency** — Government-owned firms have **no incentive** to **increase efficiency**, **take risks** or **innovate**, because they **don't** need to make profit.

4) **Market failure** happens when free markets result in **undesirable outcomes** — for example, traffic congestion is seen as a market failure.

See Section 4 for more about market failure.

5) **Governments** often intervene when there's a market failure.
   - They might **change the law**, or **offer tax breaks** (e.g. reduce taxes for anyone carrying out particular activities), or create some other kind of **incentive** to try to influence people's behaviour.
   - Governments can also intervene in the economy by **buying** or **providing** goods or services.
6) When both the **government** and **markets** play a part in allocating resources, this is called a **mixed economy**.

Markets and Economies

A Mixed Economy has a Public Sector and a Private Sector

1) In a mixed economy, the government is known as the **public sector**.
2) Businesses that are privately owned make up the **private sector**.
3) Private-sector organisations usually have to **break even** or make a **profit** to survive.
4) **Most** countries have a mixed economy, including the UK — there are **no** purely free market economies where the government doesn't intervene in some way.
5) In a **pure free market economy** there would be **no public sector** and in a **pure command economy** there would be **no private sector**.

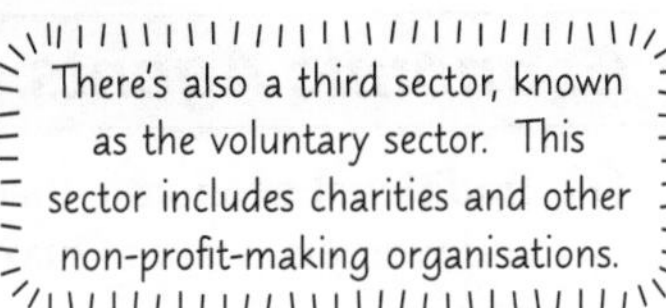

There's also a third sector, known as the voluntary sector. This sector includes charities and other non-profit-making organisations.

EDEXCEL ONLY

Smith, Marx and Hayek were Influential Economic Thinkers

Adam Smith (1723-1790)

- Smith's ideas have shaped **traditional economic theory**. He was a big believer in the **free market** and described how its '**invisible hand**' would **allocate resources** in **society's best interests.**
- He said that this came about because **consumers** and **producers** are motivated by **self-interest** — consumers are motivated to **maximise** their **own benefits** and **producers** are **motivated** to **maximise profit** (this is known as **rational self-interest** — see p.12). In the free market, consumers' **demand** and producers' **supply** will lead to price levels being set at a point which benefits them **both** (for more on the price mechanism, see p.26).
- Smith pointed out that in order for the free market to **work properly** there **couldn't** be any **monopolies** and there would have to be **low barriers to entry** (see p.46) to **maximise competition** (see p.44).
- Smith also wrote about **specialisation** and the **division of labour** — there's more on that on p.37.

Karl Marx (1818-1883)

- Marx was **critical** of the **free market** and argued that it created a situation where a **small ruling class** of **producers** (the **bourgeoisie**) **dominated** and **exploited** the **larger** working class of **wage earners** (the **proletariat**).
- Marx argued that **profit-maximising** bourgeois producers would **exploit** workers (e.g. paying them low wages and giving them few rights) until the proletariat eventually rose up in a **revolution** and took over. This would then lead to the workers **controlling production** and **everyone** having a **share** in the **ownership** of **resources**.
- Marx's ideas led to the rise of **communism** in the **20th century**, but his ideas contained little about **how command economies** would work. Many communist countries **collapsed** in the late 20th century, which led to the **discrediting** of communism and command economies, but Marx's ideas are becoming more popular now.

Friedrich Hayek (1899-1992)

- Hayek was a **keen supporter** of the **free market system** and a **critic** of **command economies**. He argued that governments **shouldn't intervene** to **allocate resources** because governments **lack** the **information** required to allocate them in the way that's most beneficial to society.
- Hayek believed that **individual** consumers and producers have the **best knowledge** of what they **want** or **need**, and so the allocation of resources should be left to them and the **price mechanism**.
- Hayek saw the price mechanism as a way for producers and consumers to **communicate** (this is the idea of price acting as a **signalling device** between consumers and producers, see p.26). The price level set by the forces of supply and demand would show what both consumers and producers **want** and will naturally allocate resources in a much more **efficient** way than governments can.

Practice Questions

Q1 Give two advantages and two disadvantages of a free market economy.

Q2 Explain what is meant by the terms: 'mixed economy', 'public sector' and 'private sector'.

Exam Question

Q1 Explain why a command economy tends to lead to a lack of efficiency. [5 marks]

Do some economics exam practice — but don't forget to market...

Free markets are one of those things that sound really good in theory, but in practice one or two problems tend to crop up. This is why mixed economies are currently all the rage in world economics (apart from in a couple of places).

Economic Objectives and Rationality

Before we get stuck into the objectives of different economic agents and how these agents act rationally (or not), you need to learn a little bit of background theory on maximising utility. Worry not, it'll all make sense soon. ***All boards.***

Economic Agents are assumed to be *Utility Maximisers*

Utility roughly means 'well-being', 'happiness' or 'satisfaction'.

1) **Traditional economic theory assumes** that economic agents (e.g. producers, consumers and workers) want to **maximise** their **utility**.
2) **Different** economic agents will have **different ways** of maximising their utility, e.g. a consumer may want to maximise their happiness, and a producer may wish to maximise their profit (see below).
3) Traditional economists argue that in order to maximise utility, economic agents must act **rationally**. This means that they'll make decisions based **solely** on trying to gain the maximum utility possible and **nothing else** will influence their decision making.

You can read about profit-maximising on p.43.

You need to understand How Consumers act Rationally

1) To fully understand how **consumers** act rationally you need to know about **marginal utility**, **total utility** and the **law of diminishing marginal utility**:
   - **Marginal utility** is the **benefit** gained from consuming **one additional** unit of a good.
   - **Total utility** is the **overall benefit** gained from consuming a good.
   - The **law of diminishing marginal utility** states that for **each additional unit** of a good that's consumed, the **marginal utility** gained **decreases**. For example, each additional biscuit eaten gives a consumer **less satisfaction** than the previous one.
2) A **rational consumer** will choose to consume a good at the point where **marginal utility = price**. E.g. if the utility a person gains from eating a chocolate biscuit is worth 10p, then a rational consumer will pay 10p for it. If the utility gained from consuming a second biscuit is worth 8p, then that consumer will only want to pay 8p for the second biscuit.
3) If marginal utility **decreases** with each extra good consumed then the **price** a consumer is willing to pay for each extra good will **decrease**. It's this law of diminishing marginal utility that explains why the **demand curve slopes downwards** (see p.14).

"Biscuits... diminish in utility? Not likely!"

Different Economic Agents will have different Economic Objectives

Economic agents will usually have different **objectives**, but quite often these objectives are to **maximise** a particular quantity (e.g. profit). This page describes some of the **traditional assumptions** made about the objectives of economic agents, but includes a few other objectives too.

PRODUCERS

1) A firm's **profit** is their **total revenue** (money received by the firm, e.g. from sales) minus their **total costs**.
2) Firms are traditionally assumed to want to maximise **profit** — this could be for **various** reasons:
   - Profit means the firm can **survive** — loss-making firms might eventually have to close.
   - Greater profits allow firms to offer better **rewards** to the **owner** (or **shareholders**) and **staff**...
   - ...or profit can be **reinvested** in the business in the hope of making even more profits later. For example, a firm might want to invest in order to **expand**.
3) But firms may want to maximise other quantities instead, such as **total sales** or the firm's **market share**.
   - A large **market share** could lead to some **monopoly power** (see p.46) — this would mean that the firm could charge higher prices due to a lack of competition.
   - Bigger firms are often considered more **prestigious** and **stable**, so they can attract the best employees.
4) Some firms may also have **ethical objectives** — i.e. 'doing some good', even if it **doesn't** increase profits. For example, a firm may decide to buy all its raw materials from nearby suppliers in order to support the **local economy**, even if cheaper alternatives are available elsewhere.

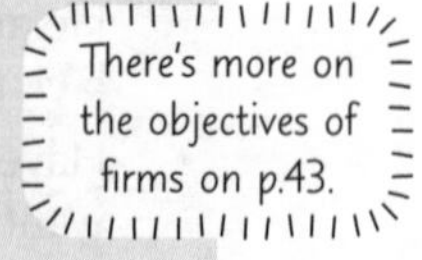
There's more on the objectives of firms on p.43.

CONSUMERS

1) **Consumers** are traditionally assumed to want to **maximise** their **utility**, while not spending more than their income (i.e. while living within their means).
   - **Utility** will involve **different things** for different people — e.g. some people might value the **security** of making large pension contributions, while others might want to **spend** their money on things like holidays.
   - But whatever someone spends their money on, it's assumed they'll act **rationally** to increase their utility in the way that makes most sense to them.
2) Consumers can also act as workers — **workers** are assumed to want to **maximise** their **income**, while having as much **free time** as they need or want.

Economic Objectives and Rationality

GOVERNMENTS

1) **Governments** try to balance the **resources** of a country with the **needs and wants** of the population — i.e. economists assume that governments try to **maximise the 'public interest'**.
2) This is likely to include some or all of the following:
   - **Economic growth** — usually measured by growth in a country's **GDP**. ← Gross domestic product (see p.72).
   - **Full employment** — everybody of a working age, who is capable of working, having a job.
   - **Equilibrium in the balance of payments** — a balance between the payments **into** the country over a period of time and the payments **out**.
   - **Low inflation** — keeping prices under control, as high inflation can cause serious problems.
3) In practice, these are **competing objectives** — policies that help achieve one objective may make it **more difficult** to achieve another (e.g. extra government spending may help create jobs, but it could lead to higher inflation). See p.107-109 for more information.

Rationality is used to explain the actions of Economic Agents

EDEXCEL ONLY

1) Using the concept of utility maximisation, it's **assumed** that a **rational individual** (sometimes referred to as '***homo economicus***') will attempt to **maximise** their **utility** (or economic profit). They do this by **comparing** the **costs** and **benefits** of **alternatives**, and then choosing the option that maximises their net utility (or net profit).
2) However, acting rationally requires all economic agents to have the **information** they need to be able to **correctly** choose between alternatives. Traditional economic theories assume that everyone has **perfect** (or **symmetric**) **information** and the **ability** to **use** this information to make a **rational decision**.
3) In **real life**, economic agents will likely have **imperfect information** — they **won't** have all the information they need to make a rational decision and this will lead to **market failure** (for more see p.56).
4) **Asymmetric information** is another problem that **prevents rationality**. Asymmetric information occurs when **one party** has **more information** than the other in a transaction. For example, sellers often have more information than buyers as a seller will know how much a product actually cost to make and what its true value is (see p.56).
5) As a result, some economists believe that **rationality alone** can't be used to **predict** consumer behaviour.

There are Many Reasons why consumers Don't act Rationally

EDEXCEL ONLY

There are several reasons why people might not make rational decisions. These include:

- **Habitual behaviour** — doing the **same thing over and over again**, e.g. individuals often choose to shop at the **same place** regardless of any rational reason for going **somewhere else**.
- **Weakness at computation** — people **might not** be able to **process** and **evaluate** the **vast amounts** of **data** involved in making a decision, and they **might not** be very good at **calculating** the **costs** of alternatives.
- **Social norms** — an individual's behaviour can be **influenced** by the behaviour of their **social group** (this could be anything from a friendship group to the population of the whole world). For example, an individual may stop buying cigarettes if none of their friends smoke.
- **Consumer inertia** — individuals may be **too busy** to make a rational decision, or they might be **resistant to change** as it seems like too much effort. For example, individuals might be unwilling to spend the time and energy needed to shop around for the best value deal on car insurance.

Practice Questions

Q1 Describe two economic objectives a firm might have.

Q2 What are governments assumed to be trying to maximise?

Q3 Describe one reason why consumers might not make rational decisions.

Exam Question

Q1 Explain what is traditionally assumed to be the main economic objective of consumers. [2 marks]

Economic agents — they like to maximise stuff and they're deadly with a gun...

The objectives of economic agents discussed here are based on traditional views of what these agents wish to maximise. However, these views are challenged by some economists who don't believe that all economic agents are rational. For example, they think that consumers' decisions can be influenced, so they won't always make fully informed, rational decisions.

Demand

Section 2 is all about markets, and to understand markets you'll need to know everything there is to know about demand and supply. Working out what demand is seems like a good place to start — so go on, get reading... ***These pages are for all boards.***

Markets *are where* ***Goods*** *and* ***Services*** *are* ***Bought*** *and* ***Sold***

1) A **market** is anywhere **buyers** and **sellers** can exchange **goods** or **services**.
2) **Sub-markets** are smaller markets that **make up** a **market**. For example, the labour market is made up of lots of sub-markets, e.g. the markets for teachers, engineers and doctors.
3) The **price charged** for and **quantity sold** of each good or service are **determined** by the levels of **demand** and **supply** in a market.
4) The levels of demand and supply in a market are shown using **diagrams**. These diagrams demonstrate the price level and quantity demanded/supplied of goods or services.

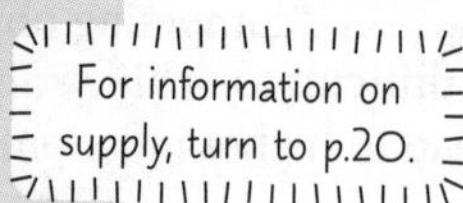
For information on supply, turn to p.20.

Demand *for* ***Goods*** *or* ***Services*** *is* ***Different*** *at* ***Different Prices***

1) **Demand** is the **quantity** of a good/service that consumers are **willing and able** to buy at a **given price**, at a **particular time**.
2) A **demand curve** shows the relationship between **price** and **quantity demanded**. At any given point along the curve it shows the **quantity** of the good or service that would be bought at a particular **price**.
3) Here's an example of a demand curve:

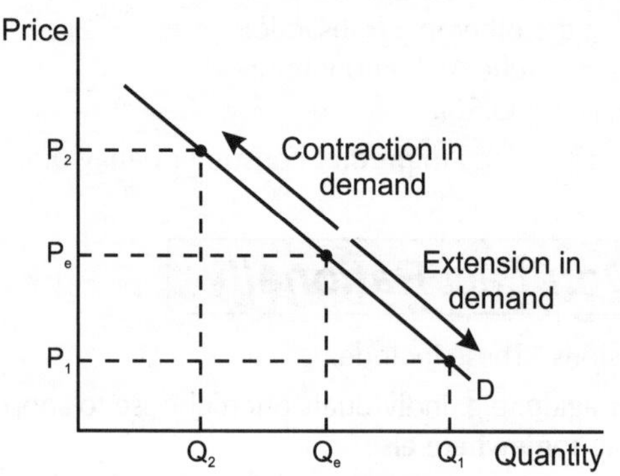

- At price P_e the quantity Q_e is demanded.
- A **decrease** in price from P_e to P_1 causes an **extension** in demand — it **rises** from Q_e to Q_1.
- An **increase** in price from P_e to P_2 causes a **contraction** in demand — it **falls** from Q_e to Q_2.
- So, **movement along the demand curve** is caused by **changes in price**.

Demand curves can be curved but are more often drawn as straight lines. They're usually labelled with a 'D'.

4) Demand curves usually **slope downwards**. This means that the **higher** the **price** charged for a good, the **lower** the **quantity demanded** — as shown by the diagram above.
5) In general, consumers aim to pay the **lowest price possible** for goods and services. As prices decrease **more consumers** are **willing and able** to purchase a good or service — so **lower prices** means **higher demand**.
6) The **relationship** between **price** and **quantity demanded** can also be explained using the **law of diminishing marginal utility** (see p.12).

Changes in Demand *cause a* ***Shift*** *in the* ***Demand Curve***

1) A demand curve moves to the **left** (e.g. D_1) when there is a **decrease** in the **amount demanded** at **every price**.
2) A demand curve shifts to the **right** (e.g. D_2) when there is an **increase** in the **amount demanded** at **every price**.

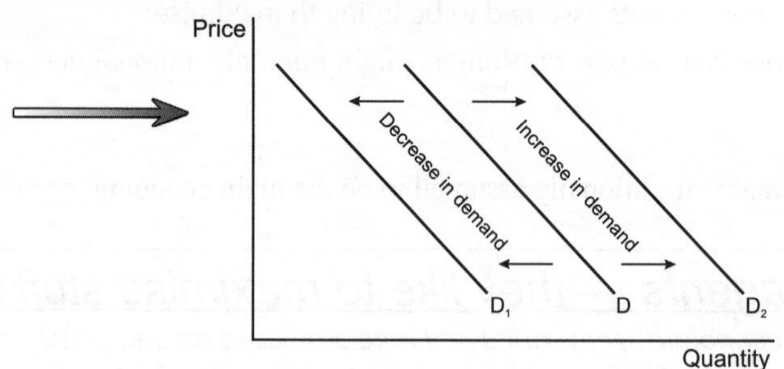

Demand

There are lots of **Factors** that can **Cause** a **Shift** in the **Demand Curve**

1) Changes in tastes and fashion can cause demand curves to shift to the **right** if something is **popular** and to the **left** when it is **out of fashion**.
2) Changes to people's **real income**, the amount of goods/services that a consumer can afford to purchase with their income, can affect the **demand** for **different types** of goods differently.

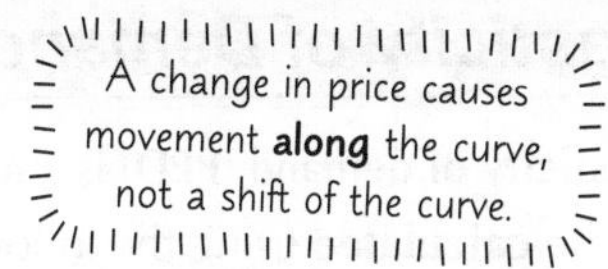

A change in price causes
movement **along** the curve,
not a shift of the curve.

- **Normal goods** (e.g. DVDs) are those which people will demand **more** of if their **real income increases**. This means that a **rise** in real income causes the **demand curve** to **shift** to the **right** — people want to buy more of the good at each price level.
- **Inferior goods** (e.g. cheap clothing) are those which people demand **less** of if their real income increases. This means that a **rise** in real income causes the **demand curve** to **shift** to the **left** — people demand less at each price level since they'll often switch to more expensive goods instead.
- A more **equal distribution** of income (i.e. a reduction in the difference between the incomes of rich and poor people) may cause the demand curve for **luxury goods** (e.g. sports cars) to shift to the **left** — and the demand curve for other items to shift to the **right**. This is because there'll be **fewer** really **rich** people who can afford **luxury** items, and **more** people who can afford **everyday** items.

Changes in demand in **One Market** can affect demand in **Other Markets**

Some markets are **interrelated**, which means that changes in **one** market **affect** a **related** market.

- **Substitute goods** are those which are alternatives to each other — e.g. beef and lamb. An **increase** in the **price** of one good will **decrease** the **demand** for it and **increase** the **demand** for its **substitutes** (this is also known as '**competitive demand**').
- **Complementary goods** are goods that are **often used together**, so they're in **joint demand** — e.g. strawberries and cream. If the **price** of strawberries **increases**, demand for them will **decrease** along with **demand** for cream.
- The introduction of a **new product** may cause the demand curve to shift to the **left** for goods that are **substitutes** for the new product and to the **right** for goods that are **complementary** to it.
- **Derived demand** is the demand for a good or a factor of production used in making another good or service. For example, an **increase** in the demand for **fencing** will lead to an **increased** derived demand for **wood**.
- Some goods have more than one use, e.g. oil can be used to make plastics or for fuel — this is **composite demand**. This means changes in the **demand curve** for **fuel** could lead to changes in the **demand curve** for **plastics**.

Practice Questions

Q1 What causes a movement along a demand curve?

Q2 What causes a shift in a demand curve?

Q3 What are normal goods?

Q4 Give four examples of complementary goods.

Exam Questions

Q1 The decline in the housing market experienced in the UK during the period 2008-2012 led to building firms reducing their workload and to many tile retailers cutting down or delaying expansion plans. Explain the likely impacts of the decline of the UK housing market on tile manufacturers. [8 marks]

Q2 Cheese and crackers are complementary goods. Explain the likely impacts on the demand for crackers if the price of cheese dramatically increases. [4 marks]

I love complementary goods — always make me feel good about myself...

A market determines the price of a certain good (or service), and price will often affect demand. Demand links to the quantity sold — greater demand tends to lead to a greater quantity sold. There are loads of different factors that can influence demand, so make sure you learn how these affect the demand curve — those that change the level of demand cause the curve to shift.

Price, Income and Cross Elasticities of Demand

Elasticity of demand is a measure of how much the demand for a good changes with a change in one of the key influences on demand — the price of the good, the level of real income and the price of another good. ***These pages are for all boards.***

Price Elasticity of Demand shows how Demand Changes with Price

1) **Price elasticity of demand (PED)** is a measure of how the quantity **demanded** of a good **responds** to a **change** in its **price**.
2) PED can be **calculated** using the following formula:

$$\text{PED} = \frac{\text{percentage change in quantity demanded}}{\text{percentage change in price}}$$

You can think of PED as the way that consumers react (how much of a good they demand) as the price changes.

3) Have a look at this example:

- When the **price** of a type of toy car **increased** from **50p** to **70p** the **demand** for them **fell** from **15** cars to **10** cars.
- The **percentage change** in **quantity demanded** would be: $\frac{\text{change in demand}}{\text{original demand}} \times 100 = \frac{-5}{15} \times 100 = \mathbf{-33.33\%}$
- The **percentage change** in **price** would be: $\frac{\text{change in price}}{\text{original price}} \times 100 = \frac{20}{50} \times 100 = \mathbf{40\%}$
- So **PED** = $\frac{-33.33\%}{40\%} = \mathbf{-0.83}$

A common exam mistake is to write PED as a percentage — it's not.

4) Price elasticity of demand is **usually negative** because **demand falls** as **price increases** for most goods.

< means 'less than'
> means 'greater than'

PED can be Elastic, Inelastic or Unit Elastic

Elastic (Relatively Elastic) Demand: PED > 1

1) If the value of PED (ignoring any minus signs) is **greater than 1 (> 1)**, demand for the good is **elastic**. This means a **percentage change** in **price** will cause a **larger percentage change** in **quantity demanded.**
2) The **higher** the value of PED, the **more elastic** demand is for the good.
3) In diagram 1, price falls from **£50** to **£40** and an extra **45** units are demanded, which gives an **elastic** PED of -7.5.

$$\text{PED} = \frac{45/30 \times 100}{-10/50 \times 100} = -7.5$$

So a 1% change in price leads to a 7.5% change in demand.

4) **Perfectly elastic demand** has a PED of **± infinity** and any **increase in price** means that **demand will fall to zero** — see diagram 2. Consumers are willing to buy all they can obtain at P, but **none** at a **higher price** (above P).

Inelastic (Relatively Inelastic) Demand: 0 < PED < 1

1) The value of PED for goods with inelastic demand (ignoring any minus signs) is **between 0 and 1 (0 < PED < 1)**. This means a **percentage change in price** will cause a **smaller percentage change in quantity demanded.** The **smaller** the value of PED, the **more inelastic** demand is for the good.
2) In diagram 3, price falls from **£50** to **£40 (20% decrease**) and only an extra **4** units (**8% increase**) are demanded. This gives an **inelastic** PED of -0.4 which means for every 1% change in price there's a 0.4% change in demand.
3) **Perfectly inelastic demand** has a PED of **0** and any **change in price** will have **no effect** on the **quantity demanded** — see diagram 4. At any price (e.g. P_1 or P_2), the **quantity demanded** will be the same.

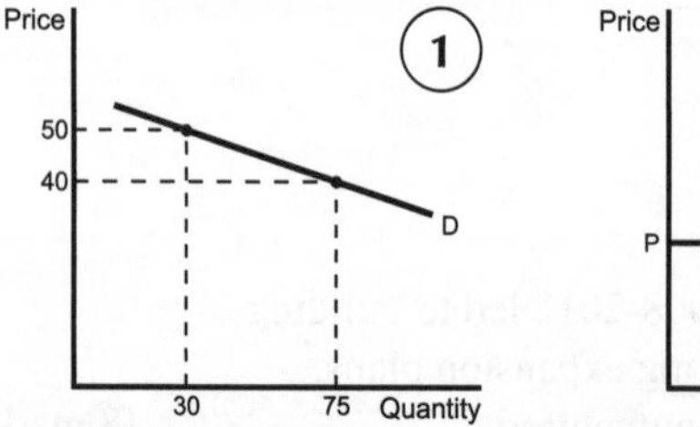

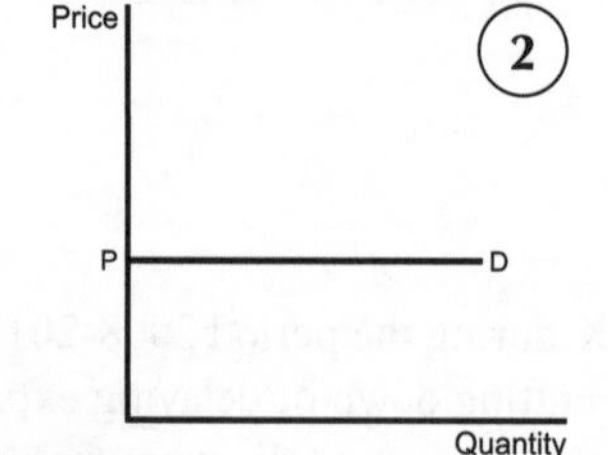

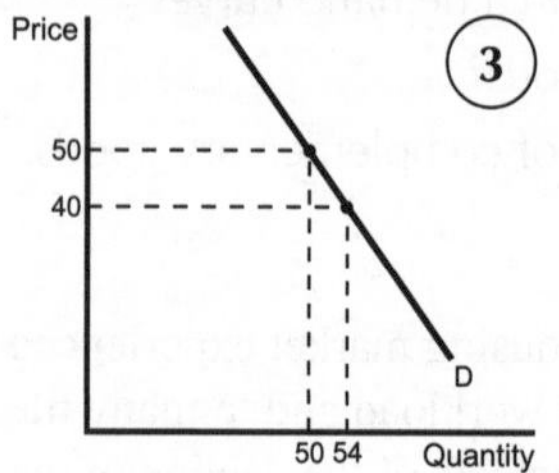

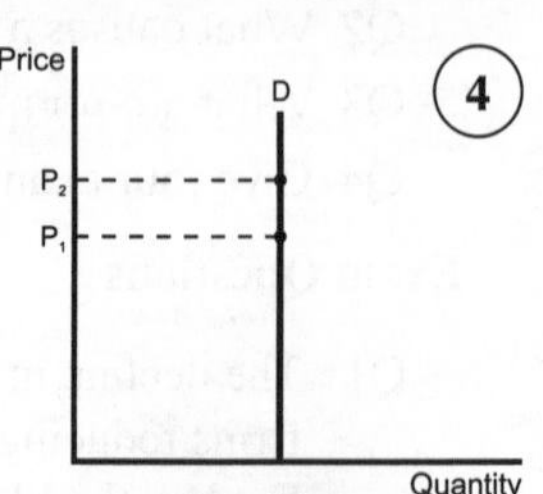

Unit Elasticity of Demand: PED = ±1

1) A good has **unit elasticity** (PED = ±1) if the size of the **percentage change** in **price** is **equal** to the size of the **percentage change** in **quantity demanded** — see diagram 5.
2) For example, here a **20% decrease** in price will lead to a **20% increase** in quantity demanded.

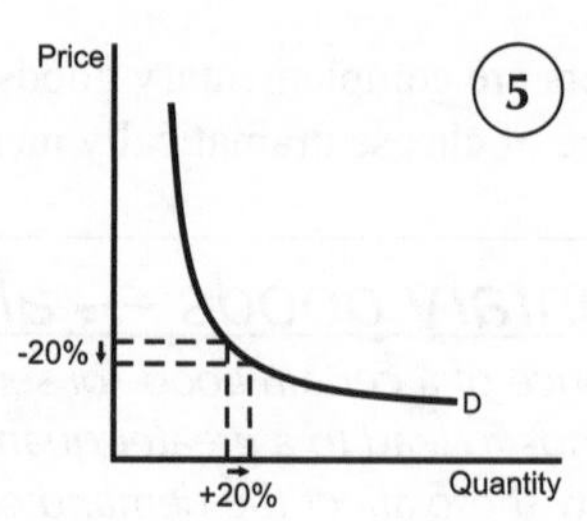

Jim's demand for bungee cord elasticity was at an all-time high.

Price, Income and Cross Elasticities of Demand

Income Elasticity of Demand shows how Demand Changes with Income

1) **Income elasticity of demand** (**YED**) measures how much the **demand** for a good changes with a **change in real income**.
2) YED can be **calculated** using the following formula:

$$\text{YED} = \frac{\text{percentage change in quantity demanded of a good}}{\text{percentage change in real income}}$$

3) Here's an example:

> If **real incomes increased** by **10%** and because of this the **demand for cameras increased** by **15%**, the income elasticity of demand for cameras would be: $\text{YED} = \frac{15\%}{10\%} = \mathbf{1.5}$

4) Here are examples of the meanings of different values of YED (ignoring any minus signs):

Income elastic: YED > 1

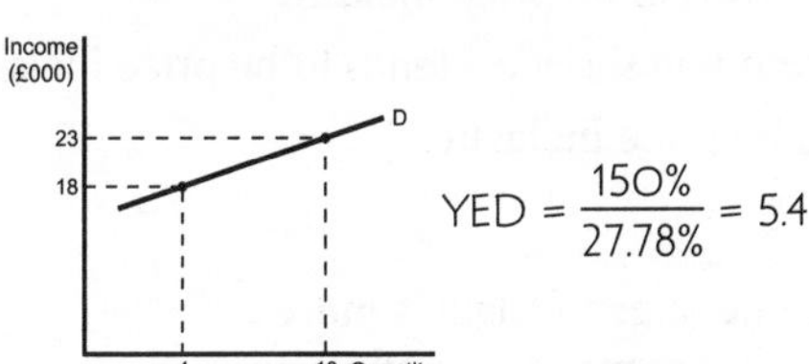

An increase in income of **£5000** leads to an increase in demand for the good of **6 units**. This gives an **elastic** (or **relatively elastic**) **YED** of **5.4**. So for every 1% increase in incomes, demand increases by 5.4%.

Income inelastic: YED < 1

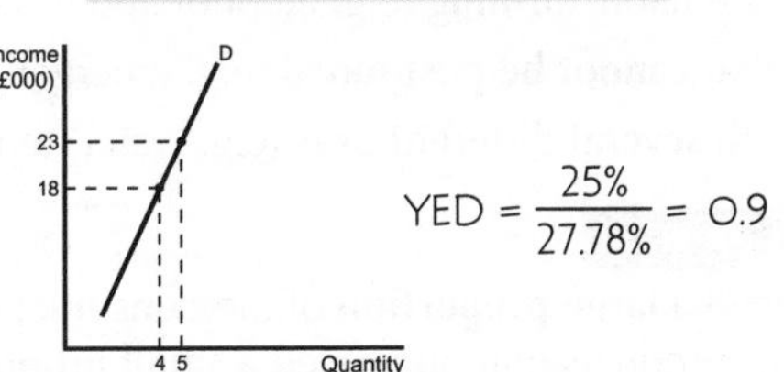

An increase in income of **£5000** leads to an increase in demand for the good of only **1 unit**. This gives an **inelastic** (or **relatively inelastic**) **YED** of **0.9**.

Perfectly inelastic: YED = 0

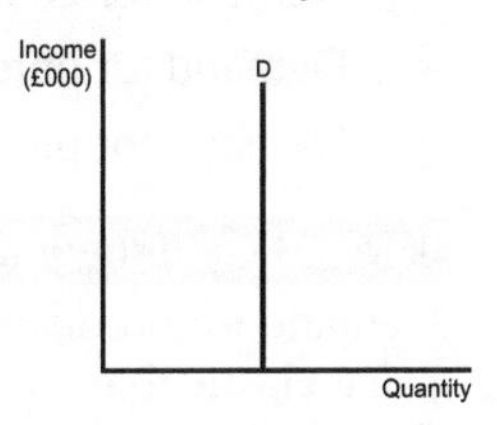

No matter how high incomes rise, **demand remains constant**.

You need to know about Cross Elasticity of Demand too

1) **Cross elasticity of demand** (**XED**) is a measure of how the **quantity demanded** of one good **responds** to a **change** in the **price** of another good.
2) XED can be **calculated** using the following formula:

$$\text{XED} = \frac{\text{percentage change in quantity demanded of good A}}{\text{percentage change in price of good B}}$$

3) If two goods are **substitutes** their XED will be **positive** and if they're **complements** their XED will be **negative**. For example:

> **Toy cars** and **teddy bears** are **substitutes**. If the **price** of toy cars **rose** by **40%**, the **demand** for teddy bears may **increase** by **20%**. $\text{XED} = \frac{20\%}{40\%} = \mathbf{0.5}$

> **Tennis rackets** and **tennis balls** are **complementary goods**. If the **price** of tennis rackets **rose** by **50%**, the **demand** for tennis balls may **fall** by **30%**. $\text{XED} = \frac{-30\%}{50\%} = \mathbf{-0.6}$

Practice Questions

Q1 Give the formula for PED.

Q2 What is income elasticity of demand?

Exam Question

Q1 The price of chococakes was reduced from £3 to £1.50, causing an increase in demand from 200 to 400.
What is the price elasticity of demand for chococakes?
A) –1.0 B) –2.0 C) –0.5 D) +2.0 [1 mark]

Cross elasticity of demand — it's elasticity of demand on a bad day...

I'm sorry, I know that's terrible. Anyway, the key things to pick up here are that there are three elasticities of demand that you need to understand. Their names should give you a clue about what affects them. Well, except XED, which is a bit less obvious — it's like PED, but it's about two different goods (or services) rather than just the one. Read it over until it's clear in your head.

Uses of Elasticities of Demand

Different factors influence the different elasticities of demand. Some factors influence more than one type of elasticity, so make sure you study them well. PED also has implications for a firm's revenue. ***These pages are for all boards.***

Many Factors Influence the Price Elasticity of Demand

1) **Substitutes**
The **more substitutes** a good has, the **more price elastic** demand is — if there are many substitutes available then consumers can easily **switch** to something else if the price rises. The **number of substitutes** a good has depends on how closely it's **defined**, e.g. peas have a number of substitutes (like carrots and sweetcorn), but vegetables as a group have fewer.

> The most important influence on elasticity is the number of **substitutes** a good has, but in the exam you'll be expected to know lots of influences.

2) **Type of good (or service)**
   - Demand for **essential items** (e.g. toilet paper) is price **inelastic**, but demand for **non-essential** items (e.g. tablet computers) tends to be price **elastic**.
   - Demand for goods that are **habit-forming** (e.g. alcohol and tobacco) tends to be price **inelastic**.
   - Demand for purchases that **cannot be postponed** (e.g. emergency plumbing services) tends to be price **inelastic**.
   - Demand for products with **several different uses** (e.g. water) tends to be price **inelastic**.

3) **Percentage of income spent on good**
Demand for products that need a **large proportion** of the **consumer's income** (e.g. a fridge) is **more price elastic** than demand for products that only need a **small proportion** of **income** (e.g. toothpaste). Consumers are more likely to shop around for the **best price** for an expensive good.

4) **Time**
In the **long run** demand becomes more **price elastic** as it becomes **easier** to change to **alternatives** because consumers have had the time to shop around. Also, in the long run, habits and loyalties can change.

Total Revenue and Price Elasticity of Demand

> Remember, PED will usually be negative, but we're ignoring minus signs here.

1) It's important for firms to understand the relationship between **total revenue** (price per unit × quantity sold) and a product's **price elasticity of demand**.
2) Elasticity **changes** along a **straight-line demand curve**:
   - PED changes along the demand curve from minus **infinity** at **high price/zero demand**, through an elasticity of minus **one** at the **midpoint**, to an elasticity of **zero** at **zero price/high quantity** demanded.
   - The n-shaped graph underneath shows how the **total revenue changes** as the point **moves along** the **demand curve** — i.e. as the price and quantity demanded change.
   - **Total revenue** is **maximised** when **PED = ±1** — the nearer a firm sets a product's price to the **mid-point** of the demand curve, the **higher** its **total revenue** will be.

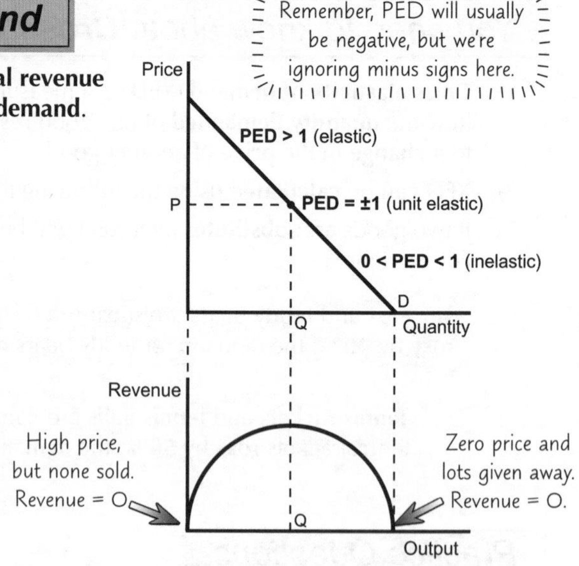

3) If a good has **elastic** demand, then:
   - A **reduction** in **price** will **increase** the firm's **total revenue**.
   - An **increase** in **price** will **reduce** the firm's **total revenue**.

   For example, a good has an **elastic** PED of -2.5. When the good's price is £5, 20 units are sold, giving a total revenue of **£100**. When **price falls** to £4, **demand rises** to 30 units and **total revenue increases** to **£120**.

4) However, if a good has **inelastic** demand, then:
   - A **reduction** in **price** will **reduce** the firm's **total revenue**.
   - An **increase** in **price** will **increase** the firm's **total revenue**.

   For example, a good has an **inelastic** PED of -0.5. When the good's price is £5, 20 units are sold, giving a total revenue of **£100**. When **price falls** to £4, **demand rises** to 22 units and **total revenue falls** to **£88**.

Uses of Elasticities of Demand

Income Elasticity of Demand is different for **Normal** and **Inferior** goods

Normal Goods

These goods have a **positive YED (0 < YED < 1)**. As **incomes rise, demand increases**. The size of the demand increase is dependent on the product's **elasticity**. If the YED of a product is **elastic (YED > 1)** then it's a **luxury** (or **superior**) **good.**

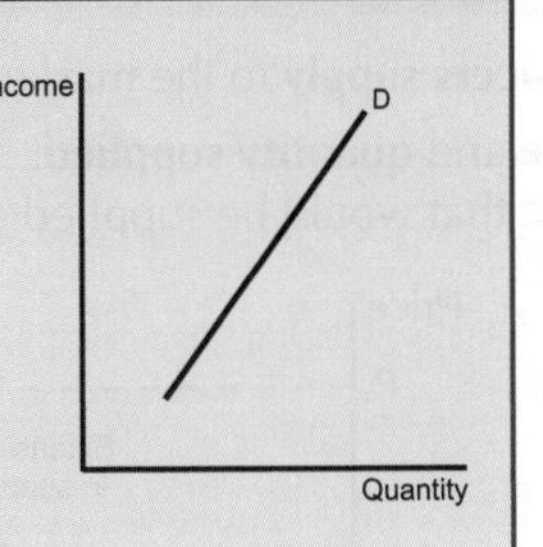

Inferior Goods

These goods have a **negative YED (YED < 0)** As **incomes rise, demand falls**. A rise in income will lead to the **inferior good** being **replaced** with one considered to be of **higher quality**.

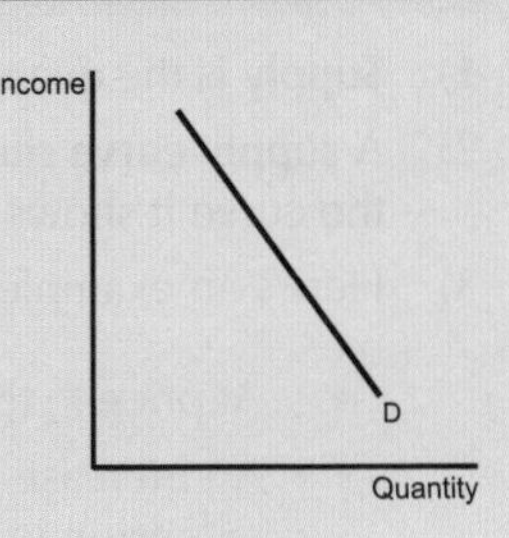

Normal goods are the most common type of good.

Cross Elasticity of Demand shows if goods are **Substitutes** or **Complements**

1) **Substitutes** have **positive** cross elasticities of demand (XEDs). A **fall** in the **price** of **one substitute** (e.g. rice) will **reduce** the **demand** for **another** (e.g. pasta). The **closer** the substitutes, the **higher** the **positive XED**. For example, ballpoint pens and fountain pens will have a **higher XED** compared to ballpoint pens and pencils.
2) Goods that are **complements** have **negative** XEDs. An **increase** in the **price** of a good (e.g. cheese) will lead to a **reduction** in **demand** for its **complements** (e.g. chutney).
3) Goods which have a **XED of zero** are **independent** (or **unrelated**) **goods** and **don't** directly affect the demand of each other — for example, bananas and slippers.

EDEXCEL & OCR

Knowledge of *Elasticities of Demand* is *Useful* for *Firms* and *Governments*

1) Information about **YED** can be used in **sales forecasting** — if the YED of a product and likely **changes** in **income** are known, then **sales levels** can be **predicted**. YED can also be used in **pricing policy** — a **reduction** in price for a normal good, when there's an **expected fall** in **incomes**, may **limit** the **expected reduction** in **demand** for the good.
2) A firm may choose to supply a **range** of goods with **various YEDs**. During a boom **demand** for a product with a **high YED** will **increase**, but demand for that product will **decrease** when the economy is in a recession. So a firm may also supply products with a **low YED** so that they can still **earn revenue** during a **recession**.
3) It's also useful for firms to know the **XEDs** of their goods because that will tell them how to **react** to **changes** in the **price** of **related products** to ensure they **maximise demand** for their products. For example, if a firm sells a product that has a close substitute and the substitute's price **drops**, they may choose to **lower** the price of their product to **reduce** the possible **fall** in demand for it.
4) It'd be very useful for governments to know how **demand** for goods might change during **booms** and **recessions** when they're setting their **policies**. For example, **demand** for **bus services** may **increase** with **falling incomes** in a recession, so a government would have to make sure that sufficient bus services were provided.

Practice Questions

Q1 List four influences on PED.

Q2 What is the PED when a firm's revenue is maximised?

Q3 Do complements have positive or negative XED?

Exam Question

Q1 Explain how a firm can use knowledge of price elasticity of demand to maximise revenue. [6 marks]

Inferior? How dare you call my bespoke carrier bag raincoats inferior...

Well, who'd have thought it? If you charge too much for an elastic good you can actually reduce revenue. If firms and governments had perfect knowledge of all the different elasticities of demand then they'd be laughing. Unfortunately, though, they don't, which means there's a bit of guesswork involved and getting it wrong can lead to some pretty costly mistakes.

Supply

Like demand, supply is a key part of the market mechanism. But whereas demand is all about what consumers are willing and able to pay for, supply is all about firms' willingness to supply goods/services at different prices. ***These pages are for all boards.***

Supply of *Goods* or *Services* is *Different* at *Different Prices*

1) **Supply** is the **quantity** of a **good or service** that **producers supply** to the **market** at a **given price**, at a **particular time**.
2) A **supply curve** shows the **relationship** between **price** and **quantity supplied**. At any given point along the curve it shows the **quantity** of the good or service that would be supplied at a particular **price**.
3) Here's an example of a supply curve:

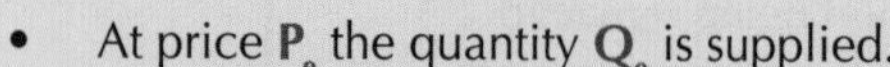

- At price $\mathbf{P_e}$ the quantity $\mathbf{Q_e}$ is supplied.
- An **increase** in price from $\mathbf{P_e}$ to $\mathbf{P_1}$ causes an **extension** in supply — it **rises** from $\mathbf{Q_e}$ to $\mathbf{Q_1}$.
- A **decrease** in price from $\mathbf{P_e}$ to $\mathbf{P_2}$ causes a **contraction** in supply — it **falls** from $\mathbf{Q_e}$ to $\mathbf{Q_2}$.
- So, **movement along the supply curve** is caused by **changes in price.**

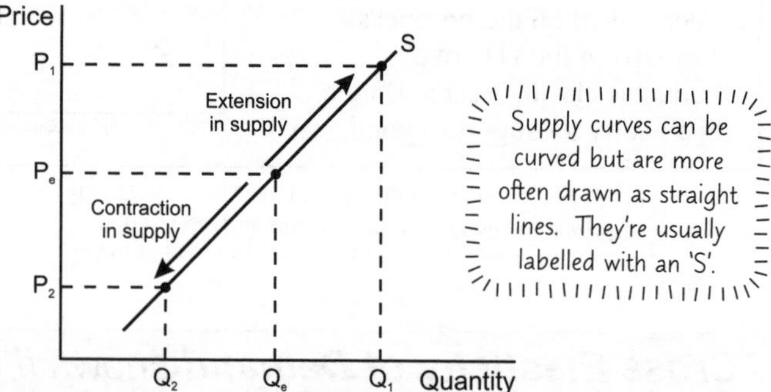

4) Supply curves usually **slope upwards**. This means that the **higher** the **price** charged for a good, the **higher** the **quantity supplied** — as shown by the diagram above.
5) **Producers** and **sellers** aim to **maximise** their **profits**. Other things being equal, the **higher** the **price** for a good or service the **higher** the **profit**. **Higher profit** provides an **incentive** to **expand production** and **increase supply**, which explains why the **quantity supplied** of a good/service **increases** as **price increases**.
6) However, increasing **supply** increases **costs**. Firms will only **produce more** if the **price increases** by **more** than the costs.
7) **Increased prices** mean that it will become **profitable** for **marginal firms** (these are firms that are just breaking even) to **supply** the **market** — increasing **market supply** levels.

Changes in Supply cause a *Shift* in the *Supply Curve*

1) A supply curve moves to the **left** (e.g. S_1) when there's a **decrease** in the **amount supplied at every price.**
2) A supply curve shifts to the **right** (e.g. S_2) when there's an **increase** in the **amount supplied at every price.**

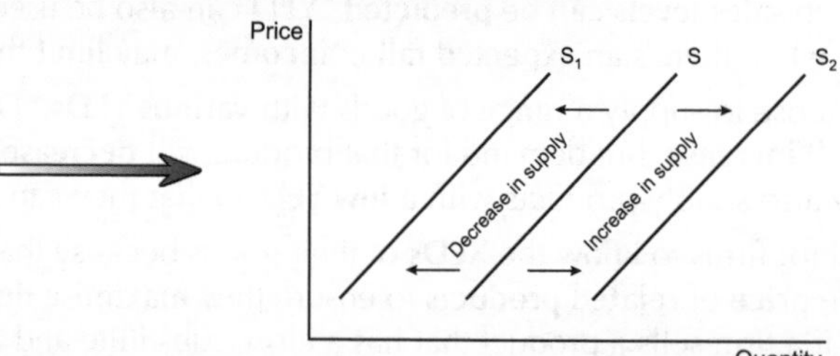

There are lots of *Factors* that can *Cause* a shift in the *Supply Curve*

Changes to the costs of production

An **increase** in one or more of the **costs of production** (e.g. raw materials, wages etc.) will **decrease producers' profits** and cause the supply curve to **shift** to the **left**. If a cost of production **decreased**, the **supply curve** would shift to the **right**. For example, an **increase** in the cost of **cocoa** will lead to a **reduction** in the **supply** of **chocolate**, but a **decrease** in the cost of **packaging** will lead to an **increase** in **supply**.

Improvements in technology

Technological improvements can **increase** supply as they **reduce** the **costs of production**. For example, improvements in the **energy efficiency** of commercial freezers could **reduce** the **energy costs** of a food company.

Changes to the productivity of factors of production

Increased productivity of a factor of production means that a company will get **more output** from a unit of the factor. For example, **more productive staff** will lead to an **increase** in **output** and shift the supply curve to the **right**.

Supply

Indirect taxes and subsidies

An **indirect tax** on a good effectively **increases costs** for a **producer** — this means that the **supply** is **reduced** and the supply curve is shifted to the **left**. A **subsidy** on a good encourages its production as it acts to **reduce costs** for **producers** — this leads to an **increased** level of supply and the supply curve **shifts right**.

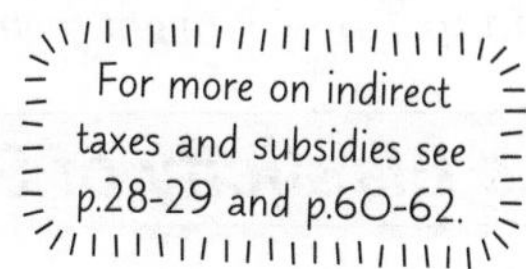

For more on indirect taxes and subsidies see p.28-29 and p.60-62.

Changes to the price of other goods

If the **price** of **one product** (A) made by a firm **increases**, then a firm may **switch production** from a **less profitable** one (B) to **increase production** of A and make the most of the higher price that they can get for it. This **decreases** the supply of **product B**.

Number of suppliers

An **increase** in the number of **suppliers** in a market (including new firms) will **increase** supply to the market, shifting the supply curve to the **right**. A **decrease** in the **number of suppliers** will shift the curve to the **left**.

Joint Supply is when *Goods* or *Services* are *Supplied Together*

AQA & OCR

1) **Joint supply** is where the **production** of **one good** or **service** involves the **production** of **another** (or several others) — it's another example of when markets are **interrelated**. For example, if **crude oil** is **refined** to make **petrol** this will also increase the supply of **butane** (another product that's made as a result of this process).
2) If the **price** of a product **increases**, then **supply** of it and any **joint products** will **also increase**. For example, if the **price** of **petrol increases**, the level of drilling for oil will rise and the **supply** of **petrol** and its **joint products** will **increase**.

You also need to know about Composite Supply and Competitive Supply

OCR ONLY

1) **Composite supply** is where **demand** for a product can be **satisfied** by the **supply** of two or more goods that are **substitutes** for each other, such as tea and coffee. When the **price** of one good **increases** (e.g. tea), the **demand** for the **substitute** good **increases** (e.g. coffee) because consumers will **switch to** the option that now appears relatively **cheap** in comparison. However, examples of perfect composite supply are **rare** as goods usually **aren't** perfect substitutes.
2) **Competitive supply** is where two (or more) **alternative goods** can be produced from the **same factors of production** (land, labour and capital). For example, land used to grow potatoes might be used to grow wheat, so it's up to the producer to **choose** the best way to use their factors of production.

Practice Questions

Q1 What does a supply curve show?

Q2 What causes a contraction of supply?

Q3 Describe two factors that can cause a supply curve to shift.

Exam Questions

Q1 Which of the following would cause a movement along a supply curve?
- A) A cut in the price of the product.
- B) A new entrant into the market.
- C) An improvement in the technology used to make the product.
- D) An increase in the costs of the raw materials used to make the product.

[1 mark]

Q2 Which of the following would most likely lead to an increase in the supply of dolls' houses?
- A) An increase in the cost of wood-cutting machinery.
- B) The exit from the market of a major toy maker.
- C) A new doll's house construction method is introduced which speeds up production by 25%.
- D) An increase in the cost of glue.

[1 mark]

Personally, I've always thought Supply was a bit shifty...

Ah supply, that's just like demand but the line goes a different way... No, no, no, wait, don't be fooled into thinking it's really similar to demand — it's still important that you learn all about supply. Although learning about it should be made easier if you're well acquainted with demand, as you've got to learn about what happens when prices change and the curve shifts.

Price Elasticity of Supply

These pages cover price elasticity of supply and the factors that can affect it. Be careful not to confuse it with price elasticity of demand (p.16) — it might seem similar but there are some differences to look out for. ***These pages are for all boards.***

Price Elasticity of Supply shows how *Supply Changes* with *Price*

1) **Price elasticity of supply** (**PES**) is a measure of how the **quantity supplied** of a good **responds** to a **change in its price**.
2) PES can be **calculated** using the **following formula**:

$$\text{PES} = \frac{\text{percentage change in quantity supplied}}{\text{percentage change in price}}$$

You can think of PES as the way that suppliers react (how much of a good they supply) as the price changes.

3) Here's an example calculation:

- When the **price** of a smartphone **increased** from **£449** to **£485** the **supply** of them **increased** from **15000** to **21500**.
- The **percentage change in quantity supplied** would be: $\frac{\text{change in supply}}{\text{original supply}} \times 100 = \frac{6500}{15000} \times 100 = \mathbf{43.33\%}$
- The **percentage change in price** would be: $\frac{\text{change in price}}{\text{original price}} \times 100 = \frac{36}{449} \times 100 = \mathbf{8\%}$
- So **PES** $= \frac{43.33\%}{8\%} = \mathbf{5.42}$

Don't forget that PES has no units — it's not a percentage.

4) PES is **generally positive** since the **higher** the **price** the **greater** the **supply**.

PES can be *Elastic, Inelastic* or *Unit Elastic*

Elastic (Relatively Elastic) Supply: PES > 1

1) If the value of PES is **greater than 1 (> 1)**, supply of the good is **elastic**. This means a **percentage change** in **price** will cause a **larger percentage change** in **quantity supplied**.
2) The **higher the value** of PES, the **more elastic** supply is for the good.
3) In diagram 1, price increases from **£5** to **£7** and an extra **7** units are supplied, which gives an **elastic** PES of **8.75**.

$$\text{PES} = \frac{7/2 \times 100}{2/5 \times 100} = \mathbf{8.75}$$

So a 1% change in price leads to an 8.75% change in supply.

4) **Perfectly elastic supply** has a PES of **± infinity** and any **fall in price** means that the **quantity supplied** will be reduced to **zero** — see diagram 2.

Inelastic (Relatively Inelastic) Supply: 0 < PES < 1

1) The value of PES for an inelastic good is **between 0 and 1 (0 < PES < 1)**. This means a **percentage change in price** will cause a **smaller percentage change in quantity supplied**. The **smaller** the value of PES, the **more inelastic** supply is.
2) In diagram 3, price increases from **£2000** to **£6000** (**200%**) and only an extra **2000** units (**100% increase**) are supplied. This gives an inelastic PES of 0.5 which means for every 1% change in price there is a 0.5% change in supply.
3) **Perfectly inelastic supply** has a PES of **0** and any **change in price** will have **no effect** on the **quantity supplied** — see diagram 4. At any price (e.g. P_1 or P_2), the **quantity supplied** will be the **same**.

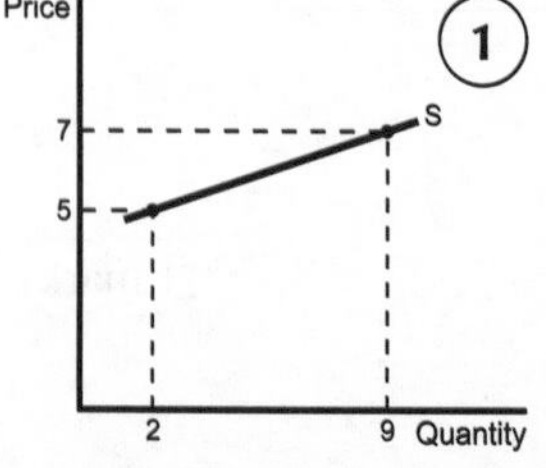

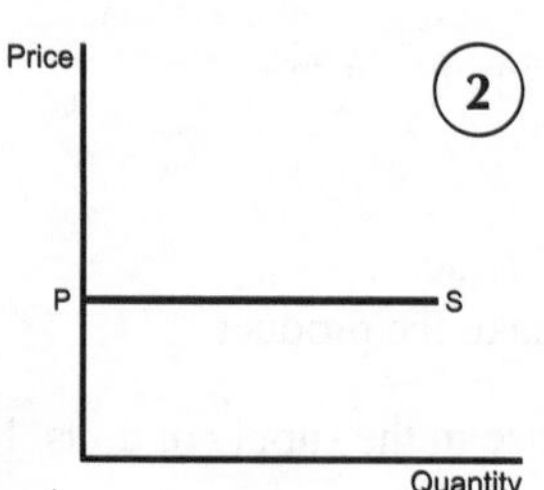

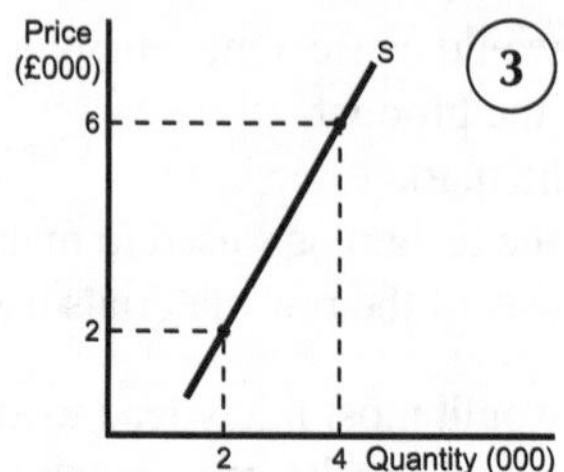

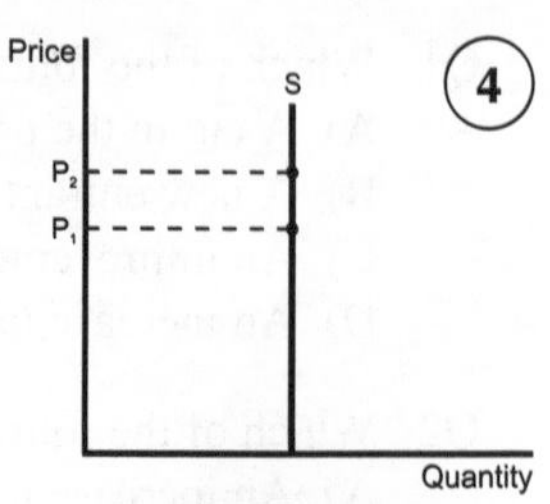

Unit Elasticity of Supply: PES = 1

1) A good has **unit elasticity** (PES = 1) if the percentage change in **quantity supplied** is **equal** to the percentage change in **price** — see diagram 5.
2) For example, a **50% increase** in price will lead to a **50% increase** in quantity supplied.

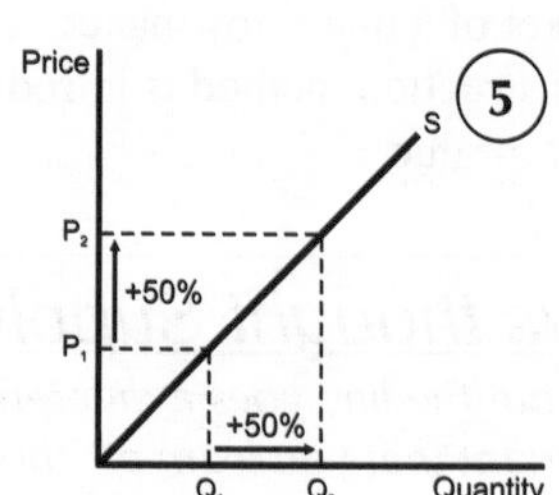

Supply of this floral outfit was low. Most people were glad about this.

Price Elasticity of Supply

A High PES is Important to Firms

1) Firms aim to **respond quickly** to **changes in price and demand.**
2) To do so they need to make their **supply** as **elastic** (i.e. responsive to price change) as possible.
3) Measures undertaken to **improve** the **elasticity** of **supply** include **flexible working patterns**, using the **latest technology** and having **spare production capacity**. For example, if a firm has spare production capacity it can quickly increase supply of a good without an increase in costs (e.g. the cost of building a new factory).

Supply is Price Inelastic in the Short Run

Over short periods of time firms can find it **difficult** to **switch production** from one good to another. This means that **supply** is likely to be **more price inelastic** in the **short run** compared to the **long run**.

SHORT RUN

- The **short run** is the **time period** when a firm's **capacity** is **fixed**, and at least one **factor of production** is **fixed.**
- **Capital** is often the factor of production that's **fixed** in the **short run** — a firm can recruit **more workers** and buy **more materials**, but it takes **time** to build additional production facilities. This means that it can be **difficult** to **increase production** in the **short run**, so supply in the short run is **inelastic.**

LONG RUN

- In the **long run** all the factors of production are **variable** — so in the **long run** a firm is able to **increase** its **capacity**.
- This means that supply is **more elastic** in the long run because firms have **longer** to react to **changes** in **price** and **demand**.

The distinction between **long run** and **short run** varies with **different industries** because **production times** and levels of **capital equipment** vary between industries. For example, the **long run** for a firm that makes sandwiches will be a **shorter time** than that of a firm that builds ships — to change production levels in ship building requires **more capital equipment**, **more planning** etc. Because ships take longer to produce than sandwiches, the **supply** of ships is more **inelastic**.

There are Several Other Factors that affect PES

The supply of agricultural products is more price inelastic in the short run than manufactured goods — plants take time to grow and livestock need nurturing over several years.

1) During periods of **unemployment** supply tends to be **more elastic** — it's **easy to attract new workers** if a firm wishes to expand.
2) **Perishable goods** (e.g. some fresh fruit and flowers) have an **inelastic supply** as they cannot be stored for very long.
3) Firms with **high stock levels** often have **elastic supply** — they're able to increase supply quickly if they want to.
4) Industries with more **mobile factors of production** (e.g. those that find it easy to expand their labour force and don't have production machinery/facilities that are difficult to relocate) tend to have **more elastic supply**. For example, industries that employ lots of unskilled workers may find it easy to increase their labour force.

Practice Questions

Q1 What is the formula used to calculate PES?

Q2 What is perfectly elastic supply?

Q3 In the short run is supply price elastic or price inelastic?

Exam Questions

Q1 It has been calculated that bananas have a price elasticity of supply (PES) in the short run of 0.62. Suggest two reasons why bananas have an inelastic PES in the short run. [4 marks]

Q2 Explain why a company that specialises in making hand-made furniture with a small highly skilled workforce could find it difficult to increase supply in the short run. [4 marks]

My morning exercise is a jog around the block — I call it the short run...

The diagrams for PES are similar to those for PED (aside from the major difference of being supply curves rather than demand curves). However, remember that the one for unit elasticity is very different — it's a straight line rather than a curved one. It's important that you understand why firms are interested in PES and how time affects PES — it's all about the short and long run.

Market Equilibrium

Here comes a key topic. On these pages you'll cover what it means when you have a pair of axes with both a demand and a supply curve on them and what they show about a market. ***These pages are for all boards.***

*A **Market** is in **Equilibrium** when **Supply Equals Demand***

1) At **equilibrium**, **price** and **output** are **stable** — there's a **balance** in the market and **supply** is **equal** to **demand**. **All products** that are presented for sale are **sold** and the market is **cleared**.
2) In a **free market**, **supply** and **demand** determine the **equilibrium price** and **quantity**.
3) This **free interaction** of supply and demand is known as **market forces**.
4) The **equilibrium point** can be found at the point where the **supply curve** and **demand curve meet**. This is shown in the example below:

When a market is cleared, the amount sellers wish to sell is equal to the amount that buyers demand.

The table below shows the **supply** and **demand** for 'Teddy-for-you' at various prices.

Price (£)	Quantity demanded per fortnight	Quantity supplied per fortnight
10	7000	1000
20	6000	2000
30	5000	3000
40	4000	4000
50	3000	5000
60	2000	6000
70	1000	7000

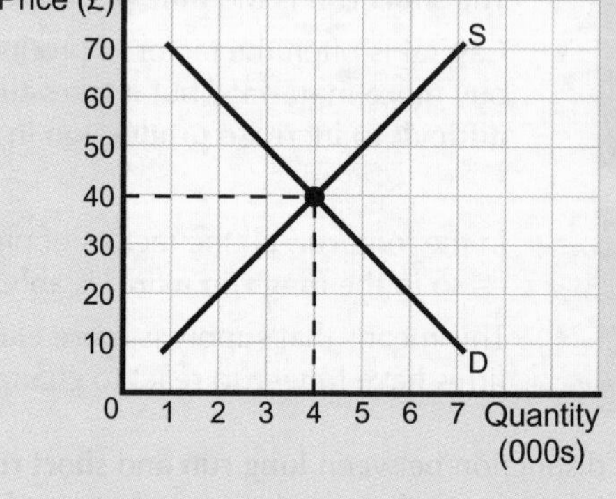

By looking at the data in this table you can see that the **equilibrium price** is **£40** — this is where the units **demanded** (4000) is **equal to** the units **supplied** (4000).

The equilibrium price and quantity are clear in the diagram above — it's at the point where the **supply** and **demand curves meet**.

5) When **supply** and **demand** aren't **equal** the market is in **disequilibrium**.
6) If there's **excess supply** or **excess demand** the market will be in **disequilibrium**.

***Excess Supply** and **Demand** won't exist in a **Free Market** for long*

Market forces act to remove **excess supply** or **demand**.

EXCESS SUPPLY

1) **Excess supply** is when the **quantity supplied** to a market is **greater** than the **quantity demanded**.
2) If the price for 'Teddy-for-you' is set **above** the **equilibrium** (e.g. **£60**) there would be **excess supply** (a surplus) of **4000 units** (6000 supplied minus the 2000 demanded). This would cause the **price** to be **forced down**, **supply** to **contract** and **demand** to **extend** until the **equilibrium** was reached (£40 price and 4000 units supplied/demanded).

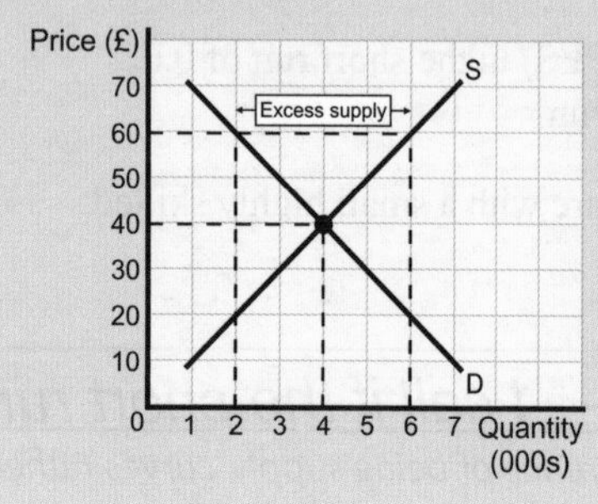

EXCESS DEMAND

1) **Excess demand** is when the **demand** for a good/service is **greater** than its **supply**.
2) If the price for 'Teddy-for-you' is set **below** the **equilibrium** (e.g. **£20**) there would be **excess demand** of **4000 units** (6000 units demanded minus 2000 supplied). This would cause the **price** to be **forced up**, **demand** to **contract** and **supply** to **extend** until the **equilibrium** was reached (again, £40 price and 4000 units supplied/demanded).

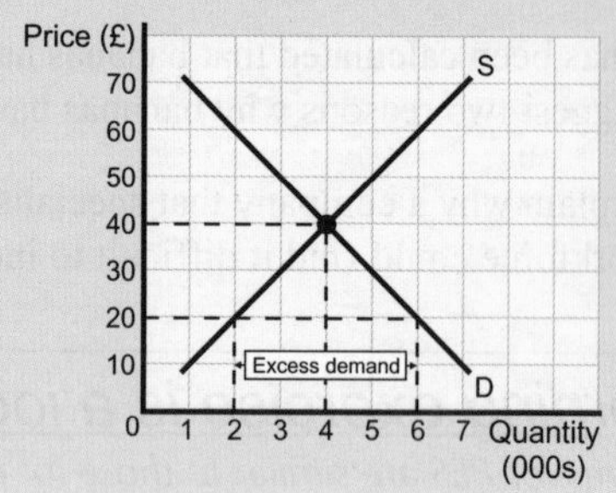

Market Equilibrium

*Shifts in **Demand** or **Supply Curves** will change the **Market Equilibrium***

1) If the **demand curve shifts**, assuming no change in the supply curve, then this will affect supply and price in the following ways:

- If **demand increases** from D to D_1 then the **price** will **increase** from P_e to P_1 and **supply** will **extend** from Q_e to Q_1, creating a new equilibrium.
- If **demand decreases** from D to D_2 then the **price** will **fall** to P_2 and **supply** will **contract** to Q_2, again creating a new equilibrium.

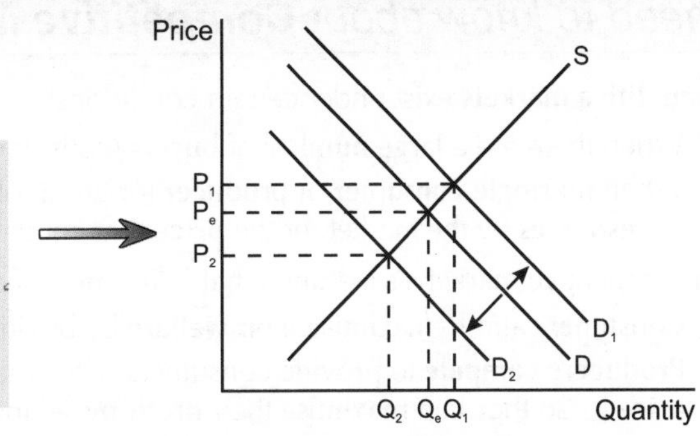

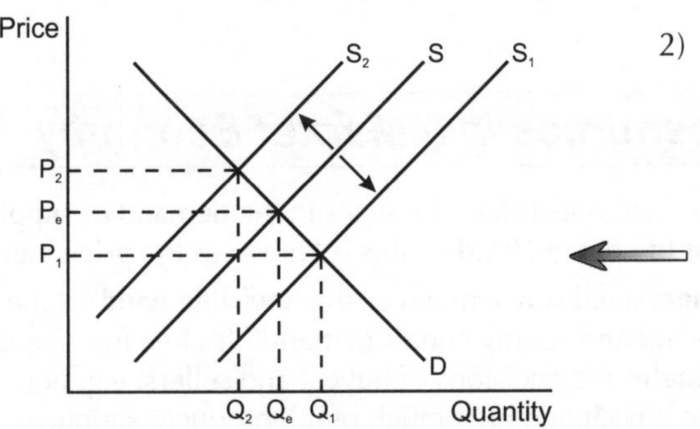

2) If the **supply curve shifts**, assuming no change in the demand curve, then this will affect demand and price in the following ways:

- If the **supply increases** from S to S_1 then the **price** will **fall** to P_1 and **demand** will **extend** to Q_1, creating a new equilibrium.
- If the **supply decreases** from S to S_2 then the **price** will **rise** to P_2 and **demand** will **contract** to Q_2, again creating a new equilibrium.

Elasticity** will affect the **Point** of the **New Equilibrium

1) **Price elasticity of supply** and **price elasticity of demand** influence the **size** of changes in the equilibrium price and quantity caused by supply and demand curve shifts.
2) For example, if the **demand curve** shifts to the **right** along an **elastic supply curve**, this will have a **larger effect** on **quantity** than price. The **opposite** is true for an **inelastic supply curve**.

Elasticity of PES/PED	Shifts in demand/supply curve has greater impact on:
Price **inelastic** supply or demand	Price
Price **elastic** supply or demand	Quantity

AQA & OCR

*The **Demand** and **Supply** model involves several **Assumptions***

1) The demand and supply model involves several **assumptions**. For example, it's assumed that:
   - Supply and demand are **independent** of each other.
   - All markets are **perfectly competitive**.
   - ***Ceteris paribus*** (see p.5) applies.
2) These assumptions mean the model has **limited use** in the **real world**. However, the model can be useful as it gives a **broad picture** of how supply and demand works in a way that's **simple** and **easy** to **understand**.

Practice Questions

Q1 When is a market in equilibrium?

Q2 What is excess supply?

Exam Question

Q1 Complete the following sentence. The equilibrium point in a free market

A) is purely dependent on supply.

B) will stay the same if there's a fall in supply.

C) determines supply and demand.

D) will move with a shift in the demand curve. [1 mark]

In my experience there's never an excess supply of cake...

...there's always a shortage. How sad. Remember, disequilibrium can exist, but in free markets the price and quantity demanded (or supplied) will head back towards equilibrium levels (equilibrium is where the supply and demand curves cross).

Price and the Allocation of Resources

Prices are crucial for determining how resources are allocated within a market. ***This page is for all boards.***

You need to know about **Competitive Markets**

1) **Competitive markets** exist under certain conditions:
   - When there are a **large number** of **buyers** (consumers) and **sellers** (producers).
   - When **no single consumer** or **producer** (or group of either) can **influence** the **allocation** of **resources** by the market, or the **price** that goods and services can be bought at.
2) In a competitive market it's assumed that consumers and producers act **rationally**:
   - **Consumers** aim to **maximise** their **welfare** by buying goods/services to **maintain** or **improve** their **quality of life**.
   - **Producers compete** to provide consumers with what they **want**, at the **lowest possible price** — so they can **maximise** their **profit** by selling to the **most customers**.

Price is the main way of **Allocating Resources** in a **Market Economy**

1) The **value** at which a good or service is **exchanged** is known as its **price**. Changes in the **demand** or **supply** of a good/service lead to changes in its **price** and to the **quantity bought/sold** — this is known as the **price mechanism**.
2) The price mechanism **allocates** goods/services in an **impersonal way** (known as the '**invisible hand**' of the market), as prices will change until equilibrium is achieved and supply equals demand. It's free from people's **biases** and **opinions**. The price mechanism also **coordinates** the decisions of **buyers** and **sellers**, e.g. how expensive something is will influence whether someone buys it and how much of it a producer supplies.
3) The price mechanism has the following **three functions**:
   - It acts as an **incentive** to firms — **higher prices** allow firms to produce more goods/services and **encourage increased production** and **sales** by providing **higher profits**.
   - It acts as a **signalling device** — **changes** in **price** show **changes** in **supply and/or demand** and act as a **signal** to producers and consumers. For example, a price increase is a **signal** to producers that demand is high, so this will encourage them to **increase production**.
   - It acts to **ration scarce resources** — if there's **high demand** for a good/service and its supply is **limited**, then the price will be **high**. Supply of the good will be **restricted** to those that can afford to pay a **high price**. The **opposite** applies for goods that are in **low demand** but in **high supply** — they'll have a **low price** and **many** will be sold.
4) The price mechanism is also used to **allocate** the **resources** used to **produce** goods/services. For example, if **demand** for **curtains increases**, the market will allocate (through the price mechanism) **more curtains** to **consumers**, **more labour** (e.g. seamstresses) for making curtains, and **more commodities** (e.g. cotton) to **curtain manufacturers**.
5) The price mechanism has **advantages** and **disadvantages**:

Advantages
- Resources will be allocated efficiently to **satisfy** consumers' **wants** and **needs**.
- The price mechanism can operate **without** the **cost** of **employing** people to **regulate** it.
- **Consumers decide** what is and isn't produced by producers.
- **Prices** are kept to their **minimum** as resources are used **as efficiently as possible**.

Disadvantages
- **Inequality** in **wealth** and **income** is likely.
- There will be an **under-provision** of **merit goods** and an **over-provision** of **demerit goods**, as the supply of and demand for these goods won't be at the socially optimal level (see p.53).
- People with **limited skills** or **ability to work** will suffer **unemployment** or receive very **low wages**.
- **Public goods** won't be produced (see p.55).

Practice Questions

Q1 Briefly explain what is meant by the term 'competitive market'.

Q2 Explain how the price mechanism acts as a signalling device.

Exam Question

Q1 Explain how prices can act as an incentive to firms. [4 marks]

So producers compete with low prices? Pretty sure some don't really try...

Prices are very important for allocating resources — they determine the levels of supply and demand for different goods/services.

Consumer and Producer Surplus

The consumer and producer surplus relate to the size of the benefit to consumers and producers from a given price level. When prices change, consumer and producer surpluses change. ***This page is for Edexcel and OCR only.***

Consumer and Producer Surpluses are above and below Equilibrium Price

Consumer Surplus

1) Everyone has **different** tastes, incomes and views on how much they're prepared to pay for a good/service.
2) When a consumer **pays less** for a good than the amount that they're **prepared** to **pay** for it, this **amount of money** is known as the **consumer surplus.** For example, if someone was prepared to pay **£10** for a good and bought it for **£8** then there would be a consumer surplus of **£2.**
3) So, the **consumer surplus** is the **difference** between the **price** that a consumer is **willing** to pay for a good or service and the **price** that they **actually pay** (the equilibrium price).

Producer Surplus

1) Different producers have **different** costs when making goods/services.
2) If a producer **receives more** for a product or service than the **price** they're **willing** to **accept**, the **extra earnings** are known as the **producer surplus.** For example, if the equilibrium price of a good is **£15** but a supplier would be happy to sell for **£10** then the producer surplus would be **£5.**
3) So, the **producer surplus** is the **difference** between the **price** that a **producer** is **willing** to **supply** a good or service at and the **price** that they **actually receive** for it (the equilibrium price).

The consumer and producer surplus can be shown on a diagram:

- **Consumer surplus** — the area **below** the demand curve and **above** the equilibrium price line.
- **Producer surplus** — the area **above** the supply curve and **below** the equilibrium price line.

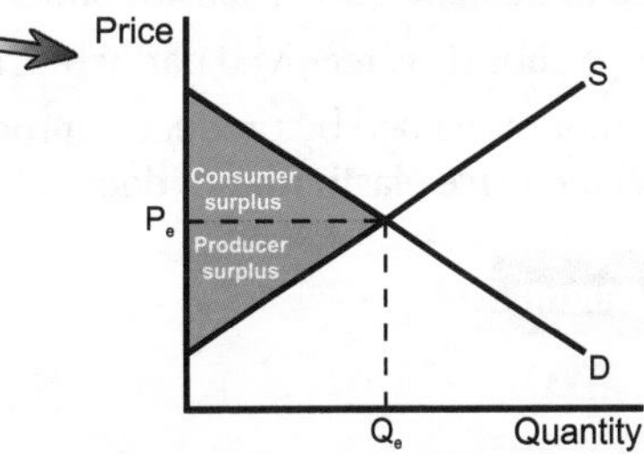

Changes in Supply and Demand affect Consumer and Producer Surplus

1) Anything that causes a **shift** in the **supply** or **demand curve** can lead to a **change** in the **price** of a good.
2) A change in price will bring a good **closer to** or **further away from** the **amount** the **buyer** was **willing** to **pay** or the **supplier** was **willing** to **sell** for — and this will **change** the **consumer** and **producer surpluses.**

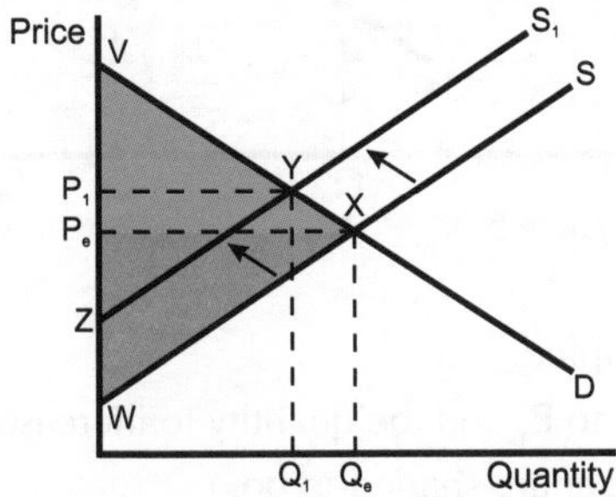

A shift in the **supply curve** from **S** to **S_1** means the **price** will **increase** from **P_e** to **P_1** and **quantity** will **decrease** from **Q_e** to **Q_1**. The **consumer surplus changes** from **VP_eX** to **VP_1Y** and the **producer surplus changes** from **P_eWX** to **P_1ZY**.

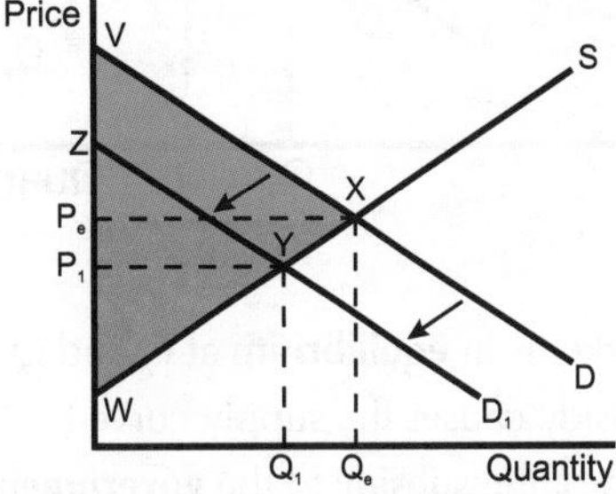

A shift in the **demand curve** from **D** to **D_1** means the **price** and **quantity** will **decrease** from **P_e** to **P_1** and **Q_e** to **Q_1** respectively. The **consumer surplus changes** from **VP_eX** to **ZP_1Y** and the **producer surplus changes** from **P_eWX** to **P_1WY**.

Practice Questions

Q1 What is consumer surplus?

Q2 What is producer surplus?

Sir Plus — King Arthur's trusty accountant...

Consumer and producer surplus — it's all about you buying stuff for less than you're prepared to and producers selling stuff for more than they need to in order to cover their costs. When you find a bargain you have a consumer surplus, which is awesome.

Subsidies and Indirect Taxes

Subsidies and indirect taxes result in gains or losses for producers and consumers. ***These pages are for Edexcel only.***

Subsidies and *Indirect Taxes* can affect *Consumers* and *Producers*

1) Governments sometimes provide **subsidies** to **encourage demand** for a good (e.g. energy-saving home insulation). A subsidy is money paid by the government to the **producer** of a good to make it **cheaper** than it would be otherwise.
2) Governments can also place a **tax** on a good (these are called **indirect taxes**) to **reduce** the **demand** for it (e.g. cigarettes and alcohol). The presence of a tax on a good aims to **discourage** people from buying it as the tax **raises** its **market price**.
3) **Taxes** and **subsidies** lead to **shifts** in the **supply curves** of **goods/services**, which cause **prices to change**.
4) The changes in price lead to an **extension** or **contraction** in **demand**.

Government subsidies for make-up increased Coco's demand.

The *Benefit* of *Subsidies* is divided between *Consumers* and *Producers*

1) Subsidies encourage **increased production** and a **fall** in **price**, which leads to an **increase in demand**. So, a subsidy **shifts** the **supply curve** to the **right**.
2) The **benefit** of a subsidy is received partly by the **producer** and partly by the **consumer**.
3) The relative amounts gained by producers (**producer gain**) and consumers (**consumer gain**) are dependent on the **price elasticities** of **demand** and **supply**. Here are a couple of examples:

For more on subsidies see p.62.

Inelastic demand

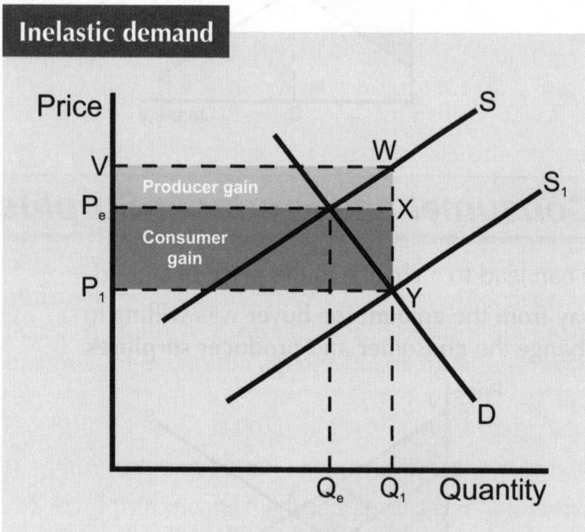

Elastic demand

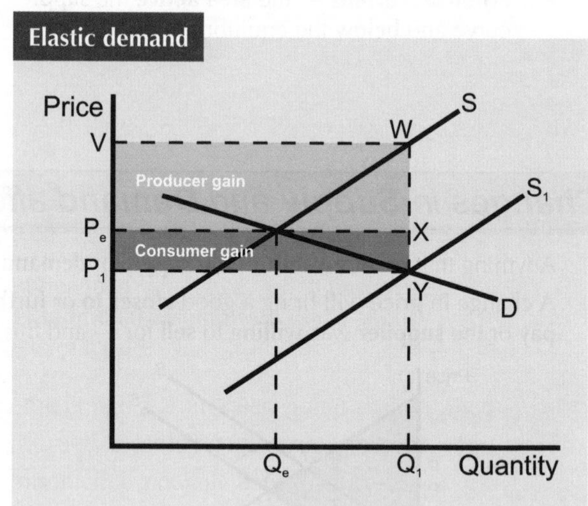

- The market is in **equilibrium** at P_e and Q_e **before** the subsidy is granted.
- The subsidy causes the supply curve to **shift** to $\mathbf{S_1}$, the price to fall to $\mathbf{P_1}$ and the quantity to increase to $\mathbf{Q_1}$.
- The **cost** of the **subsidy** to the **government** is given by $\mathbf{P_1VWY}$ (the entire shaded-in box). This subsidy can be split into two parts: the **consumer gain** and the **producer gain**.

The **consumer gain** is the fall in price from $\mathbf{P_e}$ **to** $\mathbf{P_1}$ — they gain by **paying less** for the good than they would have if there was no subsidy (this would be P_e). The area of the consumer gain is $\mathbf{P_1P_eXY}$ (dark purple).

The **producer gain** is equal to the difference between **V and** $\mathbf{P_e}$ — they gain by receiving **extra revenue** from the government that they can keep. The area of the producer gain is $\mathbf{P_eVWX}$ (light purple).

4) By comparing the two diagrams above it's clear that:
   - The **more price inelastic** the **demand curve** is, the **greater** the **consumer's gain** is from the subsidy.
   - The **more price elastic** the **demand curve**, the **greater** the **producer's gain** is from the subsidy.

Subsidies and Indirect Taxes

Indirect Taxes also affect both Consumers and Producers

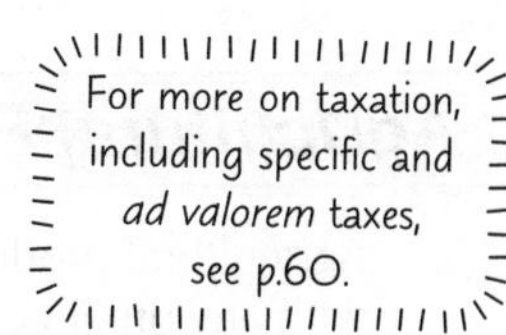

For more on taxation, including specific and ad valorem taxes, see p.60.

1) Taxes **increase** the **price** of a good, which leads to a **reduction** in **demand**. Taxation **shifts** the **supply curve** to the **left**.
2) As with subsidies, taxation has an impact on both the **producer** and the **consumer** of a good. The **relative proportion** borne by producers and consumers is again **dependent** on the **price elasticities** of **demand** and **supply**. Here are a couple of examples:

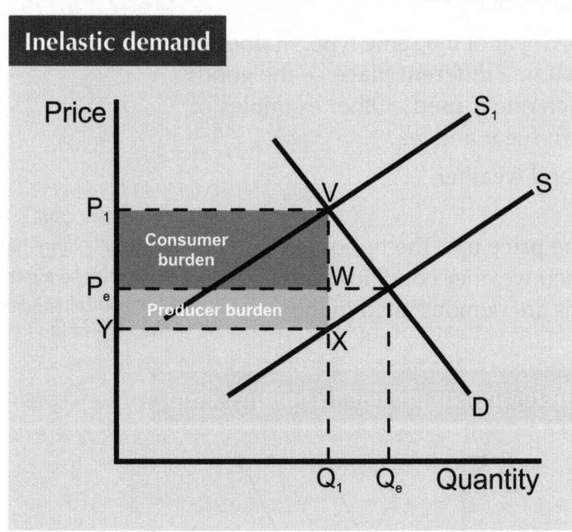

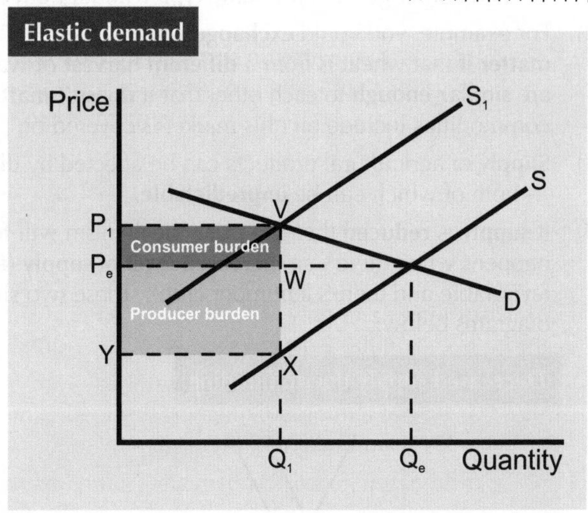

- With **no taxation** the market is in **equilibrium** at P_e and Q_e.
- The tax causes the supply curve to shift to $\mathbf{S_1}$, the price to increase to $\mathbf{P_1}$ and the quantity to decrease to $\mathbf{Q_1}$.
- The **revenue** for the **government** generated by the **tax** is given by $\mathbf{P_1YXV}$ (the entire shaded-in box). This tax can be split into two parts: the **consumer burden** and the **producer burden**.

The **consumer burden** is the rise in price from $\mathbf{P_e}$ **to** $\mathbf{P_1}$ — they lose out by **paying more** for the good than if the tax wasn't in place (this would be P_e). The area of the consumer burden is $\mathbf{P_1P_eWV}$ (dark purple).

The **producer burden** is equal to the difference between **Y and** $\mathbf{P_e}$ — they lose out by paying some of the revenue to the government. The area of the producer burden is $\mathbf{P_eYXW}$ (light purple).

3) By comparing the two diagrams above it's clear that:
   - The more **price inelastic** the **demand curve**, the **greater** the **tax burden** for the **consumer**.
   - The more **price elastic** the **demand curve**, the **greater** the **tax burden** for the **producer**.

Practice Questions

Q1 A subsidy is introduced for a good with elastic demand. Will the producer or consumer gain be larger?

Exam Questions

Q1 The diagram on the right shows the granting of a subsidy on a good. Which of the following areas represents the producer gain?

A) EGIK
B) GOHL
C) FGIJ
D) EFJK

[1 mark]

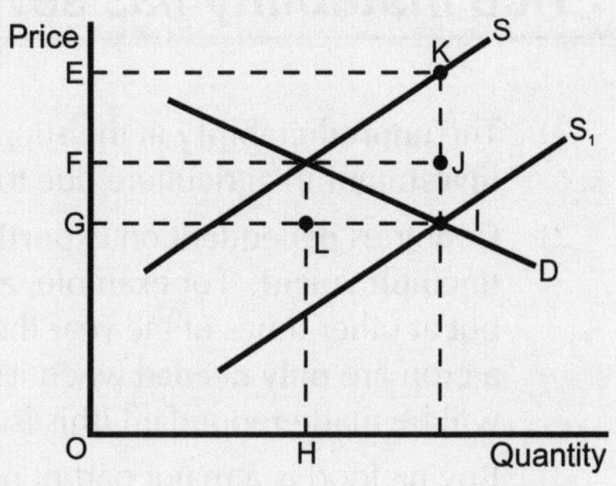

Q2 If a government places a tax on a product, explain the effect it will have on its price and demand. [6 marks]

Indirect taxis — a burden on your holiday money...

Subsidies and indirect taxation both affect consumers and producers — but who's affected more depends on the price elasticities of demand and supply. Make sure you understand how price elasticity affects the consumer and producer gains and burdens.

Demand and Supply — Agriculture

A lot of Section 2 is theoretical, but here are some pages that apply the theory to real-world markets. Many agricultural products (e.g. rice and wheat) suffer from price instability — the reasons for this can be explained using knowledge of supply and demand. ***Pages 30-35 are for OCR, but students of all boards will find these pages useful.***

Agricultural Products *display short run* ***Price Instability***

1) Agricultural products are **commodities.** A commodity is a good which could be **swapped** with any other good of the **same type** without noticeable difference.
2) For example, you could **exchange** wheat for some different wheat of the same type. It **doesn't matter** if that wheat is from a **different harvest** or was grown in a **different place** — the goods are **similar enough** to each other that it **doesn't matter** which one is used. Other examples of commodities include oil (this market is covered on p.32-33), sugar and tea.
3) **Supply** of agricultural products can be affected by **disease** and **weather** — both of which can be **unpredictable**.
4) If **supply** is **reduced** then the price mechanism will **force** the **price up**. The opposite happens when there's an **increased level** of **supply** (e.g. when weather conditions are favourable and there's a bumper crop). These two situations are demonstrated in the diagrams below:

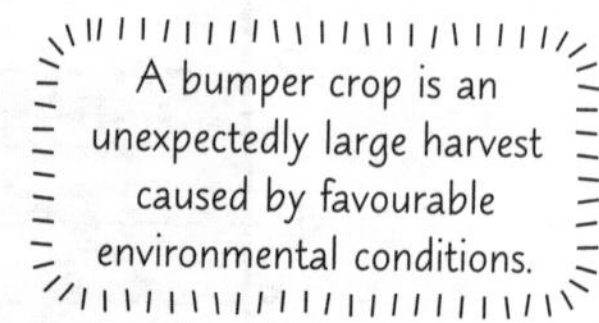

A bumper crop is an unexpectedly large harvest caused by favourable environmental conditions.

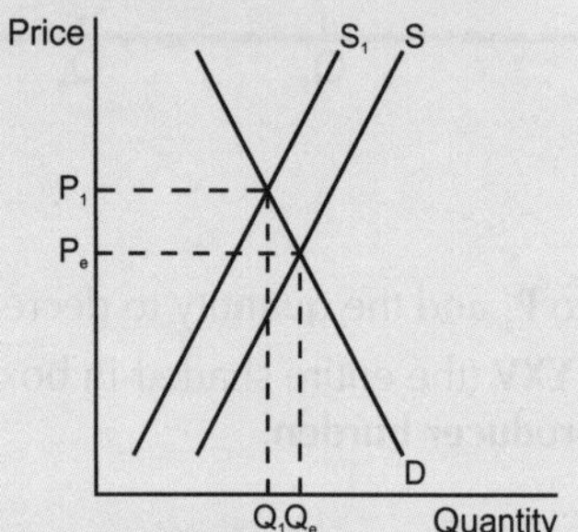

The supply curve is forced to shift to the **left** as flooding reduces the size of the crop. **Price increases** to P_1 and **quantity falls** to Q_1.

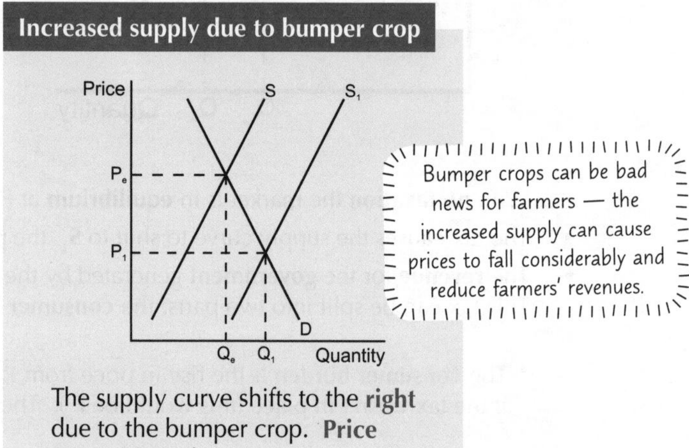

The supply curve shifts to the **right** due to the bumper crop. **Price falls** to P_1 and **quantity rises** to Q_1.

5) Agricultural products on the whole have **inelastic** price elasticities of **demand** (because food is a necessity) and **supply** (because, for example, it's difficult to store agricultural products).
6) **Price instability** can be a feature of markets for agricultural products because the **demand** for these products is fairly **price inelastic**. This means that even a **small increase** or **decrease** in the quantity supplied can have a **large impact** on **price**.

Price Instability *has several effects*

1) The **unpredictability** in the supply of agricultural products can reduce or prevent **investment** in agriculture due to the **uncertainties** about **returns** on any investment.
2) Countries **dependent** on **exporting** agricultural products can have periods of **low income** and **high unemployment**. For example, a country will receive **export revenue** after crops are harvested, but at other times of the year the revenue will be **much less**. Also, **workers employed** to harvest a crop are **only needed** when it's ready to be harvested. After this period they're **not needed** and will be made **redundant** (this is known as **seasonal unemployment**, see p.98 for more on this).
3) Buying food is a major part of people's monthly expenditure. When **food prices rise**, people become **worse off**. This has more of an impact on people on a **low** or **fixed income**.
4) Higher food prices can also have a **negative impact** on the economy as a whole. Increased prices leave **less income** to spend on other goods, which can lead to a **recession**.

Demand and Supply — Agriculture

Changes in Income have little impact on Demand for Agricultural Products

1) **Demand** for agricultural products is generally **income inelastic**. For example, as your income changes, your demand for food products isn't likely to change that much — you still need to buy enough food to survive.
2) **Increases** in **income** can lead to **changes** in the **quality** of agricultural products **demanded**. For example, consumers might switch to steak from mince or from concentrated fruit juice to freshly-squeezed juices.

Long Run Prices for Agricultural Products are Declining

1) Factors that affect the **long run supply** of agricultural products include **technological change**, the **supply of good quality land** and **changes to the climate** (e.g. caused by global warming).

For example, **technological improvements** may lead to an **increase** in the **supply** of **corn** as there will be an **increase** in the **efficiency** of **corn production**. This would cause the **supply curve** to **shift** to the **right**, and result in a **fall** in **price**.

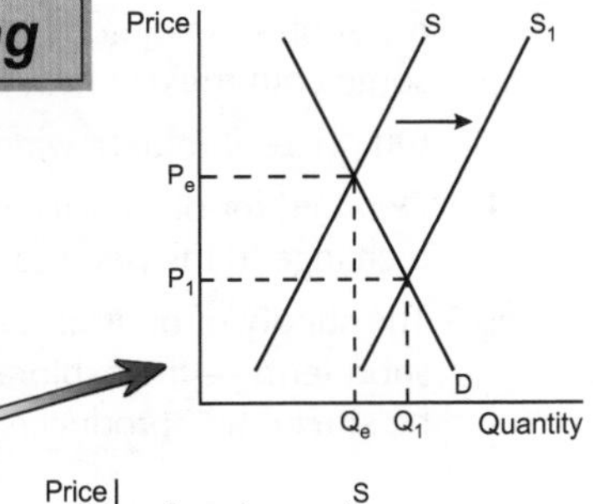

2) Factors that affect the **long run demand** for agricultural products include **changing incomes** and **consumer preferences**.

For example, the **demand** for **meat** may **fall** in the long run because of an **increase** in the number of people choosing a **vegetarian diet**. This would result in the **demand curve** shifting to the **left** and a **fall** in **price**.

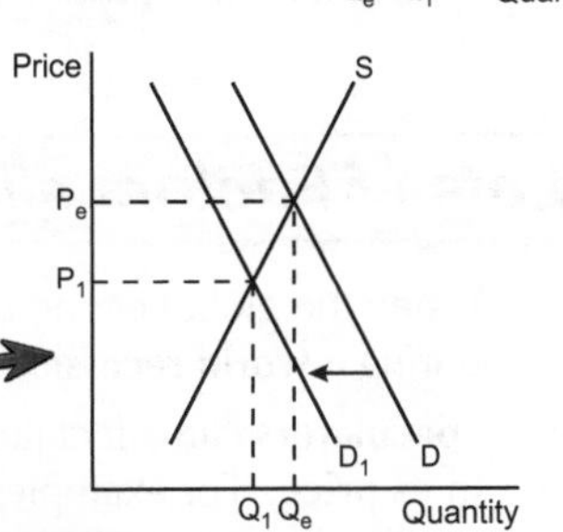

Buffer Stocks also affect the Price of Agricultural Products

1) **Buffer stocks** involve a government (or its agency) setting a **minimum** and **maximum price** for a product (e.g. wheat). The aim of buffer stocks is to **stabilise** market prices for particular products and **prevent shortages**.
2) If the price mechanism causes the price of the product to go **outside** of the **agreed price range** (i.e. too high or too low), then the government will **buy** or **sell** the product until the **price** returns to the **agreed range**.

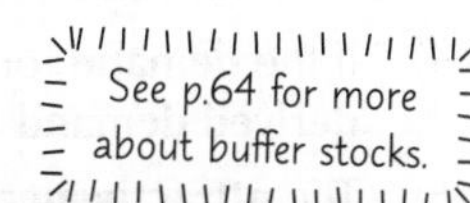
See p.64 for more about buffer stocks.

For example, if the **price falls too low**, the government will **buy** some of the product in order to **raise** the **price** — this shifts the **demand curve** to the **right** and restores the price to an acceptable level. This intervention stops prices plummeting in times of **high levels** of **supply** (e.g. after a bumper crop).

"No, no, I said bumper crop."

3) Buffer stocks of a product are **stored** and **sold** if the **price** rises **above** the **maximum allowed price**. This will **increase** the **supply** and **shift** the **supply curve** to the **right** — lowering the price.
4) A downside of buffer stock schemes is that they can be **difficult** to manage **effectively** and can be **expensive**.

Practice Questions

Q1 What are the causes of short run price instability for agricultural products?

Q2 What are the effects of short run price instability for agricultural products?

Q3 Is demand for agricultural products income elastic?

Q4 Give two reasons for the long run downwards trend in agricultural prices.

Exam Question

Q1 Using a diagram, explain the likely effect of a poor rice harvest on the global price of rice. [5 marks]

Here a moo, there a moo, everywhere a moo moo...

Price instability is a key concept here, so make sure you understand it. Increasing prices for agricultural products is bad news for everyone really, as we all consume agricultural products as food. If all food prices rocketed tomorrow we'd have to pay them.

Demand and Supply — Oil

Oil is a commodity and is one of the most important resources in the world. Oil is key to most economic activity, so changes in its price can have a big effect on global economies. So, with that in mind, take a look at these lovely pages.

The **Price** of **Oil** is **Very Important** for an **Economy**

1) Oil is used in the **production** of a huge variety of **goods** and it's **used** extensively for **transportation**. For example, many goods are made from, or packaged in, plastic and distributed using modes of transport that consume oil.
2) An **increase** in the **price** of oil can result in **inflation** (see p.100) as the **price** of many goods (and of the transportation of goods in general) **increases**. Recent **improvements** in **energy efficiency** and a **reduction**, in some countries, in **heavy industry** are helping to **reduce** the **impact** of changes in oil prices on the price of goods.
3) Oil prices **fluctuate widely**, with **rapid increases** and **decreases** over time.
4) **Demand** for oil is **price inelastic**. It's such an important and widely used resource that a change in the price causes a relatively **small change** in the **quantity demanded**.
5) The **supply** of oil is also **price inelastic**. This is partly because it's **difficult** to increase the supply of oil in the short term — the exploration for new oil and production from new wells takes **time**. Also, although oil can be **stockpiled**, producers don't want to supply lots to the market and cause **prices** to **decrease** too much.

Lots of **Factors** affect the **Demand** for **Oil**

1) When the global economy is **booming** the **demand** for oil **increases**, but **demand falls** during a **world recession**. This is because oil is used in **most economic activity**.
2) **Speculators** can affect the demand for oil because they buy and sell oil in the hope of making a **profit** from **fluctuations** in its **price**. For example, they could buy oil at **$100** per barrel **today** with the **hope** of selling it **next week** when they predict the price will have risen to **$120** per barrel — however, prices can fall and speculators can make large losses.
3) The **value** of the **US dollar** can affect the demand for oil. This is important because **oil** is priced in **US dollars** — if the **value** of the dollar is **low** then **more oil** can be **purchased** by speculators holding **other currencies**.
4) If the **demand** for **products made** from **crude oil** (e.g. plastics) **increases** then the **derived demand** for oil **increases** (see p.15 for more about derived demand).
5) The **attractiveness** of **buying oil substitutes**, e.g. biofuel, impacts demand for oil. As substitutes to oil become **cheaper**, **more reliable** and **more readily available**, this has a **negative impact** on **demand** for oil.
6) **Weather conditions** in major oil using countries can affect oil demand. For example, in cold conditions **more oil** is needed for **heating**.
7) As **living standards improve** then the **demand** for oil **increases** — this can be linked to an **increased consumption** of goods and services. Many of these goods/services will use oil in their manufacture and delivery. For example, people with a high income can afford to own a large house and several cars — this involves **higher oil consumption** than people with small houses who don't own a car.

> The growth of emerging economies is increasing the demand for oil. For example, countries such as China and India are becoming increasingly large oil consumers.

There are **Several Factors** affecting the **Supply** of **Oil** in the **Short Run**

1) **Supply-side shocks**, such as a **war** in a major oil producing country, can lead to a **disruption** of **oil supplies**. This would cause a **contraction** in the **supply of oil** as shown on the diagram.

   If the **supply** of oil **decreases** from **S** to **S_1** then the **price will rise** to **P_1** and **demand** will **contract** to **Q_1**.

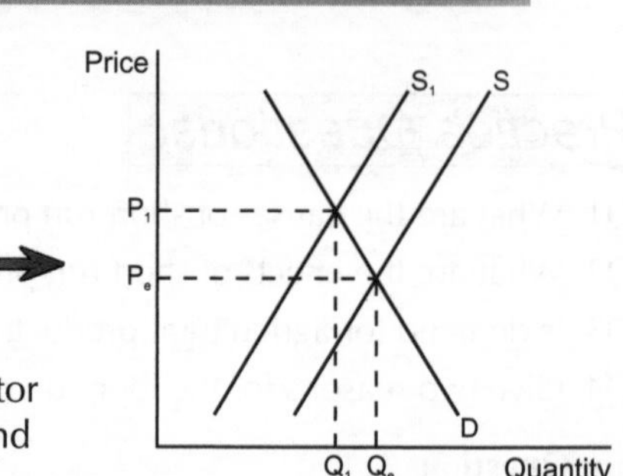

2) This price increase will **increase costs** to firms where oil is an important factor of production. These firms might **increase prices** to maintain their **profits** and this could have a knock-on effect on **demand** (it would **decrease**).
3) The **Organisation of Petroleum Exporting Countries (OPEC)** (an organisation whose members include several of the major oil exporting nations, such as Saudi Arabia and Venezuela) also has a **major influence** on the world **supply** of **oil**. This means that it can exert **significant control** over the **price** of oil.
4) OPEC members can agree to **cut** oil production levels (reduce supply), which causes oil **prices** to **increase**. Alternatively they can **increase production** levels (increase supply) to cause oil **prices** to **decrease**.

Demand and Supply — Oil

Different Factors *affect the* ***Supply*** *of* ***Oil*** *in the* ***Long Run***

1) The **size** of remaining **oil reserves** — the **bigger** the remaining oil reserves, the **higher** the **supply** of oil will be in the **long run**. The estimates of the size of world oil reserves vary.
2) The **cost** of **extracting oil** from reserves — some reserves are **too expensive** to extract oil from at the moment, but if **demand** and **oil prices increase** then it might become **worth extracting** this harder to reach oil. Also an increase in price and demand could cause an **increase** in the **exploration** for new oil reserves.
3) The **efficiency** and **cost** of **technology** used in **exploiting** and **refining** the **oil** — the **cheaper** and **more efficient** the technology, the **lower** the cost of the oil due to the increased level of supply.

Michelle couldn't hide her excitement about the discovery of a new oil well.

Examples *of changes to* ***Demand*** *and* ***Supply*** *of* ***Oil***

A large increase in the demand for oil

1) The **growth** of **emerging economies** is driving an **increased global demand** for **oil**.
2) This increase in demand can be shown on a diagram.
   - The **increase** in **demand** shifts the **demand curve** to the **right**.
   - The increase in demand can lead to an **increase** in **supply**.
3) Oil producers (e.g. OPEC) might **restrict** the use of **reserves** to keep the **price high**.
4) The **signalling effect** of the **price increase** can encourage an **increase** in **production**.
5) There will be a **delay** before this **additional supply** is **available** on the market.
6) **Demand** for oil in the **short run** is **price inelastic** — so this, with the inelastic supply curve, will lead to a large **increase** in **price**.

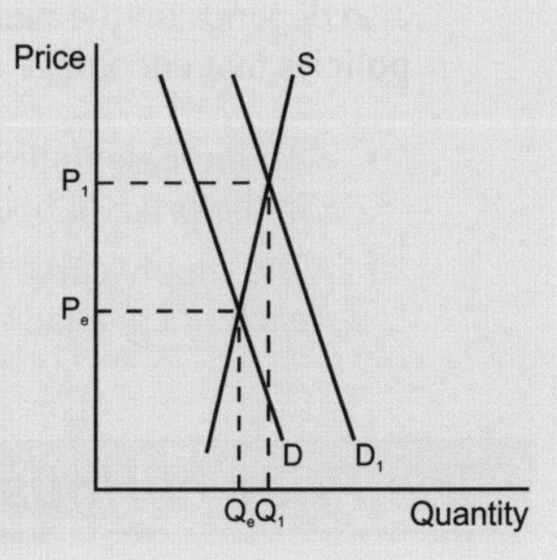

An expansion of fracking for oil

1) An **increase** in the scale of **fracking** activities (extraction of shale oil and gas) could lead to a **large increase** in the **supply** of **oil**.
2) This increase in supply can be shown on a diagram.
   - The **increase** in **supply** shifts the **supply curve** to the **right**. This increases output and causes the price to fall.
   - The **inelasticities** of supply and demand would lead to a **larger reduction** in **price** than the **increase** in **quantity**.
3) However, shale oil is **not** a **direct substitute** for **crude oil**, so the increase in its availability may not have a major effect on global oil prices.

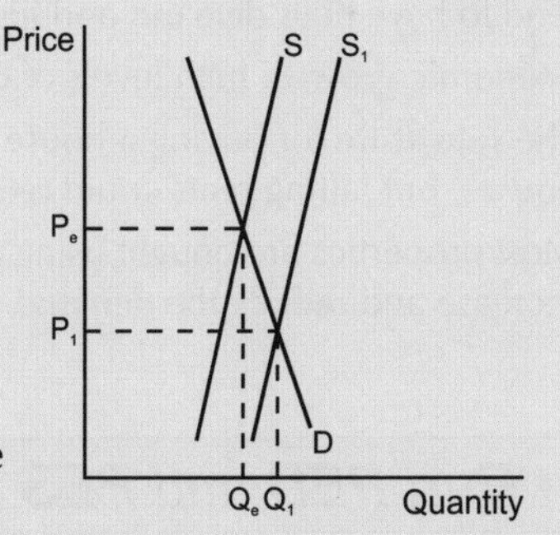

Practice Questions

Q1 Is the price elasticity of demand for oil elastic or inelastic?

Q2 Give two factors that affect demand for oil.

Q3 What factors affect the supply of oil in the long run?

Exam Question

Q1 Biofuel is a substitute for crude-oil-derived fuels and it's marketed in many countries as an alternative to diesel. How would a large subsidy granted to UK biofuel suppliers affect the demand for crude oil? [12 marks]

Crude oil — it tells the most inappropriate jokes...

In the exam you'll get extracts about different markets and you'll need to use the theory you've learnt about demand and supply to explain what happens in them. If you learn the factors that affect the demand and supply of oil, then you'll have no trouble if you're asked about the oil market. Remember, factors affecting supply can be categorised into short run and long run factors.

Demand and Supply — Housing

The housing market is really important for an economy — there's always lots of demand for places to live and it's important to have a sufficient supply of housing in order for an economy to be successful.

Buying a House is an Investment

1) Houses can **rise** in value **over time** and they're seen as an **investment** — it's possible to invest in houses and make a **return** on the investment in the future.
2) However, a **fall** in house prices can result in **negative equity** — where the value of a property's **mortgage** is **greater** than the property's **market value**. This is **bad** for **home owners** — what they sell their house for won't pay off the amount they owe on it (the remainder of the mortgage). Unless they can pay off the remainder of their mortgage they can't move house.

A mortgage is a loan taken out to contribute towards the cost of buying a house.

The Supply of Houses is the variety of houses available at a given time

1) The supply of houses is made up of **new build** and **pre-owned** houses that are available for a range of prices.
2) The supply of **new build houses** is partially dependent on the **costs** of building them (including labour, materials, land, and legal and planning costs). The supply also depends on the **number** and **size** of **building firms** and any **government policies** that encourage (or discourage) building new houses.

- An **increase** in the number of **new houses** built should lead to a **fall** in the **price** of houses. This is shown in the diagram on the right.
- The **supply curve** will shift to the **right**, leading to **more houses** being supplied at each price, a **fall** in the **equilibrium price** and a **rise** in the **equilibrium quantity**.

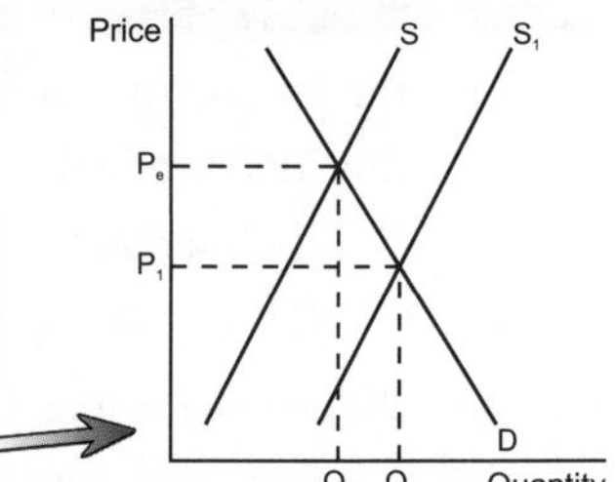

The Price of Housing is determined mainly by Demand Factors

1) The **state** of the **economy** has a big impact on the housing market — in areas of **high unemployment** houses have **lower prices** and **lower demand** (e.g. in some parts of north east England), but areas with **low unemployment** tend to have **high demand** and **high house prices** (e.g. parts of south east England).
2) **Economic growth**, high levels of **consumer confidence** and high **living standards** increase demand for housing.
3) The **substitute** for buying a house is **renting** one. A **fall** in the **cost** of renting may **decrease** the **demand to buy houses**, but falling rents could **reduce** the **supply** of properties for rent if landlords are **unwilling** to offer low rents.
4) Most properties are bought using a **mortgage**, so if, for example, **interest rates rise**, the cost of a **mortgage** will increase and **reduce** the **demand** for house purchases.

Short Run PED and PES for housing are Inelastic

1) There are **no close substitutes** for housing. This means the price elasticity of demand is **inelastic** — so a **rise** in **price** causes a **smaller reduction** in **demand**.
2) The price elasticity of supply is **inelastic** too. The **supply** of houses **can't** be quickly increased because it takes **time** to build new houses. Supply can also be **restricted** by the availability of **building materials**, **construction workers** and **suitable land**, and by **government regulations**.
3) Because supply can't increase much in the **short run**, an increase in demand can make **prices rise sharply**.

Dave was shocked to discover his builder's idea of 'minor refurbishment'.

House Prices have many Knock-on Effects

1) If house prices **rise** and lots of houses are bought and sold, then this might create more jobs in the **construction industry**.
2) **Higher** house prices **increase** the value of **people's assets** and can **increase consumer confidence** — this confidence can **encourage spending** and increase **investment**.
3) **Increased** house **sales encourage spending** on furniture, decorating and other household goods.

Demand and Supply — Transport

Finally, here's a bit of information on the transport market.

Transport *is usually a* ***Derived Demand***

1) Transport is the **movement** of freight (goods) and passengers (people) from one place to another.
2) Transport is almost always a **derived demand** — it usually results from demand for other goods and services:
   - People want to **get to places** for work, leisure activities and holidays, and shopping and other chores.
   - Firms want to bring **factors of production together**, and bring **goods to customers**.

Demand *for* ***Transport*** *is* ***Income Elastic*** *and* ***Price Elastic***

1) Transport as a **whole** has a **positive income elasticity of demand** (YED) — as real incomes increase the demand for transport increases (i.e. it's a normal good). However, each transport mode also has its **own** YED.
2) **Car** and **air travel** are generally considered to have a **positive YED**, but **bus travel** is thought to have a **negative YED** — bus travel is considered an **inferior good** (i.e. as incomes **rise**, demand for bus travel **falls**).
3) Demand for transport is also **price elastic** to some extent. People might cut back on **leisure travel** if prices rise, but **commuter travel** is less likely to be affected.
4) There's some **cross elasticity of demand** between transport modes that are suitable **substitutes** for one another.

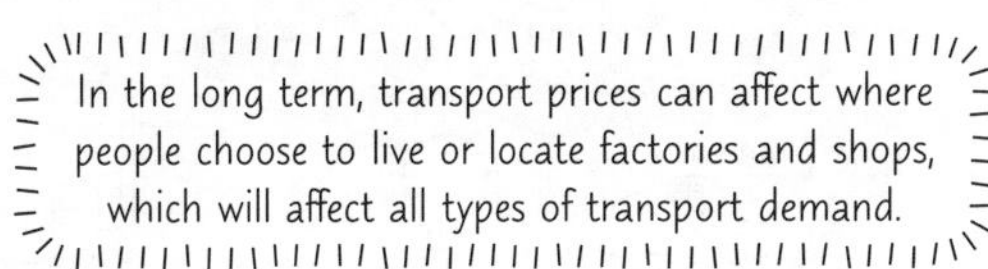

In the long term, transport prices can affect where people choose to live or locate factories and shops, which will affect all types of transport demand.

The ***Price Elasticity*** *of* ***Car Travel*** *is* ***Quite Low***

1) **Demand** for **car travel** depends on several things, for example:
   - The **cost** of a **journey**, e.g. petrol — individuals will choose whether or not to drive depending on its **cost**. However, the **price elasticity** for travelling by car is **low** because people highly value the **convenience** and **comfort** of driving. This means that changes in the cost of driving **might not** have a large effect on its demand.
   - **Income** — car ownership and usage **rise** with real income, so **economic growth** causes an **increase** in car usage.
   - **Substitutes** — there are substitutes to car travel, such as travelling by **bus** or by **train**, and a reduction in their prices **might** reduce car usage. However, these modes of transport are often considered to be **poor substitutes** for cars, so **cross elasticity of demand** is **low**.
   - **Complements** — the **price** of **complementary goods**, such as **car insurance** or **parking**, can affect the demand for driving.
2) In the **short run** the **supply** of **roads** is **fixed** (until new ones can be built). This can lead to **excess demand** (shown on the diagram) for road space during busy periods, i.e. there will be **congestion** during rush hour.
3) Congestion can be **reduced** by introducing a **price** (**P** on the diagram, e.g. a **toll fare** or **congestion charge**) for using the road network. If the price is set at the **right level** this will **reduce demand** back to the level of **supply**.

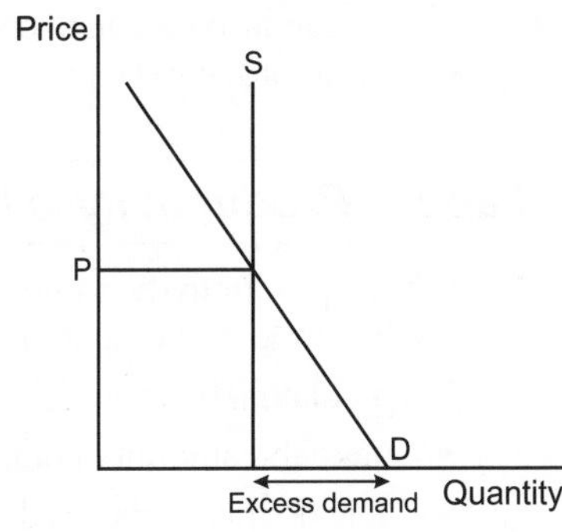

Practice Questions

Q1 Give three factors which influence the demand for housing.

Q2 Is the supply of housing in the short run price elastic?

Q3 How will demand for transport be affected by a general increase in people's real income?

Q4 Give three factors which influence the demand for car travel.

Exam Questions

Q1 Discuss reasons why average house prices might vary between two areas of a country. [10 marks]

Q2 Explain the likely impact of higher fuel prices on the usage of cars. [4 marks]

My school football coach considered me to be a poor substitute...

So, here are two very different markets, but in the end it all comes down to how the market forces act. One very important thing you should learn is how important price elasticities of demand and supply are in determining price and output levels. Lovely stuff.

Production and Productivity

Before we get down to the more complicated Business Economics topics, here are a couple of pages to gently ease you in. Businesses produce things and they try to do it efficiently — you need to know how. ***This page is for all boards.***

Production means Manufacturing something in order to Sell it

1) Production involves converting **inputs** (e.g. raw materials, labour) into **outputs** (things to sell).
2) The inputs can be any of the four **factors of production** — land, labour, capital and enterprise. **Inputs** can be:
   - **tangible** — things you can touch, like raw materials or machines.
   - **intangible** — 'abstract' things that can't be touched — like ideas, talent or knowledge.
3) The **outputs** produced should have an **exchangeable value** — they need to be something that can be sold.

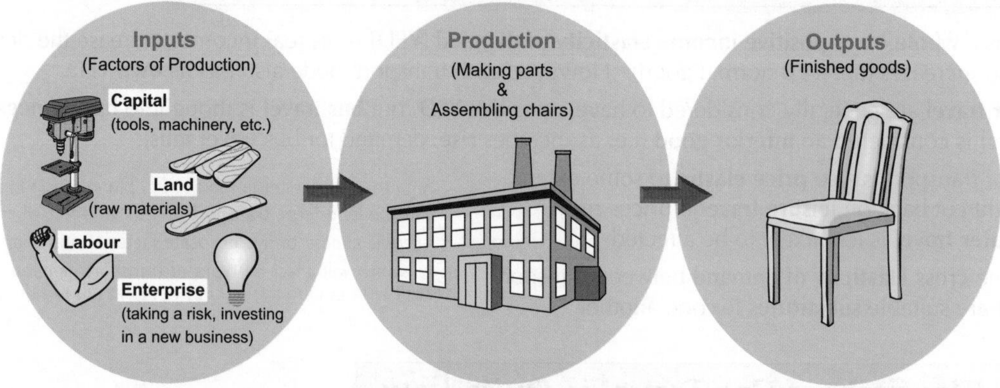

Productivity is the output per Factor Employed

- **Productivity** is a way of measuring how efficiently a company or an economy is producing its output.
- It's defined as the **output per unit of input employed**. So if one company could take the same amount of inputs as another company, but produce more stuff, their productivity would be **greater**.
- You can work out an **overall** level of productivity (involving all four possible inputs).
- But you can also calculate productivity for **any one** of the four individual factors of production, e.g. labour (see below). Improving the productivity of any one of these **separate** factors should increase **overall productivity**.

Labour Productivity is the output per Worker or output per Hour Worked

1) **Labour productivity** is one example of measuring productivity for one factor. It's the amount of output produced **per worker** (or **per worker-hour**).
2) To calculate labour productivity:
   - Take the amount of output produced in a particular time.
   - Divide this by the **total** number of workers (or the total **hours worked** by all the workers).
3) Labour productivity allows workers to be **compared** against other workers. For example, labour productivity is calculated for **whole economies**, so that the productivity of the different labour forces can be compared.
4) Improvements in labour productivity can come about as a result of better **training**, more **experience**, improved **technology**, and so on. **Specialisation** can also improve labour productivity — if each worker performs tasks that they're **good at doing**, have **practised a lot** or have been **trained** to do, then they'll **produce more** than if they did lots of different tasks.

A fitter workforce is a more productive workforce.

Practice Questions

Q1 What are the four types of input that go into producing something?

Q2 Give two examples of how the labour productivity of a firm could be improved.

Average CGP productivity — one joke per hour...

An hour well spent, eh? Right? Right...? There's no pleasing some people. Anyway, there's some pretty straightforward stuff here on production and productivity. Learning it won't get you the Nobel Prize for Economics, but it'll definitely be useful.

Specialisation

By specialising, we don't have to spend all our time making what we want or need. ***This page is for all boards.***

Specialisation *leads to a* ***Division of Labour***

1) People could **make** all the things they need and want **themselves**. They could grow their own **food**, make their own **clothes**, build their own **computers**, and so on. In **practice** though, this is very unlikely to work. What usually happens is that people and firms **specialise** — some people grow food, others make clothes, etc.
2) The **division of labour** is a **type** of **specialisation** where production is **split** into **different tasks** and **specific people** are **allocated** to each task, e.g. in making a stool — one person could make the legs and another could make the seats.
3) **Adam Smith** explained the **increase** in **productivity** that could be achieved through the division of labour. He said that **one untrained worker** wouldn't even make **20 pins per day**, but **10 workers**, **specialising** in different tasks, could make **48 000**.
4) There are **advantages** and **disadvantages** to specialisation, but overall an economy can produce **more stuff** if people and firms **specialise**. (It's not just individuals and firms that can specialise — whole **regions** and even **countries** can specialise to an extent. For example, there are loads of technology companies based in Silicon Valley in California.)

Advantages of Specialisation

- People can **specialise** in the thing they're **best** at. (Or by doing it, they learn to become better at it.)
- This can lead to **better quality** and a **higher quantity** of products for the same amount of effort overall — i.e. increased **labour productivity**.
- Specialisation is one way in which firms can achieve **economies of scale** (see p.40), e.g. a **production line** (where each person may perform just one or two tasks) is a form of specialisation.
- Specialisation leads to **more efficient** production — this helps to tackle the problem of **scarcity**, because if **resources** are used more efficiently, **more output** can be produced **per unit** of **input**.
- **Training costs** are **reduced** if workers are only trained to perform certain limited tasks.

Disadvantages of Specialisation

- Workers can end up doing **repetitive** tasks, which can lead to **boredom**.
- Countries can become **less self-sufficient** — this can be a problem if **trade** is **disrupted** for whatever reason (e.g. a war or dispute). For example, if a country specialises in **manufacturing**, and **imports** (rather than produces) all its **fuel**, then that country could be in trouble if it falls out with its fuel **supplier**.
- It can lead to a **lack** of **flexibility** — for example, if the companies eventually move elsewhere, the workforce left behind can struggle to **adapt**.

Coal mining in the UK is an example of this. When pits closed, many miners had non-transferable skills (this is structural unemployment — see p.98).

Trade *means people can* ***Buy*** *the stuff they're no longer making* ***Themselves***

1) Specialisation means that **trade** becomes absolutely vital — economies (and individual people and firms) have to be able to **obtain** the things they're no longer making for themselves. This means it's **necessary** to have a **way** of **exchanging** goods and services between countries. (See p.110-112 for more on trade.)
2) **Swapping** goods with other countries is one way a country can get what it needs, e.g. a country which mines diamonds may want oil, while another country which produces oil may want diamonds. This way of trading goods is called a **barter system** — it's **very inefficient** because it takes a lot of **time** and **effort** to find traders to barter with.
3) The most **efficient** way of exchanging goods and services between countries is using **money** (with the use of **exchange rates** where necessary — see p.113). Money is a **medium of exchange** — it's something both buyers and sellers value and that means that countries can buy goods, even if sellers don't want the things that the buying country produces.

Money has **three** other functions too:

- **A measure of value** — e.g. the value given to a good (such as a barrel of oil) can be measured in US dollars.
- **A store of value** — e.g. an individual who receives a wage may wait before buying something if they know that the money they have will be of a similar value in future.
- **A standard (or method) of deferred payment** — money can be paid at a later date for something that's consumed now, e.g. people often borrow money to buy a car or pay university fees.

Practice Questions

Q1 Give two advantages and two disadvantages of specialisation.

Q2 What are the four functions of money?

Money, eh? — Is there anything it can't do?

Money makes trade much easier, allowing specialisation — which has its own advantages and disadvantages for you to learn.

The Costs of a Firm

A firm could be anything from a dog-walking business to a giant multinational like an oil or technology company. What most firms have in common is that they sell goods or services to try to make profit. ***These pages are for AQA and OCR.***

Firms** generate **Revenue** and incur **Costs

1) A firm is any sort of **business organisation**, like a family-run factory, a dental practice or a supermarket chain.
2) An **industry** is all the firms providing **similar** goods or services.
3) A **market** contains all the firms **supplying** a particular good or service **and** the firms or people **buying** it.
4) Firms generate **revenue** (money coming in) by **selling** their **output** (goods or services).
5) Producing this output uses **factors of production** (land, labour, capital and enterprise), and this has a **cost**.
6) The **profit** a firm makes is **its total revenue minus its total costs**.
7) In the **long run** firms need to make profit to **survive**.

Revenue is explained in detail later in the section.

*Economists include **Opportunity Cost** in the **Cost** of **Production***

- When economists talk about the **cost of production** they are referring to the **economic cost** of producing the output.
- The economic cost includes the **money cost** of factors of production that have to be paid for, but it also includes the **opportunity cost** of the factors that aren't paid for (e.g. a home office that a business is run from).
- The **opportunity cost** of a factor of production is the **money that you could have got** by putting it to its **next best use**. E.g. if you run your own business the money you **could earn** doing other work is the opportunity cost of your **labour**.
- So, in economics, cost isn't just a calculation of money spent — it takes into account **all** of the effort and resources that have gone into production.

*In the **Short Run** some **Costs** are **Fixed***

1) The **short run** is the period of time when **at least one** of a firm's factors of production is **fixed**.
2) The short run isn't a specific length of time — it **varies from firm to firm**. For example, the short run of a **cycle courier** service could be **a week** because it can hire new staff with their own bikes quickly, but a **steel manufacturer** might have a short run of **several years** because it takes lots of time and money to build a new steel-manufacturing plant.
3) The **long run** is the period of time when **all factors of production** can be **varied**.
4) Costs can be **fixed** or **variable** in the short run:

FIXED COSTS

- Fixed costs **don't vary with output** in the **short run** — they have to be paid whether or not anything is produced.
- For example, the **rent on a shop** is a fixed cost — it's **the same** no matter what the sales are.

VARIABLE COSTS

- Variable costs **do vary with output** — they increase as output increases.
- The cost of the **plastic bags** that a shop gives to customers is a variable cost — the **higher sales** are, the **higher the overall cost** of the bags.

5) In the **long run all costs** are **variable**.

Total Cost** and **Average Cost** include **Fixed Costs** and **Variable Costs

Total cost (TC) is **all the costs** involved in producing a particular **level of output**.

The **total cost** (TC) for a particular output level is the **total fixed costs** (TFC) plus the **total variable costs** (TVC) for that **output level**: **TC = TFC + TVC**

Average cost (AC) is the **cost per unit produced**.

It's also called average total cost (ATC).

Average cost (AC) is calculated by **dividing** total costs by the **quantity** produced (Q): **AC = TC ÷ Q**
Average fixed cost (AFC) = total fixed costs ÷ **quantity** produced: **AFC = TFC ÷ Q**
Average variable cost (AVC) = total variable costs ÷ **quantity** produced: **AVC = TVC ÷ Q**

The Costs of a Firm

Marginal Cost is the cost of Increasing Output by One Unit

Marginal cost (MC) is the **extra cost** incurred as a result of producing **the final** unit of output.

Or think of it as the cost of producing 'one more unit' of output.

For example, the **total cost** of producing **100** ice creams is **£100** and the **total cost** of producing **101** ice creams is **£102**. So, the **marginal cost** of producing the **101st** ice cream is £102 – £100 = **£2**.

Marginal cost is only affected by **variable costs** — fixed costs have to be paid even if **nothing** is produced. As shown in the example above, you can calculate it by finding the **difference** between total cost at the current output level (TC_n) and total cost at one unit **less** (TC_{n-1}): $\mathbf{MC = TC_n - TC_{n-1}}$

Output	Total Fixed Costs (£)	Total Variable Costs (£)	Total Cost (£)	Average Cost (£)	Average Fixed Cost (£)	Average Variable Cost (£)	Marginal Cost (£)
0	60	—	60	—	—	—	—
1	60	70	130	130	60	70	70
2	60	120	180	90	30	60	50
3	60	180	240	80	20	60	60
4	60	260	320	80	15	65	80
5	60	360	420	84	12	72	100
			60 + 360	420 ÷ 5	60 ÷ 5	360 ÷ 5	420 – 320

These are the values substituted into the formulas.

Marginal cost usually means the extra cost of producing 'the final unit' of output, but there's a more general formula that gives the extra cost of 'the last few units':

$$MC = \frac{\text{Change in TC } (\Delta TC)}{\text{Change in Quantity } (\Delta Q)}$$

You need to know the Shape of the Short Run Average Cost Curve

AQA ONLY

1) The short run **average cost** (**AC**) curve of a firm is likely to be **u-shaped**.
2) Average cost tends to **initially fall as output increases**, until it reaches a minimum. Then the average cost **starts to increase**.
3) The **average cost** is the **average variable cost** (**AVC**) plus the **average fixed cost** (**AFC**) at each level of output.
4) **AVC** tends to **fall initially with output** because productivity tends to rise, but eventually this is limited by fixed factors of production (e.g. how many machines a factory has) and cost **starts to rise again**. This makes the AVC curve **u-shaped**.
5) **AFC falls as output rises**, so the AFC curve slopes downwards. This is because as the level of output increases, the total fixed cost is **spread** across the **greater level of output**.

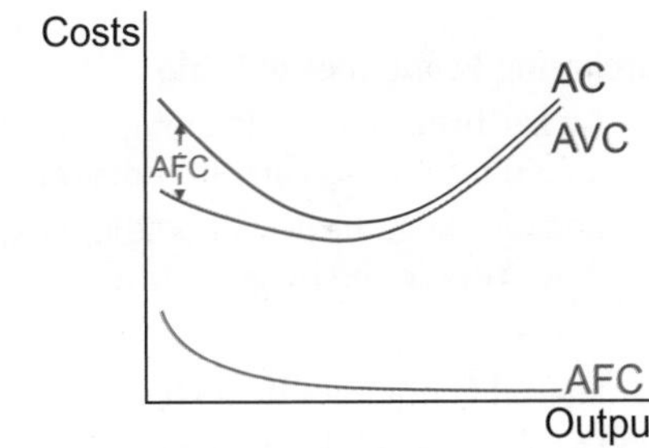

The cost curves shown in the diagram above are short run curves. For the long run average cost curve see p.59.

Practice Questions

Q1 What are fixed costs?

Q2 Give a formula that can be used to calculate total cost.

Q3 Describe what marginal cost is.

Exam Questions

Q1 Firm X and Firm Y are producing the same product at the same output level and have the same variable costs. The fixed costs of Firm X are double the fixed costs of Firm Y. Firm X and Firm Y have the same:
A) average fixed cost B) marginal cost C) fixed costs D) total costs [1 mark]

Q2 A firm's total cost for producing 50 ladders is £1421. Calculate the average cost of producing a ladder. [2 marks]

Chat-up lines for economists #23 — "I'm a big fan of you-shaped curves"...

There are loads of terms and formulas here you need to know. Make sure you've got a really good grasp of what all the different types of cost are and make sure you learn the formulas for calculating each one too. Questions involving costs are pretty common in the exams so it's important that you take in what's on these pages and can apply it when the time comes.

Economies and Diseconomies of Scale

In the long run firms can increase their scale of production by increasing all of their factors of production. ***AQA and OCR only.***

Economies of Scale can be Internal or External

1) The **average cost** to a firm of making something is usually quite high if they **don't** make very many of them.
2) But in the **long run**, the more of those things the firm makes, the more the average cost of making each one **falls**. These falls in the cost of production are due to **economies of scale**.

See the long run average cost curve on p.59.

Economies of scale — the cost advantages of production on a large scale.

3) Economies of scale can be divided into two categories — **internal** and **external**.

Internal economies of scale involve changes Within a firm

Technical Economies of Scale

- **Production line** methods can be used by large firms to make a lot of things at a very low average cost.
- Large firms may also be more able to purchase other **specialised equipment** to help reduce average costs.
- Workers can **specialise**, becoming more efficient at the tasks they do, which might not be possible in a small firm.
- Another potential economy of scale arises from the **law of increased dimensions**. For example:
  - The **price** you pay to build a new warehouse might be closely related to the **total area of the walls and roof**, say.
  - If you make the dimensions of the walls and roof **twice as big**, the total **area** of the walls and roof will be **4 times greater** — so the warehouse will **cost about 4 times as much** to build.
  - But the **volume** of the warehouse will be **8 times greater**, meaning that you're getting more storage space for each pound you spend.
  - The same is true of things like **oil tankers** — e.g. bigger tankers reduce the cost of transporting each unit of oil.

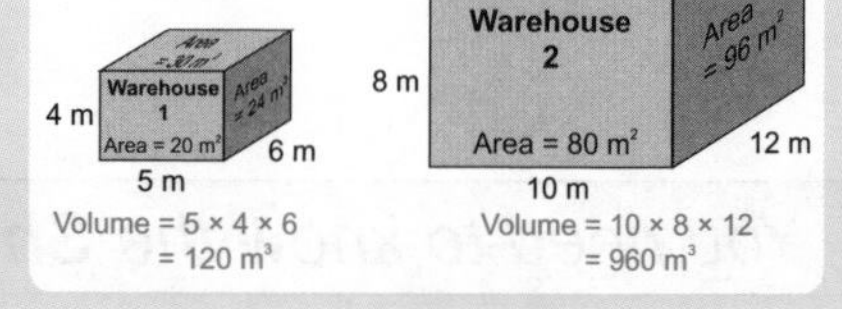

Purchasing Economies of Scale

- **Larger firms** making lots of goods will need **larger quantities** of raw materials, and so can often **negotiate discounts** with suppliers.
- Because large firms will be the **most important customers** of suppliers (as they'll put in the biggest orders), they'll be able to **drive a hard bargain**.

Managerial Economies of Scale

- **Large firms** will be able to employ **specialist** managers to take care of different areas of the business (e.g. finance, production, customer service). These specialist managers gain **expertise** and **experience** in a specific area of the business, which usually leads to better **decision-making** abilities in that area.
- And the number of managers a firm needs **doesn't** usually depend directly on the production scale — a firm probably won't need twice as many managers to produce twice as many goods. This **reduces** the management cost per unit.

Financial Economies of Scale

- Larger firms can often **borrow money** at a **lower** rate of **interest** — lending to them is seen by banks as less risky.

Risk-bearing Economies of Scale

- Larger firms can **diversify** into different **product areas** (e.g. make different things) and different **markets** (e.g. sell in different countries). This diversification leads to a **more predictable overall demand** — basically, if demand for one product in one country falls, there's likely to be a different product whose demand somewhere increases.
- It also means large firms are more able to take **risks** (e.g. by launching products that may or may not prove popular). If the product is unsuccessful, a large firm's other activities allow it to **absorb** the cost of **failure** more easily.

Marketing Economies of Scale

- **Advertising** is usually a **fixed cost** — this is spread over more units for large firms, so the cost **per unit** is lower.
- The **cost per product** of advertising several products may also be **lower** than the cost of advertising just one, e.g. a firm could advertise several products on a single flyer.
- Larger firms also benefit from **brand awareness** — products from a well-known brand will be **trusted** by consumers. This might mean a larger firm doesn't need to advertise as much to get sales.

Economies and Diseconomies of Scale

***External* economies of scale involve changes *Outside* a firm**

- Local colleges may start to offer **qualifications** needed by **big local employers**, reducing the firms' training costs.
- Large companies locating in an area may lead to improvements in **road networks** or **local public transport**.
- If lots of firms doing **similar** or **related** things locate near each other, they may be able to **share resources** (e.g. research facilities). **Suppliers** may also decide to locate in the same area, reducing transport costs.

*Extremely successful companies can gain **Monopoly Power** in a market*

1) As a firm's **average cost** for making a product **falls**, it can sell that product at a **lower price**, undercutting its competition.
2) This can lead to a firm gaining a bigger and bigger **market share**, as it continually offers products at prices that are lower than the competition.
3) In this way, a firm can eventually force its competitors out of business and become the **only supplier** of the product — i.e. it will have a **monopoly**.

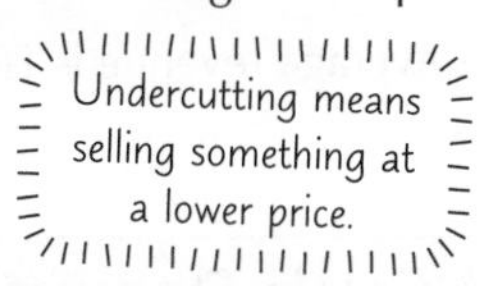
Undercutting means selling something at a lower price.

***Diseconomies of Scale — Disadvantages** of being big*

1) Getting bigger isn't always good though — as a firm increases in size, it can encounter **diseconomies of scale**.
2) Diseconomies of scale cause average cost to **rise** as output rises. Diseconomies can be **internal** or **external**.

INTERNAL

- **Wastage** and **loss** can increase, as materials might seem in plentiful supply. Bigger warehouses might lead to more things getting **lost** or **mislaid**.
- **Communication** may become more difficult as a firm grows, affecting staff morale.
- Managers may be less able to **control** what goes on.
- It becomes more difficult to **coordinate** activities between different divisions and departments.
- A '**them and us**' attitude can develop between workers in different parts of a large firm — workers might put their department's interests before the company's, leading to less cooperation and lower efficiency.

EXTERNAL

- As a **whole industry** becomes bigger, the price of raw materials may **increase** (since demand will be greater).
- Buying large amounts of materials **may not** make them less expensive per unit. If local supplies aren't sufficient, more expensive goods from further afield may have to be bought.

High Fixed Costs** create **Large Economies of Scale

1) There are **huge economies of scale** in industries with **high fixed costs** but **low variable costs.** In some cases, the **structure** of whole industries can change to take advantage of this.
2) For example, **robot-based assembly lines** are very expensive to **set up**, but reduce the **labour** required to produce each unit. This means **fixed costs** will **increase** (as the loans used to buy the equipment need to be repaid), while **variable costs** (e.g. labour costs) **fall**.
3) As a firm grows by taking advantage of its large **economies of scale**, other firms in the industry may be **forced** to follow the same strategy, or shut down. The result is an industry **dominated** by a few large firms (or even just a single firm).

This is an example of improved technology leading to changes in the structure of an industry.

Practice Questions

Q1 What's the difference between an internal economy of scale and an external one?

Q2 Give two examples of economies of scale.

Exam Question

Q1 Explain why companies do not always reduce their average cost of production as their output increases. [5 marks]

Risk-bearing economies of scale — when your business annoys grizzlies...

There are all sorts of economies of scale. But it's not all plain sailing for big firms — they can have difficulties too. This is why someone, somewhere invented the term 'diseconomy of scale'. I know, 'diseconomy' doesn't sound like a real word, but the effects are very real indeed. You know the drill... learn the stuff, cover the page, try to recall it all, and then try the questions.

The Revenue of a Firm

A firm's revenue is the money it receives from selling its production output. Revenue depends on the price a firm is able to get for the quantity of its product that it's selling. So revenue is affected by the demand curve the firm faces. ***For AQA only.***

Revenue is the Money firms receive from Selling their Goods or Services

Total revenue (TR) is the **total amount** of money received, in a time period, **from a firm's sales.**

Total revenue is equal to the **total quantity** (Q) sold multiplied by the **price** (P). It's also called **turnover**. It can be found using the formula: $TR = Q \times P$

Alicia wasn't sure why her accountant wanted to see her turn over...

Average revenue (AR) is the **revenue per unit sold.**

Average revenue is TR **divided** by quantity sold (so **average revenue = price**): $AR = TR \div Q$

A firm's Demand Curve determines how Revenue relates to Output

- Demand curves show what **quantity** of a product a firm will be able to sell at a particular **price.**
- **Price = average revenue**, so the **same** curve shows the relationship between quantity sold and average revenue. (So the demand curve could be labelled **AR.**)
- A firm's **total revenue** is given by **quantity × price.** TR at price P_1 is shown by the shaded area on the diagram.

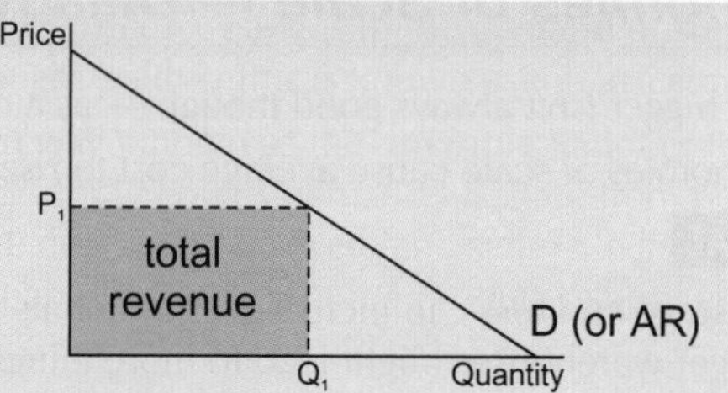

A firm that's a Price Taker has a Perfectly Elastic Demand Curve

A firm that's a **price taker** has **no power** to control the price it sells at — price takers have to **accept** the price set by the **market**.

A price taker's demand curve will be completely flat — demand is **perfectly elastic**. If the firm **increases** the price then the quantity sold will drop to **zero**. And there's no reason to decrease the price because the **same quantity** would sell at the original **higher price**.

(There's more about price takers on p.44.)

Remember, this is the demand curve for the firm, not the market as a whole.

Price (Revenue)

D (or AR)

Quantity

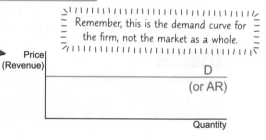

A firm that's a Price Maker has a Downward Sloping Demand Curve

Price makers (e.g. monopolists — see p.46) have **some power** to set the price they sell at.

A price maker's demand curve will slope **downwards** — this means that to **increase sales** the firm must **reduce the price**.

The **price elasticity of demand** (PED) will **change** depending on where the firm is operating on the curve. The relationship between **total revenue** and **price elasticity of demand** is covered in more detail on p.18.

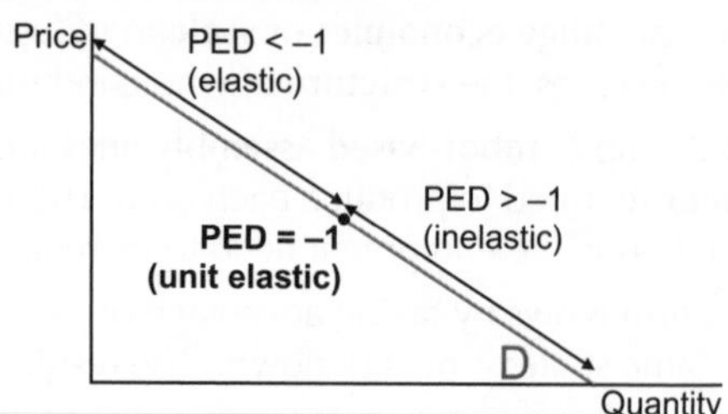

Practice Questions

Q1 Why is the average revenue curve the same as a firm's demand curve?

Exam Question

Q1 Explain why a price maker's demand curve slopes downwards. [4 marks]

Downward sloping demand curve — an economist's favourite yoga pose...

Revenue is determined by the quantity a firm is able to sell at a given price — so a firm's revenue is closely linked to its demand curve. Make sure you remember those two formulas for calculating average and total revenue.

The Objectives of Firms

Although you might reckon that the most important objective for firms is to make a profit, that isn't always the case. Often firms have a variety of different objectives in addition to (or even instead of) profit. ***This page is for AQA only.***

Profit Maximisation *is assumed to be the* ***Objective*** *of a firm*

1) The traditional **theory of the firm** is based on the **assumption** that firms are aiming to **maximise profit**. Profit is given by the following formula:

Profit = Total Revenue (TR) – Total Costs (TC)

2) But in reality, there are **other objectives** a firm might consider **more important**. For example, **revenue maximisation** and **sales maximisation** are other common objectives.
3) The objectives a firm follows will have an impact on **what they do**. For example, a firm aiming to **maximise sales** might set its **prices lower** than a firm aiming to **maximise profits**.

Maximising Profit *might* ***Only*** *be an objective for the* ***Long Run***

1) **Maximising profit** in the **long run** sometimes means **sacrificing profit** in the **short run**.
2) A firm may try to grow by **maximising sales** or **revenue** in the **short run**. For example, a firm might maximise revenue or sales to increase its **market share**, or to gain **monopoly power** so that it can make **large profits** in the long run.

There's more about monopoly power on pages 46 and 47.

3) Some firms may even be willing to operate at a **loss** in the **short run** in order to make a **profit** in the **long run**. A firm may expect **revenue to increase** in the future, for example, once they've been in the market for a while and their **brand recognition** increases. Or a firm might expect to **reduce costs** when they're able to output at higher production levels (i.e. experience economies of scale), and so they may keep operating at a loss while they **build up** the business.

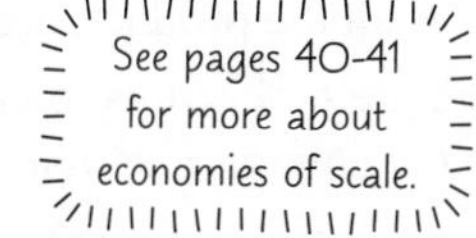
See pages 40-41
for more about
economies of scale.

4) A firm's objective may be to simply **survive** in the **short run**. Then, when it's **established** in a market, it can try to **maximise profits**.
5) Survival may be the objective of a firm operating in a **highly competitive market** (see page 44). To keep operating a firm may need to focus on keeping up with the competition and maintaining the customers that they have.

Some firms have ***Alternative Objectives***

1) Some firms might aim for something not **directly** related to profit, revenue or sales.
2) For example, some organisations are '**not for profit**' — they don't pay out profit to their owners and their **main aim** is to 'do good' or provide some kind of benefit to the public. Other firms will focus on producing **high quality products**, at the expense of maximising profits in the short run, to **gain loyal customers**.
3) Some firms may try to maximise profits by operating in a way that brings **benefit** to **society**, and so **encourages** customers to buy from them. For example:
   - A firm may try to **protect** the **environment** by using **sustainable resources**.
   - A firm may **support local businesses** by using suppliers in their region.
   - A firm may choose to **pay** its workers **above** the standard market rate.

Practice Questions

Q1 List three objectives a firm might have.

Exam Question

Q1 Explain why profit maximisation might not be a firm's most important objective. [10 marks]

Firms with a spiritual focus often aim to maximise prophets...

Traditional economics assumes firms aim to maximise profit — but in reality this often isn't the case. Other objectives that firms have include growth (e.g. by maximising sales and revenue) and even the pretty straightforward objective of survival.

Perfect Competition

Perfectly competitive markets don't happen in real life... but that doesn't mean they're not important. They show the conditions needed to achieve some really useful outcomes. ***These pages are for AQA only.***

Perfectly Competitive markets have certain *Characteristics*

1) The **model of perfect competition** is a description of how a market **would** work **if** certain conditions were satisfied.
2) It's a theoretical thing — there are **no** real markets that work quite like this. But understanding how perfect competition works makes it easier to understand what's going **wrong** with real-life markets when they have undesirable results.
3) In a **perfectly competitive** market, the following conditions are satisfied:

- There's an **infinite** number of **suppliers** and **consumers**.
  - Each of these suppliers is **small** enough that **no** single firm or consumer has any **'market power'** (i.e. no firm or consumer can affect the market on their own).
  - Each firm is a **'price taker'** (as opposed to a **'price maker'**) — this means they have to buy or sell at the current **market price**.

So all firms have 0% concentration. See p.47 for more about concentration.

- **Consumers** have **perfect information** — i.e. perfect knowledge of all goods and prices in a market.
  - Every consumer decision is **well-informed** — consumers know how much **every** firm in the market charges for its products, as well as all the **details** about those products.
- **Producers** have **perfect information** — i.e. perfect knowledge of the market and production methods.
  - No firm has any 'secret' low-cost production methods, and **every** firm knows the prices charged by every **other** firm.
- **Products** are **identical** (**homogeneous**).
  - So consumers can always **switch** between products from different firms (i.e. all the products are perfect **substitutes** for each other).

This also means there's no branding, since branding makes some products seem different from others.

- There are **no barriers to entry** and **no barriers to exit**.
  - New entrants can **join** the industry very easily. Existing firms can **leave** equally easily.
- Firms are **profit maximisers**.
  - So all the **decisions** that a firm makes are geared towards maximising **profit**.

4) The **price** in perfectly competitive markets is determined by the forces of supply and demand, i.e. the **price mechanism**.
5) The conditions for a perfectly competitive market ensure that the **rationing**, **signalling** and **incentive** functions of the **price mechanism** (see p.26) work perfectly. In particular:
   - All firms are **price takers** ('the market' sets the price according to consumers' preferences, **rationing** resources and **signalling** priorities).
   - Consumers and producers have **perfect knowledge** of the market, and there are **no barriers** to entry or exit (so firms can recognise and act on **incentives** to change their output level or enter/leave a market).

See p.46 for more on barriers to entry and exit.

Competitive markets are *Open* to *New Competitors* so *Profits* tend to be *Low*

1) In a **competitive market**, barriers to entry and exit are **low** (see p.46 for more on barriers to entry), so if **high** profits are made by existing firms in the market, **new** firms will enter the market.
   - For example, a market has supply curve S_1 and demand curve **D**. The price is P_1 and firms are making **high profits**. If the market is **competitive**, new firms will enter, **shifting** the supply curve to S_2.
   - The price **falls** from P_1 to P_2, so firms will be making **lower** profits as they're selling at a lower price.
   - If firms are **still** making high profits, **more** firms will enter the market, and prices and profits will **fall** further.

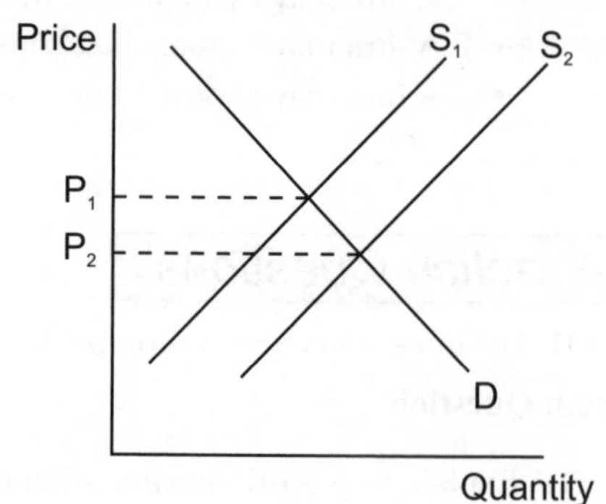
Price
S1
S2
P1
P2
D
Quantity

2) In less competitive markets there are **high** barriers to entry, which make it **difficult** for new firms to enter the market. This means profits and prices will be higher, and will **stay high** as new firms can't enter the market and bring them down. Markets like this tend to be dominated by a **few large firms**.

Perfect Competition

In Real Life there's a 'Spectrum' of different market structures

1) In the real world, there are **no** markets where all the conditions for perfect competition exist — markets fall somewhere on a 'spectrum' of different **market structures**.

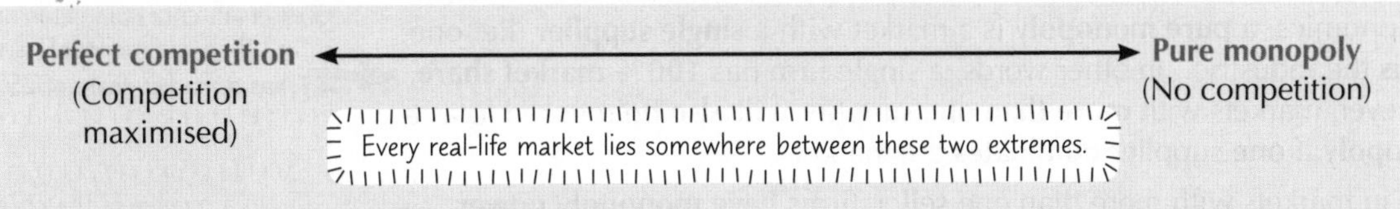
Perfect competition
(Competition maximised)
Pure monopoly
(No competition)
Every real-life market lies somewhere between these two extremes.

2) At one extreme are '**perfectly competitive** markets', and at the other are '**pure monopolies**' (where there's no competition at all — see p.46 for more info). **Real-life** markets lie somewhere between these extremes.
3) There are several factors which **determine** where a market lies on this spectrum. For example, the **number** of firms in a market, the **extent** of product differentiation and the **level** of barriers to entry (see below for more on these).
4) The **closer** an actual market **matches** the description of either a perfectly competitive market or a pure monopoly, the more likely it is to **behave** in the same way.

There are many Factors Influencing the Structure of markets

1) **Product differentiation**:
   - In a **perfectly competitive** market, all the goods produced are **identical**, so the only way for firms to compete is on **price**.
   - In practice, competition will also encourage firms to look for ways to **differentiate** their products from competitors':

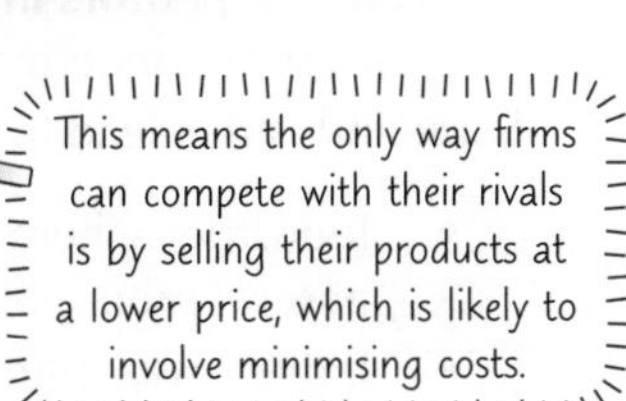
This means the only way firms can compete with their rivals is by selling their products at a lower price, which is likely to involve minimising costs.

• Improved products	• Better quality of service
• Wider product ranges	• Advertising and promotion
• Nicer packaging	• Products that are easier to use

   - If a firm manages to make its products **stand out** from its competitors', it's likely to have a **bigger** share of the market and more **monopoly power** (see next page).
2) The **number** of firms:
   - If a market was **perfectly competitive**, there would be an **infinite** number of firms — but in reality, this can never happen.
   - If there are only **a few firms** in a market, the market is likely to be **less** competitive — this suggests the market is **more** like a pure monopoly.
3) The level of **barriers** to entry:
   - In perfect competition there are **no** barriers to entry — so where barriers to entry exist, the **higher** they get, the **less** like 'perfect competition' a market becomes.

These factors are often linked — e.g. if there are high barriers to entry, there are likely to be fewer firms in the market, and both characteristics suggest the market is more towards the 'pure monopoly' end of the spectrum.

Practice Questions

Q1 List the conditions needed for a perfectly competitive market.
Q2 Why are profits likely to be higher in a market that's dominated by a few large firms than in a perfectly competitive market?
Q3 What are the two extremes between which all market structures lie?

Exam Question

Q1 Explain how product differentiation can influence the structure of a market. [4 marks]

My perfect competition is a prize crossword in the Sunday papers...

In practice, no market completely satisfies the conditions for perfect competition. However, the closer a real-life market comes to satisfying them, the more likely it is to behave in the way predicted by the theoretical model. Market structures range from perfect competition to pure monopoly — make sure you're familiar with the factors that influence a market's structure.

Monopolies

The word 'monopoly' is used by different people to mean slightly different things, but on the next couple of pages it means an industry with only one firm in it. Monopoly power is different, and more common than pure monopolies. ***For AQA only.***

*A **Monopoly** is a market containing a **Single Seller***

1) In economics, a **pure monopoly** is a market with a **single supplier** (i.e. one firm **is** the industry). In other words, a single firm has **100% market share.** However, markets with **more than one** supplier will **also** be referred to as a **monopoly** if **one** supplier **dominates** the market.

In UK law, a monopoly is when a firm has a market share of 25% or more.

2) Even in markets with more than one seller, firms have **monopoly power** if they can influence the price of a particular good on their own — i.e. they can act as **price makers** by **controlling** supply to **influence** the good's price. Firms providing **essential** goods or services with no substitutes can have the **greatest** monopoly power.

In a monopoly, the price isn't determined by 'the market'.

3) There are **very few** examples of pure monopolies in the **real world**, but **plenty** of examples of monopoly power.
4) Monopoly power may come about as a result of:
   - **Barriers to entry** preventing new competition entering a market to compete away large profits (see below).
   - **Advertising and product differentiation** — a firm may be able to act as a price maker if consumers think of its products as more desirable than those produced by other firms (e.g. because of a strong brand).
   - **Few competitors in the market** — if a market is dominated by a small number of firms, these are likely to have some price-making power. They'll also find it easier to differentiate their products.
5) Some industries lead to a **natural monopoly** — this can mean they have a great deal of monopoly power.
   - Industries where there are **high fixed costs** and/or there are **large economies of scale** lead to **natural monopolies.**
   - If there was **more than one** firm in the industry, then they would **all** have the same high fixed costs. This would lead to **higher costs** per customer than could be obtained by a single firm.
   - In this case, a monopoly might be **more efficient** than having lots of firms competing.
   - E.g. the supply of **water** is a **natural monopoly** — it makes no sense for competing firms to all lay **separate** pipes.
6) Even though firms with monopoly power are price makers, **consumers** can still **choose** whether or not to buy their products. So **demand** will still depend on the price — as always, the **higher** the price, the **lower** the demand will be.

***Barriers** to **Entry** can be used to **Create** and **Maintain** monopolies*

1) A **barrier to entry** is any obstacle that makes it **impossible** or **unattractive** for a **new** firm to enter into a market.
2) If entry into the market is **possible**, a **barrier** to entry can make it **more expensive** for a **new** firm to supply the market than an **existing** firm. For example, a large existing firm could cut its prices, losing some **short-term** profits, to **force** a new entrant **out** of the market and ensure its **market dominance** in the **long term**.
3) Other examples of barriers to entry include:
   - **Lower costs** — a large firm could use **economies of scale** to **force out** new entrants to a market.
   - **High start-up costs** which are **non-recoverable** if a firm leaves the industry — it can be **very expensive** for a new firm to **start up** in a market, e.g. it might need to buy expensive machinery. The **risk** involved might **put off** a new firm as it might not be able to recover its start-up costs if it **fails.**
   - **Patents and copyrights** — if the existing monopoly powers hold important patents and copyright (e.g. the patents for a new invention) linked to a market, this might **prevent** a new firm from supplying **competitive products** in that market.
   - **Brand loyalty** — firms can **differentiate** their products from **substitutes** made by competitors using **advertising and branding.** This can create consumers that are loyal to a firm's products and make **entry** for **new firms** (that don't have an established brand) more **difficult.**
   - **Legislation** can be used to create and maintain monopolies. For example, a government can **maintain** a monopoly, using the **law** to **protect** a firm from **competition** — this might happen with a state-owned company.

Monopolies

Concentration Ratios show **How Dominant** the big firms in a market are

1) Some industries are **dominated** by just **a few** companies (even though there may be many firms in that industry overall). These are called **concentrated markets.**
2) The **level** of domination is measured by a **concentration ratio.**
   - Suppose **three firms** control **90%** of the market, while another **40 firms** control the other **10%**.
   - The **3-firm concentration ratio** would be **90%** (i.e. the three largest firms control 90% of the market).
   - It's easy to calculate the **n-firm concentration ratio** of a market. For example, suppose a market is worth £45m and you wanted to find the **3-firm concentration ratio**. If the biggest three firms have revenues of £15m, £9m and £7m respectively, the 3-firm concentration ratio is: $\frac{(15 + 9 + 7)}{45} \times 100 = \mathbf{68.9\%}$

Monopolies have some **Potential Benefits**

1) A monopolist's **large size** allows it to gain an advantage from **economies of scale.** If **diseconomies of scale** are avoided, this means it can keep **average costs** (and perhaps **prices**) low — this can be seen on a long-run average cost (LRAC) curve (see p.59). A monopolist will produce more than any individual producer in a perfectly competitive market would.
2) The **security** a monopolist has in the market (as well as the **profit** it makes) means it can take a long-term view and **invest** in **invention** and **innovation**, e.g. coming up with new products or manufacturing processes.
3) When a market is **dominated** by a few large firms, they might still **compete** with each other — for example, they might compete on **price**, **reducing** costs and **improving** the quality of their products.
4) **Intellectual property rights** (**IPRs**) allow a form of legal **limited monopoly** that can actually be **in consumers' interests** because they'll benefit from better quality, innovative products.
   - There are various types of IPRs, such as **copyright** and **patents**. These allow a firm **exclusive** use of their **innovative ideas** (i.e. no one else is allowed to use them) for a **limited time**.
   - Without the **protection** of IPRs, firms would have **little incentive** to **risk** their resources investing in innovative products or processes — other firms would simply be able to **copy** those ideas (and immediately start to compete away any profits).

The existence of monopolies has several **Disadvantages**

1) Monopolies **restrict consumer choice** as there are **fewer products** to choose from.
2) Monopolies may have **fewer incentives** to **innovate** because they don't have to **improve** their products to make them better than their competitors' products.
3) Monopolies may have **no incentive** to **cut** costs as they're **price makers** (due to a lack of competition in the market) — they can **exploit** consumers by charging **high** prices and they may be **inefficient**, leading to a **misallocation** of resources.
4) A monopoly may use its powers to **exploit** its **suppliers**. For example, a monopoly could demand a **low price** from its suppliers — which they might agree to if the monopoly threatens to use another supplier.

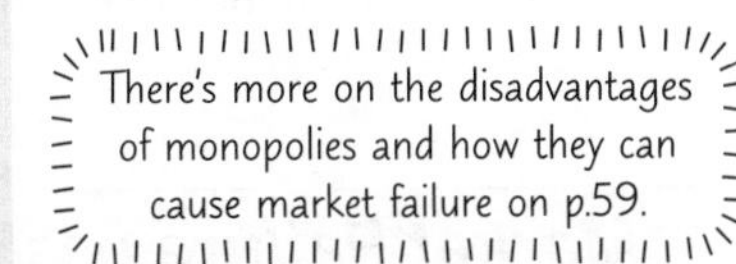

There's more on the disadvantages of monopolies and how they can cause market failure on p.59.

Practice Questions

Q1 What does it mean to say a monopoly is a 'price maker'?

Q2 Give two examples of arguments made in favour of monopolies.

Exam Question

Q1 Explain why it can be difficult for a new firm to enter a market where an existing firm has a monopoly. [8 marks]

My barrier to entry is the moat I built around my house...

And you thought it was just a game. Remember that pure monopolies are pretty rare, but monopoly power is more common. Monopolies and monopoly power aren't always a bad thing — they can bring benefits to the economy too.

Market Failure and Externalities

The price mechanism isn't perfect — this section shows you how markets fail and what governments do to try to stop this happening. Externalities are an important cause of market failure, so you need to learn about them really well. ***For all boards.***

Market Failure occurs when a market Allocates Resources Inefficiently

1) A market **fails** when the **price mechanism** (i.e. the forces of supply and demand) **fails** to allocate scarce resources **efficiently** and **society suffers** as a result — this is known as a **misallocation of resources**.
2) Market failure is a **common problem** and **governments** often **intervene** to try to prevent it (see p.60-67).

AQA ONLY

Market failure can be Complete or Partial

1) When there's **complete** market failure, **no market exists** — this is called a **'missing market'**.
2) **National defence** is an example of a **missing market** as there's **no market** which allocates national defence. This means that **governments** need to intervene and provide it.
3) When the market functions, but either the **price** or **quantity supplied** of the good/service is **wrong**, then there's **partial market failure**.
4) The provision of **health care**, if left completely to market forces, is an example of **partial market failure**. If health care was left to market forces, then some people **wouldn't** be able to **afford** the treatment they needed. As a result, **governments** might **intervene** and provide **free** health care.

Externalities affect Third Parties

1) **Externalities** are the effects that producing or consuming a good/service has on people who **aren't** involved in the making, buying/selling and consumption of the good/service. These people are often called **'third parties'**.
2) Externalities can either be **positive** or **negative**. **Positive externalities** are the **external benefits** to a third party and **negative externalities** are the **external costs** to a third party.
3) Externalities can occur in **production** or **consumption**. For example:

- A **negative externality** of producing steel could be **pollution** that harms the local environment.
- A **positive externality** of producing military equipment could be an **improvement** in **technology** that benefits society.

- A **negative externality** of consuming a chocolate bar could be **litter** that's dropped on the street.
- A **positive externality** of someone training to become a **doctor** (remember — the training is being **consumed**) could be the **benefit** to **society** that this brings.

Market Failure occurs because Externalities are Ignored

1) A **private cost** is the **cost of doing something** to either a consumer or a firm. For example, the cost a firm pays to make a good is its private cost and the price a consumer pays to buy the good is their private cost.
2) **External costs** are caused by **externalities**, e.g. if you dropped an empty crisp packet then that creates an **external cost** to the council who have to employ someone to sweep it up.
3) **Adding** the **private cost** to the **external cost** gives the **social cost**. The social cost is the **full cost** borne by **society** of a good or service.
4) A **private benefit** is the **benefit gained** by a consumer or a firm by doing something. For example, the private benefit a consumer might get from purchasing a skiing holiday is their enjoyment of the experience.
5) **External benefits** are also caused by **externalities**, e.g. a factory that **invests** in new equipment may create the **external benefit** of needing less electricity, which reduces its impact on the climate.
6) **Adding** the **private benefit** to the **external benefit** gives the **social benefit**. The social benefit is the **full benefit** received by **society** from a good or service.
7) **Market failure** occurs because in a free market the price mechanism will only take into account the **private costs** and **benefits**, but **not** the **external costs** and **benefits**.

Externalities — Social Cost and Benefit

Externalities can be shown on diagrams that include private and social costs and benefits. There are a few of these diagrams to learn, but they're pretty simple once you've got your head round them. ***These pages are for Edexcel and OCR only.***

Externalities can be shown using Diagrams

1) Here's an example of **negative externalities** from **production**.
2) The **marginal private cost** (**MPC**) is the cost of **producing** the **last unit** of a good.
3) The **marginal social cost** (**MSC**) = the **marginal private cost** + the **external cost**.
4) So, the **difference** between the **MPC** and the **MSC curves** is the **external cost** of production — the **negative externalities**.
5) If the **MPC** and **MSC curves** are **parallel** then external costs per unit produced are **constant**. If the curves **diverge** then external costs per unit increase with output.
6) An example of why the curves might diverge is **pollution** — the **external costs** per unit created by pollution can **increase** as output increases.

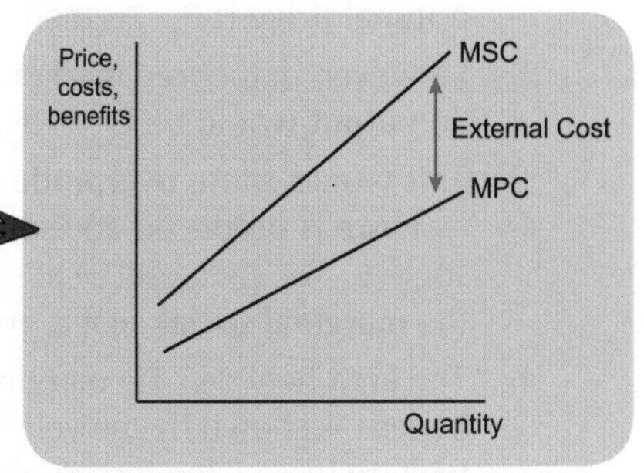

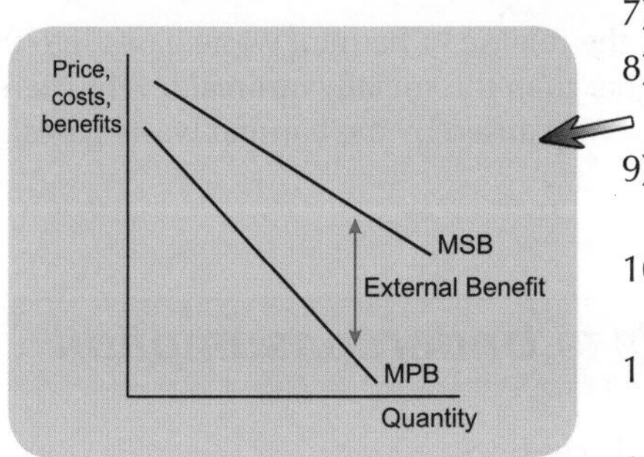

7) Here's an example of **positive externalities** from **consumption**.
8) The **marginal private benefit** (**MPB**) is the benefit to someone of **consuming** the **last unit** of a good.
9) The **marginal social benefit** (**MSB**) = the **marginal private benefit** + the **external benefit**.
10) The **difference** between the **MPB** and the **MSB** curves are the **external benefits** — the **positive externalities**.
11) Again, if the **MPB** and **MSB curves** are **parallel** then external benefits per unit are **constant**. If they **diverge** then external benefits per unit increase with output.
12) An example of when the curves might diverge is **vaccination** — the more people that are vaccinated, the **greater** the **protection** for **unvaccinated** people.

The Equilibrium Point may be Different to the Socially Optimal Point

1) When **supply** and **demand** are equal there's **equilibrium** in the free market.
2) In a free market consumers and producers only consider their **private costs** and **private benefits** — they **ignore** any **social costs** or **benefits**. As a result, the **MPC** curve can be seen as the **supply curve** of a good or service and the **MPB** curve can be seen as the **demand curve**.
3) So, **equilibrium** occurs when **MPC = MPB**. On the diagram this is where output is Q_e and price is P_e.
4) However, the **socially optimum level** of output is where **MSC = MSB**, because this includes the **external costs** and **benefits** to society.
5) This means that the **socially optimum level** of **output** is Q_1 and the **socially optimal price** is P_1. This level of output and price will give society the **maximum** benefit of any **positive externalities** and still cover the cost of any **negative externalities**.

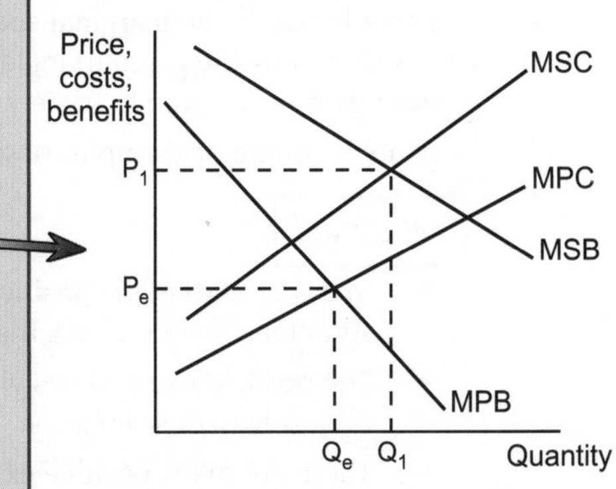

Practice Questions

Q1 What are private costs?

Q2 On an externality diagram, where is the socially optimal level of output?

Exam Question

Q1 Use a diagram to explain why the socially optimal level of output might be different to the output at the equilibrium point. [6 marks]

Socially optimal point — when all your friends think you're cool...

You've got to learn these diagrams for negative and positive externalities — it's very likely that they'll come up in the exam and you may even need to draw one. So it's worth spending a bit of time practising how to make one. Don't forget to label it.

Externalities — Social Cost and Benefit

Right, so let's get down to some of the consequences of externalities. ***For Edexcel and OCR.***

Ignoring **Negative Production Externalities** *leads to* **Overproduction**

1) In this diagram the **optimal output level** of this good is Q_1 and the **optimal price** is P_1. As there are no positive externalities, MPB = MSB.
2) However, in the **free market** only private costs are considered. So **output** would be Q_e and the **price** would be P_e.
3) This would cause **overproduction** and **underpricing** of this good — **more** is produced and sold at a **lower** price than is **desirable** for society. For each unit of this good produced between Q_1 and Q_e the **marginal social cost** is **greater** than the **marginal social benefit**.
4) The **area** between the **marginal social cost** and **marginal social benefit** is shown by the yellow triangle **ABC**. This is the area of **welfare loss** — the loss to society caused by **ignoring externalities**.

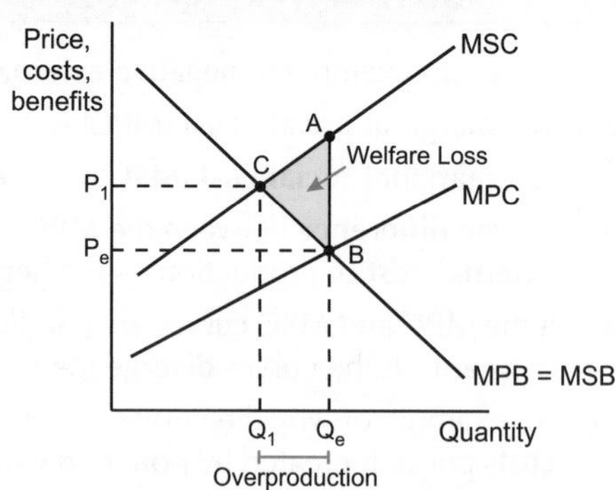

Example A **chemical factory** may **ignore** the **externalities** it produces, such as the release of harmful waste gases into the atmosphere. If this happens then **output** from the factory will be **higher** than the **socially optimal level** (where MSC = MSB) and that will lead to a **welfare loss** to society (e.g. problems caused by the harmful waste gases).

Ignoring **Positive Consumption Externalities** *leads to* **Underconsumption**

1) In this diagram the **optimal level** of **output** for this good is Q_1 and the **optimal price** is P_1. As there are no negative externalities, MPC = MSC.
2) In the free market only **private benefits** are considered. So **output** would be Q_e and the **price** would be P_e.
3) This would cause **underconsumption** and **underpricing** of this good — **less** is consumed and sold at a **lower** price than is **desirable** for society. For each unit of this good consumed between Q_e and Q_1 the **marginal social benefit** is **greater** than the **marginal social cost**.
4) The **area** between the **marginal social benefit** and **marginal social cost** is shown by the green triangle **DEF**. This is the area of potential **welfare gain** — the gain to society **lost** by **ignoring externalities**.

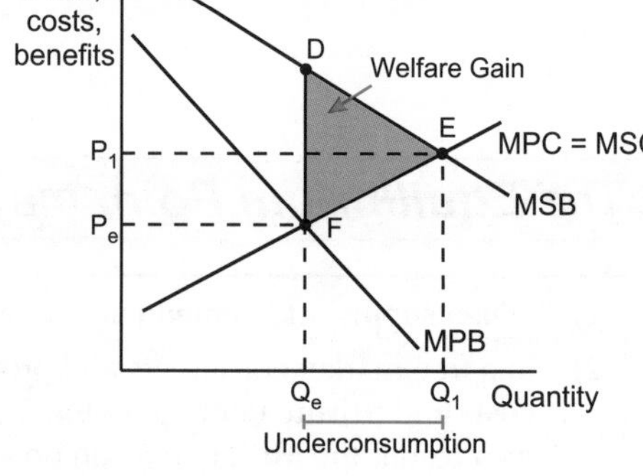

5) Here are a couple of examples of services with **positive consumption externalities**:

Education:

- In a **free market** the **positive externalities** of **education** will be **ignored** by suppliers of education. Their choices are based on **profit maximisation**.
- The positive externalities will also be ignored by **students/parents**, who will **only** consider the **benefits** to **themselves/their children** — e.g. that a good education will help someone get a better/higher-paid job.
- There are many positive externalities of education — for example, the better educated the workforce the **more productive** they are, which in turn **increases** a **country's output**. Furthermore, increasing education levels has other **social benefits** such as reduced crime levels and a happier population.

Health care:

- In the **free market**, **providers** and **consumers** of **health care** will only consider the **private costs** and **benefits**. The decisions they make will **ignore** any **positive externalities**.
- There are many positive externalities of health care — for example, a healthier workforce will be **more productive** and take less time off work, which will in turn **increase** a country's **economic output**. There are also **social benefits** to receiving health care — for example, society as a whole will benefit if people have an improved sense of personal well-being and increased life expectancy.

6) In the free market, both of these services are **underconsumed** and **potential welfare gain** to society is **lost**.

Externalities — Social Cost and Benefit

OCR ONLY

Ignoring Negative Consumption Externalities *leads to* Overconsumption

1) In this diagram the **optimal level** of **output** for this good is Q_1 and the **optimal price** is P_1 (assuming MPC = MSC). The marginal private benefit is **larger** than the marginal social benefit.
2) In the free market only **private benefits** are considered. So **output** would be Q_e and **price** would be P_e.
3) This would cause **overconsumption** and **overpricing** of this good — **more** is consumed and sold at a **higher** price than is **desirable** for society. For each unit of this good consumed between Q_1 and Q_e the **marginal social cost** is **greater** than the **marginal social benefit**.
4) The **area** between the **marginal social cost** and **marginal social benefit** is shown by the yellow triangle **KLM**. This is the area of **welfare loss** — the loss to society caused by **ignoring externalities**.

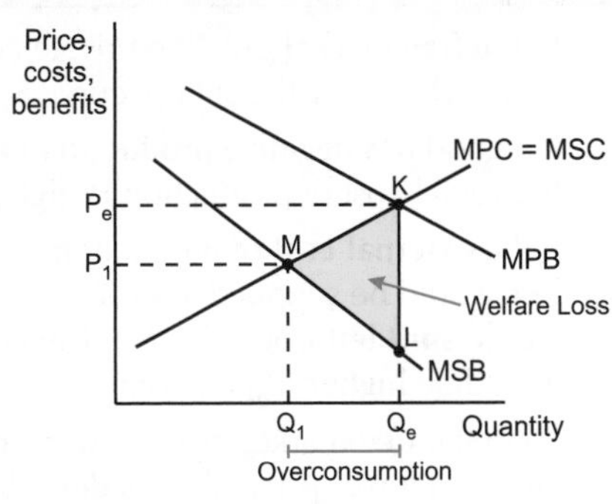

Example: **Drivers** will **ignore** the **negative consumption externalities** associated with driving their cars, such as pollution and congestion. This will result in the usage of cars being **higher** than the **socially optimal level**, causing a welfare loss to society (e.g. traffic jams reducing the productivity of workers).

OCR ONLY

Ignoring Positive Production Externalities *leads to* Underproduction

1) In this diagram the **optimal level** of **output** for this good is Q_1 and the **optimal price** is P_1 (assuming MPB = MSB). The marginal private cost is larger than the marginal social cost.
2) In the free market only **private costs** are considered. So **output** would be Q_e and **price** would be P_e.
3) This would cause **underproduction** and **overpricing** of this good — **less** is produced and sold at a **higher** price than is **desirable** for society. For each unit of this good consumed between Q_e and Q_1 the **marginal social cost** is **lower** than the **marginal social benefit**.
4) The **area** between the **marginal social cost** and **marginal social benefit** is shown by the green triangle **PQR**. This is the area of potential **welfare gain** — the gain to society lost by **ignoring externalities**.

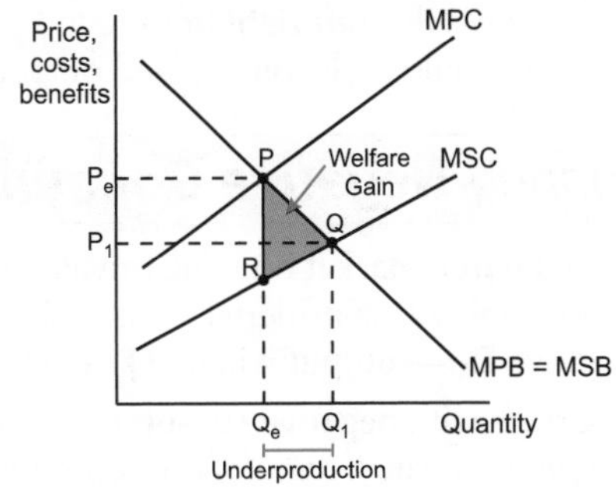

Example: **Employers** will **ignore** the **positive production externalities** associated with paying to **train** their employees, such as the benefit to society of having a more highly skilled workforce. This means resources **won't** be allocated to training employees to the **socially optimal level**, causing a **potential welfare gain** to society to be **lost**.

Practice Questions

Q1 Give an example of a negative production externality.

Q2 What will happen if the positive production externalities of staff training are ignored?

Exam Questions

Q1 Use a diagram to show how the underconsumption of education in the free market leads to the loss of a potential welfare gain to society. [12 marks]

Q2 Use a diagram to show how the consumption of cigarettes in the free market can lead to a welfare loss for society. [12 marks]

Unlike the free market — don't ignore externalities...

... you can pretty well guarantee they'll pop up at some point in the exam. Externalities are 'the' classic reason for market failure, so you'll need to know them well and be able to reproduce the diagrams from memory. So get practising.

Externalities — Demand and Supply

If you're doing AQA, you need to be able to use supply and demand diagrams to show externalities. ***For AQA only.***

Ignoring **Negative Production Externalities** *leads to* **Overproduction**

1) In the **free market** only the private cost of producing something is considered. This is shown by the supply curve **S_1**, so **output** will be **Q_1** and **price** will be **P_1**.
2) If a good has **negative production externalities** then the social cost of production is **higher** than the private cost.
3) If the **external cost** of production was taken into account, **less** would be supplied at every price level — the supply curve would **shift left** from S_1 to S_2. Then the equilibrium price would be **higher** (P_2) and output would be **lower** (Q_2).
4) So in the free market there is **overproduction** and **underpricing** of this good — **more** is produced and sold (and at a **lower** price) than is **desirable** for society, i.e. production is above the **socially optimal level**.

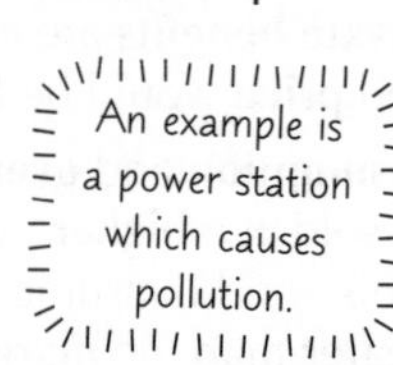

An example is a power station which causes pollution.

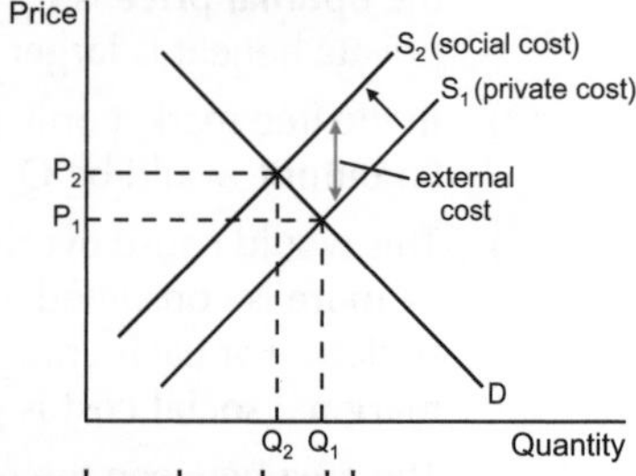

Ignoring **Positive Production Externalities** *leads to* **Underproduction**

1) If a good has **positive production externalities** then the private cost of production is **higher** than the social cost — production of the good **reduces** costs for external parties.
2) In the **free market** supply will be S_1, output will be Q_1, and price will be P_1. So there will be **underproduction** and **overpricing** of this good.
3) But if the **reduction in external cost** was taken into account, **more** would be supplied at every price level — the supply curve would **shift right** from S_1 to S_2. Then the equilibrium price would be **lower** (P_2) and output would be **higher** (Q_2).

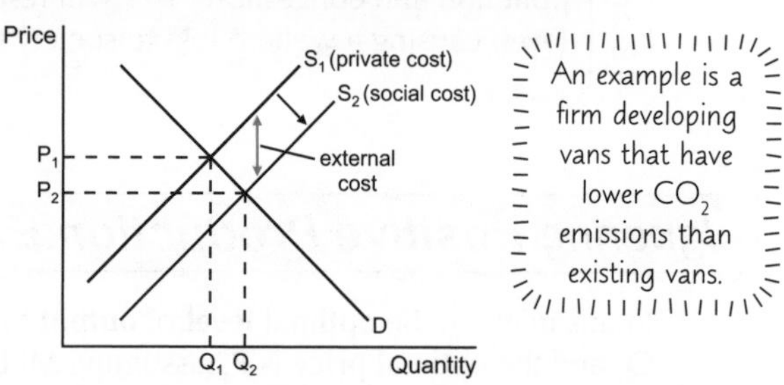

Ignoring **Negative Consumption Externalities** *leads to* **Overconsumption**

1) In the **free market** only the private benefit of consuming something is considered. This is shown by the demand curve **D_1** — **output** will be **Q_1** and the **price** will be **P_1**.
2) Goods with **negative consumption externalities** have a higher private benefit of consumption than social benefit.
3) If the **reduction in external benefit** was taken into account too, **less** would be consumed at every price level, so the demand curve would **shift left** from D_1 to D_2. Then both the equilibrium price (P_2) and output (Q_2) would be **lower**.
4) So in the free market there's **overconsumption** and **overpricing** of this good — **more** is consumed and sold (and at a **higher** price) than is **desirable** for society, i.e. consumption is above the **socially optimal level**.

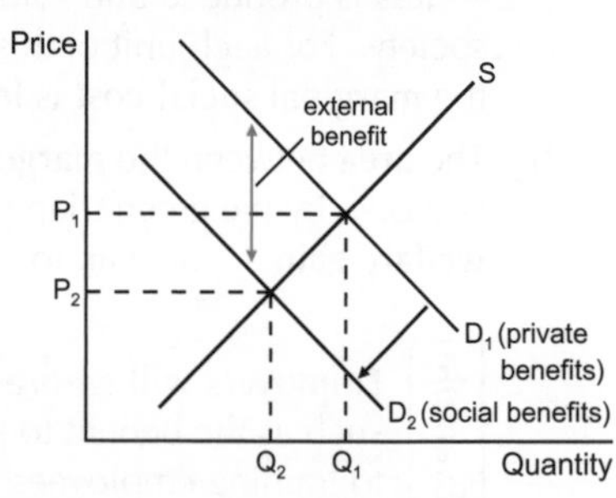

Ignoring **Positive Consumption Externalities** *leads to* **Underconsumption**

1) If a good has **positive consumption externalities** this means the private benefit of consumption is **lower** than the social benefit — consumption of the good generates benefits for external parties.
2) In the free market demand will be D_1, output will be Q_1, and price will be P_1 — there's **underconsumption** and **underpricing** of this good.
3) But if the external benefit was taken into account, **more** would be demanded at every price level — the demand curve would **shift right** from D_1 to D_2. This would raise the equilibrium price to P_2 and output to Q_2.

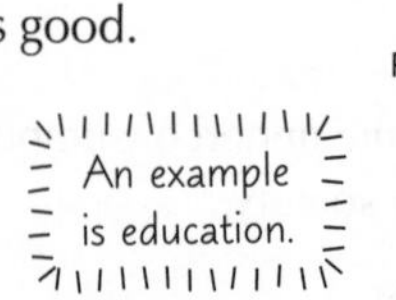

An example is education.

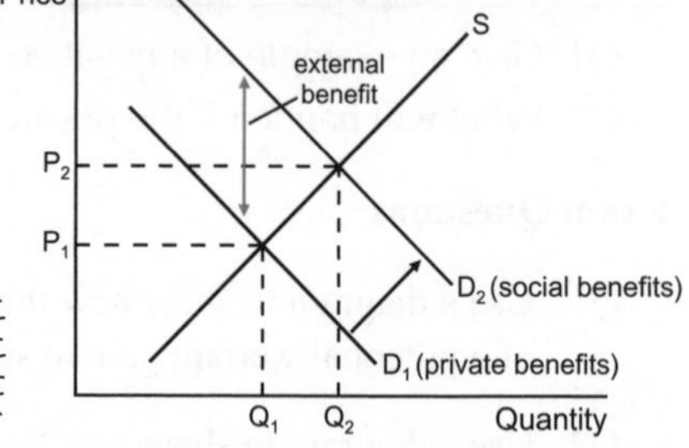

Exam Question

Q1 Use a diagram to explain how ignoring positive production externalities can lead to underproduction. [9 marks]

The supply of externality diagrams is far greater than my demand for them...

There's a lot to take in here but make sure you know all four diagrams really well, as any of them could crop up in your exam.

Merit and Demerit Goods

Classifying merit and demerit goods involves looking at the social and private benefits and costs. Some things are pretty universally agreed on, but a lot of it comes down to judgement. ***These pages are for AQA and OCR only.***

Merit Goods *benefit society but* ***Demerit Goods*** *do the opposite*

Merit goods have greater social benefits than private benefits

- **Merit goods** are goods whose consumption is regarded as being **beneficial** to **society**. They provide benefits to both **individuals** and **society** as a whole (due to the **positive externalities** that result from their consumption, see p.50 and 52), but people are usually **unaware** of the **full benefits** that merit goods provide.
- **Examples** of merit goods include **health care** and **education**.
- Merit goods tend to be **underconsumed** for two main reasons:
  i) In the free market the **positive externalities** that merit goods provide are **ignored**, and **production** and **consumption** will be **below** the **socially optimal level**. For example, producers and consumers **won't** consider the **wider benefits** to society of a **good education**, such as having a **more productive workforce**.
  ii) Due to **imperfect information** (see p.56 for more), consumers **don't always realise** the **full benefits** that merit goods provide. For example, people might not have enough information on how serious their **health problems** might be, so their **demand** for health care **isn't as high** as it should be and health care is **underprovided**.
- Not all merit goods will be welcomed by all potential consumers, and they can be **rejected** — for example, the offer of free vaccinations may be refused.

Demerit goods have greater social costs than private costs

- **Demerit goods** are goods whose consumption is regarded as being **harmful** to the people that consume them, but people are usually **unaware** (or **don't care**) about the harm that the demerit goods can cause. Demerit goods also have a **harmful effect** on **society** due to the **negative externalities** that result from their consumption, see p.51-52.
- **Examples** of demerit goods are **cigarettes** and **heroin**.
- Demerit goods tend to be **overconsumed** for two main reasons:
  i) In the free market the **negative externalities** that demerit goods cause are **ignored**, and **production** and **consumption** will be **above** the **socially optimal level**. For example, producers and consumers **won't** consider the **wider disadvantages** to society of **cigarettes**, such as smoking-related health issues putting a strain on health care services.
  ii) Due to **imperfect information**, consumers **don't always realise** the **harm** that demerit goods cause. For example, people might not have enough information on how a **harmful drug** might affect their health, so their **demand** for the drug is **higher** than it should be and the drug is **overprovided**.

1) Sometimes it's **hard to say** which goods should be classified as merit or demerit goods. Whether a good fits into one of these classifications is usually a **value judgement** — based on people's **opinions** and not on **economic theory** or **facts**.
2) For example, some people consider **contraception** to be a **merit** good, but **others** don't.
3) **Not all** goods with **positive externalities** are merit goods, e.g. planting flowers in a garden may have positive externalities, such as providing pollen for bees or an attractive sight for passers-by, but flower seeds are unlikely to be seen as merit goods whose consumption should be encouraged for the benefit of society.
4) **Not all** goods with **negative externalities** are demerit goods, e.g. driving a car can cause negative externalities (like pollution), but driving a car isn't seen as being harmful to an individual in the way that taking a drug might be.

The market ***Underprovides*** *merit goods and* ***Overprovides*** *demerit goods*

OCR ONLY

Merit *goods generate* ***Positive Externalities***

1) If it's left to the free market then price and quantity demanded of a merit good will be at $\mathbf{P_e}$ and $\mathbf{Q_e}$ respectively, where the MPB curve **crosses** the MPC/MSC curve. The **market equilibrium** is below the **socially optimal** level of consumption ($\mathbf{Q_1}$) — where MSC = MSB.
2) The area **ABC** is the potential welfare gain **lost** by underconsuming/underproducing the merit good.
3) To increase consumption to the socially optimal level of $\mathbf{Q_1}$ the government could introduce a **subsidy** (see p.62) to bring the price down to $\mathbf{P_2}$.

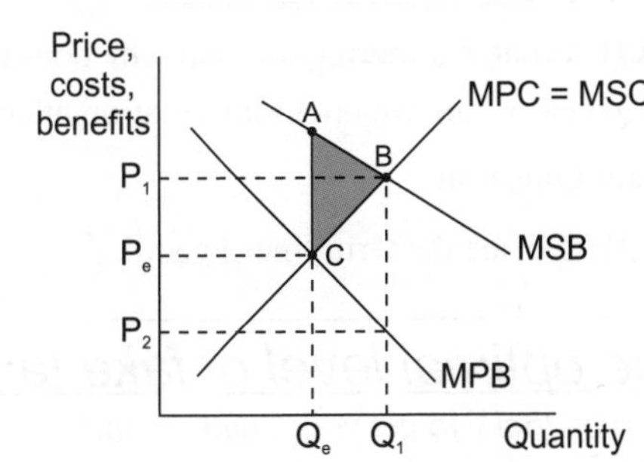

Merit and Demerit Goods

OCR ONLY

Demerit goods generate Negative Externalities

1) Again, if it's left to the free market then the price and quantity demanded of a demerit good will be at P_e and Q_e respectively, where the MPC/MSC and the MPB curves cross. The **market equilibrium** is above the **socially optimal** level of consumption at Q_1 — where MSC = MSB.
2) The area **DEF** is the **welfare loss** caused by overconsuming/overproducing the demerit good.
3) To decrease consumption to the socially optimal level of Q_1 the government could introduce a **tax** (see p.60-61) to bring the price up to P_2.

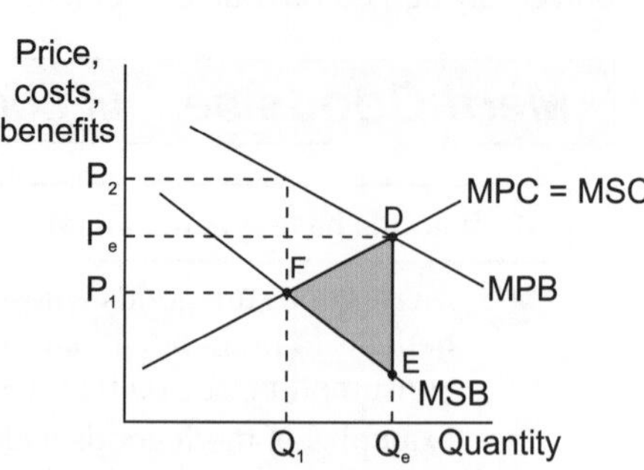

AQA ONLY

Supply and Demand diagrams can show Externalities of Merit and Demerit goods

1) **Merit goods** are **underconsumed** — because they have **positive** consumption externalities, the free market equilibrium is **below** the socially optimal level. The **positive consumption externality diagram** on p.52 shows this.
2) **Demerit goods** are **overconsumed** — they have **negative** consumption externalities, so the free market equilibrium is **above** the socially optimal level of consumption. The **negative consumption externality diagram** on p.52 shows this.

Short-term decision-making can affect the Consumption of goods

When individuals take a **short-term** approach to decision-making, it can lead to the **underconsumption** of **merit** goods and the **overconsumption** of **demerit** goods.

1) People **often** only consider the **short-term benefits** or **costs**. Individuals can **fail** to see the need to make **provision** for the **future** and for **potential changes** in their circumstances. A good example of this is paying into an old-age pension.
2) The **long-term** private benefits of **merit goods** are **greater** than their **short-term** private benefits and the **long-term** private costs of **demerit goods** are **greater** than their **short-term** private costs.
3) The **short-term benefits** of paying towards a pension (knowledge that you are saving for your old age) are **less** than the benefits of **receiving** that pension when you retire.
4) The **short-term costs** of buying cigarettes are much **less** than the **long-term** costs, e.g. serious smoking-related illness.

Go on... just think about the short-term benefit.

Governments can Intervene in markets for merit and demerit goods

1) The **failure** of the free market to supply the **socially optimal levels** of merit and demerit goods is the **main reason** why governments **intervene** to affect their supply. Governments can **directly provide** certain goods or services (see p.65) or they can uses **taxes** and **subsidies** (see p.60-62) to decrease or increase consumption of certain goods or services to the **socially optimal level**.
2) Governments have **a lot of information** regarding the **costs** and **benefits** of goods/services to both individuals and society as a whole, and can **use** this information to make decisions that benefit the whole of society.

Practice Questions

Q1 What is a merit good and why does the consideration of merit goods involve value judgements?

Q2 How can imperfect information affect the supply of demerit goods?

Exam Question

Q1 Define the term 'merit good'. [3 marks]

The optimal level of fake tan consumption is 'just' before orange...

It can be tricky to get your head around these concepts, so make sure you take the time to do so. The key thing to remember is that for merit goods social benefits exceed private benefits and for demerit goods the private costs are less than the social costs.

Public Goods

The under-provision of public goods is an important example of market failure and it's one of the main reasons for government intervention to correct market failure. ***This page is for all boards.***

Public Goods are goods that are consumed *Collectively*

1) An example of a **public good** could be a flood defence scheme or street lighting.
2) Public goods have **two main characteristics**:

- **Non-excludability** — people **cannot** be **stopped** from consuming the good even if they **haven't** paid for it, e.g. you couldn't stop an individual benefiting from the services of the armed forces. (Public goods are also said to be **non-rejectable**, e.g. you can't choose to not be protected by the armed forces — they'll do it anyway.)
- **Non-rivalry/non-diminishability** — **one person** benefiting from the good **doesn't** stop **others** also benefiting, e.g. more people benefiting from flood defences doesn't reduce the benefit to the first person to benefit.

3) Some other examples of public goods include **firework displays** and **lighthouses**.

Public goods are often provided by governments — see p.65.

Private Goods are the *Opposite* of public goods

1) **Private goods** are **excludable** (you can stop someone consuming them) and they **exhibit rivalry**. For example, biscuits are a private good — if you eat a biscuit you **stop** anyone else from eating it.
2) Unlike public goods, people have a **choice** as to whether to consume private goods — biscuits can be rejected.
3) **Most** goods are private goods — anything from **bread** to a **university education**.

Some *Public Goods* can take on the *Characteristics* of *Private Goods*

1) Some goods are **pure public goods**, e.g. lighthouses. Others can exhibit the characteristics of a public good — but **not fully**. These are known as **non-pure** (or **quasi**) **public goods**.

For example, **roads** appear to have the characteristics of a public good — often they're **free** for everyone to use (non-excludable) and one person using a road **doesn't prevent** another person from using it too (non-rivalrous). However, **tolls** can make a road **excludable** by excluding those who don't pay to use it, and **congestion** will make a road exhibit **rivalry** as there's a limit to the number of people who can benefit from the road at any one time.

2) **New technology** can **change** a good that once had the characteristics of a **public** good into a **private** good.

For example, 'analogue' television broadcasting has some characteristics of a **public good** — if you own a TV and an aerial then TV broadcasts are **non-rivalrous** and **non-excludable**. However, the **invention** of **digital technology** has meant that channels can be **encrypted** to ensure that if people want a certain channel, they have to **pay for it**.

Public Goods are *Under-provided* by the free market

1) The **non-excludability** of public goods leads to what's called the **free rider problem**.
2) The free rider problem means that once a public good is provided it's **impossible** to **stop** someone from **benefiting** from it, even if they **haven't** paid towards it. For example, a firm providing street cleaning **cannot** stop a free rider, who has **refused** to pay for street cleaning, **benefiting** from a clean street.
3) The **price mechanism cannot** work if there are free riders. Consumers **won't** choose to pay for a public good that they can get for free because other consumers have paid for it.
4) If everyone decides to **wait and see** who will provide and pay for a public good, then it **won't** be provided.
5) It's also **difficult** to set a **price** for public goods because it's **difficult** to **work out** their **value** to consumers.
6) **Producers** will tend to **overvalue** the benefits of a public good in order to **increase** the **price** that they charge. **Consumers** will **undervalue** their benefits to try to get a **lower price**.
7) These problems mean that firms are **reluctant** to supply public goods, and the problems will cause **market failure**. As a result, governments usually have to intervene to provide the public good (see p.65).

Positive externalities are a form of public good. They're consumed by those who **don't** pay for them, so they're an example of the **free rider problem**.

AQA students — No market exists for externalities, so they're an example of a missing market.

Free riders — a big problem for waves in Australia, California, Newquay...

The difference between public goods and private goods is straightforward and it's easy to see why market failure is caused by people not paying for public goods. If it's left to the market, no one would put up street lamps or provide flood defences.

Imperfect Information

Perfect information will hardly ever actually exist. Unsurprisingly, this leads to another example of market failure. ***For all boards.***

Symmetric Information means Everyone has Equal and Perfect Knowledge

1) In a **competitive market** it's assumed that there's **perfect information**. That means that **buyers** and **sellers** are assumed to have **full** knowledge regarding **prices**, **costs**, **benefits** and **availability** of products.
2) **Perfect** information which is **equally** available to **all** participants in a market is known as **symmetric information**.
3) Assuming that buyers and sellers are **rational** in their behaviour, this symmetric information will allow the **efficient allocation** of resources in and between markets. However, symmetric information **rarely** exists, e.g. **buyers** often don't have the **time** or **resources** to obtain full information on prices before **buying** a product.

Asymmetric Information involves a Lack of Perfect Information in a market

1) Usually **sellers** have **more** information on a product than **buyers**. For example, a used car salesman will have more information about the history of a car they're selling than a prospective buyer.
2) Sometimes **buyers** may have more information than **sellers**. For example, an antiques collector (buyer) may know more about the value of an antique than the person selling it.
3) When **buyers** or **sellers** have **more information** this is known as **asymmetric information**, and information is **imperfect**.
4) **Providers** of **some** services have a lack of information because the thing they provide a service for is **unpredictable**, e.g. health service providers don't know **when** someone will become ill and with **what** health problem.
5) **Moral hazard** is another possible result of asymmetric information. This happens when people take **risks** because they won't suffer the **consequences** themselves if things go wrong. For example, an individual could buy **home insurance**, but then behave **recklessly** (for example not locking their doors), safe in the knowledge that they're covered. The insurance provider **lacks information** about how the individual is acting.

Information Failure causes Market Failure

1) **Imperfect information** means that **merit** goods (e.g. education, health care and pensions) are **underconsumed** and **demerit** goods (e.g. tobacco and alcohol) are **overconsumed** (for more on merit and demerit goods see p.53-54). There are many reasons why **imperfect information** affects the **consumption** of merit and demerit goods, for example:
   - Consumers may not know the **full personal benefit** of a merit good. They may not realise that a good education could lead to improved future earnings, or that a regular medical check-up might improve their lifespan.
   - Consumers may **lack** the **information** to decide which good or service is right for them.
   - Consumers may not have the information on how **harmful** a demerit good, such as alcohol, can be.
   - **Advertising** for a demerit good may withhold or 'gloss over' any health dangers.
2) Due to **information failure**, merit goods tend to be **underprovided** and demerit goods are **overprovided**, causing a **misallocation of resources** and **market failure**. There are many reasons why **imperfect information** affects the **provision** of merit and demerit goods, for example:
   - Pension providers have a **greater knowledge** of the **pension schemes available** than their clients — this can lead to them selling **unnecessary** schemes or **more expensive** schemes than may be needed.
   - Doctors have a **greater knowledge** of medicine — they may persuade their **clients** to purchase more expensive care than is **required**.
   - Information on a good/service may be **too complex** to understand, e.g. the technical differences between computers may be confusing to a consumer, so they might struggle to work out which is best for their needs.

Practice Questions

Q1 What is symmetric information?

Q2 What is asymmetric information?

Exam Question

Q1 Describe how imperfect information can lead to the overprovision of a demerit good. [4 marks]

You won't find imperfect information in this book...

Don't get confused by all the different names on this page. Make sure you get your head around what perfect information is — when it exists there's symmetric information in a market and when it doesn't there's usually asymmetric information.

Inequity

Equity is another word for fairness, so inequity means 'unfairness'. Some people think that big differences in income and wealth between people is unfair and that this is an example of a market failure. ***This page is for AQA only.***

Consumption by an *Individual* depends on *Wealth* and *Income*

1) **Income** is the amount of money received over a **set** period of time, e.g. per week or per year.
2) Income can come from **many sources** — e.g. **wages**, **interest** on bank accounts, **dividends** from shares and **rents** from properties.
3) Wealth is the **value** in money of **assets** held — **assets** can **include** property, land, money and shares.
4) The **greater** an individual's income and wealth, the **more** goods and services they're **able** to purchase.

Income and *Wealth* are not distributed *Equally* in a market economy

1) Many people view **differences** in income and wealth as **unfair**, especially if they're **significant**.
2) In economies with **high** levels of **inequality** of income and wealth distribution (e.g. Sierra Leone), there can be people who are **starving** whilst others have **very high** levels of income and wealth.
3) Inequality can be **caused** by a number of things, such as **differences in wages** and **regressive taxes** (see p.119). Generally speaking, people who are **born** into a **poor family** will **remain poor** because they **won't** have the **income** and **wealth needed** to **improve** their **situation**.
4) This is because inequality can lead to **differences** in **access** to **resources** — it affects the **ability** of individuals to **consume** goods and services. For example, people with **very low** income or wealth may **not** be able to **afford** vital resources and services, such as **education**. As a result, a lack of education may well mean these people will **continue** to have low income or wealth as they will struggle to get a good job. People with higher income and wealth will be able to afford the **best education**, and improve their prospects of high income in future.

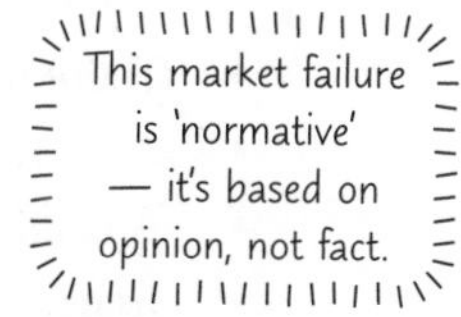

This market failure is 'normative' — it's based on opinion, not fact.

5) Some economists argue that the **unequal** distribution of income and wealth is a **consequence** of **market failure**, because the free market has led to this **inequitable** (unfair) distribution of income and wealth. As a result, they say that **redistribution** of income and wealth would lead to an **allocation** of **resources** that would **increase** the benefit to society, and society's **overall** 'happiness'.
6) The argument for this is that the **benefit** to a poor person from an **additional** £1 of income would be **greater** than the **loss** to a rich person who paid £1 extra in tax.
7) Inequality is also a **cause** of **market failure**. If, for example, some people **don't** have the income and wealth to be able to pay for things that they **need** (such as merit goods, like education), then resources **won't** be **allocated efficiently**.

Governments might try to *Distribute* income and wealth more *Equally*

1) Correcting this market failure requires **government intervention**. For example, a government might introduce progressive taxes to redistribute wealth and income.
2) The level of redistribution undertaken by governments is a **political decision** based on **value judgements** — it's up to them how much they redistribute income and wealth.
3) Some people argue that redistributing income **reduces** the **incentive** for individuals and firms to work hard. These incentives are needed to encourage **efficiency** within the market, and not having them may cause **greater market failure**.

Practice Questions

Q1 What is income?

Q2 What is wealth?

Q3 Why might the redistribution of income and wealth be considered as undesirable?

Exam Question

Q1 Explain why the unequal distribution of income and wealth is considered a market failure. [4 marks]

I'd love it if the government would distribute some more income my way...

This market failure is more opinion-based than the others — not everyone agrees that inequality of income and wealth is a market failure. Whether you agree or not, you need to know why a government may act to redistribute income and wealth.

Immobile Factors of Production

Hang in there — just a couple more pages on market failure to go. Immobile factors aren't just things which can't physically move — they also include things such as an individual with little training or education. ***This page is for AQA only.***

Factors of Production can be Immobile

1) An **immobile** factor of production is one that can't easily be **moved** to another area of the economy.
2) **Land** is an immobile factor of production — it cannot be moved from one location to another. **Land** can also be immobile because, for example, it may only be good for **one type** of agriculture (e.g. land on which rice is grown may not be suitable for growing wheat).
3) A lot of **capital** is **mobile** (e.g. computers) — it can be moved from one location (or one use) to another, but some is **immobile** because of its **size** (e.g. a steel foundry) or its **specialist nature** (e.g. a nuclear reactor).
4) Land and capital can become immobile by **human action** — e.g. a farmer may **choose** not to change the crops he grows on his land **despite** changes in climate.

Labour Immobility can be Geographical or Occupational

Labour is mobile if workers are able to move from one job to another — this movement could be between **occupations** or between **geographical areas**. However, there are several reasons why labour can be immobile:

Reasons for geographical immobility:

- **Large** house-price, rent and cost-of-living differences **between** areas can make it **very difficult** for workers to **move location** to obtain work.
- There may also be **high costs** involved in **moving** houses.
- A **reluctance** to leave family and friends.
- A **dislike** of change.
- **Imperfect information** about the jobs **available** in different areas.

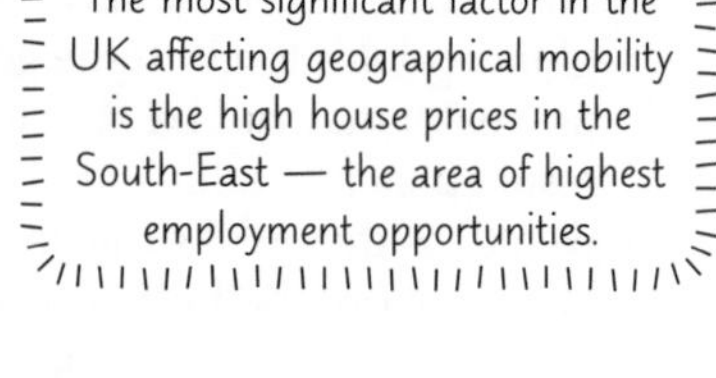

The most significant factor in the UK affecting geographical mobility is the high house prices in the South-East — the area of highest employment opportunities.

Reasons for occupational immobility:

- Lack of **training, education** and **skills** required to do a **different job**.
- Lack of **required** qualifications or **required** membership of a professional body (e.g. doctors have to be **registered** with the General Medical Council).
- Lack of **work experience**.

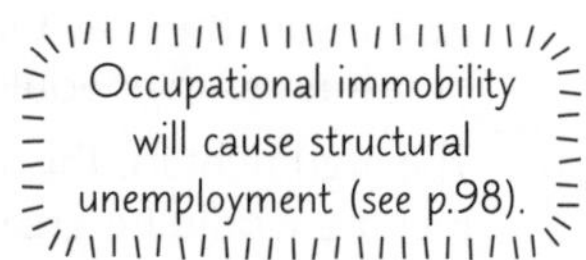

Occupational immobility will cause structural unemployment (see p.98).

Immobile Factors of Production cause Market Failure

1) Immobile factors of production mean there's often **inefficient** use of **resources** — resources are often **unused** or **underused**. This **inefficiency** in the **allocation** of resources means there's **market failure**.
2) There's a limit to how much a **government** can tackle immobile factors of production. Governments can't **move land** and most of them can't **force workers** to **relocate**.
3) However, governments can take some action to **improve labour mobility**. For example:
   - To improve **geographical** mobility governments could offer **relocation subsidies** or **mortgage relief** to make moving to a particular area **more affordable** for workers. Governments could also offer incentives to **encourage** the **construction** of housing in areas where it's needed to provide homes for workers.
   - To improve **occupational** mobility governments could provide more **training programmes** to increase people's skills.

Practice Questions

Q1 Give three examples of immobile factors of production.

Q2 What are the two types of labour immobility?

Exam Question

Q1 How can immobile factors of production lead to market failure? [4 marks]

A traffic light — a good example of a geographically immobile worker...

The stuff on this page isn't too complicated — some things that are needed for production can't be moved, whether that's land, labour or capital. This means that these resources might not be used to their full potential, causing market failure.

Market Failure in Monopolies

Monopolies (see p.46) can cause market failure through inefficiency and by restricting consumer choice. ***This is for AQA only.***

Monopolies cause **Market Failure** and the **Misallocation** of **Resources**

1) The diagram shows the supply and demand curves of a market. The **market equilibrium** would be at **point M**, where supply is $\mathbf{Q_c}$ and price $\mathbf{P_c}$.
2) However, in a **monopoly** situation there's only one firm in the market, so it could misallocate resources by **restricting supply** to $\mathbf{Q_m}$ and force the **price** up to $\mathbf{P_m}$.
3) This is a **market failure** which causes a **welfare loss** of **KLM** — there are fewer units available for consumers to buy (Q_m to Q_c are no longer available). The area of $\mathbf{P_cP_mKL}$, which would've been part of the consumer surplus, is **added** to the **firm's profits**.
4) By **restricting output** monopolies can **fail** to exploit some **economies of scale**. This means that **productive efficiency isn't achieved** and the firm isn't producing output at the lowest point on its long-run average cost curve (see below).

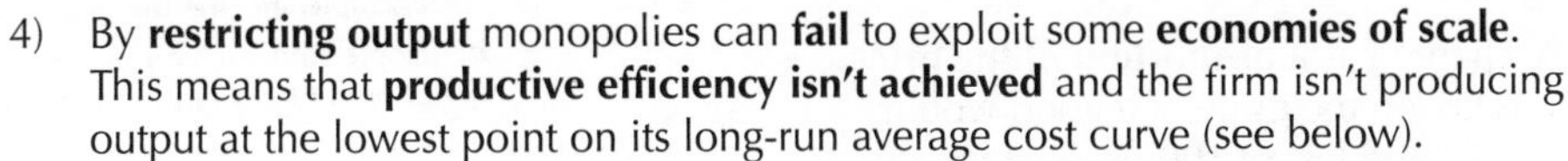

5) Monopoly firms can also experience **higher costs of production** than firms that exist in a **competitive market** — this can be because **monopolies** have less of an **incentive** to innovate to make production methods as efficient (and cost-effective) as possible. They may also have **no incentive** to **cut costs** as they're **price makers**.

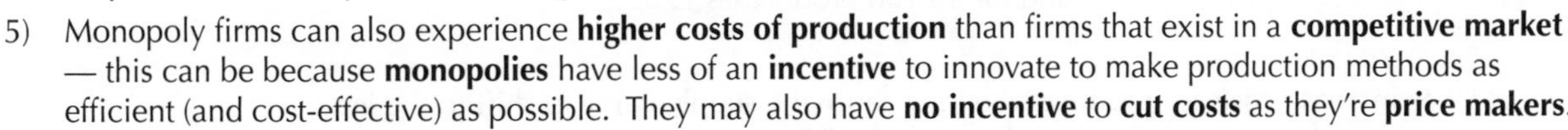

6) Furthermore, market failure will be caused by the **effect** monopolies have on **consumers**. Consumer choice is **restricted** because there are fewer products to choose from, and monopolies **won't** necessarily **react** to the **wants** and **needs** of consumers because they can set their own prices.

Monopolies can bring **Benefits** to an **Economy**

1) In the long run a firm's costs are affected by economies and diseconomies of scale (see page 40) — this determines the shape of the **long-run average cost (LRAC) curve**.

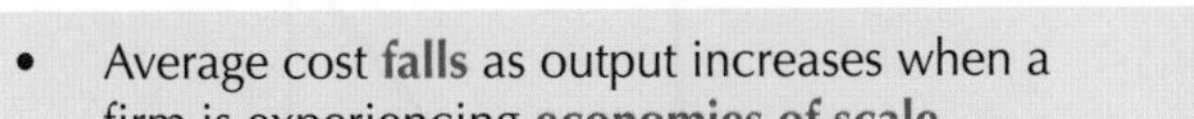

- Average cost **falls** as output increases when a firm is experiencing **economies of scale**.
- Average cost **rises** as output increases when a firm is experiencing **diseconomies of scale**.
- Firms may face **specific** economies and diseconomies of scale at the **same** output level — whether the firm is experiencing economies or diseconomies overall will depend on which is having the **greater effect**.

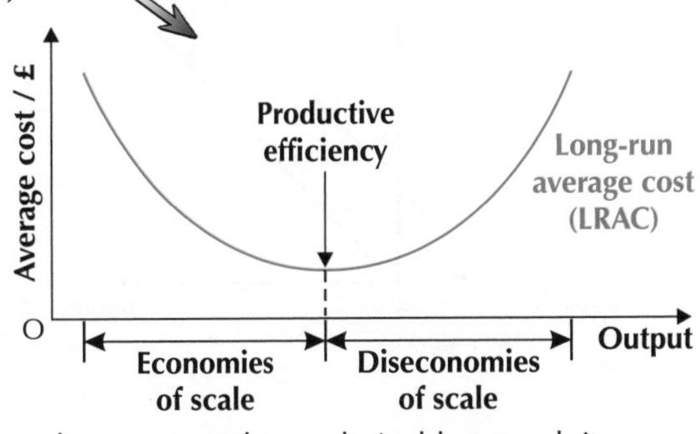

2) In some markets the most **efficient** way of allocating resources is to have **one** producer who's able to exploit **economies of scale** and achieve productive efficiency. If the market consisted of lots of **small producers** they wouldn't be able to **collectively** achieve the **same level** of economies of scale or **productive efficiency**.

Productive efficiency happens when goods are produced at the lowest possible **average cost**. So, on the diagram above, the point of productive efficiency is the output level at the **lowest point** of the LRAC curve.

3) As **large firms** can exploit **large economies of scale**, they can pass on these cost savings to their customers, who are able to take advantage of **low prices**. This will also help their **international competitiveness**.
4) Monopolies often restrict output (see above) — this increases **profits** for the monopoly, but might **not** be productively efficient. However, monopolies can use their **profits** for research into **new** production methods and products. This could lead to **innovation** and **better products** being made available for customers.

Practice Questions

Q1 In what ways might a monopoly lead to a misallocation of resources?

Q2 Why might monopolies fail to achieve productive efficiency?

Exam Question

Q1 With the use of a diagram, explain how a firm with a monopoly can cause market failure. [8 marks]

I start every day with 100% pure, freshly-squeezed monopoly...

The basic thing to take on board here is that monopolies can cause market failure. Not surprising really when they can restrict output and stop resources being allocated properly. Don't skim over the diagrams — you need to understand what they show.

Taxation

Governments use taxes to offset or reduce negative externalities caused by certain goods/services. ***For all boards.***

Governments use Indirect Taxes to affect the Supply of some goods/services

1) **Indirect taxes** can be imposed on the purchase of **goods or services.** There are **two types** of indirect tax: **specific** and ***ad valorem***:

Specific taxes — these are a **fixed amount** that's charged per unit of a particular good, no matter what the price of that good is. For example, a set amount of tax could be put on bottles of wine regardless of their price.

Ad valorem taxes — these are charged as a **proportion of the price** of a good. For example, a 20% tax on the price of a good would mean that for a £10 product it's £2 and for a £100 product it's £20.

There are also direct taxes. These are imposed on individuals or organisations. For example, income tax is paid by people who earn an income.

2) Indirect taxes **increase costs** for **producers** so they cause the **supply curve** to **shift** to the **left**. The two types of indirect taxes **affect supply curves in different ways**, as shown in the diagrams below:

A **specific** tax causes a **parallel shift** of the supply curve. The tax is the **same fixed amount** at a **low price** (P_1) and a **high price** (P_2).

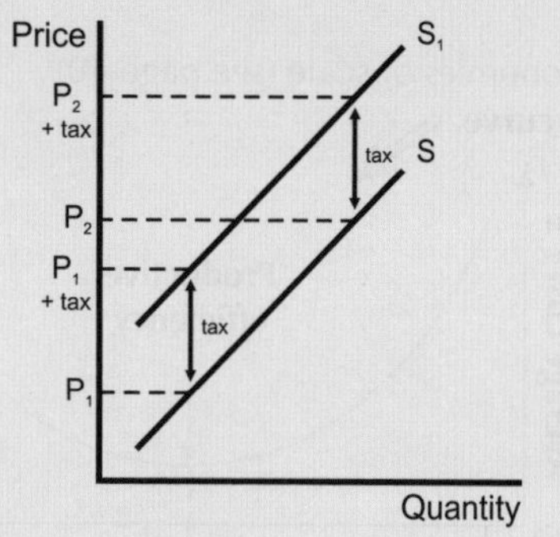

An ***ad valorem*** tax causes a **non-parallel shift** of the supply curve, with the biggest impact being on higher price goods. The tax is a **smaller amount** at a **low price** (P_1) compared to a high price (P_2).

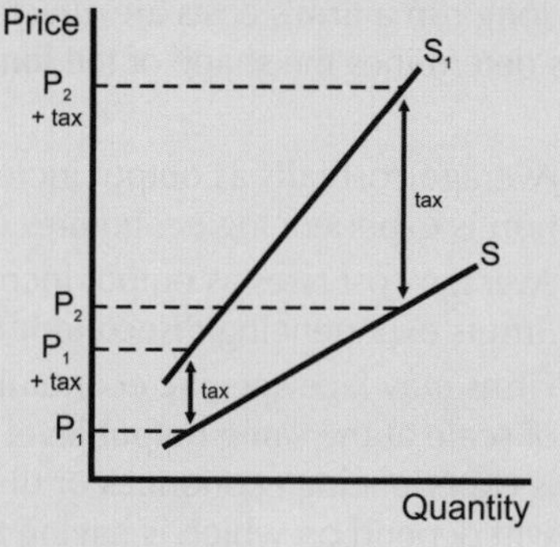

Governments Tax goods with Negative Externalities

1) Governments often put extra **indirect taxes** on goods that have **negative externalities**, such as petrol, alcohol and tobacco.
2) Governments may use **multiple** indirect taxes on **one** item, e.g. in the UK **cigarettes** have a **specific tax** (called **excise duty**) and an ***ad valorem*** tax on their **retail** price.
3) The aim of this taxation is to **internalise the externality** that the good produces, i.e. make the producer and/or consumer of the product **cover the cost** of its **externalities**. The taxes make **revenue** for the government which can be used to **offset** the effects of the **externalities** — e.g. the revenue generated from a tax on alcohol could be used to pay for the additional police time needed to deal with alcohol-related crime.
4) Another example of a specific tax used in the UK is **landfill tax**. The tax aims to **reduce** the **impacts** of **environmental market failure** linked to landfill:

James desperately wanted to see where all the non-recyclable rubbish went.

- Local authorities or firms that **dispose** of waste at **landfill** sites are charged an **environmental tax.** The tax is set at an amount which attempts to **reflect** the **full social costs** of using landfill — i.e. the external cost linked to the burying of waste in landfill, such as pollution released from landfill sites.
- The tax should **encourage recycling**, which in turn will **reduce** the **negative externalities** caused by landfill that harm the environment.
- However, the tax has led to an **increase** in fly-tipping by firms to **avoid** having to **pay** the tax. (Fly-tipping is the **illegal dumping of waste** on land that isn't designated for waste disposal, e.g. farmland and roadsides.)

Taxation

The Total Amount of Tax Paid can be shown on a diagram

1) The diagram shows the effect of an *ad valorem* tax — the **supply** curve moves **up** from S to S_1.
2) In the diagram, the **total tax paid** is ACP_1P_2. This is made up of the total tax paid by the **consumer** (BCP_1P) **plus** the total tax paid by the **producer** ($ABPP_2$). The part of the tax paid by the **consumer** is equal to the rise in price from **P** to $\mathbf{P_1}$. The part of the tax paid by the **producer** is equal to the difference between $\mathbf{P_2}$ and **P**.
3) The **amount** of tax passed on to the **consumer** will depend on the **price elasticity** of demand — if demand for a good is **price inelastic**, most or all of the extra **cost** is likely to be **passed on** to the consumer. If demand for a good is **price elastic**, then the **producer** is much **more likely** to take on most of the **extra cost**.

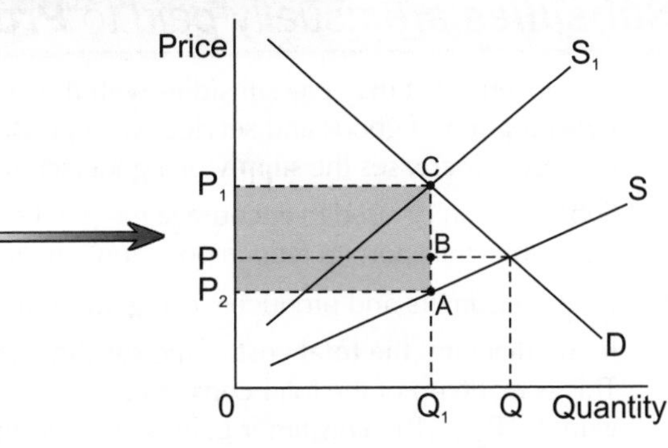

There's more detail on how indirect taxes affect producers and consumers on page 29.

There are Advantages and Disadvantages to this kind of tax

Advantages

1) The **cost** of the negative externalities is **internalised** in the **price** of the good — this **may reduce** demand for the good and the level of its production, **reducing** the **effects** of the negative externalities.
2) If demand **isn't** reduced, there's still the benefit that the revenue gained from the **tax** can be **used** by the government to **offset** the externalities — e.g. tax on **cigarettes** could be used for funding government services to help people to **stop smoking**.

Disadvantages

1) It can be **difficult** to put a **monetary value** on the 'cost' of the **negative externalities**.
2) For goods where **demand** is **price inelastic**, the demand **isn't reduced** by the **extra cost** of the tax.
3) Indirect taxes usually **increase** the cost of **production**, which **reduces** a product's international competitiveness.
4) Firms may choose to **relocate** and sell their goods abroad to **avoid** the indirect taxation. This would **remove** their contributions to the economy, such as the **payment** of **tax** and the **provision** of **employment**.
5) The money raised by taxes on demerit goods **might not** be spent on **reducing** the effects of their externalities.

Demerit goods have greater social costs than private costs and tend to be overconsumed — e.g. cigarettes. Merit goods have greater social benefits than private benefits and tend to be underconsumed — e.g. health care. For more about merit and demerit goods see pages 53-54.

Practice Questions

Q1 Describe the difference between a specific tax and an *ad valorem* tax.

Q2 Sketch a diagram to show how the supply curve shifts when an *ad valorem* tax is introduced on a good or service.

Q3 Give one advantage and one disadvantage of indirect taxes on goods with negative externalities.

Exam Question

Q1 The diagram shows the impact of an indirect tax imposed on a demerit good. The revenue received by the government would equal:

A) £2000
B) £400
C) £1600
D) £800

[1 mark]

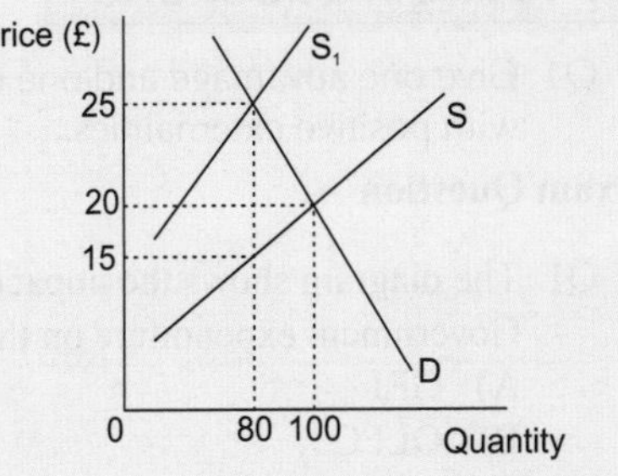

I think it's time for a government intervention — they really need help...

There are two types of indirect tax that you need to know about. Remember, they both cause the supply curve to shift, but in a slightly different way. On the diagram at the top of this page make sure you understand that the cost of the tax can be split into the parts paid by the consumer and producer. If you're doing Edexcel there's a bit more detail you need to know (see p.28-29).

Subsidies

The government can intervene in a positive way — by giving subsidies to producers or consumers. ***This page is for all boards.***

Subsidies are usually paid to Producers by the government

1) The government may pay subsidies with the aim of **encouraging** the **production** and **consumption** of goods and services with **positive** externalities — e.g. merit goods. A subsidy **increases** the **supply** of a good/service, so the **supply curve** shifts to the **right**.
2) Subsidies can be used to **encourage** the purchase and use of goods/services which **reduce** negative externalities, e.g. public transport (to reduce pollution), or as **support** for firms to help them become more **internationally competitive**.
3) Both consumers and producers can **gain** from a **subsidy**.
4) In the diagram, the **total cost** of the **subsidy** to the government is VTP_2P_1. This is made up of the total **consumer** gain ($VUPP_1$) **plus** the total **producer** gain (UTP_2P). The **consumer** gain is equal to the fall in price from **P** to $\mathbf{P_1}$. The **producer** gain is equal to the difference between **P** and $\mathbf{P_2}$.

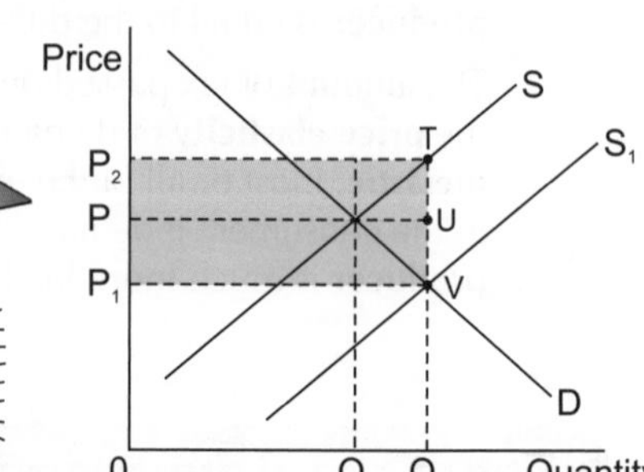

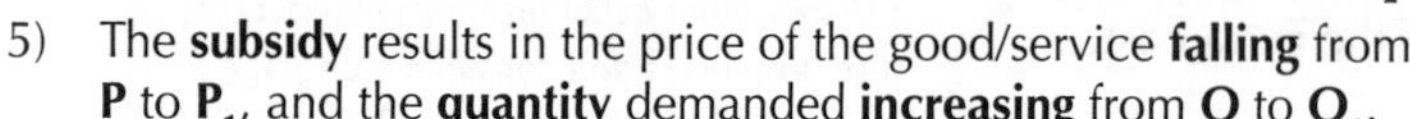

5) The **subsidy** results in the price of the good/service **falling** from **P** to $\mathbf{P_1}$, and the **quantity** demanded **increasing** from **Q** to $\mathbf{Q_1}$.
6) The **proportion** of the subsidy producers and consumers benefit from depends on the **elasticity** of the **supply** and **demand** curves.
7) Sometimes **subsidies** might be given **directly** to **consumers** instead.

There's more about this on page 28.

There are Advantages and Disadvantages to Subsidies

Advantages

1) The **benefit** of goods with positive externalities is **internalised**, i.e. the cost of these externalities is covered by the government subsidy, so the **price** of the goods is **reduced** from what it would be in the absence of the subsidy.
2) Subsidies can **change preferences** — producers will supply goods with positive externalities and consumers will consume them and receive the benefits from them. Also, making a merit good **cheaper** by the presence of a subsidy makes it **more affordable** and **increases demand** for it.
3) The **positive externalities** are **still** present. For example, if a subsidy is paid for **wind farms**, the wind farms will still **reduce pollution** levels.
4) Subsidies can support a domestic industry until it **grows** to the point that it can exploit **economies of scale** and become **internationally competitive**. (Though this could encourage inefficiency — see below.)

Disadvantages

1) It can be **difficult** to put a **monetary value** on the '**benefit**' of the **positive externalities**.
2) Any subsidy has an **opportunity cost** — the money spent on it might be better spent on something else.
3) Subsidies may make producers **inefficient** and **reliant** on subsidies. The subsidy means that producers have **less incentive** to reduce costs or innovate.
4) The **effectiveness** of subsidies depends on the **elasticity** of demand — subsidies **wouldn't** significantly **increase** demand for price **inelastic** goods.
5) The **subsidised** goods and services **may not** be as good as those they're **aiming to replace**. For example, **imported goods** may be better quality than the **domestically produced** alternatives a subsidy is promoting.

Practice Questions

Q1 Give one advantage and one disadvantage of subsidies for goods with positive externalities.

Exam Question

Q1 The diagram shows the impact of a subsidy on a merit good. Government expenditure on the subsidy would equal:

A) GFJ
B) OLFC
C) ACFJ
D) EFG

[1 mark]

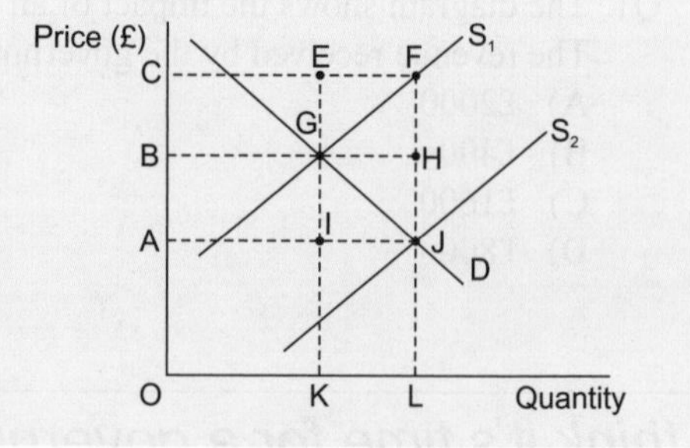

Subsidise your heating bills — move in with your next-door neighbour...

Subsidies can act as an incentive to producers or consumers, or they can help a company to be internationally competitive.

Price Controls

Setting minimum and maximum prices can have a big effect on supply and demand. ***This page is for all boards.***

Governments can set a **Maximum Price** for a good or service

1) A maximum price (or price ceiling) may be set to **increase consumption** of a merit good or to make a **necessity** more **affordable**. For example, a government may set a maximum rent price to keep the cost of renting a property affordable.
2) If a maximum price is set **above** the market equilibrium price, it will have **no impact**.
3) If it's set **below** the market equilibrium, it will lead to **excess demand** and a **shortage** in **supply** of Q_1 to Q_2. The excess demand cannot be cleared by market forces, so to prevent shortages the product needs to be rationed out, e.g. by a ballot.
4) A good's price elasticity of **supply** and price elasticity of **demand** will have a **big** effect on the **amount** of excess demand.

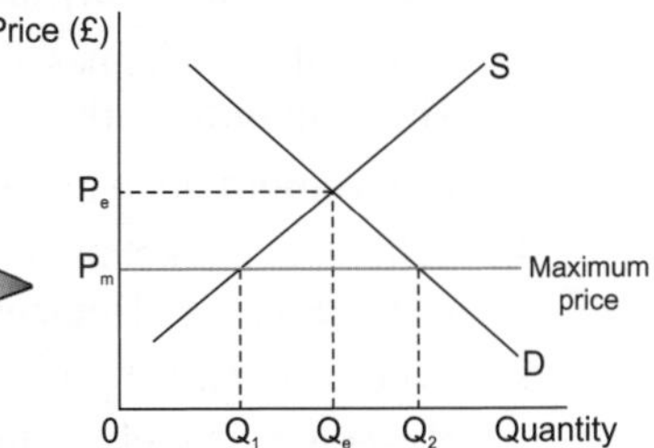

Governments can set a **Minimum Price** for a good or service

1) **Minimum** prices (or price floors) are often set to make sure that **suppliers** get a **fair** price. The European Union's Common Agricultural Policy (CAP) involves the use of a **guaranteed minimum price** for many **agricultural** products.
2) If a minimum price is set **below** the market equilibrium price, it will have **no impact**.
3) If it's set **above** the market equilibrium price, it will **reduce** demand to Q_1 and **increase** supply to Q_2, leading to an **excess supply** of Q_1 to Q_2.
4) To make a minimum price for a good work the government might **purchase** the excess supply at the **guaranteed** minimum price. The goods bought by the government will either be **stockpiled** or **destroyed**.
5) Government **expenditure** would then be ABQ_2Q_1.
6) A good's price elasticity of supply and price elasticity of demand will have a **big** effect on the **amount** of excess supply.

The CAP also involves the use of buffer stocks (see next page). For more on the CAP see page 70.

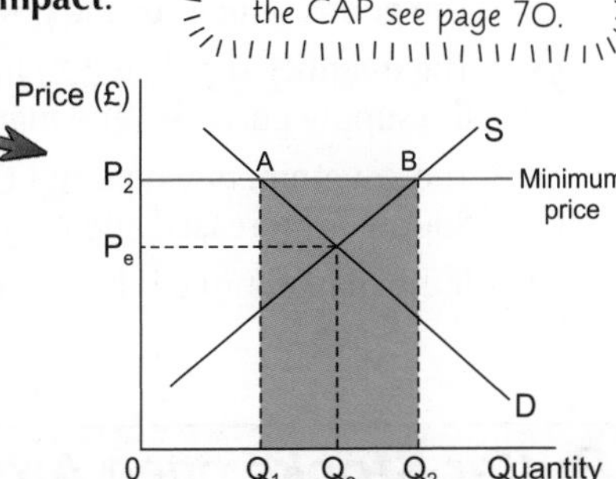

Maximum Prices

Advantages:

- Maximum prices can help to **increase fairness**, by allowing **more** people the **ability** to purchase certain goods and services.
- They can also be used to **prevent** monopolies from **exploiting** consumers.

Disadvantages:

- Since demand will be **higher** than supply, some people who **want** to buy the product **aren't** able to.
- Governments **may** need to introduce a **rationing** scheme to **allocate** the good, e.g. through a ballot.
- Excess demand can lead to the creation of a **black market** for a good.

Minimum Prices

Advantages:

- Producers have a guaranteed **minimum income** which will encourage **investment**.
- **Stockpiles** can be used when supply is **reduced** (e.g. due to bad weather) or as **overseas aid**.

Disadvantages:

- Consumers will be paying a **higher** price than the market equilibrium.
- Resources used to produce the **excess** supply could be used **elsewhere** — there's an **inefficient** allocation of resources.
- **Government spending** on a minimum price scheme could be used in **other areas** — schemes may have a **high opportunity cost**.
- **Destroying** excess goods is a **waste** of **resources**.

Practice Questions

Q1 Give two disadvantages of guaranteed maximum prices and two disadvantages of minimum prices.

Exam Question

Q1 Use a diagram to show how the setting of a maximum price for a good can result in excess demand. [8 marks]

The government egg stockpile is huge — I think it's time for a crackdown...

What a terrible yolk... anyway, moving on... setting a maximum or minimum price for something means that the market forces can't determine the price of a good or service — minimum and maximum pricing acts to restrict the price that can be charged.

Buffer Stocks

Governments might use buffer stocks to reduce market failure in agriculture. ***This page is for OCR only.***

Buffer Stocks are used to try to Stabilise commodity prices

1) **Prices** in **commodity markets**, especially for agricultural products, can be **very unstable** (see p.30).
2) **Buffer stock** schemes aim to **stabilise** prices and **prevent** shortages in supply. They can **only** work for **storable** commodities — e.g. wheat.
3) A **maximum** price (price ceiling) and **minimum** price (price floor) for a commodity are set by a government.
4) When the market price for a product goes **below** the price **floor**, the government **buys** it and stores it in stockpiles. **Demand** is **increased** and the price is brought up to an **acceptable** level.
5) When the market price goes **above** the price **ceiling**, the government **sells** the product from its **stockpiles**. Supply is **increased** and the price is **brought down** to an **acceptable** level.

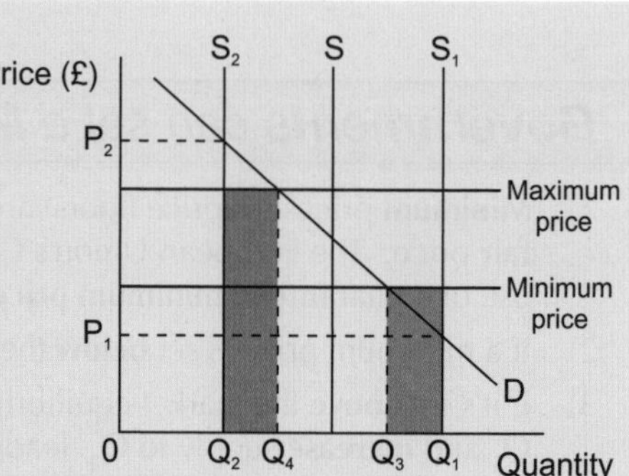

- For example, the **quantity supplied** (Q_1) in a **good** year (when levels of production have been high) is shown by the supply curve S_1, so its **market price** would be P_1.
- This price is **below** the **minimum** price, so to **prevent** this price fall, the government would **purchase** a quantity of Q_3 to Q_1 of the good at the set **minimum price**. Supply would be **reduced** and the market price would **rise** to the set **minimum** price.
- The goods **bought** by the government would be **added** to its stockpile.
- The **quantity supplied** (Q_2) in a **poor** year is shown by the supply curve S_2. The **market price** would be P_2.
- The government would **sell** Q_2 to Q_4 from its stockpile, at the set **maximum** price. Supply is **increased** and the market price would **fall** to the set **maximum** price.
- If the market price is **between** the set minimum and maximum, no action is taken.

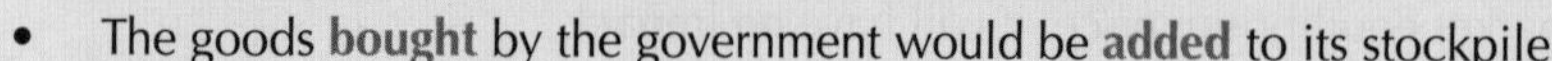

Buffer Stocks often Aren't Successful

In theory, the **income** from **selling** the product at the set **maximum** price should pay for **purchases** at the set **minimum** price and the **running** of the scheme. However, buffer schemes often don't work for a number of reasons:

- If the **minimum** price is set at **too high** a level, the scheme will **spend excessively** purchasing stocks to **maintain** this minimum price.
- If there's a **run** of **good** or **bad** harvests, then the scheme may **buy excessively** or **run out** of stock.
- **Storage** and **security** of the stockpiles can be **expensive**.
- Some commodities will **deteriorate** and go to waste over time, causing **losses** for the scheme.
- Producers may **overproduce** because they will get a **guaranteed minimum price**. This can lead to massive **stockpiles** and a **waste** of **resources**.

Practice Questions

Q1 Give three reasons why buffer stock schemes might not be successful.

Exam Question

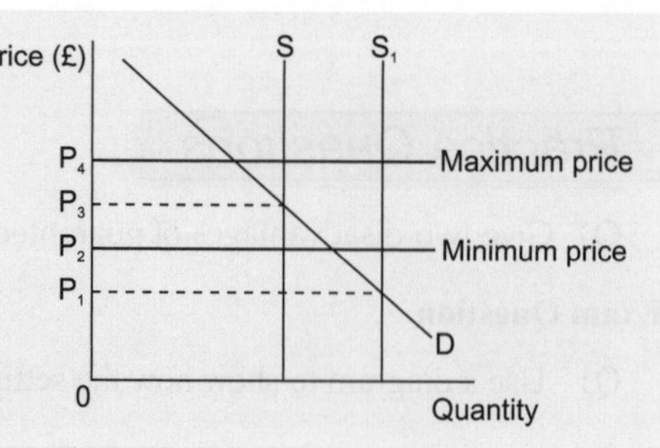

Q1 A buffer stock scheme for wheat production is being used. In a year when supply is shown by the supply curve S_1 the price per bushel received by farmers will be:

A) P_1
B) P_2
C) P_3
D) P_4

[1 mark]

I tried to stabilise prices with butter stocks — it was a tasty, tasty mess...

Buffer stocks involve maximum and minimum prices at the same time (wowser) — make sure you know how they work.

State Provision

State provision is where the government provides certain goods or services. It's often referred to as 'government expenditure' as it involves governments spending money to provide things, and they have to decide which things to provide. ***For all boards.***

Governments **Directly Provide** some goods and services

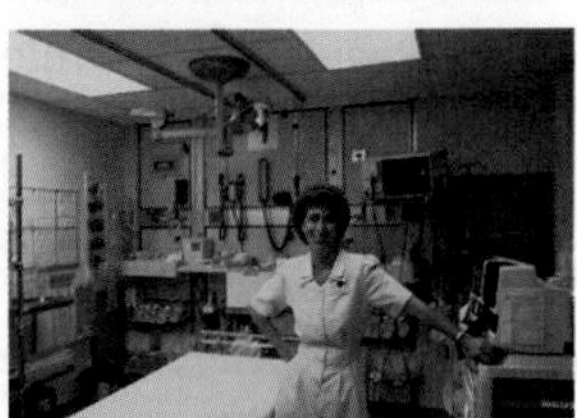

The state provided Viv with all the latest medical equipment — unfortunately, she was a chef.

1) Governments use **tax revenue** to pay for **certain** goods and services so that they're **free**, or **largely free**, when consumed. Examples in the UK **include** the NHS, state education, waste disposal and the fire and police services.
2) **Public goods**, such as **defence** and **street lighting**, are also **provided** by the state.
3) State provision can come **directly** from the government, e.g. state schools and the army, or alternatively, governments can **purchase** the good or service from the **private sector** and provide it to the **public** for **free**, e.g. in some areas **community health services** are **purchased** from private companies and then **provided free** to NHS patients.

State Provision is a way to **Overcome** market failure

1) Governments might provide certain things to **increase** the **consumption** of merit goods, such as **education** and **health care**.
2) **Free provision** of services can help to **reduce inequalities** in access, e.g. due to differences in **wealth**.
3) It can also **redistribute** income — most of the money to **pay** for the services comes from taxing **wealthier** citizens.
4) The **level** of state provision is a **value judgement** made by the government — it's up to the government to decide the **amount** of a good/service that they **provide**. This decision is likely to be based on **how important for society** they think it is that they provide the good/service.

State Provision has several **Disadvantages**

1) State provision may mean there's **less incentive** to operate efficiently due to the absence of the **price mechanism**.
2) State provision may **fail** to respond to **consumer demands**, as it lacks the motive of **profit** to determine **what's supplied**.
3) The **opportunity cost** of state provision of a good or service is that **other** goods or services **can't be supplied**.
4) State provision can **reduce** individuals' **self-reliance** — they know the good or service is there for them if they need it.

Health Care is a **Merit Good** that's sometimes **Provided** by **Governments**

1) The government funds the NHS so that **society benefits** from the **positive externalities** of **health care**. For example, the consumption of health care can contribute to a healthier, happier population and reduce the number of days people take off work due to sickness.
2) However, there are **drawbacks** to the **state provision** of health care by the NHS. These include:
   - Demand for health care in the UK has increased dramatically since the NHS was introduced. Because the NHS is **free at the point of delivery**, this has led to **excess demand** and problems like long waiting lists.
   - Hospitals and clinics can be **wasteful** of **resources**, such as money wasted on unused prescriptions.
   - The NHS may not always respond to the **wants** and **needs of patients** — e.g. local NHS officials might relocate medical services against the wishes of the population in their area for cost-saving reasons.
   - The NHS can **reduce patients' self-reliance**. For example, it can remove the incentive for patients to deal with medical issues themselves — patients might visit their doctor or hospital with problems which could be treated at home with medicines they could buy in a shop (e.g. colds or sore throats).

Practice Questions

Q1 Give two advantages of state provision of goods.

Q2 Give one example of state provision in the UK.

Exam Question

Q1 Describe the possible disadvantages of state provision of health care. [6 marks]

My bedroom is a state — it'll take some serious intervention to sort it out...

There are different reasons for state provision of goods and services. For example, the government might want to encourage the consumption of a merit good, or make a certain good or service accessible to everyone no matter how much they earn.

Regulation

Regulation is another way governments can intervene and try to reduce market failure. ***This page is for all boards.***

Government Regulation comes in Various forms

1) **Regulations** are rules that are enforced by an authority (e.g. a government) and they're usually backed up with **legislation** (i.e. laws) — which means that legal action can be taken against those that break the rules. They can be used to **control** the activities of producers and consumers and try to **change** their **undesirable behaviour**.
2) Regulations are used to try to **reduce** market failure and its impacts. They can **help** in a number of areas:
   - **Reducing** the use of **demerit** goods and services — e.g. by **banning** or **limiting** the sale of such products.
   - **Reducing** the power of **monopolies** — e.g. using a regulating body to set rules that limit prices.
   - Providing some **protection** for consumers and producers from **problems** arising from **asymmetric information** — e.g. the Sale of Goods Act **protects consumers** against firms supplying **substandard** goods.

Regulations can be Difficult to Set

1) It can be difficult for a government to work out what is 'correct'. For example, it might be **difficult** to set the **'correct'** minimum age for the purchase of alcohol — medical groups might want the legal age **increased**, alcohol producers might want it **reduced**. Or, a government might set the level of acceptable pollution by firms **too low** or **too high**.
2) There's a need for regulation in **some** areas to be **worldwide** rather than in just one country. For example, regulations to **control** greenhouse gas **emissions** might be **more effective** if they were enforced worldwide — regulations in **one country** may reduce its emissions, but this could be **offset** by an increase in emissions **elsewhere** in the world (not covered by this regulation).
3) Following excessive regulations can be **expensive** and may force firms to **close** or to **move** to a different country.
4) **Monitoring** compliance with regulations can be **expensive** for a government.
5) If the **punishment** for **breaking** regulations isn't harsh enough, then they may **not** be a **deterrent** and **change behaviours**.

Some regulations are set to Encourage the use of Renewable Energy

1) The UK government has introduced **Renewables Obligation Certificates** (ROCs) to **encourage** the use of power generated from **renewable** energy sources (e.g. wind and hydroelectric power).
2) Electricity **suppliers** are given a set **minimum percentage** of power that must come from **renewable** sources.
3) Companies who **generate** the renewable energy are issued with ROCs which link to the **amount** of renewable energy they've **generated**. They then **sell** these certificates on to **suppliers**.
4) **Suppliers** that **fall short** of the **target percentage** of **power from renewable sources** have to pay a **financial penalty**.
5) The money **raised** from these penalties is **distributed** between the suppliers who **did** reach the **target**.

AQA ONLY

Privatised Utility Companies in the UK are regulated

1) Regulating bodies, such as Ofcom (the regulator for the **telecommunications** and **media** industries), can set **rules** and impose **price controls**.
2) Regulating bodies may **use** these rules and price controls to try to **increase competition** in markets where there's a **monopoly** power. For example, Ofcom **increased competition** in the **UK broadband market** by allowing other companies to use telephone lines owned by BT to offer broadband services.

Practice Questions

Q1 Describe a market failure that regulation can be used to help solve.

Q2 Give one difficulty involved in the setting of regulations.

Exam Question

Q1 Assess how effective regulations would be for tackling the market failure caused by firms that pollute excessively. [4 marks]

Ban the sale of pink cars — reduce childhood embarrassment now...

Regulations are just rules. This page should've given you an idea of some of the many ways they can be used.

Information Provision and Pollution Permits

Information provision and pollution permits are both ways to reduce market failure. ***For all boards.***

Governments Intervene to help consumers make Well-Informed Decisions

1) Governments sometimes try to provide **information** on the **full costs** and **benefits** of goods and services. This information is given to try to help consumers make **rational choices** and prevent market failure caused by consumers and producers having **asymmetric information**. **Examples** of government-provided information include:

- School and hospital performance league tables.
- Advertising campaigns encouraging healthy eating.
- Compulsory food labelling for most foods.
- Health warnings on cigarette packets.

2) The **provision** of information will impact on the **demand** for the goods. Governments will try to **increase demand** for goods/services that they think will be **beneficial** to people and society (these will usually be **merit goods**) and **reduce demand** for goods/services that they think will be **harmful** to people and society (these will usually be **demerit** goods).
3) The **effectiveness** of government information provision is often questioned. For example, the **growing obesity problem** in the **UK** suggests that government **healthy eating campaigns** aren't having a significant impact on the public.

Tradable Pollution Permits are used to try to Control pollution levels

EDEXCEL ONLY

1) Governments may try to **control** pollution by putting a **cap** on it. The government will set an **optimal level** of pollution and **allocate** permits that allow firms to emit a **certain amount** of **pollution** over a period of time (usually a year).
2) Firms may **trade** their permits with other firms, so if a firm can keep its emissions **low**, it can **sell** its permits to other firms who want to **buy** permits to allow them to **pollute more**.
3) Tradable pollution permits use the **market mechanism** — pollution is given a **value** and firms can **buy** and **sell** permits.
4) The **EU emissions trading system (ETS)** is a tradable pollution permit scheme, with permits called **emissions allowances**. These allowances (of greenhouse gas emissions) are **distributed** between the EU's **member** governments, who in turn **allocate** these allowances to **firms**.
5) Firms will be **fined** if they **exceed** their allowances, but they can **trade** allowances between themselves, so firms can buy **extra allowances** to cover any **extra emissions**.
6) Each year the number of allowances available is **reduced**. This gives firms an **incentive** to **lower their emissions** (e.g. by investing in technology to cut emissions) — if they don't then they might have to buy more allowances.
7) Firms in the ETS are allowed to invest in **emission-saving schemes** outside of the EU to **offset** their own emissions. For example, a UK firm could invest in **low-carbon power production** in India to offset some of its emissions in the UK.

ADVANTAGES

- These schemes are a good way of trying to **reduce** pollution to an **acceptable** level, as they **encourage** firms to become **more efficient** and **pollute less**.
- Firms causing low levels of pollution will **benefit** from these schemes — they'll be able to **sell** permits, allowing them to **invest more** and **expand**.
- Governments can use any **revenue**, e.g. from fines, to **invest** in other **pollution reducing** schemes.
- These schemes **internalise** the externality of pollution.

DISADVANTAGES

- The **optimal pollution level** can be difficult to set. If the level is set too **high**, firms have **no incentive** to **lower** their emissions. If the level is set too **low**, new firms might not be able to **start up** at all, or existing firms might choose to **relocate** to somewhere they're **less restricted** (**harming** a country's **economic growth**). So, setting the optimal pollution level at the **wrong** level can lead to **government failure**.
- The pollution permit scheme creates a **new market** — there might be **market failure** within this new market.
- **High** levels of pollution in specific areas may still exist, and this would still be **harmful** to the environment.
- There are **administrative costs** involved in such schemes, to both **governments** and **firms**.

Practice Questions

Q1 Describe, using an example, how government information provision can help consumers to make rational decisions.

Exam Question

Q1 Evaluate the effectiveness of using tradable pollution permits to reduce greenhouse gas emissions. [15 marks]

'That's right Sir, without a permit I can't allow you to pollute that... or that...'

Tradable pollution permits create a new market for pollution that provides incentives for firms to decrease their emissions and therefore reduce market failure. Information provision aims to reduce market failure caused by asymmetric information.

Government Failure

Government failure is when government intervention causes a misallocation of resources in a market. ***For all boards.***

Government Intervention can cause the Misallocation of Resources

1) Government intervention can lead to **resources** being **misallocated** and a **net welfare loss** — this is **government failure**.
2) Government failure is often an **unintended consequence** of an intervention to correct a market failure.
3) When looking at government failure in a market you should consider it in relation to the market failure it was attempting to correct. For example:

- Local authorities can **charge** for some forms of non-household **waste disposal**, e.g. some county councils charge for the disposal of DIY waste. This is an attempt to force waste producers to **internalise** the **externalities of waste disposal**.
- However, there's evidence that this has led to an **increase** in **fly-tipping**. This fly-tipping produces **negative externalities** for local residents (e.g. the visual pollution caused by discarded items) and requires **resources** to be allocated to **clear up** the **fly-tipping**.
- In this instance the **intervention** that aimed to **reduce** the **negative externalities** linked to **waste disposal** has resulted in the production of **other unintended negative externalities**.

Government Intervention may cause Market Distortions

Government interventions can **cause** market distortions rather than **removing them.** There are several examples of this:

- **Income taxes** can act as a **disincentive** to working hard — if you increase your earnings by working hard then you'll have to pay more income tax.
- **Governmental price fixing**, such as **maximum** or **minimum prices**, can lead to the **distortions** of **price signals**. For example, producers will **overproduce** a product if they'll receive a **guaranteed minimum price** for it and flood the market with **surplus goods**. Without the minimum price, the price signals given by the price mechanism would **stop** large surpluses from occurring.
- **Subsidies** may encourage firms to be **inefficient** by removing the **incentive** to be efficient.

Government Bureaucracy can Interfere with the way markets work

1) Governments impose lots of **rules and regulations** — often referred to as **'red tape'**. These usually exist in order to **prevent market failure.**
2) The enforcement of these rules and regulations by government officials is known as **bureaucracy**. Excessive bureaucracy (e.g. too many regulations slowing down a process unreasonably) is seen as a form of **government failure**.
3) Red tape can interfere with the forces of **supply and demand** — it can prevent markets from working **efficiently**. For example, **planning controls** can create **long delays** in construction projects. If these delays affect housing developments then this could restrict supply for the housing market.
4) In general, lots of red tape could mean that there are **time lags** so governments can't respond quickly to the **needs** of **producers** and/or **consumers**. This might result in a country having a **competitive disadvantage** to countries that are able to respond more quickly.
5) Bureaucracy can lead to a **lack of investment** and **prevent** an economy from operating at **full capacity**.

Conflicting Policy Objectives are a source of Government Failure

1) A government's effort to achieve a certain **policy objective** may have a **negative impact** on another. For example, if a government introduces **stricter emission controls** for industry this would contribute towards its **environmental objectives**. However, this could **increase costs** for firms and **reduce their output** — causing unemployment and a fall in economic growth.
2) Politicians are also constrained by what is **politically acceptable**. For example, it's unlikely that the UK government would ban the use of private cars to reduce greenhouse gases because of the idea's **political unpopularity**.
3) Governments often favour **short-term solutions** because they're under pressure to solve issues **quickly**. For example, increasing the capacity of the UK road network will help with short-term congestion, but may increase road usage (and congestion) in the long term.

Government Failure

Government Failure can be caused by Inadequate Information

1) **Imperfect** or **asymmetric information** can mean it's **difficult** to **assess** the extent of a **market failure**, and that makes it hard to put a **value** on the **government intervention** that's **needed** to correct the failure. For example, an incorrect valuation of a market failure might lead to taxes or subsidies being set at an inefficient level.
2) Governments may not know how the population **want resources** to be **allocated**. Some economists would argue that the **price mechanism** is a better way of allocating resources than government intervention.
3) Governments don't always know how **consumers** will **react**. For example, campaigns to **discourage under-18s drinking alcohol** may lead to alcohol being viewed as desirable and **increase drinking** by this age group.

Administrative Costs can also be a cause of Government Failure

1) Government measures to correct market failure, such as policies and regulations, can use a **large amount of resources** — this can result in **high costs**. For example, the maintenance costs of a scheme to offer farmers a minimum price for a product can be substantial.
2) Some government interventions require **policing**, which can also be **expensive**. For example, for pollution permit schemes the emissions of the firms included in the scheme must be monitored to check they aren't exceeding their allowances.

There are some other causes of Government Failure

Some other reasons for government failure are:

- **Regulatory capture** — firms covered by **regulatory bodies**, such as utility companies, can sometimes **influence** the decisions of the regulator to ensure that the outcomes **favour** the **companies** and not the consumers. For example, a regulated industry might pressurise their regulatory body into making decisions that benefit them.
- It takes **time** for governments to work out where there's market failure, and then devise and implement a policy to correct it — meanwhile, the problem may have changed.
- Government policies can be affected by issues outside of its control, known as **'external shocks'** — e.g. a major oil leak would impact on the effectiveness of anti-pollution policies.

Bjorn had everything he needed to capture a regulator.

Practice Questions

Q1 What is government failure?

Q2 Give an example of how a government intervention can lead to a market distortion.

Q3 List three causes of government failure.

Exam Questions

Q1 A government banned the sale of a legal substance which has effects similar to some illegal drugs and can be hazardous to health. Which one of the following situations would be considered a government failure?

A) Public opinion of the government improved as the ban demonstrated a strong concern for public health.
B) Consumption of the substance fell dramatically and there were fewer hospital admissions due to its use.
C) The cost of imposing the ban was greater than the net benefit generated by it.
D) The public became more aware of the dangers of the substance. [1 mark]

Q2 A government has increased the level of tax on cigarettes. A neighbouring country has a lower rate of tax on cigarettes. Explain how this intervention could lead to a government failure. [6 marks]

It's taken time for me to develop my policy on blue cheese — I'm not a fan...

There are a few potential causes of government failure. This gives you an insight into how tricky it can be for governments to implement something that effectively sorts out a market failure. Maybe we should be a bit kinder to governments when they get it wrong... Anyway, conflicting policy objectives, inadequate information and administrative costs are key causes to remember.

Examples of Government Failure

To see the consequences of government failure it's useful to look at some examples of it in different markets. ***For all boards.***

*The **Common Agricultural Policy (CAP)** was set up to help farmers*

1) The main aim of the CAP is to **correct market failure** caused by **fluctuating prices** for agricultural products. By correcting these fluctuations it aims to provide a **reasonable**, **stable income** for farmers.
2) To achieve its aim the CAP uses measures such as subsidies and buffer stocks (see p.64 for buffer stocks). Another measure is import restrictions on goods from outside the EU — for example, **tariffs** can be placed on **imported goods**. Tariffs are a form of **tax** placed on certain imports to make them **more expensive** and **discourage** their consumption. By placing tariffs on imported goods this allows the guaranteed minimum price level to be maintained.
3) The CAP has had **some success** in stabilising prices and farmer incomes, but it has also caused several **problems**:
   - The CAP **encourages increased output** as farmers are guaranteed a **minimum price** for all that they produce. Increased output can lead to **environmental damage** from a greater use of intensive farming methods and chemical fertilisers.
   - The **minimum prices** have also led to an **oversupply** of agricultural products, which have to be **bought** and **stored** by government agencies at **great expense**. Governments have **sold these stocks** at a low price **outside of the EU** — negatively affecting farmers outside the EU who **cannot compete** with such **low prices**.
   - There are large amounts of **wasted food products** when perishable goods have to be **destroyed**.
   - The increased food prices caused by the CAP are particularly **unfair** on **poorer households** who spend a larger proportion of their income on food. It can be argued that the **welfare gains to farmers** brought about by the CAP are **smaller** than the size of the **welfare loss to consumers**.
   - There's a **cost to the taxpayer** of getting rid of excess agricultural produce (either by destroying it or by selling it for a very low price). This is because the produce disposed of in this way achieves a **lower price** than was paid to the producer for it by the EU.
   - The CAP can cause **conflicts** with **other countries** as it can make exports from non-EU countries **less competitive**, e.g. as products from non-EU countries can be subject to import tariffs. Also, there's **conflict between countries** within the EU about how much of the CAP budget they should each receive.
4) The CAP has resulted in **distortions** in agricultural markets — it has encouraged **oversupply**, leading to a **misallocation of resources**. This misallocation of resources causes a **net welfare loss to society**, as does the high opportunity cost of running the policy.
5) In recent years prices have **moved closer** to the **market price** as part of the EU's reforms of the CAP, but there are still problems with the policy.

*Governments may intervene in **Housing Markets** by setting **Maximum Rents***

1) Price controls, such as maximum rents, are used by governments to **protect tenants** from **excessive rental charges**.
2) The downside of the control of rent prices is that it can cause **shortages** of rental properties. This can be shown using a diagram:
   - Introducing a maximum rent would **decrease** the **rent price** from P_e to **MR**. This would cause the demand for rental properties to increase from Q_e to Q_d and supply to fall from Q_e to Q_s.
   - This could cause a shortage of rental properties of Q_s to Q_d because there's an **excess demand** for them — only some individuals demanding a rental property will get one (Q_s).

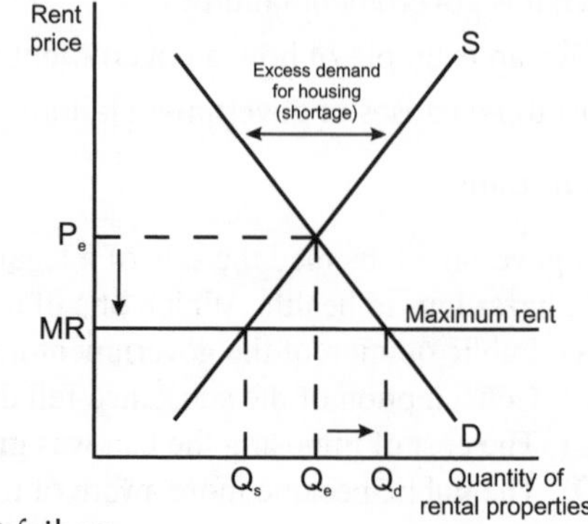

3) The problems caused by maximum rents are an example of government failure:
   - The **excess demand** for rental properties could lead to a **shortage** of available properties and cause a **black market** to develop. In a black market people are likely to end up paying more than the maximum rent level, so they won't gain any benefit from the government's maximum rent level. Also, landlords operating illegally on the black market may not offer a good service to their tenants.
   - A **shortage** of rental properties can also impact the supply of **workers**. People might not be able to find somewhere to rent near to where they work — this could affect the ability of firms to attract new staff in areas where shortages are particularly bad.

Examples of Government Failure

Governments may provide **Subsidies** to **Public Transport**

1) Bus and train journeys may be **subsidised** to **reduce car usage** and **pollution levels**.
2) Subsidies **don't always** lead to **increases** in **passenger numbers** — bus transport is often viewed as an **inferior good** so even if it's cheaper, demand might not increase. Individuals may also find travelling by car **preferable** for reasons of privacy or convenience.
3) The allocation of resources to public transport services that don't increase their usage and don't cause a reduction in pollution can be seen as a **misallocation of resources** and will lead to a **net welfare loss**. Underused public transport services may actually contribute to higher overall emissions as people aren't using their cars less.

As incomes rise, demand for inferior goods fall — see p.19.

Road Congestion Schemes aim to **Reduce Externalities** linked with **Traffic**

1) Road congestion schemes are a method of **reducing** the **external costs** linked to **road congestion** and the **pollution** (air and noise) that it creates. These schemes are also called **road pricing**.
2) The schemes work by **charging users** to travel on roads in areas where **congestion** is a **problem**.
3) Ideally the charge needs to be set at a level that will result in the **socially optimal level of traffic**. However, working out what this charge is could be very difficult.
4) Getting the charge wrong has impacts on the effectiveness of road congestion schemes:
   - If the price is set **too low** then it will have a limited impact on traffic levels.
   - If the price is set **too high** then too few cars will use the area covered by the charge. This will result in **reduced trade** for businesses within the congestion charge area, an **under-utilisation** of the road space in the congestion charge area, and may also cause congestion in **other areas**.
5) Road congestion charges may **unfairly** impact on **poorer motorists** in an area and put them off using their cars.

Fishing Quotas were introduced to help make fishing more **Sustainable**

1) Fishing quotas were introduced by the EU in an attempt to make sure **fish stocks** remain **stable** in European waters. They aim to **prevent overfishing**, which can have severe negative impacts on fish populations, by setting **limits** on the amount of fish that can be caught.
2) The system of fishing quotas has been **heavily criticised** and has a few key problems:
   - Fish stocks are **depleting** even with quotas in place. This could indicate that the quotas have been **set too high** and **overfishing** is still taking place.
   - Fishing boats that exceed their quotas often throw large amounts of dead fish back into the sea — these dumped fish are known as **discards**. As well as damaging fish stocks, these discards are also wasteful.
   - There has been **poor monitoring** of fish catches. This could mean that fishing boats have been overfishing and it hasn't been detected.
3) Problems with EU fishing quotas have led to a need for **reform**. One change is called a **landing obligation**. This means that everything fishermen catch must be kept on board and be counted against their quotas — they aren't allowed to discard any fish. This landing obligation is likely to be difficult to police — it would be a huge task to check that every fishing boat hasn't discarded any fish at sea.

Practice Questions

Q1 Use a diagram to show how setting maximum rent prices can lead to a shortage of rental properties.

Q2 Give two reasons for subsidising public transport.

Q3 Describe one problem linked with fishing quotas.

Exam Questions

Q1 It has been decided that the level of funding available for farm subsidies is to be reduced over the next 5 years. Explain two advantages of reducing the subsidies paid to farmers. [4 marks]

Q2 Evaluate the arguments for and against a nationwide system of road pricing in major cities. [10 marks]

I reckon my washing-up quota is set too high — I wish I had a dishwasher...

So, there are quite a few examples of government failure. Thankfully most governments will be trying to correct these failures, although doing this is easier said than done — it's not straightforward to iron out problems with big policies like the CAP.

Measuring Economic Growth

Instead of looking at individual markets, firms or people, macroeconomics looks at the economy as a whole — that includes the government, all firms, all individuals, other countries etc. ***These pages are for all boards.***

There are **Four** main **Macroeconomic** indicators

These four **main** macroeconomic indicators can be used to measure a country's **economic performance**:

1) The rate of **economic growth**.
2) The rate of **inflation**.
3) The level of **unemployment**.
4) The state of the **balance of payments**.

Governments use these indicators to **monitor** how the economy is doing.

GDP is a measure of **Economic Growth**

1) Economic growth can be measured by the change in **national output** over a period of time. The national output is **all** the **goods** and **services** produced by a country.
2) Output can be measured in **two** ways:

1. Volume
Adding up the **quantity** of goods and services produced in one year.

2. Value
Calculating the value (£billions) of all the goods and services produced in one year.

National output is **usually** measured by **value** — this is called the **Gross Domestic Product (GDP)**.

3) GDP can also be calculated by adding up the total amount of **national expenditure** (aggregate demand, see p.80) in a year, or by adding up the total amount of **national income** earned in a year. This means that, in theory, national output = national expenditure = national income (see p.78-79 for more on the **circular flow** of income).

Economic Growth is usually measured as a **Percentage**

1) The **rate** of economic growth is the **speed** at which the **national output** grows over a period of time.
2) Over the course of **several years**, the speed of this growth is **not** usually constant. Here are a few useful terms:
   - Long periods of high economic growth rates are often called **booms**.
   - If there's **negative** economic growth for **two consecutive quarters** (a 'quarter' is just a 3-month period of time — a quarter of a year), this is called a **recession**. A **long** recession is often referred to as a **slump**.
   - An **economic depression** is worse than a recession — it's a **sustained** economic downturn which lasts for a **long** period of time (e.g. several years).

Remember — a slowdown in the rate of economic growth means growth is still rising, but more slowly. It doesn't mean economic growth is negative — output isn't falling.

3) Over one year, a country's GDP may **increase** or **decrease**. This simply measures the **change** in the amount of goods and services produced between one year and the next. The change in GDP can be shown in **two** ways — as a **value** (£billions), or as a **percentage**.
4) To **measure** the rate of economic growth over time as a percentage, use this formula:

$$\frac{\text{Change in GDP (£billions)}}{\text{Original GDP (£billions)}} \times 100 = \text{Percentage change}$$

5) Some GDP growth may be due to **prices rising** (inflation, see p.74). **Nominal GDP** is the name given to a GDP figure that **hasn't** been adjusted for inflation. This figure is **misleading** — it'll give the impression that GDP is **higher** than it is.
6) Economists **remove** the effect of inflation to find what's called **real GDP**. For example, a 4% increase in the **nominal GDP** during a period when **inflation** was 3% means **real GDP** only rose by about 1%. The other 3% was due to rising prices.

GDP Per Capita can indicate the **Standard of Living** in a country

1) GDP can be used to give an indication of a country's **standard of living**. This is done by **dividing** the total **national output** by the country's population to get the national output **per person** — GDP per capita. Here's the formula:

$$\frac{\text{Total GDP}}{\text{Population size}} = \text{GDP per capita}$$

'Per capita' just means 'per head' or 'per person'.

2) In theory, the **higher** the **GDP per capita**, the **higher** the **standard of living** in a country.
3) Economists also use the indicators **Gross National Income** (**GNI**) and **Gross National Product** (**GNP**).
4) **GNI** is the GDP **plus** net income from abroad — this **net** income is any income earned by a country on investments and other assets **owned abroad**, **minus** any income earned by foreigners on investments **domestically**.
5) **GNP** is similar to GNI — it's the **total output** of the **citizens** of a country, whether or not they're **resident** in that country.
6) GNI and GNP per capita can be also be used to **compare living standards** between different countries. They are calculated in a **similar** way to GDP per capita — by **dividing** the **total** GNI or GNP by the country's population.

Measuring Economic Growth

Purchasing Power Parity is used in comparisons of Living Standards

EDEXCEL ONLY

1) When using **GDP per capita** (or **GNP** or **GNI per capita**) to compare **living standards** in countries that use **different currencies**, the **exchange rate** might not reflect the **true worth** of the two currencies — so comparing GDP per capita in this way might not give an **accurate** picture.
2) To **overcome** this problem, comparisons are usually carried out using the principle of **purchasing power parity** (PPP).
3) **Purchasing power** is the **real** value of an amount of money in terms of what you can **actually** buy with it. This can **vary** between countries — for example, in a **less developed** country, e.g. Malawi, $1 will buy **more** goods than in a **more developed** country, e.g. Canada.
4) Using **PPP** in comparisons of countries' living standards involves **adjusting** the GDP per capita figures to take into account the **differences** in purchasing power in those countries, with the results usually expressed in US dollars. This makes for a **more accurate** and **easier** comparison.

Using GDP to make Comparisons has Limitations

OCR & EDEXCEL

The more different the two countries are, e.g. a rich developed nation and a poor underdeveloped economy, the greater the comparison problems.

1) **GDP** and **GDP per capita** are used to **compare** the economic performance and the standards of living in **different** countries:
   - A **high GDP** would suggest a country's **economic performance** is **strong**.
   - A **high GDP per capita** suggests that a country's **standard of living** is **high**.
2) Using the GDP and the GDP per capita to make comparisons between countries has its **limitations**. There are **several** things that GDP and GDP per capita figures might **not** take into **account**:

- The extent of the **hidden economy** — economic activity that **doesn't** appear in official figures.
- **Public spending** — some governments provide **more benefits**, such as unemployment benefits or free health care, than others. For example, two countries might have **similar** GDP per capita figures, but one country might **spend** much more money **per person** on providing benefits that improve the standard of living.
- The **extent** of income inequality. Two countries may have **similar** GDP per capita, but the distribution of that income between rich and poor **may** be very different.
- **Other** differences in the standard of living between countries, such as the number of hours workers have to work per week, working conditions, the level of damage to the environment, and different spending needs (e.g. cold countries spend **more income** on heating to achieve the **same level** of comfort that exists in warm countries).

If you're doing Edexcel, p.96 explains 'happiness economics', which tries to take some of these factors into account.

Index Numbers represent percentage changes

Index numbers are useful for **making comparisons** over a period of time. The first year is called the **base year** — the index number for this year is set at **100**. Changes up **or** down are expressed as numbers above or below 100. For example:

- A 3% **rise** in real GDP over one year would mean the index rose to **103** in year 2.
- A 2% **fall** in real GDP over one year would mean the index fell to **98** in year 2.
- An index number of **108** in year 4 means an 8% rise from the **base year**.

Practice Questions

Q1 What are the four main macroeconomic indicators?

Q2 What is the difference between nominal and real national output figures? Why is this important?

Q3 What is meant by purchasing power parity? When is it used? Why is it important?

Q4 Why might comparing the GDP per capita of two countries not give an accurate comparison of their standards of living?

Q5 What can index numbers be used to show?

Exam Question

Q1 A country's real GDP in 2012 was £802 billion, and in 2013 this had grown to £831 billion. Calculate the rate of the country's economic growth in 2013. [2 marks]

I thought GDP wrote revision guides? No? GCP? PCG? Oh, forget it...

There are two key facts on these pages — GDP is the value of all the goods and services produced in a country in a year. Economic growth is measured as the percentage change in GDP over time. You'll need to learn the rest of this stuff too though. Sorry.

Measuring Inflation

Inflation is always being mentioned on the news — it's a key figure which is used to help measure how the economy is doing. ***These pages are for all boards.***

There are *Two Ways* to *Define Inflation*

1) Inflation is the sustained **rise** in the **average price** of **goods** and **services** over a period of time. Keep in mind that:
    - The prices of some goods may be rising **faster** than the average.
    - Some prices may be rising **more slowly**.
    - Some prices may even be **falling**.
2) Inflation can also be seen as a **fall** in the **value** of money. This means that:
    - A **fixed** amount of money (e.g. £10) buys **less** than before.
    - The **purchasing power** of money has fallen (for more on purchasing power, see p.73).

Inflation can be *Positive* or *Negative* (or 0)

1) **Inflation** (or positive inflation) is when the **average price** of goods and services is **rising**.
2) Sometimes the **average price** will actually be **falling**. This is called **negative inflation**, or **deflation.**
3) Other times, a country may experience **hyperinflation**. This is when prices rise **extremely quickly** and money rapidly **loses** its value.
4) If the rate of inflation is **slowing down**, e.g. from 6% to 4%, this is called **disinflation**. Prices are still rising but at a **slower** speed.

There are *Two* main *Measurements* used for *Inflation*

The *Retail Price Index* (RPI)

1) **Two** surveys are carried out to **calculate** the RPI.
2) The first survey is a survey of around 6000 households, called the **Living Costs and Food Survey**.
3) This is used to find out **what** people spend their money on, e.g. petrol, apples, haircuts. The survey also shows what **proportion** of income is spent on these items. This is used to work out the relative **weighting** of each item (this will be important in a second) — for example, if **20%** is spent on transport, then a 20% **weighting** will be given to transport.
4) The second survey is based on **prices** — it measures the **changes** in price of around **700** of the most **commonly** used **goods** and **services** (these goods and services are often referred to as the 'basket of goods').
5) The items are chosen **based on** the Living Costs and Food Survey. What is in the basket **changes** over time, because technology, trends and tastes change (see the diagram below for some examples). This ensures that the basket always **reflects** what the **average household** might spend its money on.
6) The price **changes** in the second survey are **multiplied** by the **weightings** from the first survey. These are then converted to an **index number** (see p.73 for more on index numbers). So **inflation** is just the **percentage change** to the index number over time — e.g. if the index number **rises** from 100 to 102, then **inflation** is 2%.

The weightings are important because the larger the proportion of a household's income that's spent on an item, the larger the effect a change in the price of that item will have on average spending.

Measuring Inflation

The **Consumer Price Index** (CPI)

The CPI is calculated in a **similar** way to the RPI, but there are **three main** differences:

1) Some items are **excluded** from the CPI, the main ones being:
    - Mortgage interest payments
    - Council tax
2) A slightly **different formula** is used to calculate the CPI.
3) A **larger** sample of the population is used for the CPI.

These differences mean that the CPI **tends** to be a little **lower** than the RPI — the **exception** is when **interest rates** are very low. However, they both tend to follow the same **long-term** trend.

The CPI is the official measure of inflation in the UK. Many other countries collect data on inflation in a **similar** way to the CPI, so it's often used for **international comparisons**.

The **CPI** and **RPI** have **Limitations**

The RPI and CPI can be really **useful**, but they also have their **limitations**:

1) The RPI **excludes** all households in the top 4% of incomes. The CPI covers a **broader range** of the population, but it **doesn't** include mortgage interest payments or council tax.
2) The information given by households in the Living Costs and Food Survey can be **inaccurate**.
3) The basket of goods only changes **once** a year — so it might miss some short-term changes in spending habits.
4) The RPI and CPI are likely to give an **inaccurate** representation for **non-typical** households.
5) The **differences** in prices **between regions** aren't taken into account.

The RPI and CPI are important for **Government Policy**

See pages 100-101 for more on inflation.

The RPI and CPI are used to help determine **wages** and **state benefits**.

1) **Employers** and **trade unions** use them as a starting point in wage negotiations.
2) The **government** uses them to decide on increases in **state pensions**, and other welfare **benefits**.
3) Some benefits are **index-linked** — they rise **automatically** each year by the **same** percentage as the chosen index.

They're also used to measure changes in the UK's **international** competitiveness.

1) If the rate of inflation measured by the CPI is **higher** in the UK than in the other countries it trades with, then UK goods become **less** price competitive, as they'll **cost more** for other countries to buy.
2) So — **exports** will **fall**, and **imports**, which will be made relatively **cheaper** by domestic inflation, will **increase**.

Practice Questions

Q1 In what two ways can inflation be defined?

Q2 Describe what happens to prices during a period of:

a) Negative inflation

b) Hyperinflation

c) Disinflation

Q3 In what ways is the RPI different from the CPI?

Q4 Aside from measuring inflation, give an example of a use of RPI/CPI.

Exam Question

Q1 Explain three limitations of the RPI as a measure of inflation. [6 marks]

Revision can be a bit deflating, but try to stay positive...

And there I was thinking inflation was just blowing up a balloon. The RPI and the CPI are two different measures of inflation — make sure you know what they are, the key differences between the two, and some examples of what else they're used for.

Measuring Unemployment

There are two main ways of measuring unemployment — each has its advantages and disadvantages. ***For all boards.***

There are **Two** ways of **Defining Unemployment**

1) The **level** of unemployment is the **number** of people who are looking for a job but cannot find one.
2) The **rate** of unemployment is the number of people out of work as a **percentage** of the **labour force**.

The **rate** of unemployment is used when making **comparisons** between countries, as different countries have different **population sizes**.

The labour force is all the people who are willing and able to work. This includes those working and those looking for work.

There are **Two** ways of **Measuring Unemployment**

1 The Claimant Count

The claimant count is the **number** of people claiming unemployment-related benefits from the government, known as the Jobseeker's Allowance (JSA). There are **advantages** and **disadvantages** of using the claimant count to measure unemployment:

Advantages:
- This data is **easy** to obtain (you just count the number of people claiming JSA) and there's **no** cost in collecting the data.
- It's updated **monthly**, so it's always **current**.

Disadvantages:
- It can be **manipulated** by the government to make it seem **smaller** — for example, a change in the rules (e.g. **raising** the school leaving age to 19) could reduce the **number** of people who could claim JSA, which would make it **seem** that unemployment was falling.
- It **excludes** those people who **are** looking for work but are **not** eligible to (or choose not to) claim JSA.

2 The Labour Force Survey

The International Labour Organisation (ILO) uses a **sample** of the population. It asks people who **aren't** working if they're **actively seeking** work. The **number** of people who answer 'yes' (whether they're claiming JSA or not) are added up to produce the **ILO unemployment count**. There are **advantages** and **disadvantages** to using this figure:

Advantages:
- It's thought to be **more accurate** than the claimant count.
- It's an **internationally** agreed measure for unemployment, so it's easier to make **comparisons** with other countries.

Disadvantages:
- It's less **up to date** than the claimant count because of the way the data is **collected**.
- It's **expensive** to collect and put together the data.
- The sample may be **unrepresentative** of the population as a whole — making the data **inaccurate**.

The figure from the Labour Force Survey tends to be **higher** than the claimant count because certain groups of people are **excluded** from the claimant count. For example, some people **can't claim** JSA because they have a **high earning** husband/wife, or they might have too much money in **savings**.

Unemployment comes at a **Cost** to the **Whole Economy**

See p.98-99 for more information on unemployment.

Governments want to keep track of **unemployment figures** for a number of reasons:

1) A **high** rate of unemployment suggests that an economy is doing **badly**.
2) Unemployment means there's **unused** labour in the economy, so **fewer** goods and services can be **produced**.
3) Unemployment will lead to **lower incomes** and **less spending**. This will have an impact on **companies** too — they might sell **fewer goods**, or need to **cut prices** and make **less profit**.

Measuring the Balance of Payments

The balance of payments is all about the money coming into and going out of the country. ***This page is for all boards.***

*The **Balance of Payments** refers to **International Flows** of money*

If goods are exported, they leave the country and money moves the other way, i.e. into the country to pay for them. For imports, it's the opposite.

The balance of payments records:

- The flow of money **out** of a country, e.g. to **pay** for **imported** goods.
- The flow of money **into** a country, e.g. **payments** from **exported** goods.

It's the **value** of **exports** and **imports** that's calculated in the balance of payments, **not** the **volume**.
So if **prices change**, but **volume** remains the **same**, then the **value** of exports and imports will **change**.

*There are **Four** sections to the **Current Account***

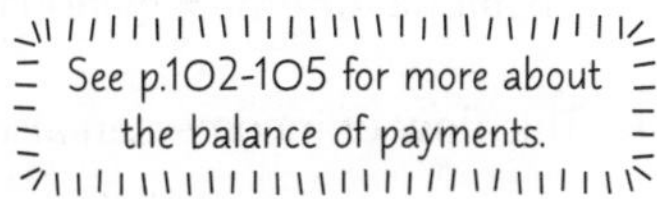

See p.102-105 for more about the balance of payments.

The **main** part of the balance of payments you need to know for your exam is the **current account**, which records the **international exchange** of goods and services. It consists of **four** sections:

1) **Trade in goods**, often called '**visible** trade' — so goods will either be **visible imports** or **visible exports**.
   Examples: cars, computers, food.
2) **Trade in services**, often called '**invisible** trade'. These can be **imported** or **exported** too.
   Examples: tourism, insurance, transport.
3) **International** flows of **income** earned as salaries, interest, profit and dividends.
   Examples: interest on an account held in a foreign country, dividends from a company based abroad.
4) **Transfers** of money from one person or government to another.
   Examples: foreign aid, transfer of money to or from a family member who lives in another country.

*The balance of payments **Isn't** always **Balanced***

1) The flows of money coming **into** a country **may not** balance the flows of money **out**.
   - If the money flowing **in** exceeds the money flowing **out**, there's a **surplus**.
   - If the money flowing **out** exceeds the money flowing **in**, there's a **deficit**.
2) In recent years, the UK has had a **deficit** in its balance of payments. Although the UK has usually had a **surplus** in **invisible trade**, it has also had a **large deficit** in **visible trade**.
3) A deficit **isn't** necessarily a bad thing — but it might be a sign that a country is **uncompetitive**.
4) Governments want to **avoid** a large, long-term deficit — this **would** cause bigger problems, for example job losses (see p.104).

Tom had always been good at balancing anything.

Practice Questions

Q1 Give two negative effects unemployment has on an economy.

Q2 For each of the items below, identify where it would appear in the current account of the balance of payments and whether it is a flow into or out of the UK.

Item 1 A British car company increases its sales to the Far East.

Item 2 Dividends from shares in an American company paid to a British shareholder.

Item 3 A British family holidaying in Spain who pay for a taxi in Madrid.

Exam Questions

Q1 Name the two main measures of unemployment, giving one advantage and one disadvantage of each. [4 marks]

Q2 Explain what a surplus and a deficit are on the current account of the balance of payments. [4 marks]

Labour Force be with you...

There's a lot on these two pages — definitions, advantages, disadvantages... You'll need to understand it all before you move on.

The Circular Flow of Income

Before you learn about the joys of aggregate demand and supply, you'll need to know about the circular flow of income. It explains the link between national output, national income and national expenditure. ***These pages are for all boards.***

Income Flows between *Firms* and *Households*

1) In simple terms, an **economy** is made up of **firms** and **households**.
2) Firms **produce** goods and services, and **all** of these **goods** and **services** make up the **national output**.
3) The **households** in a country **provide** the labour, land and capital that **firms** use to produce the national output. The money **paid** to households by firms for these **factors of production** is the **national income**.
4) Households **spend** the money they get from the national income on the goods and services (outputs) that firms create — the **value** of this spending is the **national expenditure**.
5) So, all of this creates a **circular flow of income**, which can be shown by the formula:

National **output** = National **income** = National **expenditure**

At full employment (i.e. when everybody of working age who wants a job at current wage rates has one), national income, national output and national expenditure are all equal to the "full-employment income".

6) This **flow** of income can also be shown as a **diagram**:

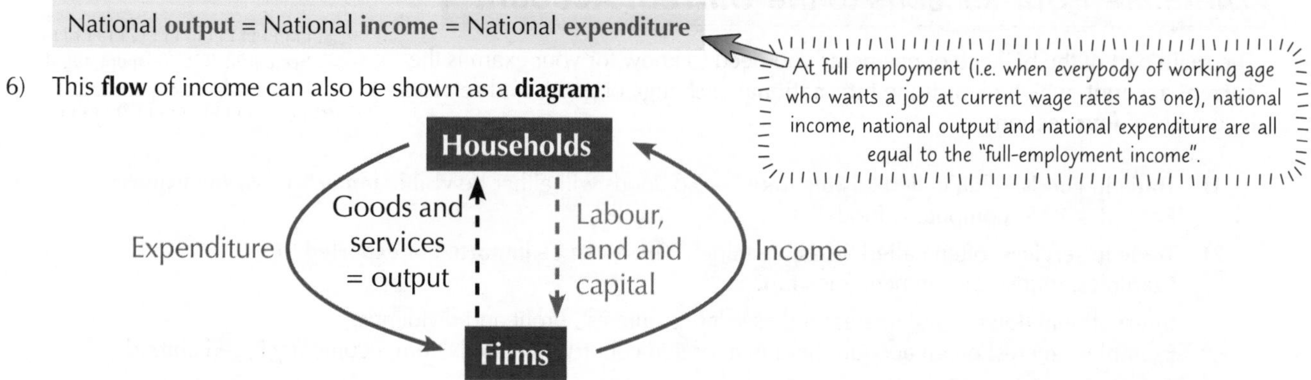

There are actually **two** flows here:

- A **physical flow** (shown by **straight arrows**) of **'real things'** — i.e. goods, services, labour, land and capital.
- A **monetary flow** (shown by **curved arrows**) — i.e. the **money** that **pays for** the 'physical things'.

There are Injections into and Withdrawals from the flow of income

1) The **circular flow** suggests that as long as **households** keep spending what they earn, and **firms** keep using their revenues to produce more goods using the same inputs, then national output (and national income) **won't change**.
2) However, an economy's circular flow of income is **affected** by **injections** and **withdrawals** (or leakages).
3) **Injections into** the circular flow of income come in the form of **exports**, **investment** and **government spending** — these go directly to **firms**.
4) **Withdrawals** come in the form of **imports**, **savings** and **taxes** — these withdrawals can be made by **households** or **firms**.
5) **Injections** and **withdrawals** can be shown in a circular flow like this:

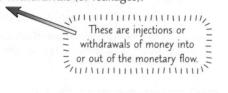

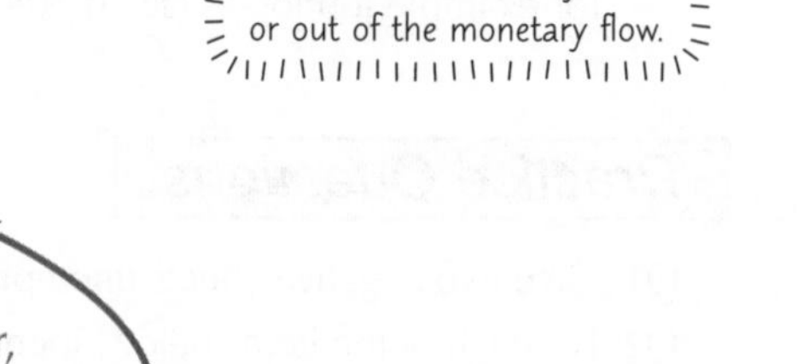

These are injections or withdrawals of money into or out of the monetary flow.

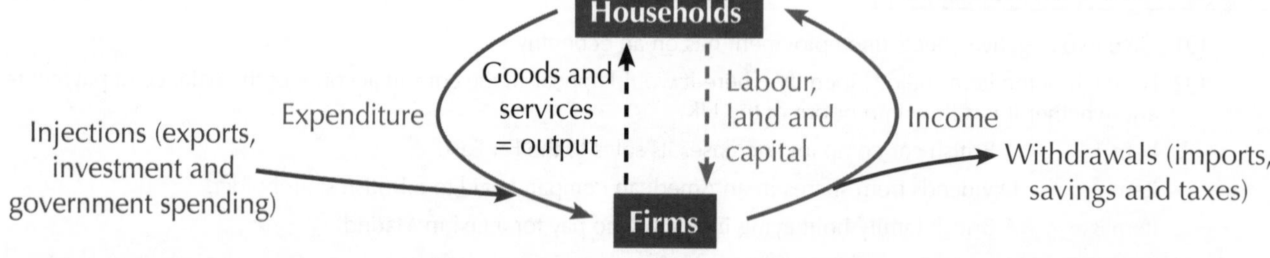

- If **injections** and **withdrawals** are **equal**, then the economy is in **equilibrium**.
- If **injections** into the circular flow are **greater** than **withdrawals**, this means that **expenditure** is **greater** than **output** — so firms will **increase output**. As a result national output, income and expenditure will all **increase**.
- If **withdrawals** from the circular flow are **greater** than **injections**, this means that **output** is **greater** than **expenditure** — so firms will **reduce output**. As a result national output, income and expenditure will **decrease**.

The Circular Flow of Income

Injections have a Multiplier Effect on the circular flow

1) When an **injection** is made into the circular flow, the **actual change** in the **national income** is **greater** than the **initial** injection — this is called the **multiplier effect**. Take a look at the following **example**:

- The government gives a firm £50 million to **invest** in new machinery. The money is used to pay households for land, labour and capital, so it's an **injection** of £50 million of **new income** into the circular flow.
- £12 million of this income **leaks** out of the circular flow as withdrawals (savings, tax and imports), but the **remaining** £38 million is **spent** on goods and services, so all £38 million goes to firms as **expenditure** — increasing **output**.
- Another £10 million **leaks** out of the circular flow as withdrawals from firms (savings, tax and imports), but the remaining £28 million is paid by firms as **income** to households.
- The cycle will continue, with households and firms **spending** some of the money and the rest **leaking** out of the circular flow, until there's nothing left of the **initial** investment.
- So the **original** £50 million has gone **round** the circular flow **multiple** times, though some of it has **leaked away** at each stage. This means the **total effect** of the initial investment on national **output**, **income** and **expenditure** is £50m + £38m + £28m + ... etc. — it's actually much **more** than £50 million.

The multiplier effect works on all kinds of things.

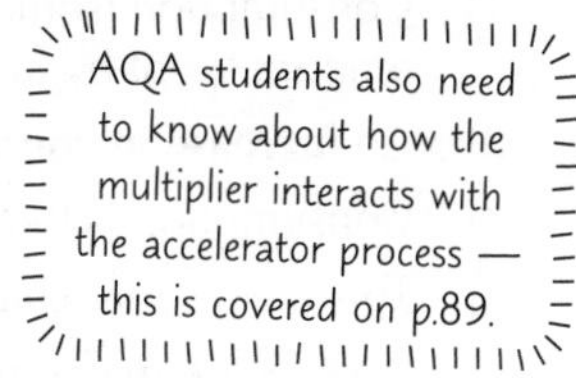

AQA students also need to know about how the multiplier interacts with the accelerator process — this is covered on p.89.

2) The **size** of the multiplier effect depends on the **rate** at which money **leaks** from the circular flow — e.g. the **bigger** the leakages, the **quicker** the money will **leave** the circular flow and the **smaller** the multiplier effect will be.
3) So, if **lots** of money is being spent on **imports** (or used as savings or tax), then the **multiplier effect** will actually be quite **small** because the injection will **quickly** leak out of the circular flow.

Wealth is Different to Income

1) Wealth is the total **value** of all the **assets** owned by individuals or firms in an economy.
2) Assets can include **actual money**, e.g. savings, and **physical items**, e.g. houses or cars.
3) Unlike income, which is a **flow** of money, wealth is a **stock** concept — you can think of it as a **stockpile** of **resources**. These resources **aren't** currently being **used** in the circular flow of income, but they **could** be at some point.
4) Although income and wealth are **different** things there's a **correlation** between them. For example, it's likely that an individual with a **high income** will also have **high wealth**, because they'll be able to **purchase** more **expensive** assets and have **more money** to save.

Practice Questions

Q1 What are the three injections into the circular flow of income?

Q2 What are the three withdrawals from the circular flow of income?

Q3 Give a definition of wealth.

Exam Question

Q1 Comment on the potential multiplier effect on the circular flow of income of a large increase in government spending on the NHS. [6 marks]

My assets include good looks, charm and modesty...

If there are no injections or withdrawals, or if injections = withdrawals, then national output, national income and national expenditure are all equal. If injections and withdrawals aren't balanced, this will lead to a change in the national income. It can be a bit tricky to get your head around, but you should be able to use the diagrams to help you figure out what's going on.

The Components of Aggregate Demand

Here's another delightful economics term — aggregate demand. 'Aggregate' is basically just a fancy economics way of saying 'total' — so aggregate demand means the 'total demand' in an economy. ***These pages are for all boards.***

Aggregate Demand *is the* ***Total Spending*** *on goods and services*

1) **Aggregate demand** (AD) is the **total demand**, or the **total spending**, in an economy over a given period of time.
2) So aggregate demand is made up of all the **components** that **contribute** to spending/demand in an economy.
3) It's calculated using the **formula**:

AD = Consumption (C) + Investment (I) + Government spending (G) + (Exports (X) – Imports (M))

Consumption *and* ***Saving*** *are affected by a number of factors*

1) Consumption (sometimes referred to as consumer spending or consumer expenditure) is the **total** amount spent by **households** on goods and services. It **doesn't** include spending by **firms**.
2) An **increase** in **consumption** will mean an **increase** in **AD** — a **reduction** in **consumption** will mean a **reduction** in **AD**.
3) Consumption is the **largest** component of aggregate demand — it makes up about **65%** of AD in the UK.
4) This means that **changes** in the level of **consumption** will tend to have a **big impact** on aggregate demand.
5) Savings are made **instead of** consumption — so income can be consumed **or** saved.
6) When consumption is **high**, saving tends to be **low**, and **vice versa**.
7) Here are some of the **main factors** affecting consumption and saving:

Disposable income is money available to spend after income tax and National Insurance have been paid.

- **Income** — generally, as disposable income **increases**, consumption will **rise**. The **rate** at which **consumption** rises is usually **lower** than the **rate** at which **income** increases because households tend to **save** more as well.
- **Interest rates** — **higher** interest rates lead to **less** consumer spending. Consumers **save** more to take **advantage** of the higher rates and they're **less likely** to **borrow** money or **buy** things on **credit** because it's more expensive. Consumers may also have **less money** to spend if interest rates on **existing** loans and mortgages increase.
- **Consumer confidence** — when consumers feel **more confident** about the **economy** and their own financial situation, they **spend more** and **save less**. Confidence is **affected** by a **number** of factors. For example, in a **recession** consumers are usually **reluctant** to spend because their **confidence** in the economy is **low** — they might, for example, be worried about **losing** their jobs. This reluctance can **continue** even after a **recession**.
- **Wealth effects** — a **rise** in household **wealth**, e.g. due to a rise in **share** prices or **house** prices, will often lead to a **rise** in **consumer spending** and a **reduction** in **saving**. This is because of consumer **confidence** — if house prices rise **faster** than **inflation**, home owners will feel more **confident** in their own finances.
- **Taxes** — **direct tax increases** lead to a **fall** in consumers' disposable income, so they spend **less**. **Indirect tax increases**, e.g. an increase in VAT, **increase** the cost of spending, so consumers tend to **reduce** their consumption. A **reduction** in direct or indirect taxes will lead to an **increase** in consumer spending.
- **Unemployment** — when unemployment **rises**, consumers tend to spend **less** and save **more**. (People still in employment will tend to replace spending with saving, as they become more worried about **losing** their jobs.) A **fall** in unemployment means **more** people have money to **spend**, and consumers are **less** worried about losing their jobs, so consumer spending **increases**.

Don't confuse ***Saving*** *and* ***Investment***

1) It's important to realise that **investment** and **saving** are **different** things.
2) **Savings** tend to be made by **households**, whereas **investments** tend to be made by **firms**.
3) For example, **savings** made by a household might be money put into a **savings bank account** each month. An **investment** made by a firm could be money paid to **build** a new office.

The Components of Aggregate Demand

Investment is made by Firms

1) **Investment** is money spent by **firms** on **assets** which they'll use to **produce** goods or services — this includes things such as **machinery**, **computers** and **offices**.

- **Gross investment** includes **all** investment spending.
- **Net investment** only includes investment that **increases productive capacity**.
- E.g. if a firm has 3 old trucks, but replaces these with 5 new trucks, the **gross** investment is '**5 trucks**', but the **net** investment is '**2 trucks**'.

2) Firms **invest** with the **intention** of making **profit** in the future.
3) Investment makes up **about 15%** of AD in the UK.
4) There are **several** factors that **affect** investment:

Risk

1) The **level** of **risk** involved will affect the **amount** of investment by firms.
2) If there's a **high risk** that a firm **won't** benefit from its investment then it's unlikely that the firm will invest. For example, when there's **economic instability**, **less investment** will be made.

Government incentives and regulation

1) **Government incentives** such as subsidies or reductions in tax can affect the **level** of **investment**. For example, a **reduction** in corporation tax might **encourage** firms to invest, because they'll have **more funds** available to do so.
2) A **relaxing** of **government regulations** might **reduce** a firm's costs and make it **more likely** to invest.

Interest rates and access to credit

1) Firms often **borrow** the money they want to **invest**. This means that when **interest** rates are **high** or firms are unable to **access credit** (i.e. they're unable to borrow money), **investment** tends to be **lower**.
2) **High** interest rates would **reduce** how **profitable** an investment would be (since interest charges on loans will be **higher**).
3) High interest rates will also mean there's a **greater** opportunity cost of investing **existing** funds instead of putting them into a **bank account** with a high interest rate.

Technical advances

Firms need to **invest** in **new technology** to stay competitive.
Investment will **rise** when **significant technological advances** are made.

Investment also depends on how quickly national income is changing — this leads to an effect called the accelerator process (see p.89).

Business confidence and 'animal spirits'

1) The more **confident** a business is in its **ability** to make **profits** (because **demand for exports** is high, for example) the **more** money it's likely to **invest**.
2) But 'business confidence' depends partly on the general **optimism** or **pessimism** of the company's managers. Keynes recognised that **not all** investment decisions are based purely on **reason** and **rational thinking**, and that **human emotion, intuition** and '**gut instinct**' are also important factors. He called these factors '**animal spirits**'.

Practice Questions

Q1 What is the formula for aggregate demand?

Q2 What is the difference between saving and investment?

Q3 What is 'business confidence' and how does it affect investment?

Exam Questions

Q1 How might high taxes and high interest rates affect the level of consumption? [6 marks]

Q2 Describe three factors which might affect the level of investment in an economy. [6 marks]

Take it from me — Investment gets SO annoyed if he's mistaken for Saving...

Each component of aggregate demand is affected by multiple factors. These pages have described the things that affect consumption (the biggest component) and investment. You'll see similar ideas popping up on the next couple of pages too.

The Components of Aggregate Demand

You've seen the things that affect two of the components of aggregate demand (consumption and investment) — here are a couple of pages on the factors affecting the other two components (government spending and net exports). ***For all boards.***

Government Spending *doesn't include* **Transfers** *of* **Money**

1) The **government spending** component of aggregate demand is the money spent by the government on **public** goods and services, e.g. education, health care, defence and so on.
2) Only money that **directly contributes** to the **output** of the economy is included — this means that **transfers** of money such as **benefits** (like the Jobseeker's Allowance) or **pensions** are **not** included.
3) Government spending is quite a **large** component of aggregate demand, so changes in government spending can have a big **influence** on aggregate demand.

Government Spending *doesn't have to be* **Equal** *to* **Revenue**

1) A government **budget outlines** a government's **planned** spending and revenue for the next year. Governments will usually have either a budget **deficit** or a budget **surplus**.
   - If government spending is **greater than** its revenue, there will be a **budget deficit**.
   - If government spending is **less than** its revenue, there will be a **budget surplus**.

Most of a government's revenue comes from taxation.

2) Governments use **fiscal policy** (see p.118-121) to alter their **spending** and **taxation** to **influence** aggregate demand.
   - If aggregate demand is **low** and economic growth is **slow**, or even negative, then a government may **overspend** (causing a budget **deficit**) in order to **increase** aggregate demand and **boost** economic growth.
   - If aggregate demand is **high** and the economy is experiencing a **boom**, a government might **increase taxes** and **spend less** (causing a budget **surplus**) to try to **reduce** aggregate demand and **slow down** economic growth.

The government budgetigar's planned spending on seeds would cause another deficit.

3) An **imbalance** in the budget will affect the **circular flow of income** — a **budget surplus** will indicate an **overall withdrawal** from the circular flow, but a **budget deficit** will indicate an **overall injection** into the circular flow.
4) An imbalance in the budget is fine in the **short run**, but in the **long run** governments will try to **balance** out any **surpluses** and **deficits**. A long-term **surplus** might mean the government is **harming** economic growth by choosing **not** to spend, or by keeping taxes **too high**. A long-term **deficit** is likely to mean a country has a large national **debt**.
5) Sometimes governments will **balance** the **budget** so that government spending will be **equal** to revenue. This should have little **effect** on aggregate demand.

An **Export** *from one country is* **Always** *an* **Import** *to another*

1) **Exports** are **goods** or **services** that are produced in one country, then sold in another. Imports are the opposite — they're goods and services that are brought **into** a country after being **produced elsewhere**.
2) Exports are an **inflow** of money to a country, and imports are an **outflow** — so exports are an **injection** into the circular flow of income and imports are a **withdrawal**.
3) Exports minus imports (X – M) make up the **net exports** component of aggregate demand.
4) If the amount spent on imports **exceeds** the amount received from exports (as it does in the UK), **net exports** will be a **negative** number.

The Components of Aggregate Demand

There are many **Factors** that will **Affect Imports** and **Exports**

Several factors will affect the **net exports** component of aggregate demand:

There's more on exchange rates on p.113-115.

The exchange rate

A change in the **value** of a currency will affect net exports in **different ways** in the **long** and **short run**:

- In the **long run** — if the **value** of a currency **increases**, **imports** become relatively **cheaper** and **exports** become relatively **more expensive** for foreigners. As a result, **demand** for **imports (M) rises** and **demand** for **exports (X) falls**. So a **strong** currency (i.e. a currency with a high value) will **worsen** net exports **(X – M)** in the **long run** and reduce aggregate demand, but a **weak** currency will have the **opposite effect** and **improve** net exports.
- In the **short run** — demand for imports and exports tends to be quite price **inelastic**. For example, some goods **don't** have close substitutes, e.g. oil, while others might **have substitutes**, but there's a **time lag** before countries will **switch** to them — so in the short run demand **won't change** much. This means that **initially** when the value of a currency **increases**, net exports will actually **improve** (increase) because the **overall value** of exports **increases** and the **overall value** of imports **decreases**.

Changes in the state of the world economy

- The higher a country's **real income**, the more it tends to **import**. So **net exports fall** as real income rises.
- The state of the **world economy** also affects exports and imports. For example, the USA exports lots of goods to Canada. If Canada goes through a period of **low** (or negative) **growth** then **exports** from the USA to Canada will **decrease**. Assuming imports are unaffected, this means a **worsening** in the USA's net exports. Similarly, if Canada experiences **high growth rates**, exports from the USA are likely to **increase** — **improving** net exports.

Degree of protectionism

In the short run, **tariffs** and **quotas** can increase net exports by reducing imports. However, industries that are protected from **international competition** in this way have few incentives to become more efficient, so will often export less in the long run. Also, in the long run, other countries may **retaliate** by introducing their own tariffs and quotas.

Non-price factors

These include things such as the **quality** of goods. For example, advancements in technology in a country that lead to the production of **higher quality** goods would be likely to cause an **increase** in exports from that country, because people are willing to **pay more** for something if it's really good. This would mean an **improvement** in **net exports**.

Net exports tend to make up a **small percentage** of aggregate demand, so changes in net exports have a **minor impact** on AD.

Practice Questions

Q1 What does the government spending component of aggregate demand consist of?

Q2 What will cause a budget deficit?

Q3 Define 'imports' and 'exports'.

Q4 What 'non-price factors' may lead to an improvement in net exports?

Exam Questions

Q1 Which of the following pairs of government policies is most likely to lead to an increase in aggregate demand?

A) Increase government spending and increase taxes.
B) Decrease government spending and increase taxes.
C) Increase government spending and decrease taxes.
D) Decrease government spending and decrease taxes. [1 mark]

Q2 Explain two factors which could increase the demand for a country's exports. [10 marks]

Apparently net exports have nothing to do with fishing...

That's all the components of aggregate demand. It's important that you know what the components of aggregate demand are, what affects them, and how important each component is to the overall aggregate demand. But that's not all you need to know about aggregate demand, not by a long shot — turn the page and be wowed by the majestic aggregate demand curve.

Aggregate Demand Analysis

Aggregate demand is the total demand in an economy — so the AD curve is similar to the normal demand curve. Sometimes a change in AD will cause a movement along the AD curve, other times the curve will shift. ***These pages are for all boards.***

The **Aggregate Demand Curve** is similar to the normal **Demand Curve**

1) The aggregate demand curve uses **different** axes to the normal demand curve (p.14) — along the x-axis is **national output**, and up the y-axis is **price level**.
2) The price level represents the **average** level of prices in an economy — in the UK this price level is likely to be the **Consumer Price Index** (see p.75).
3) The aggregate demand (AD) curve slopes **downwards** — the **lower** the price level, the **more** output is demanded. **Lower** prices mean consumers can buy **more** goods/services with their money.
4) A **change** in the **price level** will cause a **movement along** the AD curve — for example, if the price level **rose** from P to P_1, the total (aggregate) demand would **fall** from Y to Y_1.
5) A rise in the price level will cause output to fall because:

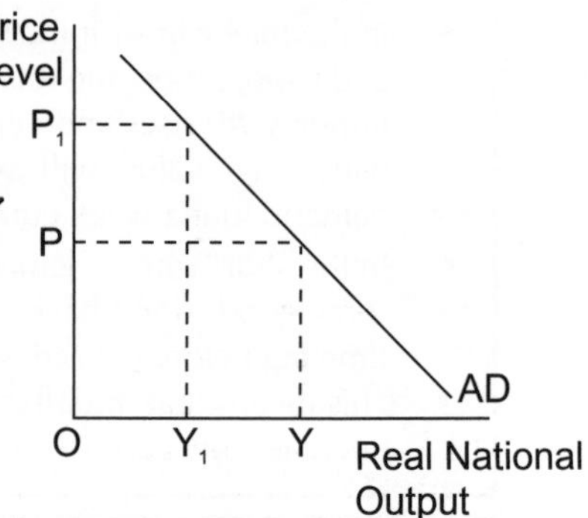

- Domestic **consumption** will be **reduced** — things become **more expensive**, so people can purchase **fewer** goods and services.
- The **demand** for **exports** will be **reduced** — domestically produced products become **less competitive**.
- The **demand** for **imports** will **increase** — if prices **haven't** risen abroad, imports will become **cheaper** in comparison.

The **AD Curve** can **Shift**

Aggregate demand can **increase** or **decrease**, causing the AD curve to shift **right** or **left**.

The **AD Curve** might **Shift** to the **Right**

1) The AD curve will **shift** to the **right** if there's a **rise** in consumption, investment, government spending or net exports that **hasn't** been caused by a change in the price level. For example:

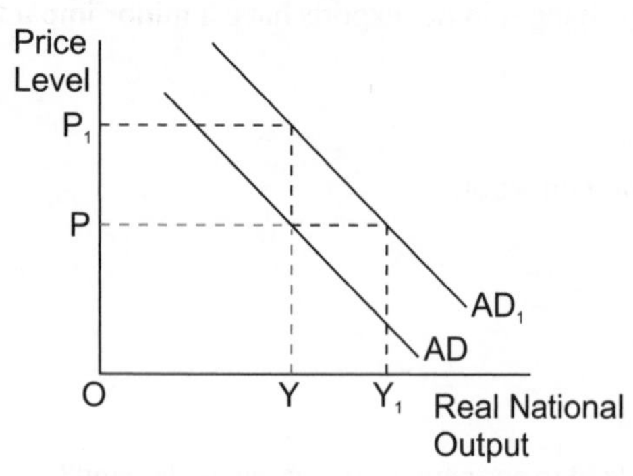

- A **reduction** in income tax will cause an **increase** in consumers' disposable income. This tends to lead to an **increase** in consumption, so there will be an **increase** in aggregate demand and a **shift** of the AD curve to the right from **AD** to **AD_1** (see the diagram to the left).
- If a government changes its fiscal policy (see p.118) and decides to **increase** its spending **above** any increase in its revenue, then this is an **injection** into the circular flow of income. It will cause an **increase** in aggregate demand and a **shift** of the AD curve to the **right**, e.g. from AD to AD_1.
- A **weak** currency will make **exports cheaper** and **imports more expensive**. This will lead to a **rise** in **net exports**, so there will be an **increase** in **aggregate demand** and a **shift** of the AD curve to the **right**, e.g. from AD to AD_1.

2) The outward shift of the curve means that at a **given price level**, **more output** can be produced — but also, a **given** amount of **output** will have a **higher** price level. For example, if there's an increase in aggregate demand from AD to AD_1 — at price level P, there's an increase in output from Y to Y_1, and at output Y, the price level increases from P to P_1.
3) Labour is a **derived demand** — an **increase** in AD means **output increases**, so the **demand** for labour **increases**. **More** jobs are created so that the **extra** output can be **produced**, and there will be an **increase** in **employment** levels.

Aggregate Demand Analysis

The AD Curve might Shift to the Left

1) The AD curve will **shift** to the **left** if there's a **fall** in consumption, investment, government spending or net exports that **hasn't** been caused by a change in the price level. For example:

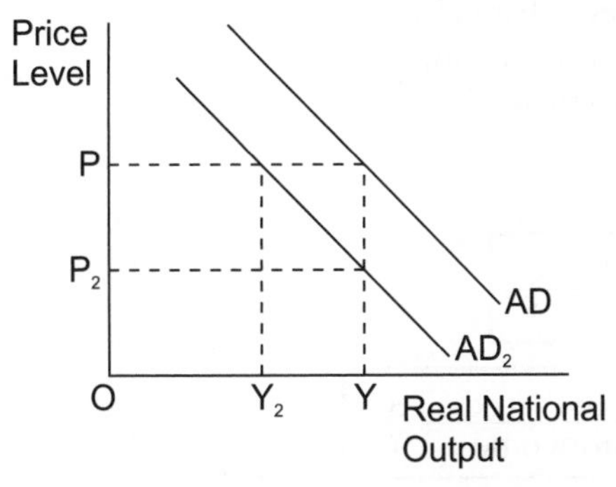

- A **rise** in **interest rates** will lead to a **reduction** in **consumer spending** because people will choose to **save** more. Higher interest rates also lead to a **reduction** in **investment** because borrowing the money to invest becomes **more expensive**. Both of these factors lead to a **reduction** in **aggregate demand**, and a **shift** of the AD curve to the **left**, e.g. from AD to AD_2 (see the diagram to the left).
- A **strong** currency will make **exports more expensive** and **imports cheaper**, so there will be a **fall** in **net exports**. This will lead to a **reduction** in **aggregate demand** and a **shift** of the AD curve to the **left**, e.g. from AD to AD_2.

2) The inward shift of the curve means that at a **given price level** (P), **less output** (Y_2) can be produced — but also, a **given** amount of output (Y) will have a **lower** price level (P_2). There will also be a decrease in **employment** levels.

The Multiplier Effect leads to a Larger Increase in aggregate demand

1) When there's an **injection** into the economy (e.g. as a result of increased government spending), the **AD curve** will **shift** to the **right**.
2) However, when money is **injected** into the circular flow of income, the **value** of the **initial** injection is **multiplied** — this is the multiplier effect that was introduced on p.79. One person's **expenditure** becomes someone else's **income**, so the money goes round the circular flow **multiple** times until it's all **leaked** out.
3) The effect is that the AD curve shifts **even further** to the right — and the bigger the **multiplier**, the greater the **shift**.

For example, if a government **injects** money into **health care**, the money might be used for **wages**. Some of this money would then be spent by **consumers** — **increasing consumption**. This would create a **second** increase in AD, and the cycle will continue until all the money from the initial injection has **leaked out**.

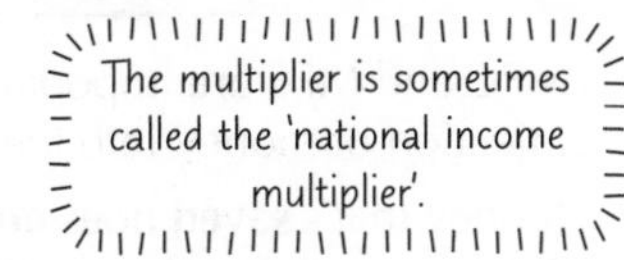

The multiplier is sometimes called the 'national income multiplier'.

4) The overall **size** of the **multiplier** will depend on the **size** of the **leakages** from the circular flow of income, but it's **very difficult** to measure in practice. This is partly because there are **time lags** and the multiplier effect of government spending can take **years** to fully show up in the economy — e.g. the **full** benefits to the economy of government spending on improving transport links may only appear **years** later.

An **initial injection** of £50m is estimated to cause a **total change** in national income of £75m. Find the size of the multiplier.

$$\text{Multiplier} = \frac{\text{change in national income}}{\text{initial injection}} = \frac{£75\text{m}}{£50\text{m}} = \mathbf{1.5}$$

You can work out the value of the multiplier if you know how an initial injection changes the national income.

5) Measuring the size of the multiplier is also made difficult because, like everything else in the economy, it's **changing all the time**. This makes it very difficult for any government to **accurately control** AD.

Practice Questions

Q1 What causes a movement along the AD curve?

Q2 What would be the likely effect on aggregate demand of a rise in interest rates?

Exam Question

Q1 Discuss the effect of an increase in government spending on aggregate demand. Refer to the multiplier effect in your answer. [10 marks]

There's more to come about AD curves — so I 'ope you 'aven't 'AD enough...

There can be movements along the aggregate demand curve, and shifts of the curve itself — make sure you understand the difference between the two. You also need to know the effect the multiplier will have on AD.

Aggregate Demand Analysis

These pages are about people's propensity (i.e. their willingness or natural tendency) to either spend or save. There's a little bit of maths, but if you can divide two numbers, then you'll be okay. ***These pages are for Edexcel and OCR only.***

Average Propensity to *Consume* or *Save* shows what happens to incomes

1) **Spending** and **saving** are both really important in an economy, and they're basically **opposite** processes. Money that's **spent** continues to circulate round the economy, while money that's **saved** is withdrawn from the circular flow described on p.78.
2) The '**average propensity**' formulas below tell you the **proportion** of the **total national income** that's either **spent** or **saved**.

$$\text{Average propensity to consume (APC)} = \frac{\text{consumption}}{\text{total income}} = \frac{C}{Y}$$

$$\text{Average propensity to save (APS)} = \frac{\text{amount saved}}{\text{total income}} = \frac{S}{Y}$$

The *Marginal Propensity to Consume* affects the size of the *Multiplier*

1) In Economics, '**marginal propensity**' is often **more important** than '**average propensity**'.
2) The **marginal propensity to consume** (**MPC**) is the proportion of any **extra** income that's **spent** on the **consumption** of goods and services. Similarly, the **marginal propensity to save** (**MPS**) is the proportion of **extra** income that's **saved**.

$$\text{Marginal propensity to consume (MPC)} = \frac{\text{Change in consumption}}{\text{Change in income}} = \frac{\Delta C}{\Delta Y}$$

$$\text{Marginal propensity to save (MPS)} = \frac{\text{Change in saving}}{\text{Change in income}} = \frac{\Delta S}{\Delta Y}$$

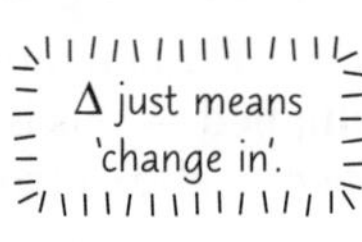

3) MPC and MPS are important, since the **size** of the **multiplier** will depend on **how much** of an injection of money into the circular flow is **spent** by those who receive it, and how much is **saved**.
4) Money that's **saved** does **not** contribute to another person's **income**. This means that the **more likely** people are to **spend** their money, the **greater** the **multiplier effect**.
5) So if the MPC is **low**, the multiplier will be **small**, because any increase in income will only lead to a **small increase** in **consumption**. The rest of the increase in income will be **saved**.
6) Generally, people with **lower incomes** tend to have **higher MPCs**. The MPC also tends to be **higher** in **less developed** countries, so the multiplier will be **bigger**.

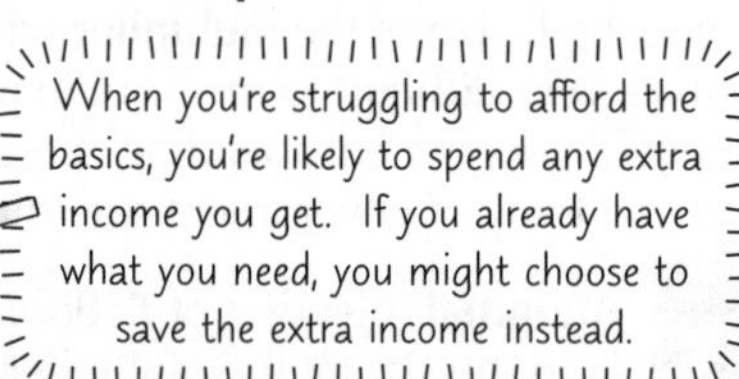

When you're struggling to afford the basics, you're likely to spend any extra income you get. If you already have what you need, you might choose to save the extra income instead.

EDEXCEL ONLY

Learn the *Formula* for calculating the *Multiplier* from the *MPC*

There's a simple formula for working out the **multiplier** if you know the **MPC**:

$$\textbf{Multiplier} = \frac{1}{1 - \text{MPC}}$$

Example: If every extra £1 of income earned in a country results in an extra 60p being spent on goods and services produced in that country, then:
a) Find the marginal propensity to consume (MPC).
b) Find the value of the multiplier for that economy.
c) What will be the total increase in national income after an injection of an extra £50m?

a) If 60p out of every extra £1 of income is spent, then:

$$\text{Marginal propensity to consume (MPC)} = \frac{\text{Change in consumption}}{\text{Change in income}} = \frac{\Delta C}{\Delta Y} = \frac{0.6}{1} = \mathbf{0.6}$$

b) $\text{Multiplier} = \frac{1}{1 - \text{MPC}} = \frac{1}{1 - 0.6} = \frac{1}{0.4} = \mathbf{2.5}$

c) Total increase in national income = size of injection × multiplier = £50m × 2.5 = **£125m**

Aggregate Demand Analysis

The **Marginal Propensity to Withdraw** can also be used to find the **Multiplier**

1) There's also another approach to working out the multiplier. Instead of looking at what proportion of extra income is **spent**, you can instead look at the proportion of extra income that's **withdrawn** from the economy.
2) The extra income can be **withdrawn** from the economy by:
   (i) being **saved**,
   (ii) being paid to the government in **taxes**,
   (iii) being used to **import** goods from abroad.
3) The **marginal propensity to withdraw** (**MPW**) is the **proportion** of any **new income** that's withdrawn from an economy. MPW can be broken down in the following way:

$$MPW = MPS + MPT + MPM$$

where:
- **MPS** = marginal **propensity to save**, the **proportion** of any **new income** that's saved.
- **MPT** = marginal **propensity to tax**, the **proportion** of any **new income** that's paid as taxes.
- **MPM** = marginal **propensity to import**, the **proportion** of any **new income** that's used to import goods.

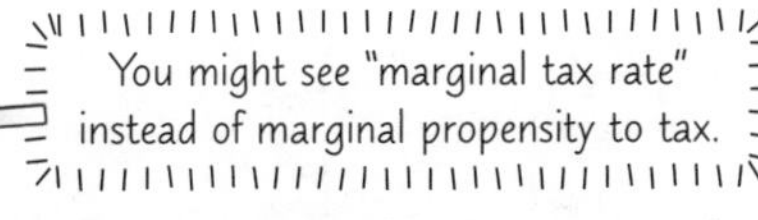

You might see "marginal tax rate" instead of marginal propensity to tax.

EDEXCEL ONLY

Learn the **Formula** for calculating the **Multiplier** from the **MPW**

1) Since extra income must **either** be spent **or** withdrawn:

$$MPC + MPW = 1$$

2) This means you can also use the formula below to find the **multiplier**:

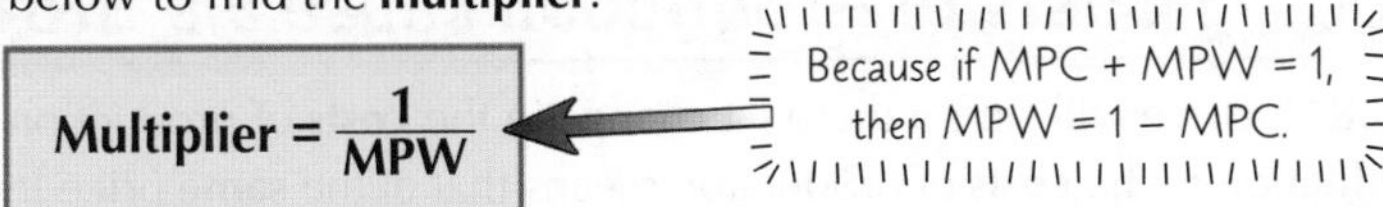

Multiplier = 1 / MPW
Because if MPC + MPW = 1, then MPW = 1 – MPC.

- The **multiplier** will be relatively **big** if **marginal tax rates** (i.e. the tax paid on the last £1 you earn) are **low**.
- This is because **low** marginal tax rates (i.e. a small value of **MPT**) means a small value for **MPW**, which means that the multiplier is **big**.

See p.80 for other factors that affect saving, consumption and the size of the multiplier.

Practice Questions

Q1 What is the average propensity to consume for an economy?

Q2 Define what is meant by marginal propensity to consume.

Q3 State the formula that can be used to calculate the multiplier from the MPW.

Exam Question

Q1 Increased government spending results in an injection of £100 million into the economy. The marginal propensities to save (MPS), tax (MPT) and import (MPM) are given by MPS = 0.3, MPT = 0.4 and MPM = 0.1.
Find the total rise in national income that results from this injection. [4 marks]

Formulas seem to be multiplying all over these pages...

Don't complain... these pages aren't as hard as they look. I realise there's a fair bit of maths going on, but it's really not that bad. If you want to complain about all the three-letter abbreviations though, that's fine with me. By the way, don't go thinking that, because working out a multiplier looks quite easy in theory (the formulas are pretty simple after all), finding the value in practice must be pretty simple too — it isn't. See page 85 for some of the practical difficulties.

Aggregate Supply

Remember, 'aggregate' means total. So you can probably work out what aggregate supply is. ***These pages are for all boards.***

*There are **Two Types** of AS curve*

1) **Aggregate supply** is the **total output** produced in an economy at a given price level over a given period of time. There are **two types** of **aggregate supply curve** you need to know about.
2) The first type is the **short run aggregate supply** (**SRAS**) **curve**. **Short run** aggregate supply (SRAS) curves slope up from left to right. They show that with an **increase** in the **price level**, there's an **increase** in the amount of **output** firms are willing to supply.

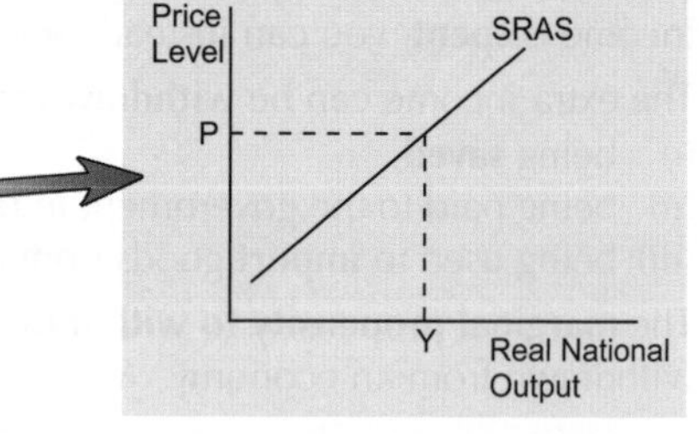

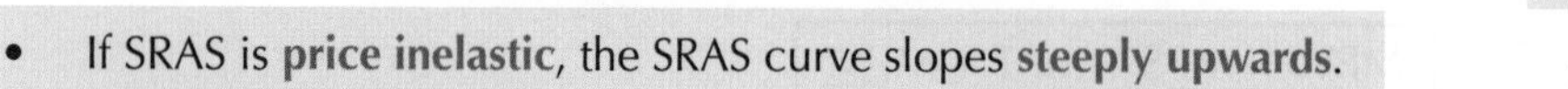
- If SRAS is **price inelastic**, the SRAS curve slopes **steeply upwards**.

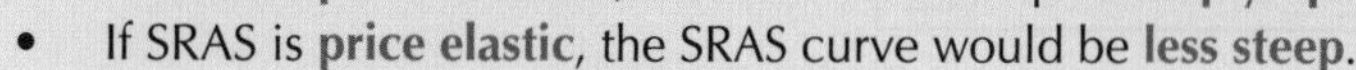
- If SRAS is **price elastic**, the SRAS curve would be **less steep**.

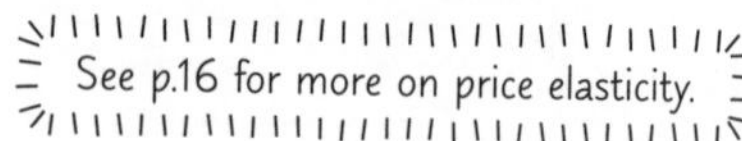
See p.16 for more on price elasticity.

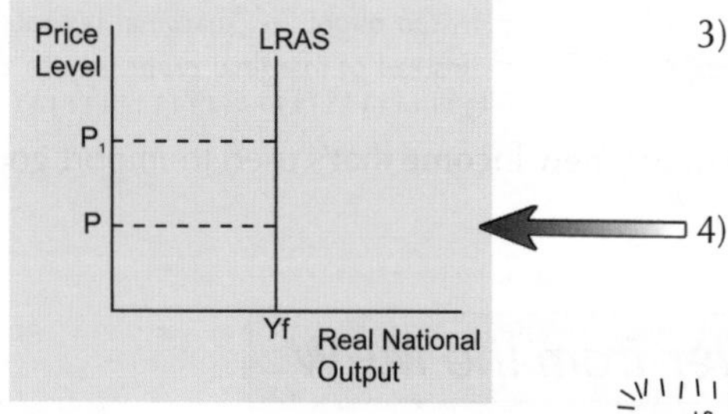

3) In the **long run**, it's assumed that an economy will move towards an equilibrium where **all resources** are being used to **full capacity** (so the economy is running at its full **productive potential**). This is shown by the **long run aggregate supply** (LRAS) curve.
4) The LRAS curve is **vertical**. An increase in the price level (e.g. to P_1) **won't** cause an increase in output because the economy is running at full capacity, so it **can't** create any more output.

If you're doing Edexcel you need to know that these are actually 'classical' AS curves. You also need to know about 'Keynesian' AS curves — these are on p.89.

*Changes in **Costs of Production** cause the **SRAS** curve to shift*

1) The SRAS curve will **shift** if there's a **change** in the **costs** of production.
2) A **reduction** in the **costs** of production means that at the **same** price level, **more output** can be **produced**, so the SRAS curve will shift to the **right**.
3) For example, a **reduction** in the price of oil might shift the curve from SRAS to $SRAS_1$ — so at price level P, **output** would **increase** from Y to Y_1.
4) **Changes** in things such as wage rates, the taxes firms pay, exchange rates and efficiency levels will cause **shifts** of the SRAS curve.
5) A sudden **decrease** in aggregate supply (leading to a price increase) could also be caused by **supply-side shocks**, such as **natural disaster** or **war**.

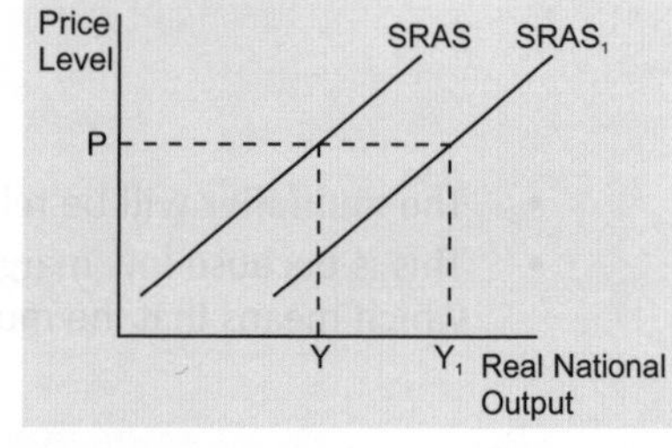

*Changes in **Factors of Production** cause the **LRAS** curve to shift*

1) Long run aggregate supply is **determined** by the **factors of production** — the LRAS curve will **shift** if there's a **change** in the factors of production which affects the **capacity** of the economy.
2) An **improvement** in the factors of production **increases** the **capacity** of the economy, and will shift the LRAS curve to the **right**, e.g. from LRAS to $LRAS_1$. This **increases** output (in other words, there's **economic growth**) from Yf to Yf_1 — the **same** price level now corresponds to a **higher** level of output.
3) E.g. **investment** that leads to **advances** in **technology** and **more efficient** production will **increase maximum** output.

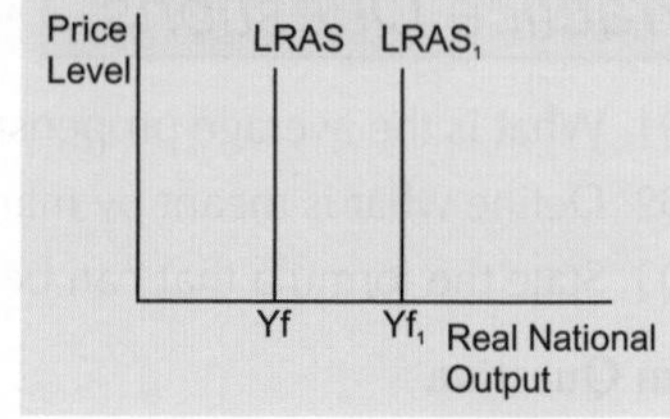

4) Other examples of **improvements** in the factors of production which might **shift** the AS curve to the **right** are:
   - An **improvement** in education and skills — better education and training should lead to **more productive** individuals, i.e. the **output** per person will **increase**, so **maximum** output is increased.
   - **Demographic changes** — e.g. skilled workers **migrating** to a country can increase the economy's capacity.
   - A **supply** of **new** resources — new resources may mean the **maximum** output of the economy can be increased.
   - **Improvements** in health care — if the **overall** health of workers **improves**, they're likely to have **less** time off work and retire at an **older** age. This means the **productivity** and **size** of the economy's labour force **increases**.

Aggregate Supply

- Changes in **government regulations** — e.g. the removal of unnecessary rules and 'red tape'.
- An **increase** in competition — greater competition in an economy will cause inefficient firms to **close** and be **replaced** by more efficient firms — **increasing** an economy's **capacity**.
- Promoting **enterprise** — e.g. by providing **economic incentives** or **guidance** for people starting new businesses.
- Increasing **factor mobility** — e.g. with training schemes to reduce **occupational labour immobility** (see p.58).

5) A **deterioration** in the factors of production that **reduces** an economy's capacity will cause the LRAS curve to shift to the **left**, e.g. if there's a massive **reduction** in the **supply** of oil then the **maximum** possible output will be **reduced**.

A **Rise** in **Demand** might cause an **'Accelerated'** increase in investment

AQA ONLY

1) One way businesses determine whether investment is needed is to look at the **current rate of change** of national income. So if national income is **growing rapidly**, then businesses will **invest heavily**.
2) This is called the **accelerator process** (or the **accelerator effect**). Firms will make 'accelerated' investment in **capital goods**, expecting to **increase output** and make **profit** in the future.
3) This is likely to occur when the economy is going through a **recovery**, or at the start of a **boom**. These are the times when **demand** will be rapidly increasing and firms will need to invest to meet this demand.
4) The multiplier (see p.79) and the accelerator work together. For example:
   - During a recovery, **AD** will be **growing**.
   - This leads to firms **increasing** their levels of **investment** — which leads to **another** increase in AD.
   - This increase in AD is then **'multiplied'**, making the growth in national income **more rapid**...
   - ...which leads to even more **'accelerated'** investment.
5) The accelerator process and multiplier effect can both also happen **in reverse** — for example, during a recession, there's likely to be a **fall** in **demand** and a **fall** in **investment**, which will then have a **reverse multiplier effect**.
6) This can lead to a constant **cycle** of output first rising and then falling.

The **Keynesian** LRAS curve is **L-Shaped**

EDEXCEL ONLY

Not everyone agrees that the LRAS curve is vertical.
Keynesian economists argue that the LRAS curve actually looks like this.

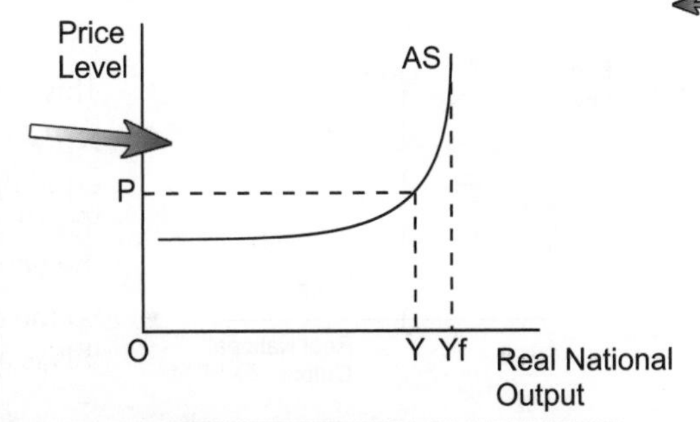

- At **low** levels of output, aggregate supply is **completely elastic** (where the curve is horizontal) — this means there's **spare capacity** in the economy, so **output** can **increase** without a rise in the **price level**. For example, if there's a lot of **unemployment** in an economy, firms will be able to employ **more** workers and **increase** output, **without** increasing price levels.
- When the curve begins to **slope upwards** this shows that the economy is experiencing **problems** with supply (known as supply bottlenecks), which are causing **increases in costs**. For example, this might be due to a **shortage** of **labour**, or a **shortage** of certain **raw materials**.
- The curve becomes **vertical** when the economy is at **full capacity** (Yf) — here, aggregate supply is **completely inelastic**. All resources are being used to their **maximum potential** and output **can't** increase any more.

Practice Questions

Q1 Give an example of a change that would shift an SRAS curve to the right.

Q2 Explain the main differences between a classical LRAS curve and a Keynesian one.

Exam Question

Q1 A shift of the LRAS curve to the right might be caused by:
A) a reduction in wages. B) the discovery of a new raw material.
C) a reduction in taxes. D) a drop in interest rates. [1 mark]

NB: if you aren't an economy, running at full capacity isn't a good idea...

Remember — a deterioration in the factors of production will shift the LRAS curve to the left, but an improvement in the factors of production will shift it to the right. You should know and understand the changes which would cause these shifts.

Macroeconomic Equilibrium

You've seen AD and AS on their own... now it's time to see how they work together to create a macroeconomic equilibrium. ***These pages are for all boards.***

Macroeconomic Equilibrium occurs where *AS = AD*

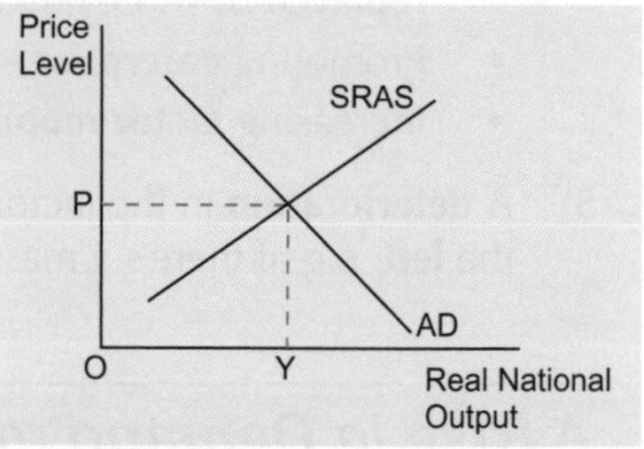

1) **Macroeconomic equilibrium** occurs where the AD and AS curves **cross**, e.g. at price level P and output Y on this SRAS curve.
2) A **shift** of either curve will **move** this equilibrium to a **different** point, but shifts of AD and AS curves affect things in **different ways**.

In particular, the government's four macroeconomic indicators (see Section 6) are affected differently by shifts in the AS and AD curves.

An *Increase* in AD alone can only increase output in the *Short Run*

1) The effect of a **shift in AD** on the equilibrium point depends on the **slope** of the **AS curve**. This means the effects of an increase in AD can be quite different in the **short** and **long run**.

Because the SRAS curve slopes upwards, while the LRAS curve is vertical.

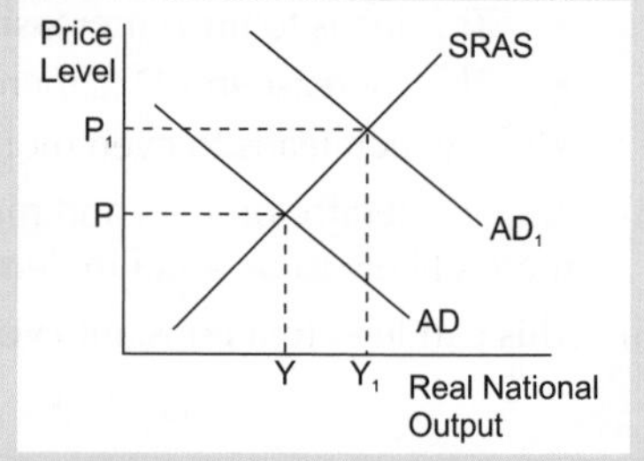

- This graph shows an **SRAS curve** along with an **AD curve**.
- When there's an **increase** in aggregate demand and the AD curve shifts from AD to AD_1, the **new** equilibrium point will be at price level P_1 and output Y_1.
- There's been an **increase in output**, which will lead to an increase in **derived demand**, so more **jobs** are created and unemployment is **reduced**.
- But there's also been a **rise in prices** — this is 'demand-pull' inflation.
- A **decrease** in AD will have the **opposite** effect — **output** will be **reduced** and there will be an **increase** in **unemployment**, but **price levels** will **fall**.

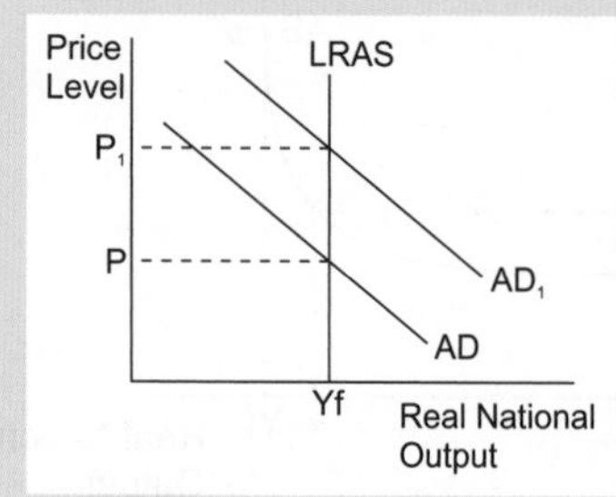

- This graph shows an **LRAS curve** along with an **AD curve**.
- Now when the AD curve shifts from AD to AD_1, the **new** equilibrium point will be at price level P_1, but the **output hasn't changed** (and **unemployment** can't fall) — because the economy is already running at **full capacity**.
- So the only effect is that **prices rise** — again, this is an example of 'demand-pull' inflation.

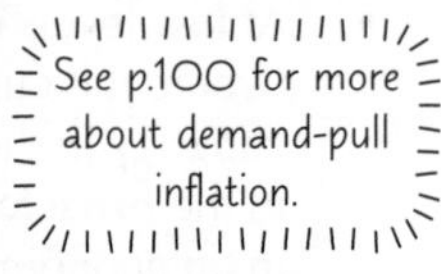

2) In both cases, the **rise** in price levels means there will possibly be a **worsening** of the balance of payments (see p.101).
3) In general, to improve **all four** macroeconomic policy indicators at the **same time**, there needs to be an **increase** in **LRAS**. See p.91 for more information.

The amount of *Spare Capacity* can *Limit* the effect of the *Multiplier*

If **supply** is already **struggling** to keep up with demand, then the **multiplier effect** after an increase in AD will probably be quite **small** — the economy just **won't** be able to cope with any further large increases in demand.

When aggregate supply (AS) is very **elastic**, there is a **lot** of **spare capacity** in the economy. In this case, after an initial injection shifts the AD curve, the **multiplier** can take effect to give a **large rise** in **output**.

When aggregate supply (AS) is very **inelastic**, there is much less spare capacity in the economy. The same initial shift in AD cannot be multiplied in the same way — there's a **smaller rise** in **output** (but a **large rise** in **prices**, i.e. inflation).

Macroeconomic Equilibrium

*Shifts in AS affect **All Four** macroeconomic indicators in the **Same Way***

A shift of the AS curve will either improve or worsen **all four** indicators at the **same time**.

- For example, an **increase** in AS, shown by a shift to the right from SRAS to $SRAS_1$, will lead to an **increase** in the **capacity** of the economy. This will result in an **increase** in output — so there's **increased** economic growth. There will be **more jobs**, reducing **unemployment**. The **price level** will tend to **fall** and the economy will become **more competitive** internationally, **improving** the balance of payments.
- On the other hand, a **decrease** in AS would **worsen** the state of all four macroeconomic indicators.

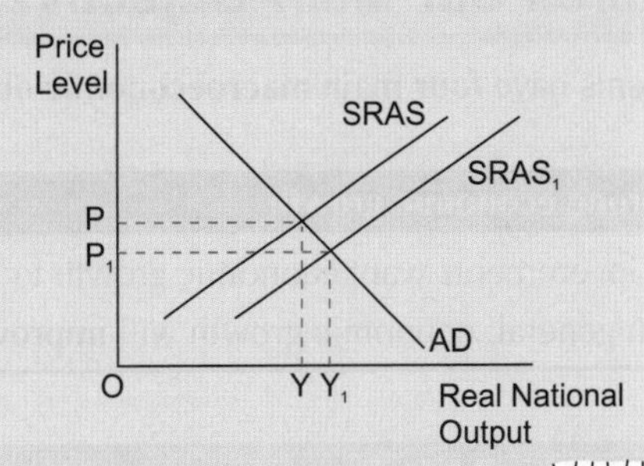

If you're doing Edexcel, remember, these are 'classical' AS curves.

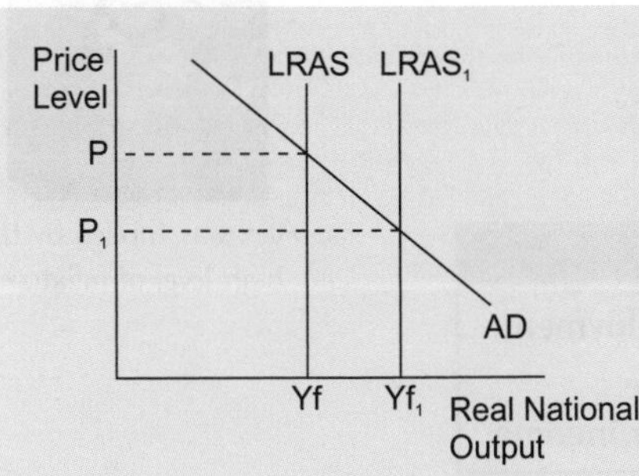

- If **LRAS** increases, then you get similar results.
- For example, if long run aggregate supply shifts from LRAS to $LRAS_1$, then in the long run **output** is **increased**, the **price level falls**, the balance of payments will potentially **improve** and the economy remains at **full employment**.
- So a **shift** of the LRAS curve will also tend to cause **all four** macroeconomic policy indicators to **improve** or **worsen** at the **same time**.

Keynesian** AS curves mean changes in AS and AD have **Different Effects

EDEXCEL ONLY

With a Keynesian LRAS curve (see p.89), the effects of an **increase in AD** can be slightly different.

- If AD increases from AD_1 to AD_2, the effects are the same as those described on p.90 — there's an **increase in prices** but **no increase in output**. This corresponds to an economy that's already operating at **full capacity**.
- If AD increases from AD_3 to AD_4, then there's an **increase in output** but **no increase in prices**. This corresponds to an economy deep in depression.
- If AD increases from AD_5 to AD_1, then there are **increases** in **both output and prices**. This corresponds to an economy operating **just under** full capacity.

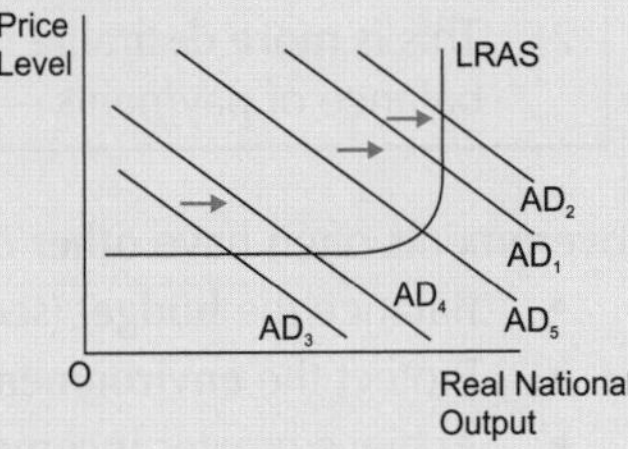

With a Keynesian LRAS curve, the effects of an **increase in AS** can also be slightly different.

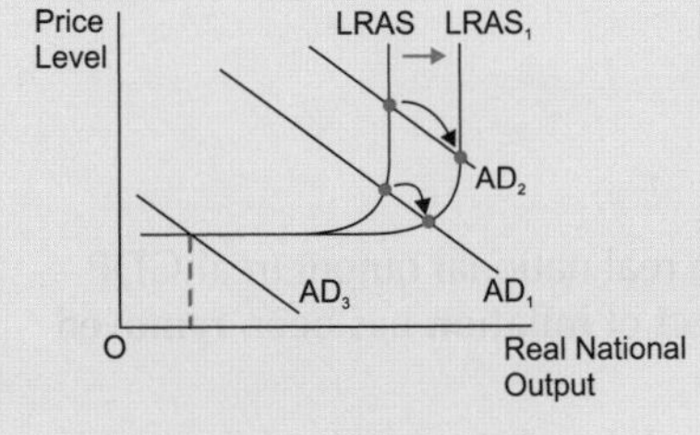

- If AS increases from LRAS to $LRAS_1$, there is a change in the macroeconomic equilibrium if AD is at **either** AD_1 **or** AD_2.
- However, if AD is at AD_3, then there is **no change** in the equilibrium.
- This is why Keynesian economists say that there is **little point** in aiming to **increase AS** during a **depression** — the macroeconomic equilibrium will **not** be affected and there will be **no increase** in **output** or **employment**.

Practice Questions

Q1 Explain why an increase in AD cannot increase output in the long run.

Q2 Explain why the multiplier effect might be limited if there's little spare capacity in the economy.

Exam Question

Q1 Describe the possible effects on an economy of a shift to the right of the short run aggregate supply curve. [8 marks]

All the curves on these pages are making me blush...

I like the way you can plot two simple curves and then the point where they cross describes a whole economy. It's nice.

Economic Growth

The government is in charge of the national economy. Sounds like fun, I know... but an economy is a tricky thing to manage and everyone hates you when you get it wrong. ***These pages are for all boards.***

There are Four Main Objectives of Government Macroeconomic Policy

Governments have **four main macroeconomic objectives** they're trying to achieve:

1 Strong economic growth

1) Governments want economic growth to be **high** (but not **too** high).
2) In general, economic growth will **improve** the **standard of living** in a country.

Alex was thrilled by the high level of inflation.

2 Keeping inflation low

1) In the UK, the government aims for **inflation** of **2%**.
2) The **Monetary Policy Committee of the Bank of England** uses **monetary policy** (see pages 122-124) to try to achieve this target rate.

3 Reducing unemployment

1) Governments aim to **reduce unemployment** and move towards **full employment**.
2) If **more** people are employed then the economy will be **more productive**. **Aggregate demand** will also **increase** as more people will have a **greater income**.

4 Equilibrium in the balance of payments

1) Governments want **equilibrium** in the balance of payments, i.e. they want **earnings** from **exports** and other **inward flows** of money to **balance** the **spending** on **imports** and other **outward** flows of money.
2) This is **more desirable** than a **long-term deficit** or **surplus** in the balance of payments — which can cause problems.

Governments often have **other** objectives too. For example, they may want to:
- Balance the **budget** (see p.82),
- Protect the **environment** (see p.106),
- Achieve greater **income equality** (see p.106).

The relative importance that governments attach to all these objectives changes over time. See Section 9 for some examples.

There are Different Types of Economic Growth

1) **Economic growth** is an **increase** in the **productive potential** of an economy.
2) In the **short run**, economic growth is measured by the **percentage change** in real national output (real GDP — see p.72). This is known as **actual** (real) growth (this just means that the **effect** of **inflation** has been **removed** from the growth figure).
3) Increases in actual growth are usually due to an **increase** in **aggregate demand**, but they can also be caused by **increases** in **aggregate supply**. Actual growth doesn't always increase — it tends to **fluctuate up** and **down**.
4) **Long run** growth (also known as **potential** growth) is caused by an **increase** in the **capacity**, or **productive potential**, of the economy. This usually happens due to a **rise** in the **quality** or **quantity** of **inputs** (the **factors of production**) — for example, more **advanced** machinery or a more **highly skilled** labour force.
5) Long run growth is shown by an **increase** in the **trend rate** of growth. The **trend rate** of growth is the **average rate** of economic growth over a period of both economic **booms** and **slumps**. It **rises smoothly** rather than fluctuating like actual economic growth, so the **actual rate** of growth often doesn't **match** the **trend rate**.
6) **Increases** in long run growth are caused by an increase in **aggregate supply**.

Economic Growth

A Production Possibility Frontier (PPF) can show Economic Growth

1) **Short run** and **long run** economic growth can be shown with a **PPF**.
2) Short run growth is shown by a **movement** from, say, point A to point B, while the PPF itself remains **fixed**.
3) Long run growth **occurs** if there's an **increase** in the **capacity** of the economy — this would make the PPF shift **outwards** to PPF_1.

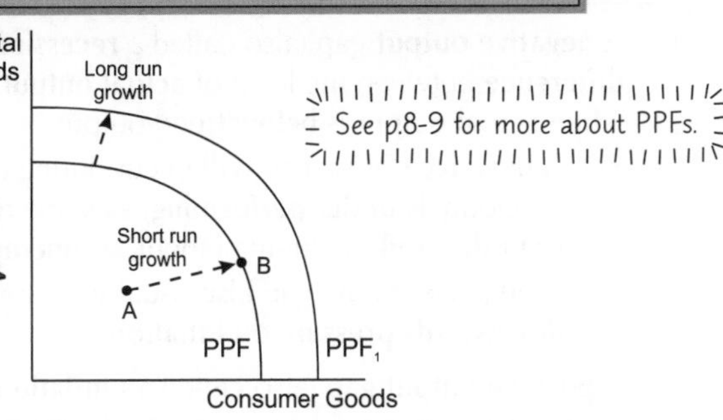

See p.8-9 for more about PPFs.

The Economic Cycle has Different Phases

'Trade cycle' and 'business cycle' are alternative names for the economic cycle.

1) The actual growth of an economy **fluctuates** over time. These **fluctuations** are known as the **economic cycle**.
2) A **boom** is when the economy is **growing quickly**. Aggregate demand will be **rising**, leading to a **fall** in **unemployment** and a **rise** in **inflation**.
3) A **recession** is when there's **negative economic growth** for at least **two consecutive quarters**. Aggregate demand will be **falling**, causing **unemployment** to **rise** and a **fall** in **price levels**.
4) During a **recovery** the economy begins to **grow again**, going from **negative economic growth** to **positive economic growth**. Aggregate demand will be **rising**, so **unemployment** will be **falling** and **inflation** will be **rising**.
5) **Long run** growth is shown by an **increase** in the **trend rate** of growth. The trend rate of growth is the **average rate** of economic growth over a period of both economic **booms** and **slumps**.

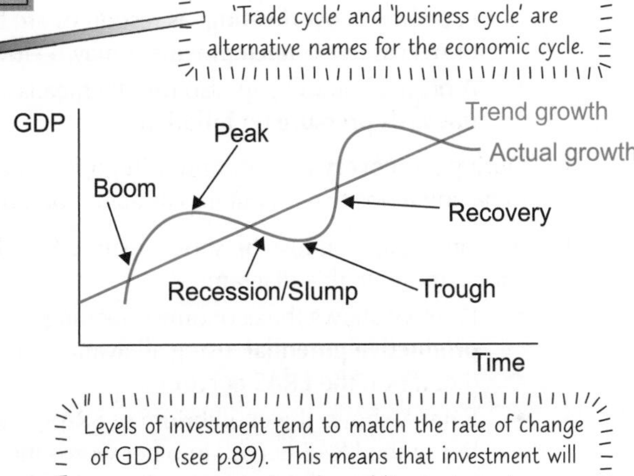

Levels of investment tend to match the rate of change of GDP (see p.89). This means that investment will be greatest when the red line is steepest.

A Recession is Bad News for Most people... but not everyone

1) A recession (period of negative growth) will usually see many firms **close down**, with many people **losing their jobs**. This means **unemployment** usually **increases**.
2) Other firms may **stop hiring** new employees — this means **young people** are often particularly badly hit.
3) **Government spending** tends to **increase** — for example, due to increased unemployment benefit payments. At the same time, the amount of **tax** a government receives usually **falls**. This leads to **increased government borrowing** and a **budget deficit** (see p.82).
4) Levels of **investment fall** — e.g. firms might reduce the amount they spend on research and development. This can have consequences for the **long run productive potential** of the economy.
5) However, some firms can benefit at times of recession — e.g. **discount retailers** can often attract more customers if people are feeling **less confident** about their economic prospects.
6) Recessions can also force firms to **face up** to their **inefficiencies**. In good times, firms might be able to **get away with** being **inefficient** in some areas. But they may need to **cut costs** to survive a recession. This can **benefit** the firm in the **long run** if it emerges from the recession **more efficient** than it was before.

Economies can suffer from Demand-side Shocks or Supply-side Shocks

1) An economy might start to shrink or grow because it's affected by a **demand-side shock** (which can cause **aggregate demand** to rise or fall) or by a **supply-side shock** (which can cause **aggregate supply** to rise or fall).
2) These shocks can be **domestic** or **global**.

Examples of demand-side shocks:

- If consumer confidence is **boosted**, e.g. due to **house prices rising**, this will **increase consumer spending**.
- If a country's **major trading partners** go into a **recession**, this may significantly reduce demand for the country's **exports**.

Examples of supply-side shocks:

- A **poor harvest** reduces the supply of food, increases its price, and **reduces** the economy's **capacity**.
- The discovery of a major **new source** of a raw material will greatly reduce its price and increase its supply — **increasing** the **capacity** of the economy.

Economic Growth

AQA & EDEXCEL

Output Gaps can occur during periods of Boom or Recession

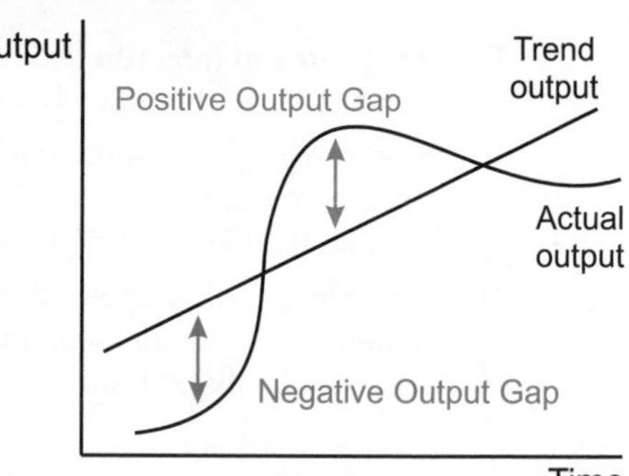

1) A **negative output** gap (also called a **recessionary gap**) is the **difference** between the level of **actual output** and **trend output** when actual output is **below** trend output.
   - A negative output gap will occur during a **recession** when the economy is **under-performing**, as some resources will be **unused** or **underused** (including labour, so **unemployment** may be high).
   - A negative output gap also usually means **downwards pressure** on **inflation**.
2) A **positive output gap** (also called an **inflationary gap**) is the **difference** between the level of **actual output** and **trend output** when actual output is **above** trend output.
   - A positive output gap will occur during a **boom** when the economy is **overheating**, as resources are being fully **used** or **overused** (so **unemployment** may be low).
   - A positive output gap also usually means **upwards pressure** on **inflation**.

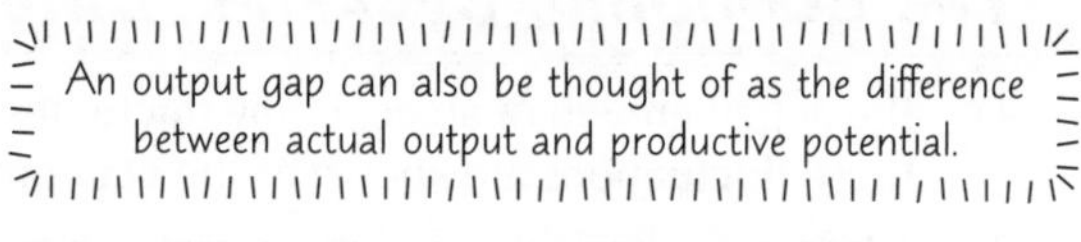

3) During a **recovery** an economy will go from having a negative output gap to having a positive output gap as actual output **rises above** trend output.

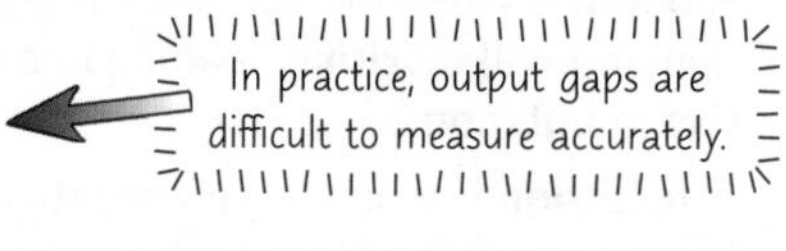

4) An output gap can also be shown using AS and AD curves. For example, in this diagram:
   - Point W shows the economy operating at its full **productive potential**, using all available resources (i.e. it's on the LRAS curve).
   - Point X shows the equilibrium of $SRAS_1$ and AD_1 to the **left** of the LRAS curve. In other words the economy has the **potential** to supply at a **greater level**. The distance between Y_1 and Y_f is a **negative output gap**.
   - Point Z shows the equilibrium of $SRAS_1$ and AD_2 to the **right** of the LRAS curve. The distance between Y_2 and Y_f is a **positive output gap**.

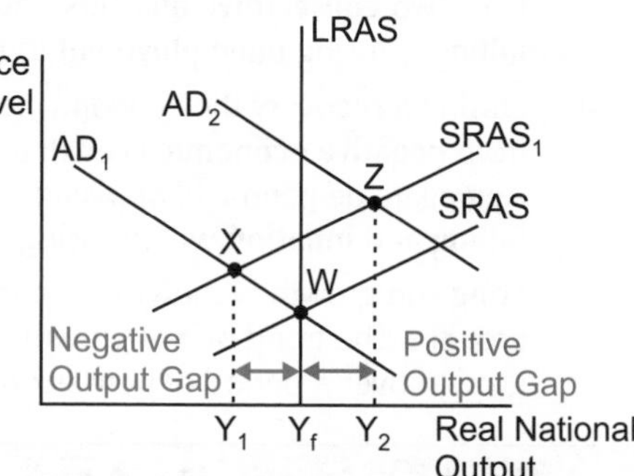

EDEXCEL & OCR

There are many Benefits of Economic Growth

1) **Economic growth** will **increase demand** for labour, leading to a **fall** in **unemployment** and **higher incomes** for individuals.
2) Economic growth usually means that firms are **succeeding**, so employees may get **higher wages**. This will also produce a **rise** in the **standard** of **living**, as long as prices **don't** rise more than the increase in wages.
3) **Firms** are likely to earn **greater profits** when there's economic growth, as consumers usually have **higher incomes** and **spend more**. Firms can use these profits to **invest** in better machinery, make **technological advances** and **hire** more employees — causing an **increase** in the **economy's productive potential**.
4) As firms are likely to **produce more** when there's economic growth then this can **improve** a country's **balance of payments** because it will sell **more exports**.
5) **Economic growth** causes wages and employment to **rise**, which will **increase** the **government's tax revenue** and **reduce** the amount it pays in **unemployment benefits**. The government can use this **extra revenue** to **improve** public services or the country's infrastructure **without** having to **raise taxes**, which is good for individuals.
6) Economic growth will **improve** a government's **fiscal position** (see p.118) because if it receives greater tax revenues and spends less on things like unemployment benefits then this will **reduce** the government's need to **borrow money**.
7) There might be some **benefits** to the **environment** brought about by economic growth, e.g. firms may have the resources to **invest** in **cleaner** and **more efficient** production processes.

Economic Growth

Unfortunately, there are some Costs of Economic Growth

1) Economic growth can create **income inequality** — **low-skilled workers** may find it hard to get the **higher wages** that other workers are benefiting from.
2) **Higher wages** for employees are often linked to an **increase** in their **responsibilities** at work (e.g. if they've been promoted). This can **increase stress** and **reduce productivity**.
3) Economic growth can cause demand-pull inflation (see p.100) because it causes **demand** to **increase faster** than **supply**. It can also cause cost-push inflation (see p.100) as economic growth **increases** the **demand** for **resources**, pushing up their prices. However, the effects of inflation will be **reduced** if **aggregate supply** (or long run aggregate supply) also **increases**.
4) A **deficit** in the **balance of payments** can be created because people on **higher incomes** buy **more imports**. Furthermore, **firms** may **import more resources** to increase their production to meet the higher levels of demand.
5) **Industrial expansion** created by economic growth may bring **negative externalities**, such as pollution or increased congestion on the roads, which **harm** the **environment** and **reduce** people's quality of life.
6) **Beautiful scenery** and **habitats** can be **destroyed** when **resources** are **overexploited**.
7) **Finite resources** may be **used up** in the creation of economic growth, which may **constrain** growth in the **future** and threaten future living standards.

In moments of quiet reflection, Stephen often worried about the increased stress and reduced productivity that could arise as a result of employees' higher wages.

See p.97 for more about sustainable economic growth.

Short Run economic growth can be created by Increasing Aggregate Demand

1) A rise in **aggregate demand** (**AD**) will create **short run** economic growth. When **AD** rises the **AD** curve **shifts** to the **right**.
2) An increase in AD will be caused by **demand-side factors**. For example:
   - **Lowering** interest rates **encourages** investment and **increases** consumption.
   - **Increasing** welfare benefits **increases** government spending and consumption.
3) How much the AD curve shifts depends on:
   - people's **marginal propensity to consume**, **MPC** (see p.86),
   - how big the **multiplier effect** is (see p.79).
4) The higher the MPC and the **bigger** the **multiplier**, the **greater** the shift to the right of the AD curve.
5) In the diagram, national output has **increased** from Y to Y_1.

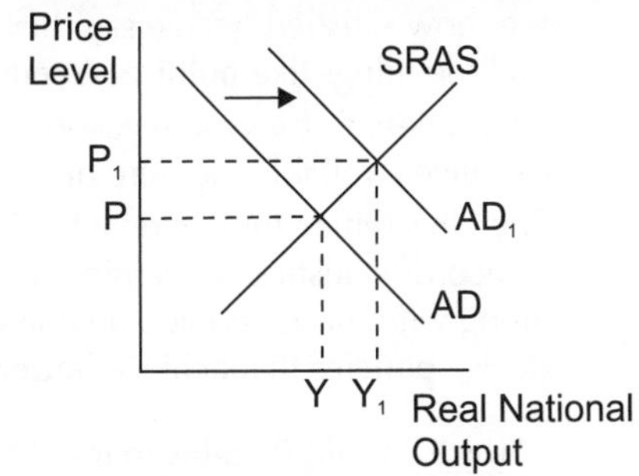

There's a lot more detail about the effects of increasing AD and AS in Section 7. The policy conflicts that can result are dealt with on pages 107-109.

Short Run Aggregate Supply Increases also create Short Run growth

1) A **rise** in **short run aggregate supply** (**SRAS**) will also create short run economic growth. When SRAS **rises** the SRAS curve **shifts** to the **right**.
2) Any factor which **reduces production costs** will cause an **increase** in SRAS. Here are some examples:
   - A **fall** in the price of oil will **reduce** production costs and increase SRAS.
   - A **fall** in wages will **reduce** production costs and increase SRAS.

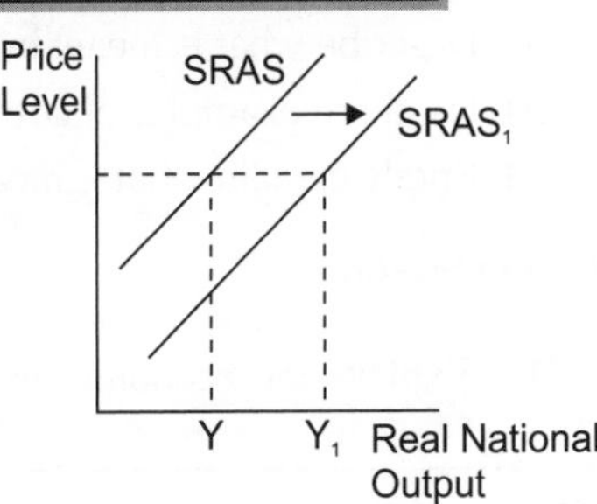

Economic Growth

There are several ways to create **Long Run Economic Growth**

1) **Long run** economic growth is the result of **supply-side factors** that increase the **productive potential** of the **economy**.
2) The **productive potential** of a country can be **increased** by **raising** the **quantity** or **quality** of the **factors of production**, for example:

- Through **innovation** — e.g. new technology.
- **Investing** in more **modern** machinery (i.e. improving **capital stock**).
- **Raising** agricultural **output** by using genetically modified (GM) crops.
- **Increasing** spending on **education** and **training** to improve **human capital**.
- **Increasing** the **population size**, e.g. by encouraging immigration, to increase the size of a country's **workforce**.

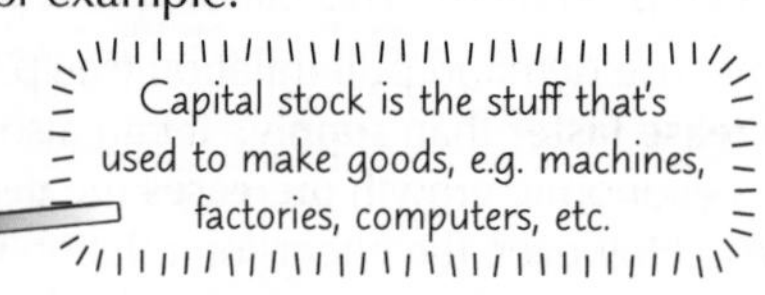

Capital stock is the stuff that's used to make goods, e.g. machines, factories, computers, etc.

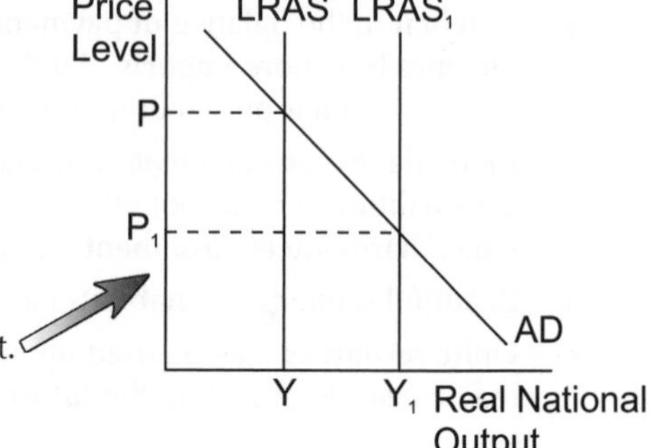

3) An **increase** in productive potential **shifts** the LRAS (or AS) curve to the right.
4) A **government** can also help to create long run economic growth by creating **stability** in a country — see the next page for more information.

EDEXCEL ONLY

'Happiness' can be linked to **Economic Growth**

1) **'Happiness economics'** tries to measure any factor that is associated with **increased** (or **decreased**) levels of **subjective well-being** (i.e. how satisfied people say they feel with their lives) — this might include things like **political freedom** or **family relationships**.

This is different from traditional economics, which concentrates on financial measures.

2) 'Happiness' is tricky to measure, but many economists claim that '**psychological surveys**' can give a reliable measure of how happy and satisfied people are with their lives.
3) The UK's Office for National Statistics (ONS) now runs a **Measuring National Well-being** programme. It records statistics concerning, for example, people's **health**, **relationships**, **education** and **finances**, along with those people's **own assessment** of their **personal well-being**. The aim is to help the government devise **policies** that achieve **better outcomes** in those areas that are particularly important to people.

The **Easterlin Paradox** (named after the economist Richard Easterlin) describes how **increases in GDP** are **not always** associated with **increases** in people's happiness levels. Easterlin found that:

- When incomes are **not** sufficient to meet **basic needs**, increasing GDP **does** lead to greater happiness.
- But people in **rich countries** tend **not** to be much happier than those in **poor countries**. And as people get **richer**, their happiness levels generally **don't increase** along with their income.
- In these richer countries, it seems that a person's **absolute income** isn't as important as their **relative income**. **'Being rich' doesn't** make someone happy if everyone else around them is equally rich, but **'being richer than the people around them' does**.

Practice Questions

Q1 What are the four main government macroeconomic objectives?

Q2 Describe what is meant by an 'output gap', and how it can be shown on a PPF.

Q3 List three examples of costs of economic growth.

Q4 Briefly explain what is mean by 'happiness economics'.

Exam Question

Q1 Explain how economic growth might contribute to an improvement in the standard of living in a country. [8 marks]

Clap along if you feel like happiness economics is the way to improve policy...

There's lots to learn on these five pages — make sure you understand the difference between long and short run growth. Also, economic growth might sound like a good thing, but in the exam you might be asked to write about its costs — so learn 'em.

Economic Stability

Sustainable growth is in part about being able to expand the economy every year. ***This page is for all boards.***

OCR ONLY

Sustainable Growth is Difficult to Achieve

Sustainable economic growth is an objective of the UK government.

1) **Sustainable economic growth** means making sure the economy **keeps growing** (now and in the future), **without** causing **problems** for future generations. Sustainable growth relies on a country's ability to:
   - **Expand output** every year.
   - Find a **continuous supply** of raw materials, land, labour and so on, to continue production.
   - Find **growing markets** for the increased output, so it's always being bought.
   - **Reduce negative externalities**, e.g. pollution, to an acceptable level so they don't hamper production.
   - Do all of the above things at the **same time** as many **other** countries who are pursuing the **same objectives**.
2) It's **very difficult** for a country to do all of these things at the same time, so sustainable growth is **hard** to achieve.
3) To be able to achieve sustainable growth, countries will need to **develop renewable** resources. Non-renewable resources will **run out** and, for growth to be sustainable, a **continuous supply** of raw materials is **necessary**.
4) Countries will also need to **innovate** to create **new technologies** that **reduce negative externalities**, such as pollution, and the **degradation** of resources, such as land or rivers, **without** stopping output from expanding.
5) A country that achieves **sustainable** growth will gain **long-term** benefits to society — it can more easily **plan ahead**, since it can be more confident about its long-term economic prospects.

You need to know about the UK's ***Recent Macroeconomic Performance***

1) It's **important** for the exam that you've got some idea of the **UK's recent macroeconomic performance**.
2) You should keep an eye on the **news** and look for any **important developments** about the **UK's economy** — e.g. there might be a rise in interest rates or a large fall in unemployment. Here are a few **general points** to get you started:
   - From **2000** until **2008** the UK enjoyed **continuous GDP growth** of, on average, **just under 3%** each year. However, in 2008 the UK went into a **recession** that lasted for **several months** and was followed by a long, **slow recovery**.
   - During the recovery the UK economy went through **short bursts** of growth followed by **slow-downs** — it almost went **back** into a **recession** in **2012**. From **2013 onwards**, the UK has had much more **consistent GDP growth** and, by **2014**, **GDP returned** to the level it was **just before** the recession — suggesting that the **recovery** is **complete**.
   - Between **2000** and early **2015** the rate of **inflation** in the UK, as measured by the **Consumer Price Index** (**CPI**), has been quite **steady** — generally inflation has been **between 0.5** and **3%**.
   - There have been **some exceptions** to this steady level of inflation. On a **couple** of occasions, inflation rose to about **5%**, **well above** the government's target of **2%**. This happened just at the **start** of the **recession** in **2008** and **again** in **2011**. Inflation then **fell** again and remained between 0 and 3% for some time.
   - **Unemployment** in the UK remained **quite low** between **2000** and **2008** — **between** about **1.4** and **1.7 million**.
   - Between **2008** and **2011** unemployment **rapidly rose**, reaching about **2.7 million** (an **unemployment rate** of **8%**). Since then unemployment has **fallen**, but, by January 2015, it was still **higher** than it was at the start of 2008.
   - The UK has had a **current account deficit** in its **balance of payments** for the **whole period** between **1984** and **2014**. The deficit was at its **largest** during this period towards the **end of 2014**.
   - The UK economy is currently dominated by its **service sector**, which accounts for approximately 77% of GDP. **Manufacturing** now accounts for just around 10% of GDP.

Practice Questions

Q1 Briefly explain the recent UK trend in economic growth.

Q2 Describe the state of the current account of the UK's balance of payments since 1984.

Exam Question

Q1 Describe two things a country must do in order to achieve sustainable economic growth. [4 marks]

Sustainable growth is the Holy Grail of economics...

Right, there's a lot of stuff here, but it's important. Basically, everyone wants sustainable growth, but it's easier said than done. Make sure you know the UK's recent macroeconomic performance so you can slip some useful points into your answers.

Unemployment

Make sure you properly understand the easy stuff on this page — it'll definitely help when you get to the trickier stuff that's coming up in a bit. ***These pages are for all boards.***

Governments want Full Employment

See p.76 for more info about unemployment.

1) Governments aim for **full employment**, which is where everybody of working age (excluding students, retirees, etc.), who wants to work, can find employment at the **current** wage rates.
2) Full employment **doesn't mean** everyone has a job — in most economies there will **always** be people **between jobs**. Governments **want** full employment because this will **maximise production** and **raise standards of living** in a country.
3) If there's **unemployment** in an economy then it **won't** be operating at **full capacity**, so it'll be represented by a point **within** the **PPF curve** (e.g. point A). At **full employment** the economy can **operate** at **full capacity**, so it can be represented by a point **on** the **PPF curve** (e.g. point B).

Capital Goods
B
A
PPF
Consumer Goods

4) **Under-employment** would also mean an economy is not operating at full capacity, and it will be represented by a point **within** its PPF curve. Under-employment is when someone has a job, but it's not a job that utilises that person's **skills**, **experience** or **availability** to the best effect. For example, a qualified accountant serving drinks in a pub might count as under-employed, as might someone who could only find **part-time** employment when they actually wanted a **full-time** position.

Economic Growth and the Time of Year affect Unemployment

1) Labour is a **derived** demand — an employer's demand for labour is derived from **consumers'** demand for goods/services. So when demand in the economy is **low** (e.g. when there's negative economic growth), unemployment will **rise** — but when demand is **high**, unemployment will **fall** (e.g. when there's positive economic growth).
2) **Cyclical** unemployment (or demand-deficient unemployment) usually happens when the economy is in a **recession** — when aggregate demand falls, employment will **fall** too. A country suffering from a **negative output gap** (see p.94) is likely to have cyclical unemployment too.
3) **Seasonal unemployment** occurs because demand for labour in certain industries **won't** be the **same** all year round. For example, the **tourism** and **farming** industries have 'peak seasons' where the need for labour is much higher than at other times of year. **Retailing** is also affected by seasonal unemployment (many shops will be particularly busy at Christmas, for example).
4) **Seasonal** unemployment tends to be **regular** and **predictable**, and it only affects **certain industries**. **Cyclical** unemployment, on the other hand, can affect **any** industry.

Recessions don't bother Clive — he has cyclical employment.

Structural Unemployment is made worse by Labour Immobility

1) Structural unemployment is caused by a **decline** in a certain **industry** or **occupation** — usually due to a **change** in **consumer preferences** or **technological advances**, or the availability of **cheaper alternatives**. It often affects **regions** where there's a decline in **traditional manufacturing** (e.g. shipbuilding or the steel industry) and it's made worse by **labour immobility**:
   - **Occupational immobility** is when workers **aren't able** to **move** from **one occupation to another** with ease. This often occurs when some occupations **decline** over time, but the workers in these occupations **don't** have the skills required to be able to do the jobs that are available.
   - **Geographical immobility** of labour is when workers aren't able to (or are reluctant to) **move to different locations** to find the best jobs for themselves. This might be because they can't **afford** to move to a different region, or they have **family ties**. Geographical immobility occurs when workers are unable to **leave** a region which has high unemployment to go to another region where there are jobs.
2) If a **region** is affected by structural unemployment then it could also suffer from the **negative multiplier effect** — unemployment will lead to less **spending**, and so cause **more** unemployment in the region.
3) Structural unemployment can be affected by changes in **other countries** — e.g. if another country started to produce a good at a **low** price, this could **negatively** affect the domestic industry for the same product and result in **job losses**. If these newly unemployed people were **occupationally immobile**, they might find it **difficult** to find another job.
4) The **problem** of structural unemployment may become **more common** in the future:
   - **Technological change** in both products and production methods is **accelerating quickly**. This will **speed up** the **decline** of out-of-date industries and **reduce** the number of workers needed to make products.
   - Consumer spending is **more likely** to change as consumers are better **informed** (through the internet and social media) than ever before — making them more likely to **switch** to **lower priced** or **higher quality** goods.

Unemployment

Frictional Unemployment is caused by the Time it takes to find a New Job

1) **Frictional** unemployment is the unemployment experienced by workers **between** leaving one job and starting another.
2) Even if an economy is at **full employment**, there will be **some** frictional unemployment. There will always be some employees **changing jobs** — maybe because their contract has run out or because they want to earn higher wages.
3) The **length** of time people spend looking for a **new** job (the 'time lag' between jobs) will depend on several things:
   - In a **boom** the number of job vacancies is much **higher**. So frictional unemployment is likely to be **short-term**.
   - In a **slump** frictional unemployment could be much **higher** as there will be a **shortage** of jobs.
   - **Generous welfare benefits** will give people **less incentive** to look for a new job, or they can mean people can afford to **take their time** to look for a good job — so the time spent between jobs **may** increase.
   - The **quality** of **information** provided to people looking for jobs is important too. If people **don't know** what jobs are available or what skills they need to get the job they want, then they're likely to **remain unemployed** for **longer**.
   - **Occupational** and **geographical** labour immobility (see p.58) will also affect the length of time between jobs.

Real Wage Unemployment is caused by wage increases Above equilibrium

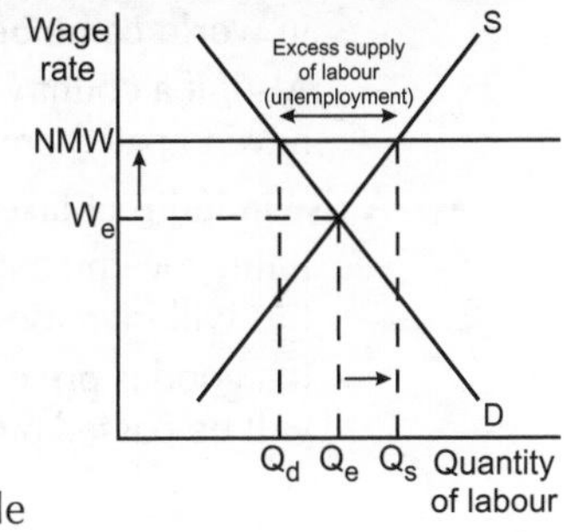

1) **Real wage unemployment** is caused by **real wages** being pushed **above** the **equilibrium level** of employment (where labour demand **equals** labour supply). It's usually caused by **trade unions** negotiating for **higher wages** or by the **introduction** of a **national minimum wage** (**NMW**) (see p.125).
2) Introducing a **national minimum wage** (**NMW**) **above** the **equilibrium wage rate** (**W_e**) would cause the labour **supply** to **increase** from **Q_e** to **Q_s** and demand to fall from **Q_e** to **Q_d**. This would cause **unemployment** of **Q_s** to **Q_d**, due to the **excess supply**.
3) **Real wage flexibility** refers to the ability of real wages to **change** in response to changes in **demand for and supply of labour**. **Performance-related pay** (when the amount you're paid depends on how well you're performing at your job) is an example of the use of flexible wages, whereas a **NMW** will make wages more **inflexible**.
4) Real wage **inflexibility** can lead to **increased** unemployment. For example, a **fall** in demand for labour will **shift** the demand curve to the **left**. If wages are inflexible, e.g. due to a NMW, unemployment will **increase**.

Migration may affect unemployment during a Recession

EDEXCEL ONLY

1) **Migration** of **workers** into a country increases the **supply** of **labour**.
2) When the economy is **strong**, **national income** should increase as a result of migration — especially if the **skills** and **knowledge** of the migrant workers is **different** from the mix of skills of the country's **native population**. There's little evidence from the UK that migration during a **boom** increases unemployment among the native population.
3) During a **recession**, unemployment among **native** workers (especially **low-skilled** workers) may increase, especially if migration levels are particularly **high**. However, even these effects **weaken** over time.

There are several Costs and Consequences of Unemployment

EDEXCEL & OCR

1) The unemployed will have **lower incomes**, which means that they'll spend less and this could **reduce** firms' **profits**.
2) Unemployment will mean **less** income tax revenue for governments, and **less** consumer spending will reduce their indirect tax revenue. The government will also have to **spend** more on unemployment **benefits**.
3) Areas with high unemployment can have high **crime** rates, and reduced incomes can cause people to have **health problems**.
4) Workers who are unemployed for a **long** time may find that their skills and training become **outdated**. This will **reduce** their **employability** and make it **more** likely that they'll stay unemployed.

Practice Questions

Q1 Briefly explain why unemployment will rise during a recession.

Q2 What might cause a region to be affected by structural unemployment?

Exam Question

Q1 Explain how high unemployment may affect a country's economic growth. [8 marks]

Structural unemployment — when buildings have no work to do...

Most unemployment is involuntary (i.e. people want to work but can't find a job), but some types can be voluntary — e.g. frictional unemployment would be voluntary if someone left their job and wanted to take time off before finding a new one.

Inflation

Inflation can rise because of higher costs and increased consumer demand. ***These pages are for all boards.***

Inflation can be caused by *Cost-Push Factors*

1) **Cost-push inflation** is inflation which is caused by the **rising cost** of **inputs** to production.
2) Rising costs of inputs to production force producers to **pass on** the **higher costs** to **consumers** in the form of **higher prices**, which causes the **aggregate supply curve** to shift to the left (from AS to AS_1). For example:

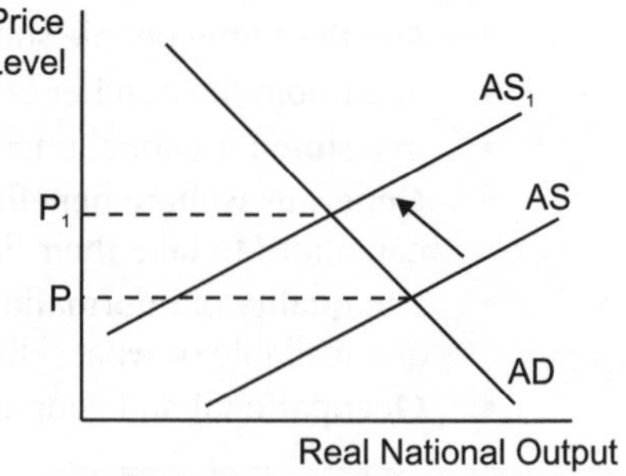

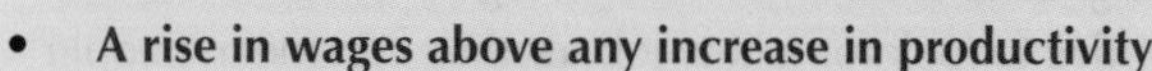

- **A rise in wages above any increase in productivity**
  - If wages make up a **large proportion** of a firm's **total costs** then this could lead to a **significant rise** in **prices**.
  - Price rises could lead to **further** wage demands, which **in turn** could lead to price increases, and so on (this is a **wage-price spiral**).

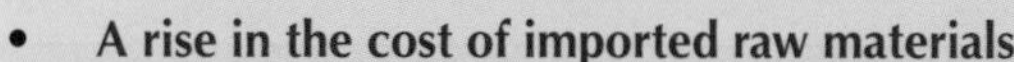

- **A rise in the cost of imported raw materials**
  - If the **world prices** of inputs **rise** then, in the short run, **producers** will pay the **higher** cost and set higher prices. This is how price increases in **world commodity markets** can lead to **higher domestic inflation**.
  - Also, if a country's currency decreases in value then producers will have to pay more for the **same imports**.
- **A rise in indirect taxes**
  - If the government raises indirect taxes (see p.60), this will increase costs and, in turn, prices.
  - If a good is **price inelastic** then **more** of the cost of the **tax** will be passed on to the **consumer**.

Inflation can *Also* be caused by *Demand-Pull Factors*

Demand-pull inflation is inflation caused by **excessive growth** in **aggregate demand** compared to supply. This growth in demand **shifts** the **aggregate demand curve** to the **right** (from AD to AD_1), which allows sellers to **raise prices**. It could be caused by:

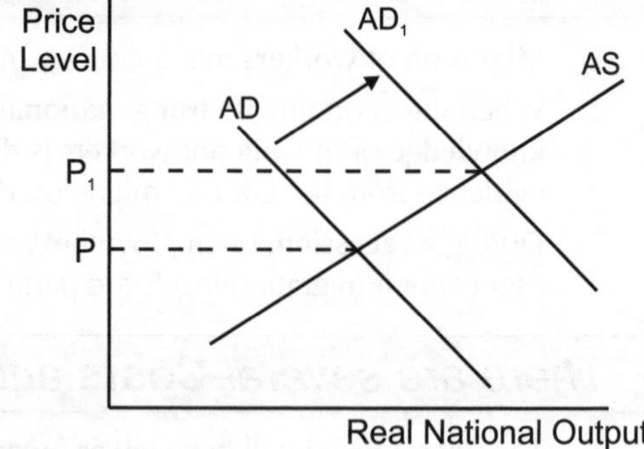

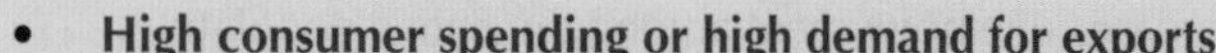

- **High consumer spending or high demand for exports**
  - High consumer spending could be caused by **high levels** of **confidence in consumers' future employment prospects** (e.g. during a period of low unemployment). **Low interest rates** encourage **cheap borrowing** and greater **spending**.
  - **High foreign demand** for **exports** could be caused by rapid economic growth in **other countries**.

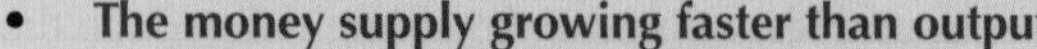

- **The money supply growing faster than output**
  - If the **amount of money** in the economy is **not matched** by the **output** of goods and services (sometimes termed 'too much money chasing too few goods'), this can lead to a rise in prices. This might be the case, for example, when **interest rates** are **low** and consumers are spending more.
- **Bottleneck shortages**
  - If **demand** grows **quickly** at a time when labour and resources are already being **fully used**, then increasing output may lead to **shortages** (i.e. there may be a positive output gap). These shortages will cause **prices to rise** and firms' **costs** to **increase**.
  - Price rises caused by shortages (e.g. a rise in wages for skilled labour) in **one area** of the **market** may be **copied** by other markets (e.g. higher wages for low-skilled labour), leading to more **general inflation**.

Inflation

There are several **Costs** and **Consequences** of **Inflation**

EDEXCEL & OCR

1) Inflation will cause the **standard of living** of those on **fixed**, or **near-fixed**, **incomes** to **fall**. This will have the **biggest impact** on those in **low income employment** or on **welfare benefits**.
2) A country's competitiveness will be **reduced** by **inflation** as exports will cost **more** to buy and imports will be **cheaper**. If **exports fall** and **imports rise**, then this could create a **deficit** in the **balance of payments** and **increase unemployment**.
3) Inflation **discourages saving** because the value of savings falls. This makes it **more attractive** to spend (creating demand-pull inflation) **before** prices rise further.
4) A **reluctance** to **save** creates a **shortage** of funds for **borrowing** and **investment**, which means that it's harder for firms to make improvements, e.g. buy new machinery. If **interest rates** go up to reduce inflation, this will also **reduce investment**.
5) Inflation creates **uncertainty** for firms as rising costs will **reduce investment** — harming future growth.
6) Inflation can cause **shoe leather costs**, which are the costs of the **extra time** and **effort** taken by consumers to search for **up-to-date** price information on the goods and services they're using, and **menu costs**, which are the **extra costs** to firms of **altering** the **price information** they provide to consumers.
7) An extreme case is **hyperinflation**, where inflation grows very quickly to very high levels (e.g. **several hundred percent** or more). It's often the result of governments creating **too much** money (e.g. because of a war or some other crisis).

Deflation Isn't a good thing

EDEXCEL & OCR

Don't confuse deflation with disinflation. Disinflation is when inflation rates fall, e.g. from 3% to 2%.

1) When the **rate of inflation** falls **below 0%** it's called **deflation**. Although there are many costs and consequences of inflation, deflation **isn't** very good either.
2) Deflation is often a sign that the economy is **doing badly**, as it's usually caused by **falling aggregate demand** and **increased unemployment**.
3) However, deflation can also be caused if firms' **costs fall** (e.g. because of new technology) and these **benefits** are then **passed on** to consumers in the form of **lower prices**.
4) Deflation can cause **big problems**. For example, if consumers think that prices are falling then they may choose **not** to spend in the hope that prices will **fall further**.
5) **Less spending** and **lower prices** will also mean **lower profits** for firms and reduced economic growth.

However, if the economy is healthy and people feel generally confident, deflation may not cause problems.

Inflation of **2%** is **Acceptable**

- In the UK, the Bank of England and the government consider **low and stable inflation (up to 2%** per year) to be **acceptable**. **Excessive inflation (above 2%**) is undesirable and can cause the problems mentioned above.
- The government uses a **combination** of **monetary policy**, **fiscal policy** and **supply-side policies** to try to keep the rate of inflation at 2% (see Section 9). However, to achieve this the government has to make **trade-offs** between their **inflation target** and their **other three** main economic objectives (see p.107-109 for more on the conflicts between objectives).
- Some economists, called **monetarists**, believe that bringing down inflation in the **short run** will **help** the government in the **long run** to achieve the other main economic objectives.

Practice Questions

Q1 What is cost-push inflation?

Q2 Give two possible causes of demand-pull inflation.

Q3 How might deflation be damaging to an economy?

Exam Question

Q1 The UK government aims to keep inflation at 2%.
Evaluate the reasons why the UK government might want to keep inflation at this rate. [12 marks]

I inflated by an unacceptable 2% over Christmas...

The diagrams aren't here just to look pretty — they should help you to understand what's going on. You'll need to know reasons for cost-push and demand-pull inflation, and why the UK government wants to keep inflation at around 2%.

The Balance of Payments

In Section 6 (p.77), you'll have seen a bit about the balance of payments — I imagine you've been eagerly waiting to find out more, so here are some pages just for you. I know, I'm too good to you. ***These pages are for all boards.***

*The **BOP** records **All Financial Transactions** of a country with other countries*

1) The **balance of payments** (**BOP**) records **all** flows of money **into** and **out of** a country.
2) The UK BOP is made up of the **current account**, the **capital account** and the **financial account**.

OCR students need to know a bit more about the financial and capital accounts — see p.105.

*There are **Four** sections of the **Current Account***

1. Trade in goods

1) Trade in goods measures **imports** and **exports** of **visible** goods — e.g. televisions, apples, potatoes, books.
2) The UK's **biggest** goods exports include things such as **machinery**, **mechanical appliances** and **pharmaceuticals**.
3) The UK's **biggest** goods imports also include **machinery** and **mechanical appliances**, along with **mineral fuels** (e.g. coal) and **oils**.

2. Trade in services

1) Trade in services measures **imports** and **exports** of **services** such as insurance or tourism.
2) Some of the UK's biggest **exported** services are **banking** and **insurance**.
3) The UK's biggest **imported** services include **tourism** (e.g. holidays abroad).

3. Investment and employment income (or 'primary income')

This covers flows of money **in** and **out** of a country resulting from **employment** or **earlier investment** — e.g.:

- Deposits in **foreign banks** receive **interest payments**.
- Businesses set up **overseas** by a UK company will earn **profits** for the UK **parent company**.
- Shares bought in **foreign firms** will bring **dividend payments** to the UK shareholder — the shares themselves **won't** appear on the current account.
- **Salaries** paid to UK residents working abroad.

4. Transfers (or 'secondary income')

1) Transfers are the **movements** of money **between** countries which **aren't** paying for goods or services and aren't the result of investment.
2) Transfers include **payments** made to family members **abroad** and **aid** paid to or received from **foreign countries**.

*Add up the **Individual Balances** to find the overall **Current Account Balance***

		£ million	£ million
Trade in Goods			
	Export of goods	306 765	
	Import of goods	419 364	
	Balance		-112 599
Trade in Services			
	Export of services	209 127	
	Import of services	130 261	
	Balance		78 866
Investment income			
	Credits	157 675	
	Debits	172 639	
	Balance		-14 964
Transfers			
	Credits	19 296	
	Debits	46 458	
	Balance		-27 162
Current balance			**-75 859**

Subtract imports from exports to get the balances for trade.

Subtract debits from credits to get the balances for investment income and transfers.

Add up the balances for the individual sections to find the overall balance. Remember, a positive balance is a surplus, and a negative balance is a deficit.

Recent data on the **UK's balance of payments** shows:

- A **large deficit** on the balance of **visible** trade — the UK **imports more** goods than it **exports**.
- A small **surplus** on the balance of **invisible** trade — the UK **exports** slightly **more** services than it **imports**.
- A **surplus** on flows of **investment income** — the UK receives more payments from investment than it pays out.
- A **deficit** on transfers — the UK **pays** money to the EU and also makes **foreign aid payments**.

As a result, the UK has a **large deficit** on its current account, and it has had a deficit **every year** since 1984. This means that the UK's current **macroeconomic policy** includes having to deal with a balance of payments **deficit**.

The Balance of Payments

There are usually **Many Causes** of a BOP **Surplus** or **Deficit**

A country might experience a **current account deficit** if:

1) There are high levels of consumer spending (low savings rate)

- When there's **economic growth**, consumers and firms **buy** more **imports**.
- If the **income elasticity of demand** for imports is **high** then there will be a **greater increase** in imports.

2) It's struggling to compete internationally

- Countries that **can't compete** internationally will see a **reduction** in exports.
- Some countries (especially more developed countries) may not be able to **compete** with **low** costs of **production** in other countries, e.g. **newly industrialised** nations.
  - When the costs of production in a country rise **faster** than in **competitor** countries — e.g. due to higher labour costs, production inefficiencies, a **fall** in labour productivity etc., then exports will **fall** and imports will **rise**.
  - Other countries may **struggle** to **compete** with countries that have access to more **advanced** technology or more **efficient** methods of production, which can **lower** costs and **improve** the **quality** of the products they make.
  - If the country has **structural problems**, e.g. labour immobility, this could be making domestic products and exports **more expensive**.
- A **rise** in the value of a currency will make goods **more expensive** to foreign buyers, so **exports** will **fall**. At the same time, foreign goods will be **cheaper** to buy, so **imports** will **rise**.
- If inflation **rises** exports will **fall** because they'll become **more expensive** and **less competitive** in **foreign** countries. Imports will **rise** because it'll become **cheaper** for consumers and firms to buy **imports** rather than domestic products.

The UK's large deficit in visible trade is partly caused by a lack of competitiveness in its manufacturing industries.

3) It has to deal with external shocks

- If there's a **rise** in the world prices of imported **raw materials**, e.g. oil, timber or metals, and the **demand** for these materials is relatively **price inelastic**, then a country will end up **paying more** for these imports — at least in the **short run**.
- An **economic downturn** in countries to which a country **exports** can cause a sudden **reduction** in the amount of **exports** that are demanded.
- The imposition of **trade barriers** on goods by a trading partner could mean a sudden reduction in exports made to that country. Trade barriers are anything that **restricts** trade — for example, a government could **limit** imports into its country.

Ellie was suffering from a different kind of external shock.

A country might experience a **current account surplus** if:

1) It's been experiencing a **recession** — sometimes domestic producers will **struggle** to sell products domestically, so they'll focus their efforts on competing in **international** markets instead. There may be a **fall** in imports too as a result of an **overall reduction** in spending.
2) Its domestic currency has a **low value** — this will make exports **cheaper** and imports **more expensive**.
3) **High interest rates** are causing **more** saving and **less** spending.

Practice Questions

Q1 Describe the four sections of the balance of payments current account.

Q2 Explain the term 'external shock', with reference to an economy's balance of payments.

Exam Question

Q1 In recent years the UK economy has had a balance of payments deficit. Explain why. [8 marks]

Deficit? No, it can hear perfectly well...

You've got to learn what the four sections of the current account are and how a balance of payments deficit might be caused. Make sure you can see how the BOP links to other aspects of the economy, e.g. exchange rates and economic growth.

The Balance of Payments

I know what you're thinking... the balance of payments is basically the best thing ever. So if you're an OCR student, then you're in luck — here's a page just for you. ***This page is for OCR only.***

*There can be **Consequences** of a **BOP Surplus** or **Deficit***

Consequences of a BOP deficit

1) A balance of payments **deficit** could indicate that an economy is **uncompetitive**.
2) A deficit **isn't always** a bad thing — it might mean that people in that country are **wealthy** enough to be able to afford **lots of imports**. A deficit may also allow people to enjoy a **higher** standard of living, as they're importing the things they want and need. But, a **long-term deficit** is likely to cause problems.
3) The consequences of a deficit include a **fall** in the value of a currency, leading to **higher import prices** — at least in the **short run**. This can lead to an increase in **inflation**.
4) A balance of payments deficit may also lead to **job losses** domestically — for example, if more goods are being **imported**, that may mean fewer goods need to be produced **domestically**, so **unemployment** may increase.

Consequences of a BOP surplus

1) **Surpluses** can show that an economy is **competitive**.
2) However, if a country has a **surplus** for a **prolonged** period of time, e.g. Japan, they may experience **stagnation**. This means that, for example, due to **low domestic demand**, they'll experience **low**, or even **negative**, **economic growth** — which also has the potential to lead to **other** problems, such as **high unemployment**.
3) A large surplus on a current account may also be a result of an economy's **overreliance** on **exports**.
4) If a surplus is created by a country having an **undervalued currency**, this will create **inflationary pressures** — the price of **imported components** for use in **production** will **rise**, meaning a **rise** in the **costs of production** and therefore a **rise** in the **price level**.

Governments** often try to **Correct Imbalances** in the **BOP

1) Governments might try to correct a **BOP deficit**:
   - They might use **policies** to **reduce** the price of **domestic** goods — this should **increase** exports and **reduce** imports. For example, a government might use **supply-side policies** to remove **structural** problems (see p.125 for more).
   - Governments might impose **restrictions** on **imports** — for example, a government might impose **tariffs** (see p.70) on **imports** to make them **relatively** more expensive (compared to domestic goods) for **domestic consumers**. This might cause **inflation** if demand for imports is too **price inelastic**.
   - They may **devalue** (fixed exchange rate systems) or **depreciate** (floating exchange rate systems) the **currency** (see p.113) — this will make exports **cheaper** and imports more **expensive**. For this to be **successful**, the Marshall-Lerner condition must hold (see p.115).
   - Governments might use **fiscal** or **monetary policy** to reduce spending in the economy (see p.118-124 for more) — however, as well as **reducing imports**, it's likely to also **reduce domestic demand** and harm economic growth.

These are expenditure-switching policies — they switch consumer spending away from imports, towards domestically-produced goods instead.

These would be examples of expenditure-reducing policies.

2) Governments might try to correct a **BOP surplus** — for example, they might **raise** the value of their currency. This will **reduce** the demand for **exports** and **increase** the demand for **imports**. However, this is likely to result in a **reduction** in output and has the potential to cause a **rise** in unemployment.
3) When the governments of **major economies** try to correct imbalances in their BOP, it can have **global impacts**:
   - **Supply-side policies** to correct deficits may lead to an **increase** in **world trade** and **growth**.
   - **Restrictions** on imports can lead to **trade wars**, **reducing** international trade and leading to **lower** global efficiency.
   - If a government's attempts to reduce its BOP deficit lead to a **fall** in exports from **developing** countries, this may have many **negative** consequences. For example, **economic growth** in those developing countries will be **limited**, leading to a **rise** in **unemployment**. **Reduced** economic growth in developing countries has the potential to **hold back** global improvements in **efficiency**.

The Balance of Payments

And here's one final page on the balance of payments. ***This page is for OCR and Edexcel only.***

The **Capital** and **Financial** accounts show **Asset Transfers**

OCR ONLY

1) The **capital** account includes **transfers** of **non-monetary** and **fixed** assets — the most important part of this is the flow of non-monetary and fixed assets of **immigrants** and **emigrants**, e.g. when an immigrant comes to the UK, **their assets** become part of the UK's **total assets**.
2) The **financial** account involves the movement of financial assets. It includes:
   - **Portfolio investment** — investment in financial assets, such as **shares** in overseas companies.
   - **Financial derivatives** — these are **contracts** whose value is based on the value of an asset, e.g. a foreign currency.
   - **Reserve assets** — these are financial assets held by the **Bank of England** to be used as and when they're **needed**.
3) **Income** from the financial account, e.g. in the form of interest, is recorded in the **current account**.
4) The current account **should balance** the capital and financial accounts, e.g. a deficit of £5bn on the current account should be offset by a surplus of £5bn on the capital and financial accounts. However, due to **errors** and **omissions**, the current account and capital and financial accounts often **don't** balance, so a **balancing figure** is needed.

There are both **Short-term** and **Long-term** capital and financial flows

OCR ONLY

1) **Long-term** flows are due to things such as investment from foreign firms and portfolio investment. They're usually quite **predictable** as, for example, investment by foreign firms is often made when a country gains a **comparative advantage** in producing something, which tends to happen over a **long** period of time.
2) **Short-term** flows (sometimes called '**hot money**' — see p.123 for more) are based on **speculation** and people/firms trying to **quickly** make money — e.g. by **moving** money from one currency to another expecting to make a profit through **changes** in **exchange rates**.

Private financial flows come from individuals and firms, and official financial flows go to and from governments and other official organisations (e.g. the EU).

International economies are more **Interconnected** than ever before

1) **International trade** and **capital flows** mean that many firms and governments have **interests** and **investments** in lots of different countries.
2) This allows those firms and economies to **grow** in ways that wouldn't be possible otherwise.
3) However, it also means that economies are now **dependent** on each other much more than ever before. For example, a **banking crisis** in one country can now cause **economic problems** in many different countries — e.g. if **foreign** firms or governments have **borrowed** or **lent** money to banks that have **collapsed**.
4) Similarly, if one country enters a **recession**, then this might cause **problems** for countries that **trade** with it.
5) These connections mean that **global trade imbalances** carry a serious risk. For example, the USA currently has a very large **current account deficit**, while China has a very large **surplus**. If the USA introduced policies to **limit** imports to try and **reduce** their deficit, then other countries could **retaliate** with their own policies, **harming trade** and **damaging economies**.

Private individuals may also invest and trade internationally.

Practice Questions

Q1 Briefly explain the difference between the current, capital and financial accounts of the balance of payments.

Q2 List four methods a government might adopt to remove a persistent trade deficit.

Exam Question

Q1 The US has a current account deficit on its balance of payments, and it imports a lot of goods from China. Evaluate the possible benefits to the US balance of payments current account of a rise in the value of the Chinese renminbi. [15 marks]

As the Chancellor often reminds us — "Hip hop, the BOP don't stop"...

Phew — there's quite a lot to learn on the balance of payments, but don't let it overwhelm you. Just keep in mind that a balance of payments deficit can bring some pretty undesirable consequences if it gets out of control.

Other Economic Policy Objectives

Governments have lots of other objectives for the economy. Here are a couple more objectives they might try to achieve — but remember that different governments will have different priorities. ***This page is for Edexcel only.***

Governments try to **Distribute Income** more **Equally**

1) In any economy, there is a wide **range** of **earnings**. Earnings **depend** on a number of things, including:
   - **Labour skill** — training and education raises a person's **labour productivity** and, usually, their **pay rate**.
   - **Market forces** in the **labour** market — **shortages** or **surpluses** of various kinds of labour **influence** the **wage rate**, e.g. a **shortage** of electricians may **increase** an electrician's wage, a **surplus** may **reduce** it.
   - **Geography** — in **less** prosperous parts of the country, **earnings** are **lower**.
   - **Level** of **responsibility** — in general, the greater the **authority** and **responsibility** of a job, then the **higher** the **pay**.
2) Governments may want to **distribute** income more **equally** to **increase** overall **welfare** or **reduce** poverty so there's a better overall **standard of living**. Governments may also consider **too much** inequality in society to be **unfair**.
3) The redistribution of income can also **benefit** the **economy**. **High** earners tend to **save** more of their income and **low** earners tend to **spend** most or all of it — so income redistribution will **increase overall** consumer spending, and **raise** aggregate demand, output and employment.
4) The government can redistribute income by **reducing** the **net income** (take-home pay) of **high earners** and **increasing** the **net income** of people with **no** or **low incomes** — this can be done by:
   - **Tax** — especially income tax.
   - **Welfare payments** — paid to those on no, or low, incomes.
5) However, redistributing income carries a **risk**, as some income differences are **beneficial**:
   - The **reward** of **higher wages** acts as an **incentive** to hard work, training and risk-taking — so **too little** inequality would mean these **incentives** are **lost** and people will not work as hard.
   - **Wealth creation** can produce **employment** and **income opportunities** for others.
   - **Spending** by people with **high incomes** (e.g. on luxury goods that might not be purchased by those on lower incomes) creates **jobs** for others.

Governments try to **Protect** the **Environment**

Environmental protection has become **more important** to governments. Two of the **main** factors governments recognise are:

1 Damage/pollution to the environment

The role of the government is to:

1) **Identify** environmental damage caused by firms/individuals, e.g. **carbon emissions** from factories or cars.
2) Measure the **cost** of this damage.
3) Use **financial penalties** or certain **restrictions** or **bans** to **reduce** environmental damage and provide an **incentive** for firms/individuals to **decrease** the damage they cause. These might include:
   - Non-market policies — outright bans or limits on **polluting practices**. For example, **banning** cars which produce **unacceptable** levels of **carbon dioxide**.
   - Market policies — influencing the **cost** of polluting and therefore changing the behaviour of firms/individuals. For example, **tradable pollution permits** (see p.67) — these put a **restriction** on the **amount** of pollution a firm can produce, but firms are allowed to buy/sell permits between themselves.

2 Depletion of finite resources caused by continued economic growth

1) Some governments feel it's necessary to use **non-renewable resources**, such as oil and copper, more **wisely** to either **avoid** a future without them, or just to make them last for **longer**.
2) For example, governments might want to **encourage** the **development** and **use** of **renewable** energy resources, so that non-renewable resources such as coal and oil can either be **replaced** or will last for **longer**. They might try to achieve this by giving **financial incentives** to firms to develop or use **renewable** energy.

Financial penalties — a cause for dread for any England fan...

Not all governments will have these objectives, but you should learn the principles behind them. Remember that governments might not choose a policy that's best for a country economically — they might choose one that's the most popular with voters.

Conflicts Between Economic Objectives

Here's a bit about what governments want to do and the problems they face in doing it.
These pages are for all boards.

Governments make **Trade-offs** between their objectives

1) Remember... most governments have the same four **main macroeconomic objectives** (see p.92):
   - Strong economic growth,
   - Reducing unemployment,
   - Keeping inflation low,
   - Maintaining an equilibrium in the balance of payments.
2) They may also have **other objectives** (see previous page), such as:
   - A more equal distribution of income and wealth,
   - Protecting the environment.
3) However, trying to achieve **one** of these objectives may make it **more difficult** to achieve **another** — in other words, there may be **conflicts** between **policy objectives**.
4) In the short run, governments decide which objectives they think are **most important** and **accept** that these decisions may have an adverse effect on their other objectives — i.e. they make **trade-offs** between their objectives.
5) Governments may have to use **short-term policies** to correct **sudden problems**, such as major unemployment caused by a severe recession. In a scenario like this the government may **accept** that inflation will result from a policy designed to reduce unemployment quickly because it's more important to get people back to work.

Changes in **Aggregate Demand** are likely to cause **Conflict** between objectives

1) **Short run economic growth** is caused by the AD curve shifting to the **right**. This could be due to an **increase** in any of the **components** of **aggregate demand** (C + I + G + (X – M)).
2) For example, if the AD curve shifts to the right from AD to AD_1 then there will be an **increase** in **output** (i.e. economic growth) from Y to Y_1 and, as a result, there will be a **decrease** in **unemployment** (because of the derived demand for labour).
3) However, a shift to the right of the AD curve will also result in an **increase** in the **price level** from P to P_1. Higher prices may also lead to a **lack** of **competitiveness** internationally, meaning a **decrease** in exports, a **rise** in imports and therefore a **worsening** in the current account of the **balance of payments**.
4) So, in this case, an increase in aggregate demand will only help the government to achieve **two** of its macroeconomic objectives.

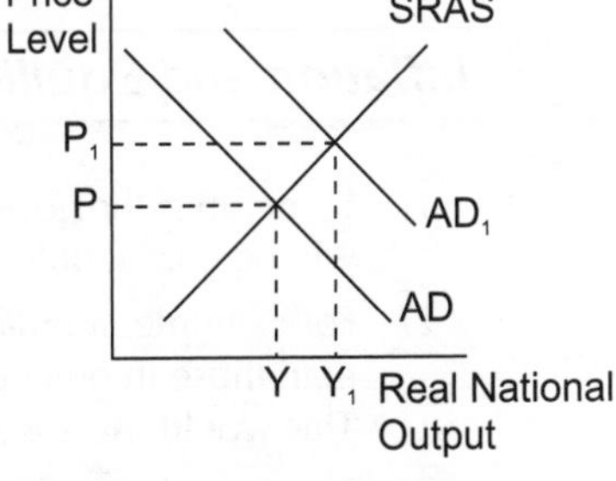

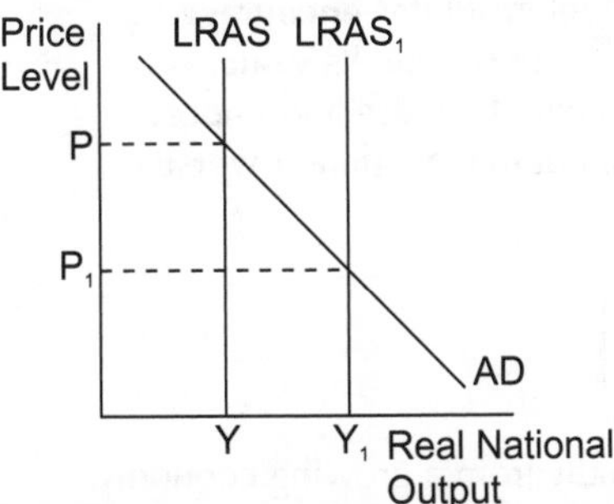

5) However, a shift in the LRAS (or AS) curve will enable a government to achieve **all four** of the main macroeconomic objectives at the **same time**.
6) For example, if the LRAS curve shifts to the right to $LRAS_1$ then this will lead to an **increase** in **output** (from Y to Y_1) and **reduce unemployment**. The **price level** will also **fall** (from P to P_1) and this will **improve** the country's **competitiveness** — **improving** the **balance of payments**.
7) This suggests that if the government **only** used **demand-side policies** (see p.118) to achieve its macroeconomic objectives then this would lead to **conflict** between the objectives. However, **supply-side policies** (see p.125) are more likely to help a government achieve their four main macroeconomic objectives in the **long run**.

Learn the **Main Causes** of **Conflict** between the **Macroeconomic Objectives**

Make sure you understand the **cause** of these **key conflicts** between **government objectives**. Remember, these objectives are likely to conflict in the **short run**, but in the **long run** these conflicts may **not** occur if **aggregate supply increases**.

See p.94 for how output gaps link to unemployment and inflation.

Inflation and **Unemployment**

- When unemployment is **reduced** and the economy begins to **approach** full capacity, there are **fewer** spare workers, so **demand** for workers increases — especially for **skilled** workers. This will lead to an **increase** in wages and the **extra cost** of this may be passed on by producers to consumers in the form of **higher prices** — causing **cost-push** inflation.
- Low unemployment may cause consumers to **spend** more because they feel more **confident** in their **long-term** job prospects. This may cause **prices to rise** due to **demand-pull** inflation.
- So reducing unemployment makes it more **difficult** to keep inflation at the **preferred low rate**.

Conflicts Between Economic Objectives

Economic Growth and *Environmental Protection*

Economic growth can put a **strain** on the **environment**. For example:

- New factories and increases in production can raise levels of air and water **pollution**, as well as increase the amount of **waste** that needs **disposing** of.
- Economic growth will tend to increase the use of **natural resources** — this can be a major problem if these resources are **non-renewable**.
- Ecosystems might be **damaged** or even **destroyed** by the **construction** of new factories, housing, etc. — in the most **extreme** cases, this can lead to the **extinction** of certain animals or plants.

Economic Growth and *Inflation*

1) A rapidly **growing** economy can cause large **increases** in **prices**, due to an increase in **demand**. This will cause a **higher** than desirable level of **inflation**.
2) Similarly, attempts to keep **inflation low** can **restrict** growth. For example, if **interest rates** are kept **high** to reduce inflation by **discouraging** spending (and encouraging saving), this can **restrict economic growth**.

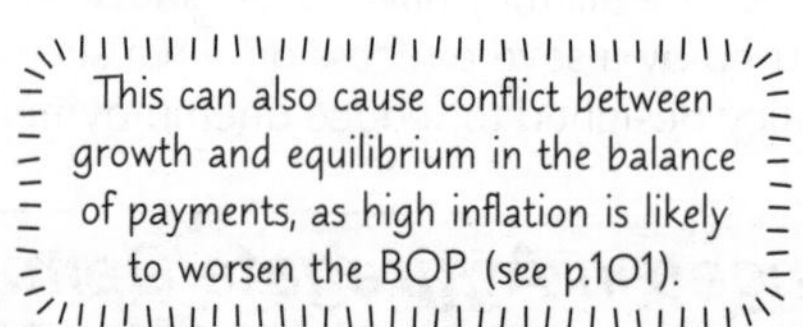
This can also cause conflict between growth and equilibrium in the balance of payments, as high inflation is likely to worsen the BOP (see p.101).

Inflation and *Equilibrium* in the *Balance of Payments*

1) **Sometimes** the government's objectives for low inflation and equilibrium in the balance of payments will be **compatible**, but at other times they'll **conflict**.
2) For example, if **inflation** is **low**, this implies that prices are **rising slowly**. If prices rise **more slowly** than those in other countries, then **exports** to other countries will **increase** and **imports** will **decrease**. This would **increase** a **surplus** on the balance of payments, but **reduce** a balance of payments **deficit**.
3) However, low inflation is often **maintained** by **high interest rates**. High interest rates **encourage** foreign investment, which **increases demand** for the domestic currency — **increasing** its **value**. This will make exports **more expensive** and imports **cheaper**, so **exports** will **decrease** and **imports** will **increase**. This would **reduce** a **surplus** on the balance of payments, but make a **deficit worse**.

Economic Growth and a Reduction in *Wealth Inequality*

1) Economic growth can **increase inequality**, as not everyone benefits **equally** from a growing economy.
2) For example, as an economy grows, **highly skilled** workers (e.g. those that work in hi-tech industries) may become **more** in demand, while the demand for **low-skilled** workers (e.g. those that carry out routine manual tasks which can be done instead by machines) may **fall**.
3) Governments can choose to use **increased** tax revenue from economic growth to **decrease** this inequality by:
   - Increasing **welfare payments**.
   - Using **progressive taxes** (i.e. taxes where the rich pay a higher rate than the poor).
   - Increasing the **minimum wage** in line with increases in the **average wage**.
4) However, increasing taxes or welfare payments may **damage** future economic growth. For example:
   - High taxes may be a **disincentive** for individuals and businesses to earn and grow.
   - Extra welfare payments may **not** encourage people to **work**.

However, some welfare benefits can help the economy to grow (e.g. help with childcare costs might allow parents to return to work).

5) **Supply-side policies** that help people back to **work** and reduce geographical and occupational **labour immobility** would encourage **growth**, while reducing the **welfare budget** and **unemployment**.

Conflicts Between Economic Objectives

EDEXCEL ONLY

The *Short Run Phillips Curve* shows an *Inflation/Unemployment Trade-off*

1) The **short run Phillips curve** shows an apparent **trade-off** between inflation and unemployment. By plotting **historical** inflation and unemployment data, the economist A.W. Phillips found that as **inflation falls**, **unemployment** seems to **rise**, and vice versa.
2) So it looks like if the government wants to **reduce unemployment**, then it can **increase aggregate demand** to achieve this... as long as it's prepared to **accept higher inflation**.
3) However, **not** everyone **agrees** that it's quite this simple. One problem is that once inflation has gone **up**, people seem to **expect** it to **remain high**, and they change their behaviour accordingly.

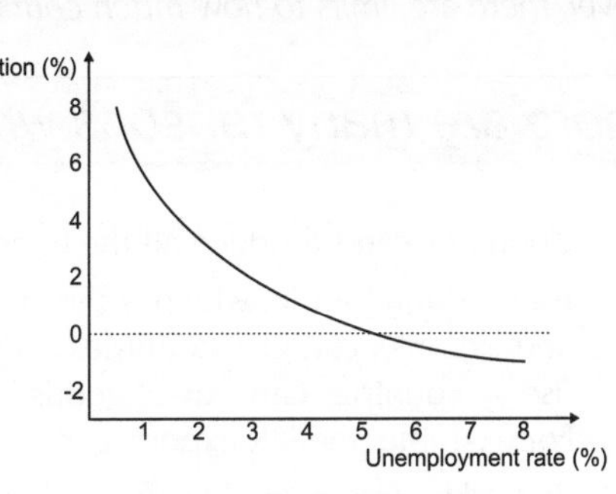

Supply-side Policies can help governments to achieve the four main objectives

1) Governments use various **demand-side** and **supply-side policies** to tackle problems that **prevent** them from achieving their macroeconomic objectives.
2) However, supply-side policies are often seen as the **more effective** way of achieving **all four** macroeconomic objectives at the same time — there's more on this on p.107 and 126.
3) For example, a government may use supply-side policies to **reduce unemployment** (which should boost **economic growth**), and tackle **cost-push inflation**. This may also improve a **balance of payments deficit**, as if domestically-produced goods become cheaper, **imports** will fall and **exports** will rise. The policies a government uses will depend on the type of unemployment they face:

Frictional unemployment will be reduced by policies which **encourage** people to find a job and **speed up** this process:

- **Reducing benefits** will give unemployed workers a greater **incentive** to find a job. The supply of labour is likely to **increase**.
- Similarly, **income tax cuts** will **increase** the **incentive** for workers to find a job, or encourage them to **work longer hours**.
- **Increased information** about jobs will help workers find the **right job** for themselves **more quickly**.

Structural unemployment will be reduced by policies which tackle **geographical** and **occupational immobility**:

- Governments can improve **occupational mobility** by **investing** in **training schemes** that help workers to **improve** their **skills**, or by **encouraging firms** to set up their **own training schemes**.
- **Geographical immobility** can be tackled by giving workers **subsidies** to move to different areas or by building **affordable houses** in areas that need workers. However, workers will still often be **reluctant** to leave their homes and families.
- Governments can **bring jobs** to areas with **high unemployment** by providing benefits to firms that locate in certain areas. This might be **combined** with **training schemes** to give local workers the skills required for the jobs provided.

Practice Questions

Q1 Explain why a government aiming for low unemployment and low inflation might encounter policy conflicts.

Q2 Briefly explain how a government's objectives for economic growth and inflation might conflict.

Exam Question

Q1 Explain, using a diagram, how a government could improve all four of its main macroeconomic objectives at the same time. [12 marks]

My macaroni-economic policy involves eating lots of pasta and cheese...

Eeeh... running an economy sounds tricky. You need to know about all the bear-traps awaiting unsuspecting governments as they go about trying to achieve useful things. The stuff on these pages is hated by governments, but loved by Economics examiners.

Trade

When countries trade internationally, they tend to start to specialise in the products they're best at producing. The law of comparative advantage can be used to help judge the amount of output that countries should produce. However, there are limits to how much countries should specialise. ***This page is for AQA and OCR only.***

There are many reasons why countries **Trade Internationally**

- Countries **can't** produce all the things they **want** or **need** because resources are **unevenly distributed.**
- **International trade**, which is the **exchange** of goods and services **between** countries (i.e. imports and exports), can give countries **access** to resources and products they otherwise **wouldn't** be able to use — countries can **export** goods in order to **import** the things they can't **produce** themselves. For example, the UK exports goods so that it can import things such as tea, rice and diamonds.
- By trading internationally, not only do a country's consumers enjoy a **larger variety** of goods and services, but increased **competition** resulting from international trade can lead to **lower** prices and **more** product innovation — so people's **standards of living** are raised by having more **choice**, and **better quality** and **cheaper** products.
- **Additional markets** (i.e. markets abroad) allow firms to exploit more **economies of scale** — if the additional markets mean there's an **increase** in **demand** for their products.

International Trade allows countries to **Specialise**

1) International trade allows countries to **specialise** in the goods and services they're **best** at **producing**.
2) Countries specialise because:
   - They have the **resources** to produce the good or service **efficiently**.
   - They're **better** than other countries at producing the good or service.
3) Specialisation **reduces costs**, which can be passed on to **consumers** in the form of **lower prices**.
4) It also means the world's resources are used **more efficiently**, global output is **increased** and living standards are **raised**.

OCR ONLY

It's useful to consider **Absolute Advantage** when looking at **Trade**

1) A country will have an **absolute advantage** when its output of a product is **greater per unit of resource used** than any other country.
2) To explain absolute advantage economists make a number of **simplifying assumptions**.

Example 1 — absolute advantage

Assume:

- There are only **two countries** in the world, **A** and **B**, who each have the **same amount** of resources.
- They both produce **only crisps** and **chocolate**.
- If each country splits its resources **equally** to produce the **two** goods, then output would be:

	Units of crisps output per year	Units of chocolate output per year
Country A	1000	5000
Country B	2000	3000

Before specialisation, world production of crisps is 1000 + 2000 = 3000 units, and of chocolate is 5000 + 3000 = 8000 units.

- Country A has the **absolute advantage** in producing chocolate and country B has the **absolute advantage** in producing crisps.
- So if the countries **specialised** in the products they have an absolute advantage in, then **world production** of crisps would rise to 4000 units (all produced by country B) and of chocolate to 10 000 units (all produced by country A). (Remember — each country **splits** its resources **equally** between the two products, so if country A **only** made chocolate, then the **half** of its resources that **were** used to make **crisps** would be used for **chocolate** instead, and chocolate production would **double**.)
- Through specialisation, **more output** is produced using the **same amount** of resources — so the **cost per unit** is **reduced**.

Trade

There's plenty more on trade if you're an OCR student... You must feel like it's your birthday. ***These pages are for OCR only.***

Comparative Advantage uses Opportunity Costs

1) **Comparative advantage** uses the concept of **opportunity cost** — the opportunity cost is the **benefit** that's **given up** in order to do something else. In this case, it's the number of units of one good not made in order to produce one unit of the other good.
2) A country has a comparative advantage if the opportunity cost of it producing a good is **lower** than the opportunity cost for other countries.

Example 2 — comparative advantage

Make the same **assumptions** as **example 1** (previous page), but this time country A and country B produce **only wheat** and **coffee**. If they each split their resources **equally**, they can produce the following quantities:

	Units of wheat output per year	Units of coffee output per year	Opportunity cost of wheat	Opportunity cost of coffee
Country A	3000	3000	1 unit of coffee	1 unit of wheat
Country B	2000	1000	½ unit of coffee	2 units of wheat
Total output before specialisation	5000	4000	–	–

- Country A has the **absolute advantage** in producing **both** wheat and coffee.
- Country A has the **lower opportunity cost** in producing **coffee**, and therefore the comparative advantage — i.e. if country A makes **one extra unit of coffee**, it must give up **one unit of wheat**, but if country B makes **one extra unit of coffee**, it must give up **two units of wheat**.
- Country B has the **lower opportunity cost** in producing **wheat**, and therefore the comparative advantage — i.e. if country B makes **one extra unit of wheat**, it must give up **half of a unit of coffee**, but if country A makes **one extra unit of wheat**, it must give up **one unit of coffee**.

See below for what happens when the countries specialise.

3) The law of comparative advantage is based on several **assumptions**, which make it hard to apply to the **real world**. For example, it assumes that there are **no economies** or **diseconomies** of scale, there are **no transport costs** or **barriers** to trade (see p.103), there's **perfect** knowledge, and that factors of production are **mobile**. Also, externalities are **ignored**.

Specialising Fully often Won't maximise output

Example 3

- Using **example 2** above, if the countries specialise **fully** in the goods they have a comparative advantage in, allocating **all** of their resources to **one product**, total output of **coffee** will **increase** from 4000 to 6000 units, but total output of **wheat** will **decrease** from 5000 to 4000 units (see the table below).
- However, it's possible to increase the output of **both** goods by only reallocating **some** resources. Countries can **split** production and then **trade**. For example, in the bottom row of the table below, ¼ of country A's resources are allocated to wheat and ¾ to coffee, while country B just specialises in wheat. By using **partial** specialisation, wheat and coffee output are **both** greater than they were **before** specialisation.

	Units of wheat output per year	Units of coffee output per year	Opportunity cost of 1 unit of wheat (1W)	Opportunity cost of 1 unit of coffee (1C)
Country A	3000	3000	1 unit of coffee (**1C**)	1 unit of wheat (**1W**)
Country B	2000	1000	½ unit of coffee (**½C**)	2 units of wheat (**2W**)
Total output before specialisation	5000	4000		
Total output after specialisation	4000	6000		
E.g. of total output with partial specialisation	1500 (country A) 4000 (country B)	4500 (country A)	–	–

If country B specialises in wheat and stops making coffee, it can only double its wheat output to 4000 units with the resources it has.

- Countries are **unlikely** to specialise 100% — instead they produce at a level where their combined production of **both** goods is **greater** than without specialisation.
- For trade to **benefit** both countries, the **terms of trade** must be set at the right level (see next page).
- If the **opportunity cost** of production is the **same** in both nations, there would be **no benefit** from trade.

Trade

Trade should be *Beneficial* to *All* countries involved

1) Usually, for trade to occur between two countries, **both** countries must **benefit** from trading, or at least not be any **worse off** than if they **hadn't** traded. So, **neither** country will **pay more** for a good than it would **cost** for them to **produce** it themselves, and **neither** will **accept less** for a good than it **costs** for them to **produce** it.
2) Whether trade is beneficial or not depends on the **opportunity cost ratios** for each country.
   - For Country A in example 3 (see previous page), the opportunity cost ratio of wheat to coffee is **1C : 1W**.
   - For Country B, the opportunity cost ratio of wheat to coffee is **1C : 2W**.

These ratios come from either of the last two columns in the example 3 table.

3) As long as the **rate of exchange** lies between **"1C for every 1W"** (i.e. 1C : 1W) and **"1C for every 2W"** (i.e. 1C : 2W), trade will benefit at least one of the two countries, while neither will be worse off.
4) For example, suppose the countries agree to trade at a rate of exchange of **"1C for every 1.5W"** (i.e. 1C : 1.5W). Then the cost to country A of **importing** 1.5W is 1C — this is **less** than the **opportunity cost** of producing 1.5W **itself** (= 1.5C). And by **exporting** 1.5W, country B receives 1C, which is **more** than it'd be able to produce **itself** — country B would have to give up **2W** to produce **1C** itself.

*If a country's **Terms of Trade Rises** then it's **Better Off** — if it **Falls** then it's **Worse Off***

1) A country's **terms of trade** is the **relative** price of its **exports** compared to its **imports**.
2) In the real world, a country's **terms of trade** is often described using an index number. It's **calculated** using the formula:

$$\text{terms of trade index} = \frac{\text{index of average price of exports}}{\text{index of average price of imports}} \times 100$$

Think of a country's terms of trade as the 'rate of exchange' used between it and the rest of the world — i.e. the amount of imports it can buy per unit of exports.

3) If the price of a country's **exports rises**, but the price of its **imports stays the same**, its **terms of trade index** will **increase** — e.g. if a country exports lots of tea and the price of tea **rises**, its terms of trade index is likely to **rise** (e.g. from 102 to 120). This increase will mean it'll effectively become **'better off'**, as it'll be able to afford more imports.
4) And if a country's terms of trade index **falls** (e.g. from 110 to 105), it'll effectively be **worse off**.
5) For example, during the recession in 2008-2010, the UK's terms of trade index fell — this was because the price of its imports rose more quickly than the price of its exports.

World Patterns of trade are *Changing*

1) A hundred years ago, **developed** countries, such as the **UK**, had a **comparative advantage** in **manufactured** goods, whereas **developing** countries had a **comparative advantage** in **primary** goods, such as commodities.
2) Most trade took place **between developed** and **developing** countries.
3) Now, **developed** countries tend to have a comparative advantage in **high** value, **technologically advanced**, **capital-intensive** products, and **developing** countries tend to have a comparative advantage in **low** value, **labour-intensive** products.
4) **Developed** countries do most of their trade with **other developed** countries.
5) **Developing** countries also tend to do **most** of their trade with **developed** countries.
6) China and India have grown rapidly and are both now important **global** traders — China is the **largest exporter** and the **second largest importer** of goods in the world. Its **main** exports are **electronic equipment** and **machinery**.
7) China's **high-tech industry** has seen **rapid growth** in recent years — it's now the **largest** exporter of **high-tech** goods.
8) India's **main** goods exports are **fuels** and **materials**, e.g. **glass**. It's also a big exporter of **services**, such as **IT services**.

Practice Questions

Q1 What is international trade?

Q2 What is the difference between absolute and comparative advantage?

Q3 List three assumptions of comparative advantage which make it hard to measure in the real world.

Exam Question

Q1 Explain how comparative advantage has had an impact on the pattern of global trade over time. [6 marks]

The opportunity cost of not learning these pages is X marks in your exam...

Yep — some of this stuff is pretty tough to get your head around. Make sure you understand opportunity cost, absolute and comparative advantage, and the examples on the first couple of pages before you try to tackle the stuff at the top of this page.

Exchange Rates

Exchange rates have an impact on many aspects of the economy, such as economic growth, inflation and the balance of payments. Some countries set a fixed exchange rate, whilst others mainly leave a floating exchange rate to market forces. ***For OCR only.***

There are **Two** main types of **Exchange Rate Systems**

1) A **fixed** exchange rate is where the **government** or its **central bank** sets the exchange rate. This often involves **maintaining** the exchange rate at a **target rate**.
2) A **floating** exchange rate is free to **move** with changing supply of, and demand for, a currency.
3) A **hybrid** exchange rate system is a mixture of fixed and floating. There are a number of different hybrid systems, e.g.:
   - **Managed floating** — the exchange rate is mainly left to **market forces** (i.e. to float freely), but the government will occasionally **intervene** to influence the exchange rate. For example, to **reduce** the impact of an economic shock on the value of its currency.
   - **Semi-fixed** — the exchange rate is only allowed to **fluctuate** within a **set band** of exchange rates.
   - **Pegged** — the **value** of the currency is 'pegged' to **another** currency or **group** of currencies. This peg can be **moved** periodically, or as the government sees fit.

Fixed exchange rates have to stay at a **Target Rate**

1) **Fixed** exchange rate systems, and certain **hybrid** exchange rate systems, have a **target** rate.
2) A **government** or **central bank** will maintain the exchange rate at the target rate by **controlling** interest rates and by **buying** and **selling** the currency (using foreign currency reserves) to keep supply of, and demand for, the currency **stable**.

Market Forces or **Government Intervention** cause exchange rates to **Fluctuate**

1) The **devaluation** of a **fixed** exchange rate occurs when the exchange rate is **lowered** formally by the government. They can achieve this by **selling** the currency.
2) The **opposite** of exchange rate **devaluation** is exchange rate **revaluation** (achieved by **buying** the currency).
3) The **depreciation** of a **floating** exchange rate is when the exchange rate **falls**. This might occur naturally due to **market forces**, although government action (e.g. **lowering** interest rates) might **affect** it indirectly.
4) The **opposite** of exchange rate **depreciation** is exchange rate **appreciation**.
5) **Competitive devaluation** can occur in fixed or hybrid exchange rate systems. This is when governments **deliberately** devalue their own currencies to **improve** international competitiveness (see p.117).
6) **Competitive depreciation** can occur in floating or hybrid exchange rate systems — government intervention might indirectly **reduce** the value of the currency, **improving** the country's international competitiveness.

This crowd **really** appreciated the exchange rate.

Practice Questions

Q1 What are fixed and floating exchange rate systems?

Q2 Why might a government want to devalue its currency?

Exam Question

Q1 Which of the following is the exchange rate system being described here?
'*The currency is left to float freely for the majority of the time, but the government occasionally intervenes.*'
A) Pegged exchange rate system
B) Semi-fixed exchange rate system
C) Managed floating exchange rate system
D) Fixed exchange rate system
[1 mark]

Changing devalue of the currency isn't always an option...

There are many exchange rate systems — but you just need to know the basics of the ones given on this page. Make sure you remember how a government can influence its exchange rate, and why a government might want to devalue its currency.

Exchange Rates

Floating and *Fixed* exchange rates have *Advantages* and *Disadvantages*

	Advantages	Disadvantages
Floating	Under **fixed** exchange rate systems, central banks require **foreign currency reserves** so that they can intervene to maintain their exchange rate target — a **floating** exchange rate will **reduce** the need for currency reserves.	Floating exchange rates can **fluctuate** widely, which makes business planning **difficult**.
Floating	A floating exchange rate can help to **reduce** a BOP current account **deficit** — a BOP deficit will lead to a **fall** in the value of the currency, so if demand for exports and imports is moderately **price elastic**, exports will **increase** and imports will **decrease**, reducing the BOP deficit.	Speculation can **artificially strengthen** an exchange rate — this would cause a country to **lose competitiveness**, as domestic goods will become **over-priced**.
Floating	A floating exchange rate means that a government **doesn't** need to use monetary policy, e.g. interest rates, to help to maintain the exchange rate — it can use it for **other objectives**.	**Falls** in exchange rates can lead to inflationary pressures — for example, if demand for imports tends to be **price inelastic**.
Fixed	**Speculation** may be **reduced** — unless dealers feel that the exchange rate is no longer **sustainable**.	If speculators feel a fixed exchange rate **isn't sustainable**, they might take advantage of this by **selling** the currency.
Fixed	**Competitive pressures** are placed on firms — they need to keep costs **down**, **invest** and **increase productivity** to remain competitive.	The country effectively **loses control** of interest rates, as they need to be used to keep the **exchange rate** at the desired level.
Fixed	Fixed exchange rates create **certainty**, which is likely to **encourage** investment (including from firms in foreign countries).	Fixed exchange rates are **difficult** to maintain.

The various hybrid systems have a **mixture** of advantages and disadvantages of both floating and fixed systems. For example, a **pegged** system creates **more certainty** than a freely floating system, so this might lead to **more investment**. However, the country will also lose **some** control of interest rates, as they'll need to be used to **influence** the exchange rate.

Supply and *Demand* determine *Floating* exchange rates

1) Floating exchange rates are determined by **changes** in **supply** and **demand** for a currency. For example, an **increase** in the **supply** of pounds to S_1 will cause a **decrease** in the **value** of the pound to P_1. This increase in supply may be due to things such as an **increase** in **imports** to the UK and **increased selling** of the pound.
2) A **decrease** in the **demand** for pounds to D_1 will cause a **decrease** in the **value** of the pound to P_1. This decrease in demand may be due to, for example, a **decrease** in **exports** from the UK and **decreased buying** of the pound.
3) Supply and demand **fluctuations** are caused by many other factors, for example:

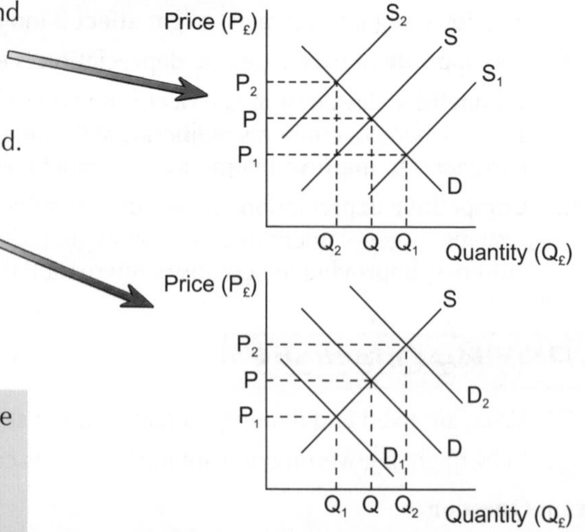

- **Speculation** — where people **buy** and **sell** currency because of changes they **expect** are going to happen in the future.
- The **official** buying and selling of the currency by the **government** or **central bank**.
- **Relative inflation rates** — if a country's inflation rate is **higher** than its **competitors'**, then the **value** of its currency is likely to **fall**. **Prices** in the country will become **less competitive**, leading to **reduced exports** and **increased imports**, so **demand** for the currency **decreases** and **supply increases**.
- **Relative interest rates** — **high** interest rates **increase demand** for a currency because there's an **inflow** of '**hot money**' (see p.105 and 123).
- **Confidence** in the state of the economy — there'll be **greater demand** for a currency if people feel confident in, for example, a country's **growth** and **stability** (this will include a country's **economic** and **political** stability — investors are **unlikely** to have confidence in **unstable** governments).
- The balance on the **current account** of the balance of payments has a **small** effect on the exchange rate — for example, a current account **deficit** will mean there's a **high supply** of the currency due to the **purchase** of **imports**.

Exchange Rates

Fluctuations in the Exchange Rate have Impacts on the economy

1) If the value of a currency **falls**:
   - **Exports** will become **cheaper**, so domestic goods will become **more competitive**.
   - This means that **demand** for **exports** will **increase**.
   - **Imports** will become **more expensive**, so **demand** for **imports** will **fall**.
   - A current account **deficit** should therefore be **reduced**, but a surplus should **increase**.
2) The current account deficit will only reduce if the **Marshall-Lerner** condition holds — see below.
3) The **J-curve** shows how the current account may actually **worsen** in the **short run**, but **improve** in the **long run** — see below.
4) A **fall** in the value of a currency can also mean:
   - If exports increase and imports decrease, there'll be **economic growth** caused by an **increase** in aggregate demand.
   - **Unemployment** may also be **reduced** through the **creation** of more jobs from economic growth.
   - **Inflation** may **rise** if demand for imports is **price inelastic**.
   - **Increased** import prices can also cause **cost-push** inflation.
5) A **rise** in the value of a currency will tend to have the **opposite** effects on an economy.
6) For example, **exports** will become **more expensive** and **imports** will become **cheaper**. This will potentially mean:
   - An **increase** in the size of a current account **deficit**, or a **reduction** in a current account **surplus**.
   - A **fall** in aggregate demand, which is likely to lead to a **fall** in output.
   - **Unemployment** may **rise**.
   - The impact on inflation will depend on the **price elasticity of demand** for imports and for domestic goods.

A Fall in the Value of a currency Might Not improve a current account Deficit

1) A fall in the value of a currency will only reduce a current account **deficit** if the **Marshall-Lerner condition** holds.
2) The Marshall-Lerner condition says that for a **fall** in the value of a currency to lead to an **improvement** in the balance of payments, the price elasticity of demand for **imports plus** the price elasticity of demand for **exports** must be **greater than one**, i.e. $PED_M + PED_X > 1$.

The J-curve shows the effect of Inelastic demand for imports and exports in the Short Run

1) The Marshall-Lerner condition might hold in the **long run**, so there'll be an **improvement** in a current account deficit if the value of a currency **falls**.
2) However, in the **short run** a current account deficit is likely to **worsen**, as demand for imports and exports will be **inelastic** — e.g. because it takes time for people to switch to a cheaper substitute.
3) In the short run, the **overall** value of **exports falls** and the **overall** value of **imports rises**, so the current account deficit worsens.
4) This is shown on the **J-curve**.

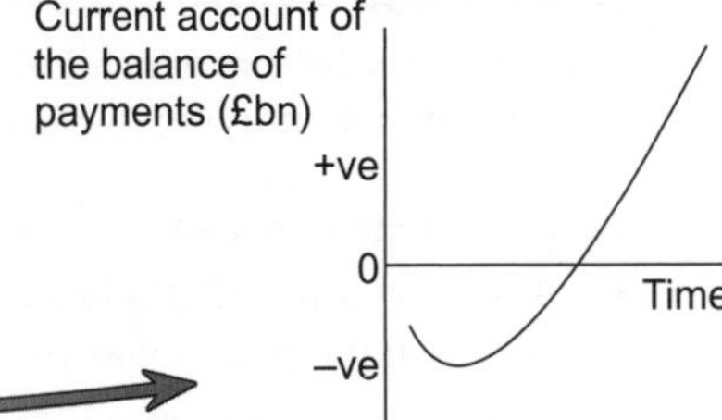

Practice Questions

Q1 Give one advantage and one disadvantage of floating exchange rates.

Q2 Give one advantage and one disadvantage of fixed exchange rates.

Q3 What impact might a fall in the value of a country's currency have on a current account deficit?

Exam Question

Q1 Explain the likely impact of hosting a major sporting event on a country's currency. [4 marks]

I lost £7 learning that floating exchange rates are nothing to do with water...

Exchange rates play an important part in all economies — they directly affect exports and imports, which have knock-on effects on other aspects of the economy, such as economic growth, unemployment, inflation and the balance of payments. As well as understanding the exchange rate's impact on the economy, make sure you know the factors which can affect the exchange rate.

International Competitiveness

International competitiveness is all about making sure that, as a country, you're making things that people want to buy and selling them at prices that they're happy to pay. ***These pages are for OCR only.***

Competitiveness involves a lot of **Price Factors**

1) International **competitiveness** is a complex thing to try to **measure** — it involves trying to measure a country's **ability** to provide better-value goods and services than its rivals.
2) This will, to a large extent, depend on the **price** at which a country can produce and sell those goods and services. Various measures give an indication of this:

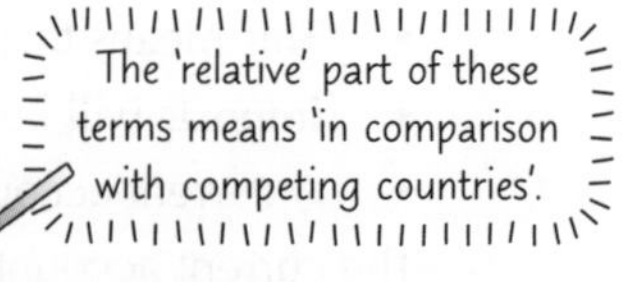

The 'relative' part of these terms means 'in comparison with competing countries'.

- **Relative unit labour costs** — unit labour costs measure the cost of the **labour** needed to generate output. If one country has **lower** unit labour costs than another country, then (all other things being equal) that country will be **more competitive** — i.e. better able to sell its products. To **compare** unit labour costs in different countries, you need to convert each country's unit labour costs to the **same currency**. In fact, comparisons are usually carried out by converting the costs to an **index number** that tries to allow for differences between countries, to make comparisons more valid.
- **Relative productivity** — increasing productivity (e.g. the output per worker per hour) will have a similar effect on competitiveness to reducing unit labour costs — i.e. all other things being equal, **higher** productivity means **greater competitiveness.**
- **Relative export prices** — exchange rates (see below and p.113) are a key determinant of relative export prices. For example, if the value of a country's currency **falls**, its exports will become **relatively** cheaper and its competitiveness will **increase**. The cost of **labour** will also have a significant effect on relative export prices, especially in **labour-intensive** industries, such as many manufacturing industries. (In **capital-intensive** industries, it's **less useful** as a guide to overall competitiveness.)

3) These are all **price factors**, but often **non-price factors** are used to judge competitiveness too. For example:

- **Design** — are a country's products what people want to buy?
- **Quality** — are products well made, and do they work properly?
- **Reliability** — do a country's products keep working?
- **Availability** — is it easy to buy a country's products?

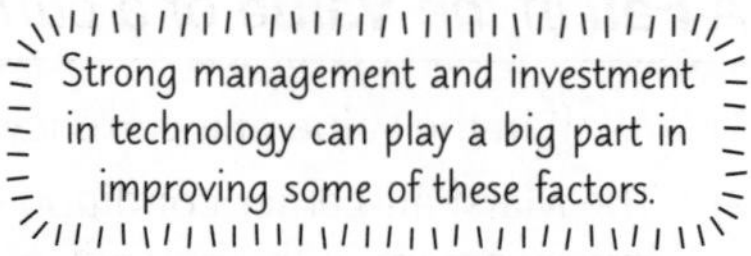

Strong management and investment in technology can play a big part in improving some of these factors.

Competitiveness is **Influenced** by many factors

There are many factors which influence competitiveness and that can therefore be taken into consideration when trying to decide **how competitive** a country is. For example:

Real Exchange Rates and Relative Inflation Rates

- **Real exchange rates** affect the **relative export prices** of different countries, impacting on a country's competitiveness — e.g. if the **pound** was **strong** compared to the **dollar**, then other countries would be more likely to buy **US exports.**
- The **real exchange rate** is the **nominal exchange rate** (the exchange rate determined by the foreign exchange rate markets), but it's **adjusted** to take into account the **price levels** within the countries being compared.
- It's worked out using the following **formula**:

$$\text{real exchange rate} = \text{nominal exchange rate} \times \frac{\text{price level in a country}}{\text{price level abroad}}$$

- So, the real exchange rate will be **affected** by changes to the **nominal exchange rate** and the **rate of inflation** in a country or abroad. This means, for example, the real exchange rate will **fall** if the nominal exchange rate **falls** or if the price levels abroad **rise** relative to domestic prices.

Productivity

- Productivity will be affected by the level of **human capital** in workers...
- ...which is affected by the levels of **education** and **training** of the population.
- The amount and sophistication of **capital equipment** used by workers will also be a factor here.

International Competitiveness

Wage Costs and Non-Wage Costs

- As well as **wage costs** (what a firm spends on wages), **non-wage costs** will affect the competitiveness of a country's firms.
- Non-wage costs will include things like:
  - employers' **national insurance** contributions and **pension** contributions,
  - costs incurred as a result of **environmental protection** or **anti-discrimination** laws, or **health-and-safety** regulations.

Labour Market Flexibility

- A flexible labour market is one where the **supply** of labour is able to **adapt** quickly to the **changing** needs of businesses — for example, workers can **transfer between activities** quickly.
- So factors affecting flexibility include the strength of **trade unions**, levels of **skills** and **qualifications** amongst workers, the ability for firms to hire/fire workers **easily**, and the willingness of workers to work **part-time** or on **flexible** contracts.

Research and Development

A country that's able to **innovate** and create **new products** (and perhaps even whole **new markets** as a result) or new, more efficient **methods of production** is likely to have an advantage when it comes to competing internationally.

Regulation

Regulations often **increase costs** for firms, forcing them to **raise** prices and become **less competitive** internationally.

Governments can Influence prices more directly

1) Some governments may **devalue** their currency — i.e. **reduce** its **value** against other currencies (see p.113).
2) Devaluing a country's currency can lead to **increased demand** from abroad for that country's **exports**. But it also means **imports** become more expensive, so people in that country are more likely to buy **domestically** produced goods.
3) Overall, the country should become **more competitive**, and there should be improvements in the **balance of payments**.
4) But devaluation can lead to **cost-push inflation** (see p.100) if imports are used in the production of other goods. It may also mean that firms aren't under as much pressure to **reduce their costs**, something that will be necessary in the long run if they're hoping to compete with foreign firms.

Decreasing interest rates would usually lead to a fall in the exchange rate — so you might think a government could devalue the currency that way. But in the UK, interest rates are set by the Bank of England rather than the government.

Competitiveness is Usually a good thing

1) In general, being internationally competitive is a **good** thing — if a country's **exports** are **relatively cheap**, there'll be **higher** demand for them. This'll mean **increased** aggregate demand, economic growth and levels of employment. Many countries have current account **deficits** — increasing exports (and reducing imports) helps to **correct** this imbalance.
2) Falling competitiveness can have **serious consequences** — a country that's less able to sell its products is likely to experience a worsening in its **balance of payments**, because **exports** will **fall** while **imports increase**. In addition, as economic activity generally decreases, **unemployment** will probably **increase**. Remaining competitive is particularly important for countries whose industries rely on **international trade** to achieve **economies of scale**.

Practice Questions

Q1 How can real exchange rates influence a country's competitiveness?

Q2 How might a devaluation of a currency help a country regain its competitiveness?

Exam Question

Q1 State two factors which will influence a country's competitiveness. [2 marks]

My competitiveness peaks during family games of charades...

International competitiveness is important to countries — if they're not competitive, they're likely to face all sorts of problems, such as struggling to grow their economies. There are loads of things that can affect competitiveness, so time to get learning.

Fiscal Policy

The next few pages are about the macroeconomic policy tools that governments can use to achieve their macroeconomic objectives. Before you tackle this section, make sure you're clear on aggregate demand and aggregate supply (pages 80-91), and on policy objectives (pages 92-109). ***This page is for all boards.***

You've got to learn the Key Features of Fiscal Policy

1) **Fiscal policy** (or budgetary policy) involves **government spending** (public expenditure) and **taxation**. It can be used to **influence** the **economy as a whole** (macroeconomic effects) or **individual firms** and **people** (microeconomic effects).
2) **Traditionally**, fiscal policy has been used to influence **aggregate demand** (AD) — this is a **macroeconomic** effect.
3) The aim of managing demand in this way is to 'smooth out' the fluctuations in the **economic cycle**.
4) Governments do this by **boosting demand** when the economy is in a **recession/slump** using **reflationary** policy, and **reducing demand** when the economy is **booming** by using **deflationary** policy:

This is known as 'Keynesian demand management'.

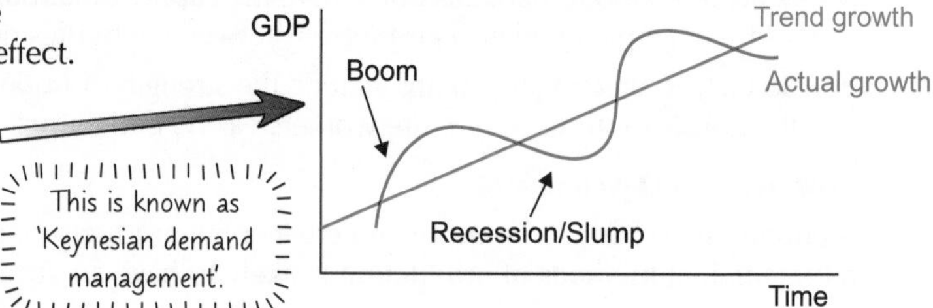

- **Reflationary fiscal policy** (sometimes called 'expansionary' or 'loose' fiscal policy) involves **boosting** aggregate demand (causing the AD curve to shift to the right) by **increasing** government spending or **lowering** taxes. It's likely to involve a government having a **budget deficit** (government spending > revenue).
- **Deflationary fiscal policy** (sometimes called 'contractionary' or 'tight' fiscal policy) involves **reducing** aggregate demand (causing the AD curve to shift to the left) by **reducing** government spending or **increasing** taxes. It's likely to involve a government having a **budget surplus** (government spending < revenue).

5) A reflationary fiscal policy is likely to be used during a **recession** or when there's a **negative output gap**. It'll **increase economic growth** and **reduce unemployment**, but it'll also **increase inflation** and **worsen** the **current account** of the **balance of payments** because as incomes increase, more is spent on imports.

Reflationary and deflationary fiscal policy is known as demand-side fiscal policy — it affects aggregate demand.

6) A deflationary fiscal policy is likely to be used during a **boom** or when there's a **positive output gap**. It'll **reduce economic growth** and **increase unemployment**, but it'll also **reduce price levels** and **improve** the **current account** of the **balance of payments** because as incomes fall, less is spent on imports.
7) A government's **fiscal stance** or **budget position** describes whether their policy is reflationary (known as an **expansionary** stance), deflationary (a **contractionary** stance), or neither (a **neutral** stance). If a government has a neutral fiscal stance then government spending and taxation has **no net effect** on AD.

Deflationary policy reduces demand — it doesn't necessarily cause deflation.

8) The **discretionary policy** of a government will affect its fiscal stance:

Discretionary policy is where governments **deliberately** change their level of spending and tax. At **any given point** a government might choose to spend on improving the country's infrastructure or services, and increase taxes to pay for it. On other occasions the government might take action because of the **economic situation**, e.g. during a recession the government might spend more and cut taxes to stimulate aggregate demand.

Changes to government spending and taxation (i.e. fiscal policy) can also be used to increase aggregate supply (AS) — see p.125.

OCR ONLY

Cyclical and Structural Budget Positions are Different

1) A **structural budget position** is a government's **long-term** fiscal stance. This means their budget position over a whole period of the **economic cycle** (see page 93), including booms and/or recessions.
2) A **cyclical budget position** is a government's fiscal stance in the **short term**. This is affected by where the economy is in the economic cycle — there's likely to be a **surplus** (i.e. a contractionary budget position) during a **boom** and a **deficit** (i.e. an expansionary budget position) during a **recession**.

Government spending can be split into **current expenditure** — repeated spending on things which are **used up** quickly (e.g. wages), and **capital expenditure** — spending on **assets** (e.g. infrastructure) which will last a long time.

A government may have a budget position on **current expenditure** which is different from their overall position. For example they may want current expenditure to be funded from **revenue**, but be willing to borrow for **capital expenditure**. So their budget position on current expenditure would be **neutral** or **contractionary**, but their **overall position** may be **expansionary** because of their capital expenditure.

This is the 'golden rule' that the UK government aimed to follow before 2008 — see page 121.

Fiscal Policy

Most of the money that governments spend comes from taxation. Taxes aren't just about paying the bills though. For example, they can also have a social impact by redistributing income. Who knew tax could be so exciting? ***This page is for all boards.***

Taxation** can promote **Equity** and **Equality

1) Taxes should be **cheap to collect**, **easy to pay** and **hard to avoid**, and they **shouldn't** create any **undesirable disincentives**, e.g. discouraging people from working or from saving.
2) On top of this, governments may want taxes to achieve **horizontal** and **vertical equity**.
   - **Horizontal equity** will mean that people who have **similar incomes** and **ability** to **pay taxes** should pay the **same amount** of tax.
   - **Vertical equity** will mean that people who have **higher** incomes and **greater ability** to **pay taxes** should pay **more** than those on **lower incomes** with **less ability** to **pay** taxes.
3) Governments may also want taxes that **promote equality** in an economy. This might involve using taxes to **reduce major differences** in people's **disposable income**, or to **raise revenue** to pay for **benefits** and the **state provision** of **services**.
4) Governments **raise tax revenue** through **direct taxation** (e.g. income tax) and **indirect taxation** (e.g. VAT or excise duty).

A 'good' tax will have all of these features.

See page 60 for direct and indirect taxation.

AQA & OCR

*There are **Different Types** of **Tax System***

1) Governments also use **different tax systems** to achieve different economic objectives — the ones you need to know are **progressive taxation**, **regressive taxation** and **proportional taxation**.
2) **Progressive taxation** is where an **individual's taxes rise** (as a percentage of their income) as their **income rises**, and it's often used to **redistribute income** and **reduce poverty**. A government can use the tax revenue from those on high incomes and **redistribute** it to those on low incomes in the form of benefits or state-provided merit goods (e.g. health care or education) — **increasing equality**. Progressive taxation follows the **'ability to pay' principle** (the tax achieves **vertical equity**).
3) **Regressive taxation** is where an **individual's taxes fall** (as a percentage of their income) as their **income rises**, and they're used by governments to **encourage supply-side growth**. By **reducing** the taxes of the **rich** the government will hope that the economy will **benefit** from the rich **spending more**. A regressive tax system gives people more of an **incentive** to **work harder** and **earn more income**, but it may **increase inequality**.
4) **Proportional taxation** (a 'flat tax') is where everyone pays the **same** proportion of tax **regardless** of their **income** level. This tax system can achieve **horizontal equity**, but setting a fair tax rate to apply to all members of society is **difficult**. For example, a 25% tax on income might be too high for those on lower incomes to afford, and it might not raise enough revenue from those on higher incomes for the government to be able to pay for all of the public goods and services it provides.

- Supporters of a flat tax argue that it can **simplify** the tax system, **reduce** the incentive to **evade and avoid** paying taxes (flat taxes often charge high earners less than variable rates), and **increase** the incentive to **earn more**.
- However, flat rate tax systems may bring in **less tax overall** than variable rate tax systems.
- Flat rate tax systems also don't have **vertical equity**, but they can be made more **progressive** by having a **tax free allowance** (where you don't pay any tax until you earn a certain amount).

AQA & OCR

*The **UK Government** uses **Various Different Taxes***

1) In the UK there's a **sales tax** on most products, known as **VAT** (value-added tax). VAT is a **proportional tax** — it's a **fixed percentage** regardless of the selling price of a product. However, it can also be seen as a **regressive tax**. This is because the **percentage** of **total income** that the **rich** spend is **less** than that of the **poor** (e.g. because the rich can afford to save more of their income), so that means the percentage of total income that the rich spend on VAT will be **less** than it is for the **poor**.
2) A more **progressive system** of **VAT** might be to tax **luxury goods** at a **higher tax rate**.
3) It's argued that the UK has a **progressive income tax system**. There's a **tax-free allowance** (£10 600 for 2015/16), and then individuals on **low-to-middle income** have their extra income over the allowance taxed at **20%**. Those on a **high income** are taxed at **40%** on their extra income over a certain threshold, and those on a **very high income** are taxed at **45%** on their income over a further threshold.
4) But it's also argued that the UK tax system is **regressive** because if you consider **direct** and **indirect** taxes **together**, the **lowest earners** in the UK economy have to pay a **higher proportion** of their income as tax than the **highest earners** do.

Fiscal Policy

The 'budget balance' is the difference between a government's spending and the revenue it brings in (e.g. from tax). It's important, because both a deficit (spending > revenue) and a surplus (spending < revenue) have their downsides. Read on... ***All boards.***

The Size of Government Spending can be affected by several things

1) The **size** and **structure** of a **country's population** will affect levels of government spending. For example, a country with a **large population** may require greater levels of government spending than a country with a **small population**, and a country with an **ageing population** will have **greater demand** for **state-funded health care**.
2) Government policies on **inequality**, **poverty** and the **redistribution of income** will alter the amount of government spending — this might vary from government to government depending on their **political views**. For example, a government that wants to redistribute income may **spend more** on **benefits**.
3) The **fiscal policies** governments use to tackle **certain problems** in a country will also have an effect. During a **recession** a government may increase public spending to **encourage growth** and **reduce unemployment**, but if these policies lead to a **large national debt** then the government may introduce '**austerity measures**' and **severely reduce** their spending.

AQA & OCR

Deficit and Debt are Different

1) A **budget deficit** is what a government borrows in a single year — governments borrow when they want to spend **more money** than they **receive** in **revenue**. A budget deficit is also known as **public sector net borrowing** (**PSNB**).
2) The **national debt** is the total government debt (run up over time) — it's also known as **public sector net debt** (**PSND**).
3) A government may **deliberately** run a budget deficit (or surplus) to try and influence **aggregate demand** (see page 82).
4) If a government has a **long-term** budget deficit then this borrowing will **increase** the national debt. A **short-term** deficit will probably be balanced out by a surplus later, so **won't** increase national debt.

OCR ONLY

Large Budget Deficits can cause Big Problems

1) A **budget deficit** must be **paid for** by **public sector borrowing**. In the UK, the government can borrow the money it needs from **UK banks**, which will create **deposits** that the government can spend. It can also **borrow money** from the private sector by selling **Treasury bills**, which the government will **pay off over a period of time** (e.g. 3 months), or it can borrow money from foreign **financial markets**.
2) This kind of borrowing is **fine** in the **short run**, especially if the borrowed money is used to **stimulate demand** in a country. But there will be **problems** if there's **excessive borrowing**:
   - Excessive borrowing could cause **demand-pull inflation** (see p.100), partly due to the fact that government borrowing **increases** the **money supply**, so there's **more money** in the economy than can be **matched** by **output**.
   - As borrowing may cause inflation, it can also lead to a **rise** in **interest rates** to curb that inflation (see p.122). **Higher** interest rates will **discourage investment** by firms and make a country's **currency rise in value**, meaning that its **exports** are **less price competitive**.
3) **Continued government borrowing** will **increase** a country's **national debt** (see above). A **large** and **long-term** national debt can cause **several problems** too:
   - If a country's debt becomes very large then it may cause **firms** and **foreign countries** to **stop lending** money to that country's government. This will **constrain** the country's ability to **grow** in future.
   - **Future taxpayers** will be left with **large interest payments** on **debt** to pay off. Debt repayments have an **opportunity cost** as future governments may have to **cut spending** to pay off a debt, which may **harm economic growth**.
   - A **large national debt** suggests that there's been **excessive borrowing**, which **causes inflation** and **interest rates** to **rise** (see above).
   - A country with large debt is **less attractive** to **foreign investment**, as foreign countries will be **uncertain** how the debtor nation's economy will do in future and whether it will be a good bet for investment.

OCR ONLY

Budget Surpluses are Not Ideal either

- A budget surplus is **generally more desirable** than a budget deficit — however, it's **not** always a good thing either.
- A budget surplus might suggest that **taxes** are **too high** or that governments **aren't spending** enough on the economy. Both of these things could **harm** or **constrain economic growth**.
- **Lowering taxes** or **increasing government spending** would **correct** a budget surplus.

Fiscal Policy

OCR ONLY

Governments follow Fiscal Rules to Avoid Overspending

1) The **UK government** first brought in **fiscal rules** in 1997. One of these was the **golden rule** — over the economic cycle (see page 93) the government can borrow to **invest** in things like infrastructure (which should generate future growth), but cannot borrow to fund **current expenditure** (e.g. wages).
2) Following fiscal rules like these should help to **prevent** a government from **continuously borrowing** and **overspending** to promote growth, which increases national debt and inflation. It'll also help governments to achieve **economic stability** as they'll **avoid** uncertainty and fluctuating inflation.
3) Fiscal rules can also influence the behaviour of **businesses** and **consumers**, by increasing **confidence** in future economic stability. For example, consumers may be more willing to spend and firms may increase investment if they're confident in the country's economic stability.
4) However, this will only work if there is a belief that governments will **keep to** the rules they've set.
5) In 2010 the UK government created the **Office for Budget Responsibility** (**OBR**) — an independent body that:
   - Publishes reports **analysing** UK **public spending**, **taxation**, and government **predictions** of future spending.
   - Assesses the **performance** of the government against the **fiscal targets** it's set for itself.
   - Uses **long-term projections** to analyse how **sustainable** government spending and revenue is.
6) By doing this, the OBR **helps** the government to keep its fiscal policy **under control**.

For example, there was disagreement over whether the golden rule was actually being followed between 1997 and the 2008 financial crisis, as it's not clear how an economic cycle is defined. (The rule was abandoned after 2008.)

The Government Spends Tax Revenue on Benefits and Services

1) A government's budget is all about **where** it gets its money from, and how it **spends** it.
2) These are the taxes that the UK government gets most of its **tax revenue** from:
   - **Income tax** (roughly 30% of central government tax revenue)
   - **VAT** (about 20%)
   - **National Insurance** payments (about 20%)
   - **Excise duties** on goods like **alcohol** and **fuel** (about 10%)
   - **Corporation tax** (about 8%)
   - **Council tax** and **Business rates** (paid to local government)

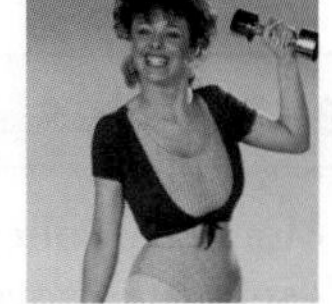

Nina was thrilled to hear that exercise duties would be falling.

3) And these are the main areas of **government expenditure** (i.e. where they spend their revenue):
   - **Social support** including pensions (about 40%)
   - **National Health Service** (about 20%)
   - **Education** (about 15%)
   - **Debt interest** (about 7%)
   - **Police, law courts and prisons** (about 5%)
   - **Defence** (about 5%)

Practice Questions

Q1 How can demand-side fiscal policy help smooth out the economic cycle?

Q2 Give three examples of problems caused by large, long-term national debt.

Q3 Explain the role of the Office for Budget Responsibility.

Q4 Which taxes are the main sources of tax revenue for the UK government?

Exam Questions

Q1 Loose fiscal policy is most likely to be used when:

A the economy is in a boom phase.
B a country has a large national debt.
C there is a negative output gap.
D the government's budget position is neutral. [1 mark]

Q2 Define the term 'progressive taxation'. [3 marks]

Q3 Evaluate whether fiscal rules are effective in creating economic stability. [12 marks]

I've found these pages pretty taxing to be honest...

Governments sometimes aim for a balanced budget. This is one of those terms that's used in different ways by different people (hurray). It can mean government spending is equal to revenue (so the 'budget balance' is zero), or that spending is no more than revenue (i.e. spending ≤ revenue). Getting a more balanced budget is also called 'improving the budget balance'. Simple, eh?

Monetary Policy

Monetary policy is largely about setting interest rates. But there's a lot of things to take into account as you do it. ***All boards.***

Monetary Policy is about *Controlling Money*

The money supply is measured in different ways — here, it means the amount of notes and coins in circulation, plus the amount of money held in bank accounts.

1) **Monetary policy** involves making decisions about **interest rates**, the **money supply** and **exchange rates**.
2) Monetary policy has a huge effect on **aggregate demand** — it's a **demand-side** policy.
3) The most important tool of monetary policy is the ability to set **interest rates**. Changes to interest rates affect **borrowing**, **saving**, **spending** and **investment**.
4) Interest rates also affect the other components of monetary policy — the **money supply** and **exchange rates**. For example, a **high** interest rate can **restrict** the money supply as there'll be **less demand** for loans.
5) Monetary policy can either be **contractionary** ('tight') or **expansionary** ('loose'):
   - **Contractionary monetary policy** — this involves **reducing** aggregate demand (AD) using high interest rates, restrictions on the money supply, and a strong exchange rate.
   - **Expansionary monetary policy** — this involves **increasing** aggregate demand using low interest rates, fewer restrictions on the money supply, and a weak exchange rate.
6) As with **demand-side fiscal policy** (see p.118), monetary policy **can't** help achieve **all** of a government's macroeconomic objectives simultaneously — there's a **trade-off**. For example, using monetary policy to **increase economic growth** and **reduce unemployment** may mean **increasing inflation** and **worsening the current account** of the balance of payments.
7) In the UK, the main aim of monetary policy is to ensure **price stability** — i.e. **low inflation**. But it also has the aims of **promoting economic growth** and **reducing unemployment**.

See page 113 for more about exchange rates.

Interest Rates are set by the *Monetary Policy Committee (MPC)*

1) The **Monetary Policy Committee** (**MPC**) of the **Bank of England** sets interest rates in order to meet the inflation target that's set by the government — this target is currently **2% inflation**, as measured by the **Consumer Price Index** (CPI). This is known as **inflation rate targeting**.
2) If the inflation rate misses the 2% target by more than 1% **in either direction** (i.e. if it's less than 1% or more than 3%), then the governor of the Bank of England has to write to the Chancellor (see below).
3) So if the MPC believed that inflation was likely to go **above 3%** with current interest rates, it would **increase** the official rate of interest (sometimes called the **Bank Rate** or **Base Rate**) to **reduce** aggregate demand and keep inflation close to 2%.
4) A low rate of inflation that's **stable** and **credible** (i.e. trustworthy and accurate) helps a government achieve **macroeconomic stability** — a high or rapidly changing rate of inflation creates **uncertainty**, prevents **investment**, and makes it difficult to **plan** for the future.
5) To achieve this **stability** and **credibility**, the Bank of England is **independent** and **accountable**:
   - The Bank of England's **independence** means that interest rates **can't** be set by the government at a level that will win votes, but which might not be right for the economic circumstances at the time.
   - The Bank of England is **accountable** — if the inflation rate is **more than 1%** away from the **target rate** (either above or below), then the Bank's governor must write an open letter to the Chancellor explaining why, what action the MPC is going to take to deal with this, and when they expect inflation to be back to within 1% of the target.
6) Although price stability is the **main objective** of monetary policy, the Bank of England must pursue this in a way that **doesn't harm** the government's other macroeconomic policy objectives (e.g. economic growth or low unemployment).
7) When the MPC is making a decision on interest rates it will look at important **economic data**, such as:
   - house prices,
   - the size of any output gaps,
   - the pound's exchange rate,
   - the rate of any increases or decreases in average earnings.
8) The MPC has to consider interest-rate changes very carefully, since these changes can have a **huge** effect.

There's more about this on page 124.

A Rise in Interest Rates causes a Ripple Effect

Even very small changes in interest rates can create a '**ripple effect**' through the whole economy.
Here are some likely effects of an **increase** in interest rates:

- less **borrowing**,
- more **saving**,
- less **investment** by firms,
- less **consumer spending** (i.e. less **consumption**),
- a decrease in **exports**,
- less **confidence** among consumers and firms,
- an increase in **imports**.

A decrease in interest rates will have the opposite effects.

Monetary Policy

Markets affect *Interest Rates* too

1) The **Bank Rate** is the lowest rate at which the Bank of England will lend to financial institutions (e.g. banks). But it **isn't** the rate of interest that you'd pay if you applied to a high-street bank for a **mortgage** or took out a **bank loan**.
2) However, these various types of interest rates are **linked** — if the Bank Rate goes **up**, then that will usually lead to interest rates charged on mortgages and bank loans also **increasing**. The same happens in reverse if the Bank Rate **falls** — i.e. other interest rates in the economy will also **fall**.
3) But the Bank Rate is **not** the **only** thing that affects these 'market' interest rates.
4) For example, banks often need to **borrow** the money that they then **lend out** to firms and consumers from other lenders. If lots of banks are trying to borrow money at the same time, then they'll have to pay a **higher rate** of interest themselves, which will affect the cost of mortgages and loans they offer to **consumers**.

Interest rates are affected by other things as well as the Bank Rate and the supply and demand for credit. But these are the things you need to be particularly aware of.

Interest Rates affect *Exchange Rates*

1) When interest rates are **high** in the UK, big financial institutions (such as large banks or insurance companies) want to **buy the pound**. They do this so that they can put their money into UK banks and take advantage of the **high rewards** for savers brought about by the high interest rates. This is likely to be a short-term movement of money and it's called '**hot money**'.
2) An **increased demand** for the pound means its **price goes up** — i.e. the pound's exchange rate **rises**.
3) Unfortunately, a **high exchange rate** makes UK exports **more expensive**.

- Suppose the **exchange rate** of the pound against the dollar is **£1 = $2**. And suppose a British firm makes pens that cost, say, £1.
- To buy one of these British pens, someone in the USA would first have to buy the pound. This would mean that the price of one of these pens in the USA is effectively **$2**, since it costs them **$2** to buy **£1**, and then they can spend this £1 on buying a pen.
- Now suppose the exchange rate **changed** to **£1 = $4** (i.e. the pound's exchange rate goes up, or the pound becomes **stronger**).
- Someone in the USA would now have to spend **$4** to pay for the same £1 pen. Remember, the pen's price in the UK **hasn't changed** at all — this **extra cost** to the person in the USA is **all** to do with the **cost** of **buying pounds**.

4) When this happens **exports go down**, **worsening** the current account on the **balance of payments**.
5) For the same reason (but in reverse), **high** UK interest rates mean **imports** from abroad become **cheaper**. Again, this **worsens** the current account.
6) And remember... imports are a **leakage** in the circular flow of income, and so more spending on imports means a **reduction** in AD.
7) When UK interest rates **fall**, the opposite happens:

- The **exchange rate** of the pound **falls**.
- UK **exports increase** (as UK goods become cheaper) and **imports decrease** (as foreign goods become more expensive).
- The **balance of payments improves**.

Remember though, this depends on the price elasticity of demand of exports and imports.

Jimmy always got excited when the decisions of the Monetary Policy Committee were about to be announced.

Monetary policy needs to look about *Two Years* into the *Future*

1) The effect of changing interest rates is **not** felt straight away — it takes time for the effects to feed through into the rest of the economy.
2) For example, reducing interest rates **won't** usually cause a **sudden surge** in investment or house buying.
   - Firms **plan** investment projects **very carefully** — it can take months or years before they increase their spending.
   - **House buying** can also take a long time — people need to **find** a suitable home, and the purchase can take a long time too. **Fixed-rate mortgage** holders won't notice the effect of an interest rate change until their fixed-rate period ends.
3) In fact, the **time lags** between changes in the Bank Rate and its effect on the economy can be very long indeed.
   - The maximum effect on **firms** is usually felt after about **one year**.
   - The maximum effect on **consumers** is usually felt after about **two years**.
4) So the Bank of England has to look up to **two years** into the future when it's making a decision about interest rates.

These are 'typical' lags — actual lags may be different.

Monetary Policy

When the economy's in a slump, lowering interest rates might not be enough to stop inflation from falling... ***All boards.***

EDEXCEL & OCR

Quantitative Easing injects *New Money* into the Economy

1) **Quantitative easing** (QE) is used when it's necessary to adopt a 'loose' monetary policy to **stimulate aggregate demand** (or create upwards pressure on **inflation**) at a time when interest rates are already very **low** (or **negative**).
2) QE **increases** the **money supply**, which will enable individuals and firms to spend more.
3) It involves the Bank of England (or another central bank) 'creating new money' and using it to **buy assets** owned by **financial institutions** and other firms. The hope is that these will then either **spend** the money or **lend** it to other people to spend.

Aggregate demand was low because the 2007 'credit crunch' meant that banks suddenly cut back the amount they were willing to lend.

4) QE was introduced in the UK in 2009. **Aggregate demand** needed to be stimulated after the **2008 recession**, but **interest rates** were already at a very **low** rate (0.5%).

Treasury bills are a form of government debt.

- The Bank of England **bought assets** (e.g. government Treasury bills) from firms such as insurance companies and commercial banks.
- However, QE was **slow to work** at first because the banks were still reluctant to lend money after the credit crunch. Instead they used it just to increase their reserves of money.
- Eventually these banks did begin to **lend** money to other firms and individuals — who used the money to, for example, invest in new machinery, start new businesses or buy houses.
- All of this spending boosted **aggregate demand** and led to an increase in the rate of **inflation** (see below).

5) Using QE to bring up the rate of inflation (rather than decreasing interest rates) has the added benefit that it will keep a **currency weak** (i.e. its exchange rate will remain low). This can increase the **competitiveness** of an economy and **boost exports**.
6) QE also provides a boost to overall **confidence** in an economy (especially during a recession), as consumers and firms see the central bank taking action.
7) One **danger** of using QE is that financial institutions may initially use this 'new money' to increase their reserves, and only **lend** it out when the **economy improves**. This **extra lending** at a time when **inflation** may already be **increasing** can lead to demand-pull inflation becoming harder to control.

Although the Bank of England could use QE 'in reverse' — i.e. sell assets to institutions to decrease the amount of money in circulation.

The Bank of England also has to consider the ***Wider Economy***

1) The **main aim** of monetary policy in the UK is to ensure **price stability** — i.e. keep **inflation** close to its **target rate**. Under normal circumstances, this would mean that during a period of **high inflation**, interest rates would **increase**.
2) But between January 2010 and March 2012, inflation was **3%** or **higher** (and so was outside the 1% limit above the 2% target), but the Bank of England **kept** interest rates at 0.5% during this entire period and **continued** its use of QE.
3) The reason is that the UK economy had suffered some '**economic shocks**', and there were concerns about the possibility of entering the second dip of a '**double dip**' recession.
4) The Bank of England reasoned that raising interest rates was **unnecessary** — it said inflation would fall **naturally** even without an interest rate rise, and that if it did increase interest rates, then a double dip recession was **more likely**.
5) Remember... as long as inflation is under control, the Bank has a duty to support the government's economic objectives. The Bank therefore continued with its very **loose monetary policy** in order not to further harm the economy.

Practice Questions

Q1 List five effects a **fall** in interest rates is likely to have on an economy.

Q2 Explain quantitative easing.

Exam Question

Q1 Outline the objectives of the Monetary Policy Committee when setting the UK's official interest rate. [4 marks]

I use quantitative easing to squeeze into my favourite jeans...

Monetary policy looks complicated, but the basic idea's fairly straightforward. Governments use it to try to achieve macroeconomic objectives, e.g. a low and stable rate of inflation. Central banks (e.g. the Bank of England) tend to be in charge of trying to control inflation. Interest rates are the main tool they use for this, but they've got other options — quantitative easing, for example.

Supply-side Policies

Supply-side policies are very popular at the moment among economists. That goes for Economics examiners too. ***All boards.***

Supply-side Policies** aim to **Increase** the economy's **Trend Growth Rate

1) The aim of supply-side policies is to **expand** the **productive potential** (i.e. long run aggregate supply) of an economy, or to increase the **trend rate** of growth, as shown in these diagrams.

Price Level
LRAS LRAS$_1$
Y Y_1
Real National Output

Real National Output
Trend growth rate increases
Time

2) Supply-side policies are about the government creating the **right conditions** to allow **market forces** to create **growth**, as opposed to the government creating growth **directly** by, for example, increasing its spending.
3) Supply-side policies involve making **structural changes** to the economy to allow its 'individual parts' to work **more efficiently** and **more productively**. For example, they might do this by helping **markets** function more efficiently, or creating **incentives** for **firms** or **individuals** to become more **productive** (or more **entrepreneurial**).

High taxes can create unhelpful disincentives to work — supply-side policies may aim to correct these.

4) Supply-side policies can be divided into **free market** and **interventionist** policies:
   - **Free market supply-side policies** aim to increase efficiency by **removing** things which **interfere** with the free market. They include tax cuts, privatisation, deregulation, and policies to increase labour market flexibility. (There's more about these policies below.)
   - **Interventionist supply-side policies** are usually aimed at **correcting market failure**. They include government spending on education (see below), subsidies for research and development, funding for improvements to infrastructure (e.g. ports that help firms to export their goods), and industrial policy (this is policy aimed at developing a particular industry or sector of the economy, e.g. through subsidies).
5) Supply-side policies can make an economy more **robust** and **flexible**.

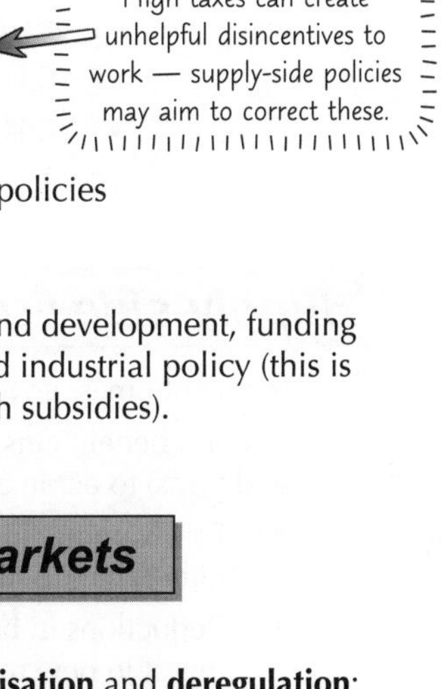

*Supply-side policies can **Increase** the **Efficiency** of various **Markets***

Here are some examples of **supply-side policies** that a government might use:

- **Encourage competition** — to increase **efficiency** in a market. For example, through **privatisation** and **deregulation**:

Many economists believe the **private sector** is more efficient and less wasteful than the **public sector**. So **privatisation** (when a firm or a whole industry changes from being run by the **public** sector to the **private** sector) is a popular supply-side policy with some economists.

Deregulation involves getting rid of rules imposed by the government ('red tape') that can restrict the level of **competition** or efficiency in a market. For example, regulations stopping private firms entering a market which contains only a state-owned monopoly could be scrapped, or governments could reduce the amount of 'red tape' and bureaucracy involved in getting planning permission. When there's more **competition** and **efficiency** in a market, **productivity** should **increase**.

There's more on this on the next page.

- **Reform taxes and benefits** — to create **incentives** for people to work hard. For example, reducing the **marginal income tax rate** (the rate you pay on the last £1 you earn) might encourage people to earn more.
- Bring in a **national minimum wage** (NMW) — this is a legal minimum hourly rate of pay:
  - A NMW means there's **greater reward** for doing a job that pays the NMW. It gives people more **incentive** to get a job rather than be unemployed.

  The UK has had a NMW since 1999.

  - A NMW can be set at the '**living wage**'. This is a wage that'll cover an individual's **basic cost of living**. Introducing a living wage may mean the government has to **pay out less** to support people on **low incomes**.
  - However, a NMW can **increase wage costs** for firms. This might mean they have to **cut jobs**, resulting in increased **unemployment**, and it could decrease the **international competitiveness** of firms. Firms may also have to **pass on** increased wage costs to consumers by **increasing prices**, and this could contribute to **inflation**.
- Improve **education and training** — this will allow employees to become more **productive**.
- Encourage **immigration** — to expand the **workforce**. This could be targeted at people with **specific skills** that are needed.
- Improve **labour market flexibility** — e.g. by increasing **labour mobility** (see page 58), or through **trade union reforms**:
  - A major supply-side policy in the UK in the 1980s was to **reduce** the **power** of **trade unions**.
  - Strong trade unions can reduce the ability of a firm to react to changing **market conditions**, e.g. by making it **harder** for firms to **lay off** workers.
  - Reducing the power of trade unions has resulted in a **more flexible** workforce. In practice, this means that **short-term**, **flexible** contracts are more common than they used to be, allowing firms to 'hire and fire' workers according to the current demands of the business.

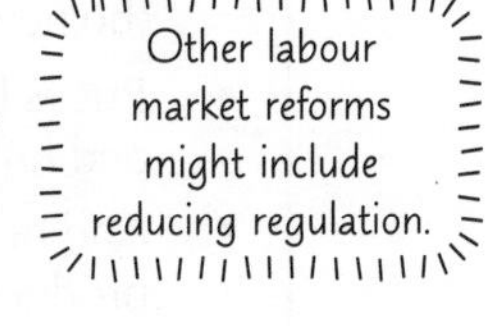

Other labour market reforms might include reducing regulation.

Supply-side Policies

Supply-side policies are good... but they have their downsides too. ***These pages are for all boards.***

Supply-side Policies can have Powerful effects

1) Supply-side policies tend to be implemented in a **microeconomic** way — they affect the way individual consumers and firms behave (e.g. a policy might encourage a firm to train its workforce differently). But usually supply-side policies, such as privatisation and increasing the competitiveness within a market, will also have a **macroeconomic** effect.
2) Improving the supply side of the economy is not just down to the government — **businesses** can take the initiative and improve things themselves by investing in **new machinery** or paying for **extra staff training**.
3) In a **free market** it's in a firm's own interests to improve its **productivity** and **competitiveness**. When firms do this, the country's economy is helped too.

- For example, supply-side improvements introduced by a firm might increase its **competitiveness** and the **quality** of its products.
- This could increase the quantity of products that the firm sells as **exports**.
- This then improves the **current account** on the balance of payments.

Supply-side fiscal policies are currently more popular than Demand-side ones

1) In recent times, governments have focused on implementing **supply-side fiscal policies** rather than **demand-side** ones.
2) Tax and benefit cuts have often been introduced to create **incentives** for **individual** economic agents (e.g. consumers and firms) to act in a way that will be good for the economy, and not to manage aggregate demand (AD).
   - For example, **income tax cuts** have been implemented to give workers an incentive to **work harder** rather than to **directly** increase people's **disposable income**.
   - Reductions in **business taxes** have aimed to provide an incentive for **entrepreneurs** to take more risks, invest in new machines and technology, and allow them to build successful, innovative companies.
   - Reductions in **welfare benefits** have aimed to increase people's incentive to **work** rather than stay on benefits.
3) If these supply-side policies are successful then **tax receipts** (i.e. the money the government gets from taxes) should go **up** rather than down. This is because:
   - **More people** are **in work** (meaning less money is spent by the government on welfare benefits).
   - People are **working** longer and harder (meaning they end up paying more income tax overall).
   - Businesses are more **successful** (meaning they have larger profits to tax).
4) So successful supply-side fiscal policies should **reduce** the size of a **budget deficit** (or **increase** the size of a **budget surplus**).

Supply-side policies involve Fewer Trade-offs between objectives

1) A problem with demand-side expansionary fiscal and monetary policies is that while they might help the **economy to grow**, there's also a **danger** of **inflation rising** as a result.
2) Supply-side policies avoid this risk — they increase the **productive potential** of the economy, causing an **increase** in growth, jobs and output.
3) Policies that increase growth, jobs and output will shift the **AD curve** and create a risk of **higher inflation** (see p.84). But successful supply-side policies, which also shift the **LRAS curve**, can avoid this.

- Initially the macroeconomic equilibrium is at **point S**.
- When the LRAS curve shifts from LRAS to $LRAS_1$ as a result of the supply-side policies, and AD increases from AD to AD_1, the new macroeconomic equilibrium is now at **point T**.
- Prices haven't increased — supply has kept up with demand and **no demand-pull inflation** has been caused.
- And because supply-side policies aim to make firms more productive and efficient, the risk of **cost-push** inflation is also low.

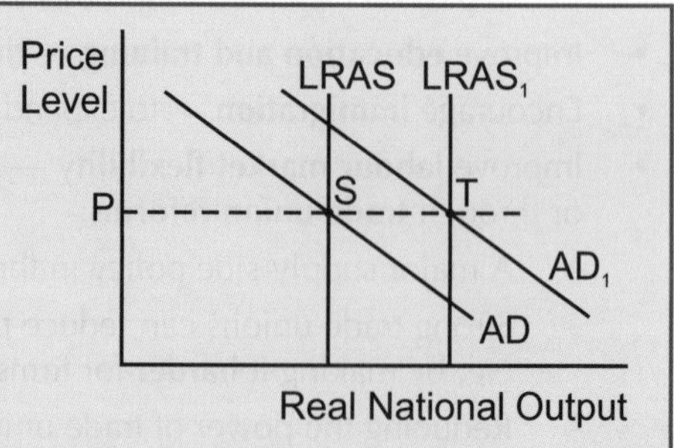

Supply-side Policies

Supply-side policies can make an economy **Less Dependent** on **Imports**

1) Supply-side policies can make an economy **less dependent** on **imports**. If an economy can provide **high-quality** goods and services at **low prices**, people are less likely to buy imports.
2) Supply-side policies that keep UK exports competitive are vital for **future growth**.
3) **Foreign export markets** are becoming more and more important for UK firms. The economies of China and India are **growing quickly** and their **demand** for high-quality goods is **increasing**.

Thanks to the newly developed shrink ray the UK's annual exports to the USA could now fit into a single container.

Supply-side policies **Won't Work** in all circumstances

1) **Supply-side** policies are aimed at improving AS, but **without** sufficient AD, supply-side policies don't work.
2) For supply-side policies to be successful, they need **demand-side** policies to support any growth.
3) For this reason some economists argue that during a **recession**, when demand is weak, supply-side policies are **not** appropriate.
4) Supply-side policies also take **time** to work. Again, in a recession, the economy might need **more immediate** help. **Demand-side** policies can have a more immediate effect in these circumstances.
5) However, **supply-side** policies do make an economy more **resilient** and better able to **cope** with shocks. For example, in a recession, it's an advantage to have a **highly-trained** and **flexible** workforce.
6) Nowadays, supply-side and demand-side policies are often used together, but to achieve different aims:
   - **Supply-side** policies create **long-term growth**,
   - **Demand-side** policies **stabilise** the economy in the **short term**.

Exporting is one way to increase AD — see above.

The credit crunch in 2008 was a major shock to many economies — this is a situation where supply-side policies alone wouldn't have been appropriate (see p.129).

Supply-side policies are **Not Perfect** in every way

1) It can take a **long time** to see the results of supply-side policies, so they **can't** be used to fix the economy **quickly**. For example, it'll take **many years** to see the effects on an economy's labour supply that occur from **improvements** in **education**.
2) There can be **unintended consequences** — e.g. the deregulation of financial markets (starting with the 'Big Bang' in 1986) led to excessive **risk-taking** in financial markets, which contributed towards the recent recession.
3) Supply-side policies can be **unpopular**, and there are also concerns about whether some are **inequitable** (i.e. **unfair**).
   - For example, **benefit cuts** can lead to the poorest people in society worrying about their ability to cope financially.
   - **Greater flexibility** in the labour market and **trade union reforms** could lead to some people having **less job security**.
4) So while a government may hope that improved economic performance will lead to **greater prosperity** overall in the **long term**, it can be very difficult in the short term to introduce some of these policies.

Inequality has increased in the UK since the early 1980s (see p.57 for more on inequality).

Practice Questions

Q1 What is privatisation?

Q2 How do successful supply-side policies shift the LRAS curve?

Q3 Why are suitable demand-side policies important if supply-side policies are to be effective?

Q4 Explain some of the possible criticisms of supply-side economic policies.

Exam Question

Q1 To what extent should government macroeconomic policy focus on supply-side policies rather than demand-side policies? [25 marks]

Supply-side policies aren't perfect — they're useless for making a lasagne...

In practice it's actually quite difficult to create increases in trend growth rate using supply-side policies. But at the moment, supply-side policies are economists' and governments' favourite tool for trying. So they're probably just going to have to try quite hard and for quite a long time, given that there are few alternatives around that are clearly better. Okay... see what you remember.

Different Approaches to Macroeconomic Policy

Government macroeconomic policy changes over time. One reason for this is that people's understanding of economics develops by seeing how successful (or unsuccessful) different policies have been in the past. ***These pages are for all boards.***

EDEXCEL ONLY

Government Intervention became *Popular* as a result of the *Great Depression*

1) The **Great Depression** was a period of **falling output**, **deflation** and **high unemployment** around the world — the depression spread from the US, where it began in **1929**, and lasted until the late 1930s.
2) As the Great Depression hit the UK, **government revenue** fell, and the cost of providing **unemployment benefits** rose. The government was expected to face an increasing **budget deficit**.
3) In the 1920s the classical economic idea that **balancing the budget** is the government's **most important economic goal** was the mainstream view. This meant that the UK government followed **deflationary** fiscal policy of cutting government spending during the Great Depression. There were major cuts to **public sector pay** and **unemployment benefits**.
4) These cuts made things **worse** — unemployment kept rising, and the economy stayed in **recession**.
5) **Monetary policy** was also **contractionary**, because of Britain's membership of the **Gold Standard**:
   - The **Gold Standard** is a system where currency can be **swapped** for a fixed amount of gold from the **central bank**, so the amount of currency in the system is fixed, depending on how much gold the central bank holds.
   - This meant that countries in the Gold Standard couldn't use **expansionary monetary policy** (see page 122) such as expanding the **money supply** or lowering **interest rates**. It also meant that **exchange rates** were effectively **fixed** (with the pound **overvalued**, so British **exports** weren't competitive).
6) The economy only began to recover when Britain left the Gold Standard in 1931, and could then lower interest rates and devalue the pound. This had an **expansionary** effect — **consumption** and **investment** increased. For example, more houses were built, which provided **jobs** and contributed to **growth**. Increasing **defence spending** (in response to the rise of Nazi Germany) also had an expansionary effect.

> The US experienced similar problems with the Gold Standard, and similar positive effects when they left in 1933.

7) Economic policies in the US during the Great Depression (under President Hoover) were **laissez-faire** — this means leaving the economy to market forces, with minimal interference by the government.
8) Taxes were generally kept low to encourage businesses to **invest more** and consumers to **spend more**. However, as **government revenue** fell during the Great Depression, taxes were increased (as in the UK) to avoid a **budget deficit**.
9) As the depression **worsened** the government was criticised for not intervening to help the **unemployed** and **poor**.
10) In 1933, **Franklin D. Roosevelt** became the new President of the USA. Roosevelt ended laissez-faire policies, and introduced the '**New Deal**' — this included **expansionary policies** which increased government spending, for example government-funded **jobs** for the unemployed and large **infrastructure projects**.
11) These projects reduced **unemployment** and **poverty**. However, unemployment began to **rise** again in the late 1930s. It eventually fell when **defence spending** during WW2 contributed to economic recovery (as it had in the UK).

Keynesian Fiscal Policy was *Widely Used* in the *Mid 20th Century*

1) The experience of the Great Depression contributed to rising interest in the work of **Keynes**, which argued that **government spending** could boost an economy during recession and get it back on track.
2) **Keynesian** demand management policies of adjusting **government spending** to control **economic growth** (see page 118) were popular in the middle of the 20th century — in the UK the government focused on **full employment**, and adjusted **taxation** and **spending** to influence demand and try and smooth out the **economic cycle**.
3) There was **steady growth** and near **full employment** in the UK in the 1950s and 1960s, as well as fairly **low and stable inflation**. There were boom and bust cycles, but the downturns were fairly weak.

> This relies on the multiplier effect (page 79) to create an increase in national income that's bigger than the government spending.

The government's approach to fiscal policy has Changed

Governments now generally use fiscal policy **differently** to the Keynesian approach:

Supply-side fiscal policy is used to increase **aggregate supply**, which will help a government to achieve all four of its main economic objectives (unlike demand-side fiscal policy). See page 126 for more on this.

Government spending can be directed at **specific regions** that need extra help. For example, if a region loses a big employer and is suffering from **structural unemployment**, then the government could **invest** in that region to **create jobs**, or encourage **firms** to move there with **subsidies** and **tax breaks**.

Different Approaches to Macroeconomic Policy

Fiscal policy is used on a **microeconomic** level to influence the behaviour of **consumers** and **firms**. For example, **demerit goods** are **taxed** to decrease consumption, and **merit goods** can be provided by the state or **subsidised** to increase their consumption. Fiscal policy can also be used to help governments achieve their **environmental policy objectives**. For example, the government could introduce '**green taxes**' that discourage the use of coal or oil, or provide **subsidies** to firms that use renewable energy (e.g. solar or wind power).

Progressive taxation allows the government to **redistribute** wealth from those who are **better off** to those who are **less well off** (for more see p.119).

But Keynesian fiscal policy was used during the 2008-2010 recession (see below).

There are a **few reasons** why demand-side fiscal policy became **less popular**:

- The government spending **multiplier effect** is **small** — partly because government spending is **paid for** by **taxes**, so **increases** in **government spending** may be **matched** by **increases** in **taxes** (a withdrawal from the circular flow).
- **Continuous** government spending, paid for by **borrowing**, will lead to **inflation**, a **budget deficit** and an **increase** in **national debt** (see p.120).
- Policies that **only** affect aggregate demand will lead to **conflicts** between **macroeconomic objectives** (see p.107-109).

EDEXCEL ONLY

Inflationary Policy was used in the UK and the US after the 2008 Financial Crisis

1) Fiscal policy has generally moved away from the **Keynesian** demand-side approach since the 1970s. But during the recession which followed the **2008 financial crisis** the UK government brought in policies aimed at stimulating the economy which used a more Keynesian approach. Inflationary **fiscal policies** were used, such as:
   - A temporary **cut to VAT** from 17.5% to 15%, aimed at increasing consumer spending.
   - Bringing forward planned **capital expenditure** (see p.118), to raise national income during the downturn.
2) Expansionary **monetary policy** was also used — the **base rate** was lowered to 0.5%. As this wasn't considered enough to boost demand, other monetary policies such as **quantitative easing** were also followed (see page 124 for more).
3) This approach was influenced in part by the lesson of the **Great Depression**, where deflationary fiscal policy aimed at balancing the budget and an inability to use expansionary monetary policy had made the problem **worse** (see page 128).
4) Another contrast between the Great Depression and the 2008 financial crisis was the reaction to **bank failures**. During the Great Depression banks were allowed to **collapse**, which reduced the **money supply**, **damaged the economy** further, and caused **widespread panic** as people feared losing their savings. During the 2008 financial crisis the UK government used **public money** to take over several major banks and prevent them from failing. The US government followed a similar policy.
5) The post 2008 recession ended up being much **less severe** than the Great Depression, possibly because of these policies. However, the combined effect of the **crisis** and the **expansionary policies** resulted in the government running a large **budget deficit**, and **national debt** levels increased sharply.
6) After the worst of the crisis had passed, the government brought in **tax increases** to begin to deal with this, and after the change of government in 2010 policy became particularly focused on reducing the **budget deficit**. Deflationary fiscal policy was brought in, mostly in the form of **spending cuts**. There was also a **VAT increase** from 17.5% to 20%.
7) GDP growth per capita **fell** in the UK from 2010 to 2012. The Office for Budget Responsibility has stated that deflationary fiscal policy **reduced growth** in this period, but that other factors such as rising **oil prices** also contributed to falling GDP.
8) In the US, the initial response to the financial crisis was very similar — **interest rates** were lowered and **quantitative easing** was used. There was also a programme of **government funding** of banks and **investment** in the motor industry.
9) However, these inflationary measures have been phased out more **slowly** in the US than they were in the UK. Some economists think that this is one reason why the **recovery** from the financial crisis was **faster** in the US than in the UK. But there may have been **other factors** which contributed to this — the UK is more heavily affected by economic problems in the **EU** than the US. Also, **oil prices** increased much more in the UK than the US, which affected household income.

Practice Questions

Q1 Why has demand-side fiscal policy become less popular?

Exam Question

Q1 Briefly discuss differences in the UK policy responses to the Great Depression and the 2008 Financial Crisis. [6 marks]

I'm having a financial crisis — choosing a new wallet is pretty tough...

So, demand-side fiscal policy had gone out of fashion before the financial crisis, but recently it's had a bit of a comeback. Supply-side policy is still pretty popular too though — there's more about how the two are used together on page 127.

Get Marks in Your Exam

These pages explain how you'll get marks in the exams. To do well you need to satisfy four different Assessment Objectives (AO1, AO2, AO3 and AO4), each of which requires different skills. Prove you've got the skills and you'll get the marks.

Make Sure You Read the Question Properly

It's easy to **misread** a question and spend 10 minutes writing about the **wrong thing**. A few simple tips can help you avoid this:

1) **Underline** the **command words** in the question (the ones that tell you **what to do**). Here are some common ones:
   - **Calculate** — you'll need to do some **maths** to find the **value** you're asked for (pretty obvious really).
   - **Explain** — you should write about **why** it's like that (i.e. give reasons). You might also need to do some **analysis** (see below).
   - **Assess, evaluate, discuss** — these words basically mean the same thing. You'll need to write about the **advantages** and **disadvantages** OR the **arguments for** and **against**. You'll then need to give your **opinion** on which side is **stronger**, and **back this up** with reasons why.
2) **Underline** the **key words** (the ones that tell you **what it's about**), e.g. productivity, sustainability, market failure.
3) **Re-read** the question and your answer **when you've finished** to check that your answer addresses **all parts** of the question. A **common mistake** is to **miss a bit out** — like when questions say 'refer to the data from...' or 'illustrate your answer with...'.

There are Four Assessment Objectives the questions will cover

These are the **assessment objectives** you'll be marked on in your exams:

AO1 marks are for **content** and **knowledge**.
- This means things like knowing the **proper definitions** for **economics terms**.
- **Most** questions will include **at least one** AO1 mark. It's always good to give a **definition** of the key term(s) from the question, or to give the **formula(s)** if you're doing a calculation, to make sure you get your AO1 marks.

AO2 marks are for **application**.
- This means **applying** your knowledge to a situation. Again, **most** questions will include AO2 marks.
- Use your knowledge to **explain** your answer and give **reasons**. You'll need to **apply** your **own ideas** and your **economic knowledge** to show **why** you think something has happened or will happen.

AO3 marks are for **analysis**.
- This means thinking about benefits, costs, causes, effects and constraints.
- If there's **disagreement** about something (e.g. whether a particular policy is good or bad for economic growth), then consider **both sides** of the argument — you'll only get **limited** analysis marks by looking at **one side**.
- If there's data, say what the figures **mean**, talk about what might have **caused** them and say what **effect** you think they will have on the economy in the **future**.

AO4 marks are for **evaluation**.
- This means using your **judgement**. Questions with AO4 marks will **always** have AO3 marks too — you'll have to **weigh up** both sides of the argument **before** using your judgement.
- You need to give a **balanced** answer, so talk about the **different viewpoints** on the subject (i.e. consider the **advantages** and **disadvantages**).
- It's good to say which **side** of the argument you think is **strongest**, but you **don't need** to give a **definite** answer. You can point out that it **depends** on various factors — as long as you say **what those factors** are, and say **why** the issue depends on them. Use your judgement to say what the **most important factors** are. The main thing is to **justify** why you're saying what you're saying.

1) The **command words** can give you a bit of a clue about **which** assessment objectives the question includes:
   - '**Define**' or '**state**' questions will **only** have AO1 marks.
   - '**Explain**' questions **won't** require you to evaluate (AO4), but **could** involve all the other objectives (see below).
   - '**Evaluate**', '**discuss**' and '**assess**' questions will have marks for **each** of the four assessment objectives.
2) You should **always** look at the **number of marks** a question is worth — this gives you a **good indication** of how much you need to write. For example:
   - If you're asked to **explain** something and the question is worth **3 marks**, you **won't** need to write very much to earn all the marks — there'll probably only be **AO1** and **AO2** marks.
   - If you're asked to **explain** something and the question is worth **10 marks**, you'll need to write **more** — there'll almost certainly be some **AO3** marks too, so you'll have to include some **analysis** in your answer.

Get Marks in Your Exam

It's **Important** that you make your answers **Clear**

Some of the following might sound **pretty obvious** — but you'd be surprised how **easy** it is to panic in an exam and focus **too much** on getting all the facts down, and **not enough** on making your answer clear and understandable:

- It's really **important** that your answers are **clear** and **well-written**, particularly in **extended** answer questions (i.e. questions worth 9 or more marks).
- Try to write **formally** and **arrange relevant information clearly** — write a **well-structured** 'essay', not a list of bullet points.
- You should use **specialist vocabulary** when it's appropriate — it's well worth **learning** some of the **technical terms** used in this book.
- Try to write **neatly** enough for the examiner to be able to read your answer.
- **Spelling**, **grammar** and **punctuation** are important too — using them correctly will help you to make your answers **crystal clear**.
- If your handwriting, grammar, spelling and punctuation are **so** far up the spout that the examiner **can't understand** what you've written, **expect problems**.

Impressive... but it won't get you any marks.

Jotting down a quick 'essay' plan will help you to structure your essay-style answers.

If you're taking the **OCR** exams, there are **specific** questions that assess the **quality** of your extended responses — these are marked with an **asterisk** (*). For these questions, you **must** write your answers clearly as described above — you **won't** be able to get full marks for them if you don't.

Data-response questions will ask you to refer to extracts given in the exam. These could be tables of data, or pieces of text.

Use the **Data** for **Data-Response Questions**

Again, that sounds pretty obvious, but there are some things you need to bear in mind:

1) If a question asks you to **refer** to a table of data, a graph, or some text, make sure you **use** it in your answer.
2) **Don't** just copy out loads of data — any data you use in your answer must be **relevant** to the specific point you're making.
3) If a data-response question asks you to 'explain', you'll need to use the data as well as your **economic knowledge** to **back up** the points you make.
4) You'll need to show that you **understand** the information, and you might need to **analyse** and **evaluate** it.
5) If you need to draw a diagram, do it in **pencil** so you can rub it out if you make a mistake. However, label your diagrams in **pen** so they're nice and clear.
6) Sometimes you might need to do a **calculation**. You can use a calculator to find the answer, but **write down** your **working out**. If you get the answer **wrong** you can still **pick up marks** for using the correct method.
7) '**Quantitative skills**' questions (i.e. questions involving some **maths**) will make up at least **15%** of the marks in your exams. Don't worry though — a lot of these marks are just for **reading** tables or graphs and **using** the data in your answers.

Don't forget to include **All** the **Skills** in **Extended Answer Questions**

1) Longer essay-style questions need a bit of **planning**. Jot down a **rough outline** of what you want to say — remember, you need to make your answer **balanced**, so make a list of the **advantages** and **disadvantages**, or the arguments **for** and **against**.
2) **Diagrams** are a quick and easy way of explaining quite difficult concepts in your answers, but make sure you **explain** what your diagrams show and **always** refer to them in your answers. **Label** your diagrams properly so they're clear.
3) In an essay answer you need to show **all** the skills — **don't jump** straight to the **evaluation** part. So, if you're asked to evaluate the extent to which lowering the price of exports can bring about the recovery of the UK economy, you need to:
   - **Define** what is meant by exports and recovery (this will get you your **AO1** marks).
   - Explain how an increase in exports is **relevant** to the recovery of the UK economy (for **AO2** marks).
   - Give the **advantages** and **disadvantages** of lowering the price of exports (for **AO3** marks).
   - Finally, for the **AO4** marks, **weigh up** both sides of the argument and **decide** how successful, in your opinion, lowering the price of exports would be in helping the UK economy to recover.

Learn this stuff for some inflation of marks...

Of course, to do well in the exam, you've got to know all that economics stuff inside out — but these pages will give you an idea of how you can put that knowledge to best use in the exam. Keep in mind that you don't just need to learn the facts — you've got to prove to the examiner that you understand them and can apply them to various scenarios. So all very simple, really...

What to Expect in the Exams

It'll be handy if you're familiar with how the exams are structured for your exam board, and the types of question you might face. All exam boards use multiple-choice questions, so make sure you have a look at the last section on this page.

AS Economics is divided into Two Exams

1) Whichever exam board you're doing, you'll sit **two exams** for AS Economics. You'll have **1 hour 30 minutes** for each exam.
2) Paper 1 will be on **microeconomics** and paper 2 will be on **macroeconomics**.
3) Each **exam board** has a slightly different format for the papers:

AQA

- Each paper is worth a total of **70 marks**, so you should aim to pick up a mark every **minute or so**.
- For both papers:
  - **Section A** is made up of **twenty multiple-choice** questions worth **1 mark** each.
  - **Section B** is worth **50 marks**. You'll have to **choose one** of **two** contexts to answer a series of **data-response** questions on — these questions will be based on some **extracts** of information that you'll be given in the exam. Some questions will be **short** answer and some will need **extended** answers, and there'll be one **25 mark, essay-style** question at the end.

EDEXCEL

- Each paper is worth a total of **80 marks**, so you should aim to pick up a mark every **minute or so**.
- For both papers:
  - **Section A** is made up of a mixture of **short** answer and **multiple-choice** questions, worth a total of **20 marks**.
  - **Section B** is worth **60 marks**. You'll be given a series of **data-response** questions based on some **extracts** of information — these will range from **short** answer to **extended** answer questions, including **one** from a **choice** of two **20 mark, essay-style** questions.

OCR

- Each paper is worth a total of **60 marks**, so you should aim to pick up a mark every **minute and a half**.
- For both papers:
  - **Section A** is made up of **fifteen multiple-choice** questions worth **1 mark** each.
  - **Section B** is worth **25 marks**. You'll be given some **extracts** of information and will need to answer a series of **data-response** questions. There'll be **one extended** answer question, and the rest of the questions will be **short** answer.
  - **Section C** gives a choice of two **20 mark, essay-style** questions — you just need to answer **one**.

Here's an example Multiple-Choice Question and Answer

For **multiple-choice** questions, you'll have to indicate the **correct answer**:

1 The diagram shows the competitive market for oil.
If the price of oil is set at P_1, then

A there will be a surplus of Q_e to Q_2
B demand will decrease from Q_e to Q_1
C the quantity demanded will be Q_2
D the quantity supplied will stay the same.

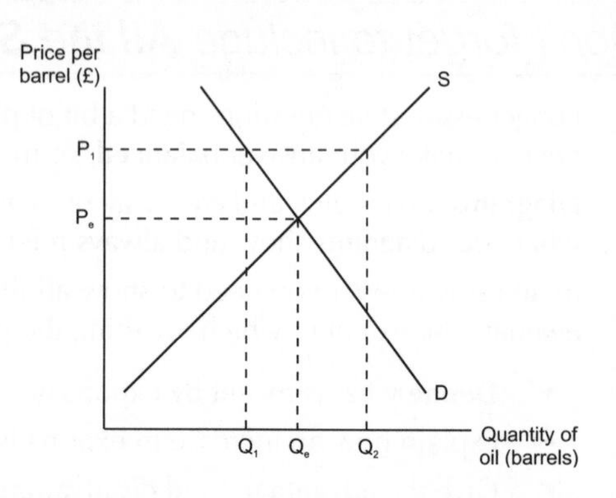

Answer 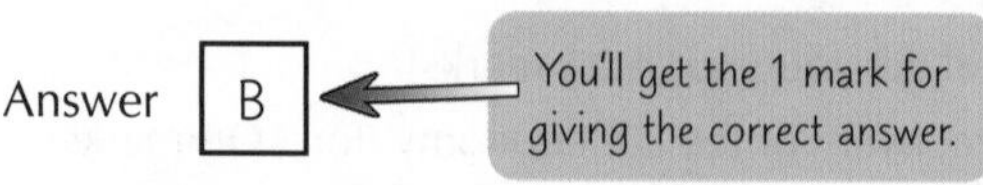

1 mark

To answer multiple-choice questions, go through each option **one by one**. You should be able to spot the **correct** answer, but it can help to **rule out** answers you **know** aren't right too — e.g. for the question above, you might think:

Option A is incorrect because the surplus supplied by the market at the new price is Q_1 to Q_2. When the price is increased and set at P_1 the quantity demanded decreases to Q_1, and the quantity suppliers are prepared to supply changes to Q_2 — so B is the correct answer and options C and D are incorrect.

Sample Questions and Worked Answers

You've seen an example multiple-choice question already — but there are loads of types of questions you could get in the exams.

The **Next Three Pages** give some **Example Questions** and **Answers**

1) These three pages **don't** cover **all** the question types that might come up in your exams — just a small selection.
2) There are **five** sample questions with worked answers. Each example includes **notes** on the answer, pointing out **good** features and areas for **improvement**, and an **explanation** of the number of marks that answer would earn.
3) **Don't** just read what's here — where the example answer **wouldn't** earn full marks, it's a good idea to try to write your own **improved answers**.

Here are some example **Data-Response Questions** and **Answers**

Extract A: Consumer Price Index (CPI) inflation in Brazil 2007-2014.

Year	2007	2008	2009	2010	2011	2012	2013	2014
Inflation (%)	3.6	5.7	4.9	5.0	6.6	5.4	6.2	6.3

Extract B: Inflation and Economic Growth in Brazil.

Brazil's inflation target is 4.5%, with an allowance of 2 percentage points either side. Despite a general trend of rising inflation in recent years, Brazil generally managed to stay within this band until the end of 2014. However, inflation started to rise sharply again at the start of 2015.

Brazil's growth rate has generally been falling since 2007, when GDP growth was 6%. In 2014 GDP growth fell to 0.1%.

2 With reference to **Extract A**, explain what happened to inflation in Brazil between 2007 and 2014. 4 marks

Inflation is the sustained rise in the average price of goods and services over a period of time. Overall, inflation rose in Brazil between 2007 and 2014, from 3.6% to 6.3%. There were some years in this period where inflation fell, but each time this happened inflation rose again the following year. For example, inflation fell from 5.7% in 2008 to 4.9% in 2009, but rose again to 5.0% in 2010.

Defining the main term(s) given in the question will often earn you a mark or two.

If a question asks you to refer to an extract of some data, then make sure you use the data in your answer.

This answer would receive all 4 marks. It gives a definition of inflation, then accurately explains what happened to inflation in Brazil with reference to the given data.

3 With reference to **Extract B**, explain why trying to reduce inflation in Brazil could cause further problems for the country's growth. 5 marks

Low inflation and economic growth are conflicting policy objectives. Rapid growth often leads to high, undesirable levels of inflation, and maintaining low inflation can restrict growth. For example, the Brazilian government could use monetary policy to try to restrict inflation by raising interest rates to encourage saving and discourage spending. However, a reduction in spending is likely to further restrict and harm economic growth, which had already fallen to 0.1% in 2014.

The first sentence here isn't a definition, but it's a key bit of economic knowledge that's relevant to the question and answer.

This answer could get 4 marks. The economic knowledge and analysis are good, but it only refers to extract B at the very end. It's important to use the data you're given to back up your answer in a question like this one — referring to the data more would improve the answer.

Sample Questions and Worked Answers

An example question using a Diagram

Extract A: Drought causes severe shortage of wheat

Two consecutive dry winters have led to a severe shortage of British wheat. Reservoir levels in the south of England have fallen to an all-time low and the government has enforced strict restrictions on the amount of water farmers can use for their land. As a result, the recent wheat harvests have been very poor and there is a serious decline in the supply of British wheat. The fall in the supply of wheat has forced many thrifty shoppers to switch to buying non-wheat-based products as they search for better deals. If this continues then many farmers could be put out of business.

4 Draw a demand and supply diagram to show how the market for British wheat might be affected by the recent droughts. 4 marks

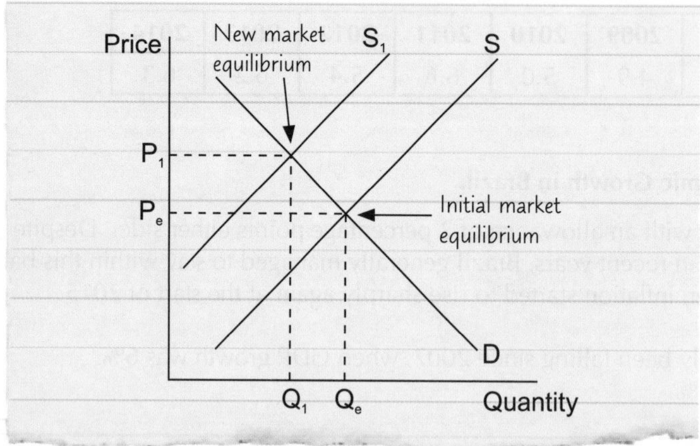

This answer would get all 4 marks — the diagram is accurate and correctly labelled. You can get all 4 marks without giving any further explanation.

Here's an example Calculation Question and Answer

This question is like the data-response ones (including a calculation) that you might get in your exams.

Extract A: Average hourly wage for full-time employees in the UK in 1986 and 2011 and the % change in this period (1986-2011).

Full-time employees		Hourly wage (£)*		Percentage change (%)
		1986	2011	
Lowest earners	Bottom 1% earn less than	3.48	5.93	+ 70
	Bottom 10% earn less than	4.80	7.01	+ 46
Average		7.78	12.62	?
Highest earners	Top 10% earn more than	14.78	26.75	+ 81
	Top 1% earn more than	28.18	61.10	+ 117

*1986 wages converted to 2011 prices

5 Using **Extract A**, calculate to the nearest whole number the percentage change in the average wage of a full-time employee between 1986 and 2011.

2 marks

Answer:

$$\text{Percentage change} = \frac{12.62 - 7.78}{7.78} \times 100 = \frac{4.84}{7.78} \times 100 = 62\%$$

This answer would get both marks. You'd get both marks just for the correct answer, but it's important to show your working — if your final answer was wrong but your working was correct, you could still earn 1 mark.

Sample Questions and Worked Answers

*An example **Essay-Style Question** and **Answer** to give you some tips*

6 Evaluate the effectiveness of the use of government fiscal policy to achieve the main macroeconomic objectives. 20 marks

The four main macroeconomic objectives of governments are strong economic growth, low and stable inflation, reducing unemployment, and equilibrium in the balance of payments.

Fiscal policy is one tool governments can use to try and achieve these objectives. Fiscal policy involves government spending and taxation and can be used to influence the economy as a whole. Traditionally it has been used to influence aggregate demand. This is known as demand-side fiscal policy. During a slump a government may use reflationary fiscal policy to boost aggregate demand. This will involve increasing government spending, or lowering taxes. During a boom they may use deflationary fiscal policy to reduce aggregate demand, which will involve reducing government spending, or increasing taxes.

In the short run, using reflationary fiscal policy to increase aggregate demand, e.g. during a recession, will increase GDP. This increase will be greater than the size of the injection of government spending because of the multiplier effect, so this can be effective at achieving the objective of economic growth. The derived demand for labour will also increase, so reflationary fiscal policy can also be effective at achieving the objective of reducing unemployment.

However, in the long run, increasing aggregate demand without increasing aggregate supply cannot create growth or reduce unemployment, as the economy is already running at full capacity. So reflationary fiscal policy is only effective at achieving these two objectives in the short run.

Demand-side reflationary fiscal policy is unlikely to be effective at achieving the other two macroeconomic objectives either in the long or the short run, as increasing aggregate demand will cause demand-pull inflation. This means that using reflationary fiscal policy may prevent governments from achieving their objective of low and stable inflation. It's also likely to worsen, or cause, a deficit in the current account of the balance of payments. Inflation will reduce exports, as goods will become less competitive internationally. Imports may well increase too, as it'll become cheaper for consumers and firms to buy imports instead of domestically-produced products.

To achieve all four macroeconomic objectives at the same time a government will need to increase aggregate supply. If they can achieve this then economic growth and reductions in unemployment will be long term, as the economy will reach a new macroeconomic equilibrium at a higher level of output and lower unemployment. Demand-pull inflation should also be avoided, so inflation should stay low. In fact, prices tend to fall when aggregate supply increases, so the balance of payments should also improve as exports will become more competitive.

Increasing aggregate supply can be achieved by using supply-side policies, some of which are supply-side fiscal policies. In contrast to reflationary fiscal policy, supply-side fiscal policies often involve tax cuts, which create an incentive for firms and individuals to work harder and be more entrepreneurial. This approach may also involve cuts to government spending, for example on welfare benefits, to encourage people to work and therefore increase the supply of labour.

On the other hand, supply-side fiscal policies can include government spending on things like infrastructure investment, education and training, and subsidies for research and development. This sort of spending should help to create the conditions which allow the economy to grow.

In conclusion, fiscal policy can be effective at achieving all four of the government's economic objectives, but only if the tax and spending decisions are focused on increasing aggregate supply, which supports long-term growth. In the short term, demand-side fiscal policy is unlikely to achieve all of the four objectives, and in the long term it is unlikely to achieve any of them.

It's usually a good idea to start your answer with a definition or explanation of the key term(s) in the question.

This shows a solid understanding of the basics of fiscal policy.

You could use diagrams to support this answer — e.g. you could include a diagram to show the effect of increasing AD without increasing AS.

It's really important to balance your answer — so explaining the downside of demand-side reflationary fiscal policy is a good idea.

Some evaluation of how effective tax cuts and reductions in welfare benefits are likely to be at increasing aggregate supply would be useful here.

Concluding your answer is really important in essay-style evaluation questions. It's your chance to sum up what you think.

This answer could get around 15 marks. There's lots of information here, so it'd score well for knowledge and application. It could provide a bit more analysis and evaluation though. For example, the answer would be improved with some explanation of why supply-side policies aren't always effective. It could talk about the need for demand-side policies alongside supply-side policies, and mention that during a recession when demand is weak, supply-side policies may not be the best way of helping with the problem. Including a relevant diagram will always help you to grab some marks in this type of question — as long as you refer to it properly in your answer.

Answers

Section One — The Economic Problem

Page 7 — The Economic Problem

1 Maximum of 6 marks available. HINTS:
- Pick three factors of production that would be necessary for someone opening a new restaurant, and explain why each is important.
- E.g. 'Labour will be important, since a new restaurant will need people to carry out all the various tasks involved, such as cooking food, serving customers, managing the accounts, and so on.'

Page 9 — Production Possibility Frontiers

1 Maximum of 1 mark available. HINTS:
- The answer is B.
- W, Y and Z all show combinations that can be made using existing resources, since they all lie inside or on the PPF.
- But X lies outside the PPF, so this combination cannot be made using existing resources.

2 Maximum of 5 marks available. HINTS:
- Start by defining the term opportunity cost, e.g. 'the next best alternative that you give up in making a particular decision'.
- Then explain that only combinations of cars and butter shown by points inside or on the production possibility frontier (PPF) can be made using the existing resources.
- Now you need to show an opportunity cost on this diagram. E.g. 'Suppose the combination of goods shown by point Y is currently being produced (20 000 cars and 9000 tonnes of butter), but it was then decided that more butter was needed. This could only be achieved by producing fewer cars. For example, if production were shifted to point Z, then this would mean 11 300 tonnes of butter would be produced, but with current resources only 10 000 cars could be produced. So the opportunity cost of producing an extra 2300 tonnes of butter is the lost production of 10 000 cars.'

Page 11 — Markets and Economies

1 Maximum of 5 marks available. HINTS:
- Start by explaining what a command economy is, e.g. 'A command economy is where the government decides how resources should be allocated, rather than leaving it to the market.'
- Then you need to give reasons why a command economy could lead to a lack of efficiency, e.g. 'Because government-owned firms don't need to make a profit, they have no incentive to try to reduce inefficiency by, for example, improving their production methods to make them more efficient. This means that command economies as a whole lack efficiency because they're made up of inefficient firms.'
- You could also mention that there might be a lack of efficiency because all economic decisions need to be made by the government and this can be slow.
- You don't need to write too much — there are only 5 marks for this question.

Page 13 — Economic Objectives and Rationality

1 Maximum of 2 marks available. HINTS:
- Start by stating what is traditionally assumed to be the main objective of a consumer, e.g. 'to maximise their utility while not spending more than their income'.
- Then you need to go on to briefly explain what 'utility' is, e.g. 'Utility is about increasing well-being. Different people will have different ways of maximising utility. For example, some people might choose to spend their money on antique furniture, while others will spend it on the latest electronics.'

Section Two — Competitive Markets

Page 15 — Demand

1 Maximum of 8 marks available. HINTS:
- Start by stating that the demand for tiles is a derived demand.
- Then explain what is likely to happen to the demand for tiles — 'The demand for tiles is likely to decrease in line with the falling demand for houses.'
- To maximise your marks you need to provide more detail. So here you could say that if the housing market is in decline there would be less demand for tiles because fewer new houses would be built — so fewer tiles are needed. You could also say that there will always be some demand for tiles even when the housing market is slow (due to people redecorating and refurbishing etc.), but the fact that tile retailers are cutting back expansion plans suggests they have seen a drop-off in demand for tiles.

2 Maximum of 4 marks available. HINTS:
- Define what's meant by complementary goods, e.g. 'Complementary goods are goods that are often used together, so they are in joint demand. When demand rises for one good, then demand will also rise for the other good.'
- State what is likely to happen to the demand for crackers — 'The demand for crackers is likely to decline if the demand for cheese falls due to a price increase.'
- For full marks you could mention any complicating factors — e.g. you could say that people also buy crackers without cheese, so an increase in cheese prices may not have a dramatic impact on cracker sales.

Page 17 — Price, Income and Cross Elasticities of Demand

1 Maximum of 1 mark available. HINTS:
- The correct answer is B.
- This question is a case of calculating PED using the numbers you've been given. As it's a calculation there's only one correct answer.
- percentage change in demand $= \frac{200}{200} \times 100 = 100\%$

  percentage change in price $= \frac{-1.5}{3} \times 100 = -50\%$

  $\text{PED} = \frac{100}{-50} = -2.0$

Page 19 — Uses of Elasticities of Demand

1 Maximum of 6 marks available. HINTS:
- Start by explaining what price elasticity of demand (PED) is, and what different values for PED mean for a business — e.g. 'Price elasticity of demand shows how the quantity demanded of a product responds to a change in its price. A value greater than 1 (ignoring minus signs) signifies elastic demand — i.e. that a change in price will cause a proportionally larger change in the quantity demanded, while a value between 0 and 1 signifies inelastic demand — i.e. that a change in price will cause a proportionally smaller change in the quantity demanded.'
- Then you should explain how the firm can use this knowledge to maximise revenue — e.g. 'The firm should set the price at the level where PED = 1. If it were to set the price at a level where PED > 1, then a reduction in price would lead to a proportionally larger increase in sales, which would lead to an increase in revenue. If it were to set the price at a level where PED < 1, then an increase in price would lead to a proportionally smaller decrease in sales, which would also lead to an increase in revenue.'

Answers

Page 21 — Supply

1 Maximum of 1 mark available. HINTS:
- The correct answer is A.
- A cut in the price causes a movement down the curve. The other options are incorrect because they would all cause the supply curve to shift (as they cause an increase or decrease in the amount of the product supplied at every price).

2 Maximum of 1 mark available. HINTS:
- The correct answer is C.
- You need to work out which option would cause the supply curve to shift to the right. This is C because increased production speed results in increased output, which increases supply (and causes the supply curve to shift to the right). Options A, B and D all result in a decrease in supply and shift the supply curve to the left.

Page 23 — Price Elasticity of Supply

1 Maximum of 4 marks available. HINTS:
- There are several possible answers for this question.
- In general supply is more inelastic in the short run as at least one factor of production will be fixed (e.g. it takes time to expand banana plantations to allow for an increase in supply).
- More specific reasons include that bananas are perishable, so can't be stored for long, and take time to grow — both of which mean that suppliers can't respond that quickly to a change in price.
- Make sure you give two clear reasons for this question to get the marks.

2 Maximum of 4 marks available. HINTS:
- Your answer to this question is likely to focus on the fact that the firm employs 'highly skilled' workers to create hand-made furniture.
- For example, the firm may find it difficult to expand its workforce as it needs to find highly skilled workers and/or take time to train new unskilled staff.
- You could also mention that the furniture produced by the firm is likely to take a long time to make, which limits the ability of the firm to increase supply in the short run.

Page 25 — Market Equilibrium

1 Maximum of 1 mark available. HINTS:
- The correct answer is D.
- The equilibrium point moves when the demand curve shifts.
  A is incorrect as the equilibrium is where the demand and supply curves meet.
  B is incorrect as a fall in supply causes the supply curve to shift and the equilibrium point to move. C is incorrect because it is supply and demand which determine the equilibrium point, not the other way round.

Page 26 — Price and the Allocation of Resources

1 Maximum of 4 marks available. HINTS:
- Start by explaining what the price mechanism is — 'when a change in the supply or demand for a good/service leads to a change in its price, which in turn leads to a change in the quantity bought/sold, until supply is equal to demand'.
- Then talk about how price can act as an incentive — e.g. 'higher prices are attractive to firms because they can mean higher profits for the firm — this encourages firms to increase production/supply'.

Page 29 — Subsidies and Indirect Taxes

1 Maximum of 1 mark available. HINTS:
- The correct answer is D.
- EFJK shows the area above the market price of the good if there was no subsidy. A, B and C are incorrect — A is the total cost of the subsidy, B is not part of the subsidy and C is the consumer gain from the subsidy.

2 Maximum of 6 marks available. HINTS:
- For this question it's a good idea to draw a diagram to show what happens when a tax is put on a product.
- Draw a diagram that shows how a tax shifts the supply curve to the left.
- Explain what the diagram shows — i.e. the price of the product increasing above the free market equilibrium price and the quantity demanded/supplied of the product falling.

Page 31 — Demand and Supply — Agriculture

1 Maximum of 5 marks available. HINTS:
- You should include a diagram similar to this one:

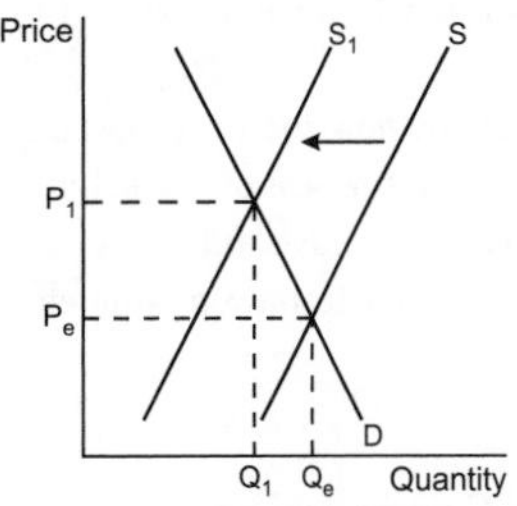

- Explain the likely effect of a bad harvest of rice on the supply of rice, e.g. 'A poor harvest of rice is likely to cause a reduction in the supply of rice and therefore shift its supply curve to the left.'
- You'll then need to explain the effect this is likely to have on the global price — e.g. 'A shift of the supply curve to the left will cause a large increase in the global price of rice, from P_e to P_1. The quantity demanded will fall from Q_e to Q_1.'

Page 33 — Demand and Supply — Oil

1 Maximum of 12 marks available. HINTS:
- Explain the influence of a subsidy on price and demand for biofuels — e.g. it lowers the price of biofuel and increases demand for it.
- Draw a diagram showing how a subsidy on biofuels would shift the supply curve to the right.
- Explain what the diagram shows — i.e. the price of the product decreasing below the free market equilibrium price and the quantity demanded/supplied of the product increasing.
- Biofuels are a substitute for oil-based fuels, so explain how a reduction in the price of biofuel could affect the demand for oil (i.e. decrease it).
- Discuss other factors that could affect demand for biofuels and crude oil — e.g. 'If it is cheap and easy to switch to biofuels, demand for biofuels could increase hugely. However, issues like expensive switching, difficulties in use, or limited uses could limit an increase in demand.'

Answers

Page 35 — Demand and Supply — Transport

1 Maximum of 10 marks available. HINTS:
- For this question you can discuss a variety of different factors that can have an impact on housing prices in different areas.
- The supply of houses in an area impacts prices — large supply leads to lower prices. Supply depends on factors such as costs and availability of land, materials and construction workers.
- Government regulations — incentive schemes to build in a certain area may lead to a large supply of houses to buy and cause house prices to be lower than other areas without such schemes.
- Levels of employment play a role — in areas with high levels of unemployment house prices will be lower due to lower levels of demand.
- Desirability of an area — in a fashionable part of the country with nearby amenities and good transport links, house prices may be higher.
- Availability of cheap rental properties — this may reduce demand for houses to buy and therefore reduce average house prices.

2 Maximum of 4 marks available. HINTS:
- Start by explaining broadly what the effect of higher fuel prices will be — e.g. 'higher fuel prices would lead to a fall in demand for car usage'.
- You then need to include details about how the price elasticity of demand for car travel would determine the size of the fall in demand — e.g. 'The price elasticity of demand for travelling by car is low, so changes in the cost of driving are unlikely to have a large effect on demand.'

Section Three — Business Economics

Page 39 — The Costs of a Firm

1 Maximum of 1 mark available. HINTS:
- The correct answer is B.
- The marginal cost is the additional cost of producing one more unit of output, so it only depends on variable costs. Because Firm X and Firm Y have the same variable costs, they must also have the same marginal cost.
- The firms have the same variable costs but different fixed costs, so they must also have different total costs and average costs. This lets you rule out options A, C and D.

2 Maximum of 2 marks available. HINTS:
- To work out the average cost you need to use the formula $AC = TC \div Q$.
  So for this question AC = £1421 ÷ 50 = £28.42

Page 41 — Economies and Diseconomies of Scale

1 Maximum of 5 marks available. HINTS:
- State that what's being described in the question is a firm encountering 'diseconomies of scale' — this is where the average cost per unit increases as the firm's output rises.
- Give examples of how diseconomies of scale can arise, e.g. 'Larger firms whose output has grown can suffer from increases in wastage and loss, as materials may seem in plentiful supply', or 'As a firm grows and its output increases, communication between workers may become less efficient.'

Page 42 — The Revenue of a Firm

1 Maximum of 4 marks available. HINTS:
- Start by defining a price-making firm — i.e. it's a firm that has enough market power to set the price they sell their goods at.
- Then explain that even for a price-making firm, the higher it sets the price, the lower demand will be, so its demand curve will slope downwards.

Page 43 — The Objectives of Firms

1 Maximum of 10 marks available. HINTS:
- Start by explaining that the traditional theory of the firm assumes that firms aim to maximise profit, but state that there are also other objectives that many firms try to achieve.
- You'll need to then describe some other objectives that are commonly pursued by firms and give possible reasons why — e.g. 'Firms may choose to maximise sales or revenue rather than profit, perhaps to increase their market share. However, pursuing any of these objectives will reduce profit, at least in the short term.'
- You could also go on to talk about objectives of firms that aren't directly related to profit, revenue or sales. E.g. 'Some firms may choose to operate in a way that benefits society. For example, they might choose to use local suppliers to support the local economy.'
- You could explain that even if a firm is prioritising an objective other than profit maximisation in the short term, this may in fact be a way to maximise profit in the long term — e.g. 'A new firm may be aiming to increase output as quickly as possible in the short run. Although this means sacrificing profit in the short run, this may allow the firm to maximise profits in the longer term.'
- Similarly, a firm's objective in the short run might just be to survive. The aim of profit maximisation may become important only once the firm is established in a market.

Page 45 — Perfect Competition

1 Maximum of 4 marks available. HINTS:
- Start by explaining product differentiation, e.g. 'Product differentiation is about firms making their products stand out from those of competing firms. For example, by making them easier to use, or of better quality.'
- Then talk about how this can influence the structure of a market, e.g. 'If one firm can differentiate its product from its competitors' this may mean that that firm gets a larger share of the market, and could gain monopoly power. This means it would be more likely for the market to be dominated by a small number of firms, and the market structure would be closer to a pure monopoly than perfect competition.'
- You could round off by saying that if it's difficult to make improvements to a product, it might be more difficult for firms to differentiate their products, and the market might be more competitive.

Page 47 — Monopolies

1 Maximum of 8 marks available. HINTS:
- This is a question about barriers to entry. Start by defining what a barrier to entry is, e.g. 'an obstacle that makes it impossible or unattractive for a new firm to enter into a market'.
- Explain some barriers to entry that might make it difficult to enter a market that already contains a firm with a monopoly.
- Examples include: the new firm may have higher costs than the monopoly firm, which can exploit economies of scale; the existing monopoly firm may have an established brand to which many consumers are loyal, which might mean that consumers are not willing to buy from a new firm with an unestablished brand; legislation may be in place to protect the monopoly firm, which prevents the new firm entering the market; and the market may have high start-up costs which might put off a new firm as these costs may be unrecoverable if the firm fails.

Answers

Section Four— Market Failure

Page 49 — Externalities — Social Cost and Benefit

1 Maximum of 6 marks available. HINTS:
- The question asks for a diagram so you must include one:

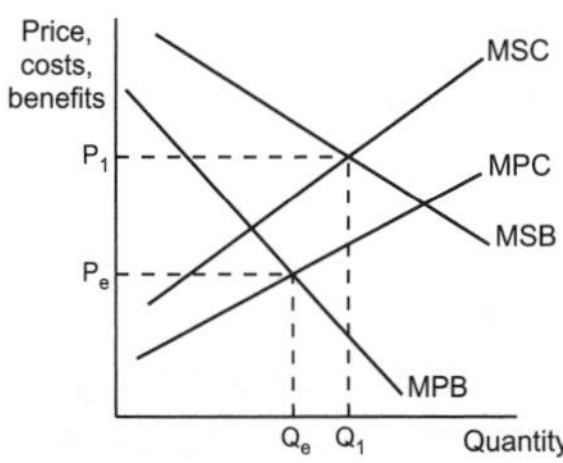

- Explain why the MPC curve can be seen as the supply curve and the MPB curve can be seen as the demand curve. Then you can say that this means equilibrium occurs where MPC = MPB and refer to the diagram, saying this is at price P_e and output Q_e.
- Say that this isn't the socially optimum level, e.g. 'This is not the socially optimal level of output — this occurs when the external costs and benefits to society have been included, which is where MSC = MSB.'
- Again, refer to the diagram by saying that this means the socially optimal price is P_1 and the socially optimal level of output is Q_1.

Page 51 — Externalities — Social Cost and Benefit

1 Maximum of 12 marks available. HINTS:
- Draw a diagram showing positive consumption externalities like the one below:

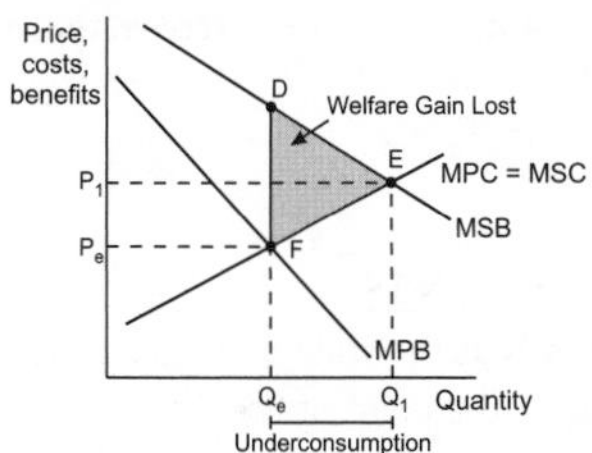

- To get all of the marks for this question you need to explain what your diagram shows. Make sure you correctly label the curves and axes.
- Explain how the consumption of education has a higher MSB than MPB and how, if it's left to the market, education will be consumed at a level below the socially optimal point (where MSC = MSB).
- Talk about how the free market level of production causes the loss of a potential welfare gain (you need to make it clear where this is on your diagram).

2 Maximum of 12 marks available. HINTS:
- Draw a diagram showing negative consumption externalities like the one below:

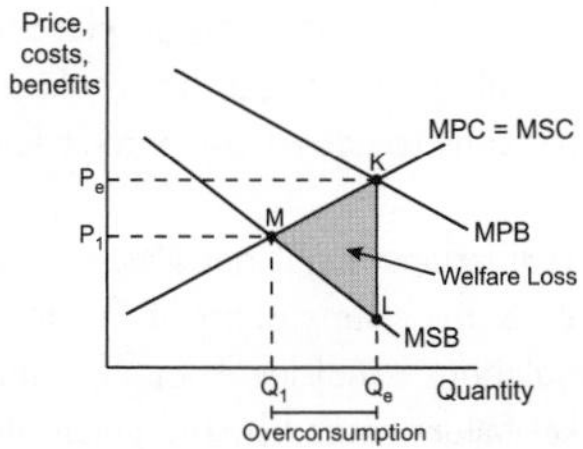

- To get all of the marks for this question you need to explain what your diagram shows. Make sure you correctly label the curves and axes.
- Explain how the consumption of cigarettes has a higher MPB than MSB and how, if it's left to the market, cigarettes will be consumed at a level above the socially optimal point (where MSC = MSB).
- Talk about how the free market level of production causes the welfare loss (you need to make it clear where this is on your diagram).

Page 52 — Externalities — Demand and Supply

1 Maximum of 9 marks available. HINTS:
- Draw a diagram showing positive production externalities like the one below:

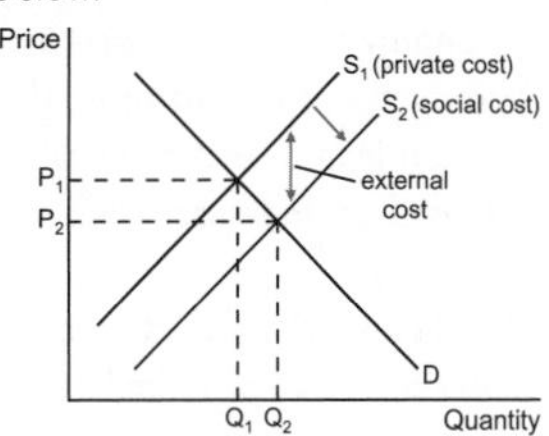

- To get all of the marks for this question you need to explain what your diagram shows. Make sure you correctly label the curves and axes.
- Explain that goods that generate positive production externalities have a higher private cost of production than social cost. In the free market these externalities are ignored, which means that the good is underproduced.
- Don't forget to explain why the supply curve shifts, e.g. 'if the reduction in external cost was taken into account then the supply curve would shift right from S_1 to S_2, and output would increase from Q_1 to Q_2'.
- You could include an example of a good with positive production externalities if it helps your explanation.

Page 54 — Merit and Demerit Goods

1 Maximum of 3 marks available. HINTS:
- Start off by saying that a merit good is considered to be beneficial to society, e.g. 'Merit goods are goods which have greater social benefits than private benefits.'
- Go on to mention that the consumption/production of merit goods generates positive externalities.
- You could also mention that merit goods tend to be underconsumed/underproduced in the free market, e.g. 'because the positive externalities of merit goods are ignored in the free market, they tend to be underconsumed'.

Page 56 — Imperfect Information

1 Maximum of 4 marks available. HINTS:
- Define what imperfect information is, e.g. 'Imperfect information is when buyers and/or sellers have incomplete knowledge of the price, costs, benefits and availability of products.'
- Give a couple of examples where this imperfect information causes market failure and the overprovision of demerit goods. For example, provision of alcohol, cigarettes and unhealthy foods.

Page 57 — Inequity

1 Maximum of 4 marks available. HINTS:
- Describe what is meant by market failure, e.g. 'Market failure occurs when the price mechanism fails to allocate scarce resources in a suitable way.'
- Then you need to explain how income and wealth inequality can be seen as market failure. Make sure you mention that this is normative market failure — it's based on opinion. E.g. 'Inequality in the distribution of income and wealth is a normative example of market failure. This is because it's the opinion of some economists that this kind of inequality is unfair (i.e. where the free market distributes income and wealth in a way that means that some people cannot afford to pay for what they need), so is a misallocation of resources. They argue that income and wealth should be redistributed for the benefit of society.'

Answers

Page 58 — Immobile Factors of Production

1 Maximum of 4 marks available. HINTS:
- Give a definition of what an immobile factor of production is, e.g. a factor of production which cannot be moved from one location to another or from one part of the economy to another, such as land.
- Explain why immobile factors of production can lead to market failure. E.g. immobile factors of production can lead to inefficient allocation of resources (resources are often unused or underused), which means there's market failure.
- Give an example of where immobile factors of production can cause market failure. For example, a jobseeker may not be able to afford to move to a different area to get a job — this is an example of geographical labour immobility.

Page 59 — Market Failure in Monopolies

1 Maximum of 8 marks available. HINTS:
- It's a good idea to start by explaining what market failure is, e.g. 'Market failure occurs when the price mechanism fails to allocate scarce resources efficiently.'
- Then you'll need to draw a diagram to show how monopoly firms can restrict output and cause an inefficient allocation of resources.

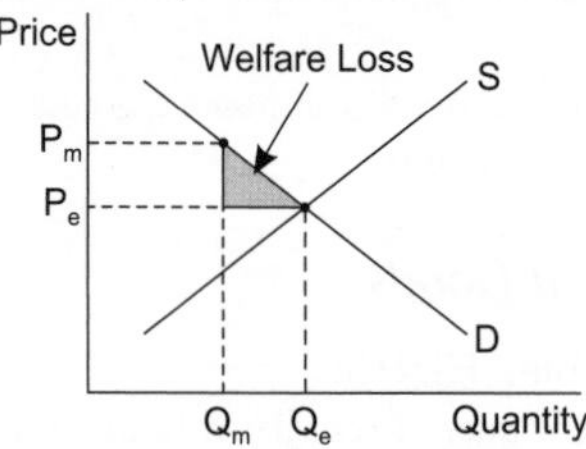

- To get all of the marks for this question you need to explain what your diagram shows, and correctly label the curves and axes.
- Explain that a monopoly is a price maker, which means that it can restrict supply (to Q_m) to get a higher price (P_m), leading to a welfare loss to society.

Section Five — Government Intervention

Page 61 — Taxation

1 Maximum of 1 mark available. HINTS:
- The correct answer is D. This is because the tax causes the supply curve to shift left to S_1. The tax revenue is equal to the difference in price (= 25 – 15 = £10) at the new level of demand multiplied by the new equilibrium quantity (80), so the tax revenue is £800.

Page 62 — Subsidies

1 Maximum of 1 mark available. HINTS:
- The correct answer is C. This is because the area ACFJ is equal to the difference between A and C (this takes into account the producer and consumer gain) multiplied by the quantity demanded when the subsidy is in place (equal to A to J). So ACFJ is the total cost of the subsidy to the government.

Page 63 — Price Controls

1 Maximum of 8 marks available. HINTS:
- Draw a diagram that shows the setting of a maximum price (P_m) like the one below.

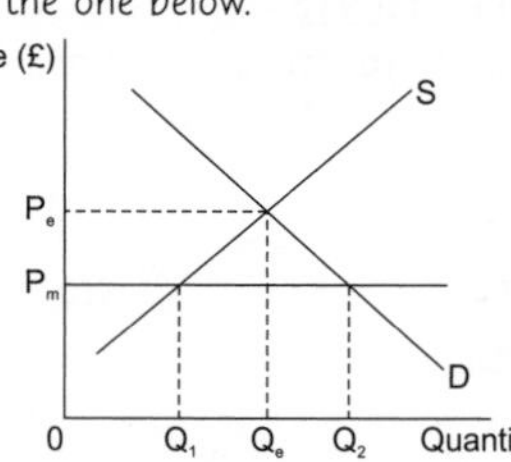

- Your diagram should have correctly labelled axes and clearly show a maximum price that's below the equilibrium price (e.g. in the diagram above P_m is below P_e).
- Give a complete explanation of what is shown on your diagram. Mention the equilibrium price and quantity and refer to the maximum price that has been set. You need to talk about the excess demand at the maximum price and indicate where this is shown on your diagram (i.e. Q_1 to Q_2 on the diagram above).

Page 64 — Buffer Stocks

1 Maximum of 1 mark available. HINTS:
- The correct answer is B. This is the correct answer because farmers would be paid the minimum price (P_2) when supply is at S_1.
- Option A is incorrect as this is the price that would be received by farmers if there was no buffer stock scheme in place.
- Option C is incorrect as this is the price farmers would receive for the level of supply shown by S rather than S_1.
- Option D is incorrect because farmers would not receive this price for the level of supply shown by S_1.

Page 65 — State Provision

1 Maximum of 6 marks available. HINTS:
- Start your answer by explaining that the state provision of health care means that it's likely to be free at the point of use.
- There are several disadvantages that you could go on to explain. These include: state provision can mean there's less of an incentive to operate efficiently due to a lack of the price mechanism; state-provided health care may fail to respond to consumers' demands as there is no profit motive to determine the services offered; self-reliance of patients may be reduced if they know the service is there if they need it; and free health care can lead to excess demand and this can lead to long waiting lists for consumers.

Page 66 — Regulation

1 Maximum of 4 marks available. HINTS:
- Start by talking about how regulations could be used to penalise firms that pollute excessively, e.g. 'Regulations could be put in place to limit the amount of pollution a firm could produce and they could be fined if they exceed this amount. This aims to correct the market failure of excess pollution.'
- You also need to explore why regulations might not always result in the correction of market failure. Some examples are: if the acceptable level of pollution set by the regulations is not low enough, it might not effectively correct the market failure caused by the pollution; if the punishment for breaking the regulation isn't large enough, it might not act as an effective deterrent meaning the firms don't change their behaviour; excessive regulation may encourage firms to move elsewhere, which could be bad for the economy; and the monitoring involved in regulations (e.g. measuring pollution levels) can be an expensive burden for governments.

Answers

- You need to make sure you discuss a couple of points in a bit of detail (but not too much, it's only a 4 mark question) and relate them back to the pollution example given in the question.

Page 67 — Information Provision and Pollution Permits

1 Maximum of 15 marks available. HINTS:
- Briefly explain what tradable pollution permits are and how they work, e.g. 'Tradable pollution permits are a way of controlling pollution by putting a cap on it, and using the market mechanism to internalise the externality of pollution. The government sets an optimal level of pollution and allocates permits that allow firms to emit a certain amount of pollution over a period of time. Firms can trade their permits with other firms and over time the number of permits will be reduced. This will create a market that assigns a cost to firms' pollution and creates incentives for firms to reduce their pollution.'
- You need to consider the advantages of using tradable pollution permits to reduce greenhouse gas emissions, such as the fact that they reward firms who cause low levels of pollution and they raise revenue for the government which could be used for other schemes to reduce greenhouse gas emissions. You also need to write about some disadvantages, such as the fact that it's difficult to set the optimal level of pollution and that the scheme has administrative costs for both firms and governments.
- A strong answer will also consider other possible schemes to reduce greenhouse gas emissions, with some evaluation of their effectiveness compared to using tradable pollution permits. For example, 'A government could impose a tax on petrol to discourage the overuse of cars and lorries and so reduce greenhouse gas emissions. This kind of tax will also internalise the externality of pollution from road transport and raise revenue for the government to use for other schemes to reduce greenhouse gas emissions. However, using taxation has problems, for example, it's difficult to put a value on the cost of pollution and set the right level of tax.'
- Finish off with some evaluation of whether you think tradable pollution permits are effective or not, e.g. 'I think tradable pollution permits are an effective way of reducing greenhouse gas emissions as they create strong incentives for firms to reduce pollution. However, their success is dependent on the government setting a level of pollution that is appropriate, otherwise the system won't work.'

Page 69 — Government Failure

1 Maximum of 1 mark available. HINTS:
- The correct answer is C. This is because the high cost involved in implementing the ban is an example of government failure.
- Options B and D are incorrect as they contribute to correcting the market failure associated with the banned substance.
- Option A is incorrect as the boosted opinion of the government hasn't contributed to a government failure.

2 Maximum of 6 marks available. HINTS:
- For this question you need to think about the effects the intervention would have and whether this actually addresses the market failure surrounding cigarette consumption.
- You should talk about how the desired impact of this intervention is to reduce demand for cigarettes and the negative externalities linked to their consumption (e.g. health problems).
- You also need to talk about the likely impact of the neighbouring country having cigarettes at a lower price, e.g. that people may purchase cigarettes from the neighbouring country to avoid the tax, and the consumption of cigarettes may not decrease as the government intended — this would be a government failure.

Page 71 — Examples of Government Failure

1 Maximum of 4 marks available. HINTS:
- There are several different advantages you can talk about for this question. If you think about the problems associated with farm subsidies, there are several of these that would be eased if the size of payments were reduced.
- For example, reducing farm subsides could: reduce the oversupply of agricultural products and save money for governments if they have to store excess produce; and reduce the cost to the taxpayer.

2 Maximum of 10 marks available. HINTS:
- For this question you need to give arguments for and against road pricing.
- Arguments for a road pricing scheme include: a scheme could reduce the external costs linked to congestion (e.g. increased journey times) and the pollution (e.g. air and noise) it creates; revenue generated by the scheme can be used to contribute to projects that benefit society; and a reduction in health problems linked to traffic emissions inside the area covered by the scheme.
- Arguments against a road pricing scheme include: businesses inside a road pricing area may experience reduced trade because of the scheme; congestion may simply be shifted to areas not covered by the scheme — i.e. the road pricing may not actually reduce the external costs it aims to, just change their location; there may be underutilisation of road space in the road pricing area; schemes have an unfairly large impact on poor motorists; if the road pricing charge is too low then it might not have much impact on congestion levels.
- Include a brief evaluation of what you think about implementing a road pricing scheme to finish off your answer. It doesn't matter whether you're for or against — you just need to back up what you say.

Section Six — Measuring Economic Performance

Page 73 — Measuring Economic Growth

1 Maximum of 2 marks available. HINTS:
- Show the steps of your calculation:

$$\text{percentage change} = \frac{\text{change in GDP}}{\text{original GDP}} \times 100$$
$$= \frac{£831 - £802}{£802} \times 100$$
$$= \frac{£29}{£802} \times 100 = 3.6\% \text{ (1 d.p.)}$$

Page 75 — Measuring Inflation

1 Maximum of 6 marks available. HINTS:
- Start your answer by defining inflation, e.g. 'Inflation is the sustained rise in the average price of goods and services over a period of time.'
- Explain what the RPI is, e.g. 'The RPI is a measure of inflation calculated using two surveys — the Living Costs and Food Survey, which looks at what people spend their money on, and a survey of the prices of the most commonly used goods and services.'
- Then give a limitation of the RPI, e.g. 'The information given by people responding to the Living Costs and Food Survey can be inaccurate.'
- The question asks for two more limitations of the RPI as a measure of inflation. You could mention that certain households are excluded from the RPI, and discuss the fact that the basket of goods only changes once a year,
so short-term changes are often missed.

Answers

Page 77 — Measuring the Balance of Payments

1 Maximum of 4 marks available. HINTS:

- State that one measure is the claimant count.
- Give one advantage and one disadvantage of the claimant count, e.g. 'The claimant count is the number of people who are claiming JSA, so it's easy to obtain the data. However, unemployed people who either choose not to claim JSA, or aren't eligible to claim it, aren't included in the claimant count.'
- State that the other measure is the Labour Force Survey.
- Give one advantage and one disadvantage of the Labour Force Survey, e.g. 'The Labour Force Survey is an internationally agreed measure for unemployment, so it's easy to use it to make comparisons with other countries. However, it's expensive to collect and compile the data.'

2 Maximum of 4 marks available. HINTS:

- Give a definition of the balance of payments, e.g. 'The balance of payments records flows of money in and out of a country.'
- Explain that if the flow of money into a country exceeds the flow of money out of that country, it will have a balance of payments surplus.
- Then say that if the flow of money out of a country exceeds the flow of money into that country, it will have a balance of payments deficit.

Section Seven — Aggregate Demand and Aggregate Supply

Page 79 — The Circular Flow of Income

1 Maximum of 6 marks available. HINTS:

- Start by defining the multiplier effect, e.g. 'The multiplier effect is the process by which an injection into the circular flow of income creates a change in the size of national income that's greater than the size of the initial injection.'
- Then explain that an increase in government spending on the NHS will represent an injection into the circular flow of income, and how this extra money will go around the circular flow of income in the form of increased expenditure and income.
- Finally, explain that the size of the multiplier will depend on the size of leakages from the circular flow of income. So if a lot of money leaks out of the circular flow then the size of the multiplier will be quite small.

Page 81 — The Components of Aggregate Demand

1 Maximum of 6 marks available. HINTS:

- Describe what is meant by consumption, e.g. 'Consumption is the total amount spent by households on goods and services.'
- Then, explain how high taxes affect consumption, e.g. 'High direct taxes (such as income tax) will reduce the amount of disposable income available to consumers, and high indirect taxes will increase the cost of spending. This means that high taxes are likely to lead to a fall in consumption.'
- And then explain how high interest rates affect consumption, e.g. 'High interest rates increase the cost of borrowing, which means that it's more expensive for consumers to borrow money to spend, and they make it more attractive for people to save their money. High interest rates may also reduce the amount consumers have to spend, as loan repayments and mortgages will become more expensive. As a result, high interest rates are likely to lead to a fall in consumption.'

2 Maximum of 6 marks available. HINTS:

- Identify three things that will have an effect on investment, such as risk, business confidence and interest rates, and say what effect they will have.
- The question asks you to describe three factors, so you don't need to provide too much detail.
- Risk — if there is a high risk that an investment will not benefit a firm then it is less likely to invest.
- Business confidence — if business confidence is high and a firm is doing well, then it is more likely to invest.
- Interest rates — if interest rates are high then investment is likely to be reduced because the cost of borrowing to invest is higher.

Page 83 — The Components of Aggregate Demand

1 Maximum of 1 mark available. HINTS:

- The correct answer is C.
- C is correct because both policies will increase aggregate demand. Government spending is a component of aggregate demand, so an increase in government spending will increase aggregate demand. A decrease in taxes will increase people's disposable income, so consumption (another component of aggregate demand) is likely to increase, which means aggregate demand will increase.
- A, B and D are incorrect. Option B will cause aggregate demand to fall, and options A and D may result in a slight rise in aggregate demand, but they're less likely to lead to an increase in aggregate demand than option C.

2 Maximum of 10 marks available. HINTS:

- Start by defining exports, e.g. 'Exports are goods or services that are produced in one country and then sold in another.'
- Then, identify two things that could increase the demand for a country's exports, such as changes to the exchange rate or non-price factors.
- The question asks you to explain two factors, so you'll be expected to give some reasons to support your answers.
- Explain how the exchange rate may affect the demand for a country's exports, and remember to consider the price elasticity of demand — e.g. 'A fall in the value of a country's currency will reduce the price of its exports, so they'll be cheaper for other countries to buy and demand for them will increase. However, the level of an increase in demand will depend on the price elasticity of demand. For example, demand can be price inelastic in the short run, so if the UK's exchange rate fell, there may be a time lag before countries switch to buying exports from the UK instead of from another country. This means that in the short run, demand for a country's exports might not increase, or increase by much.'
- Then go on to talk about the second factor, non-price factors — e.g. 'An improvement in the quality of a country's goods may increase demand for that country's exports, as people are often willing to pay more for good quality products. The level of the increase in demand may depend on who the country exports to — for example, demand for exports might be low if that country's main trading partners are quite poor or suffering from a recession.'

Answers

Page 85 — Aggregate Demand Analysis

1 Maximum of 10 marks available. HINTS:
- Give a definition of the multiplier effect.
- Use the multiplier effect to explain how an increase in government spending, e.g. on roads, hospitals and schools, would be likely to lead to a bigger increase in aggregate demand in general.
- Draw a diagram to show how an increase in government spending will cause the aggregate demand curve to shift to the right.
- Point out that the size of the increase in aggregate demand (and, therefore, the size of the shift to the right of the aggregate demand curve) depends on the size of the multiplier effect.
- Explain that the size of the multiplier depends on the size of the leakages from the circular flow of income, e.g. 'If the leakages in the circular flow are small then the multiplier will be big and cause a large shift to the right of the aggregate demand curve.'

Page 87 — Aggregate Demand Analysis

1 Maximum of 4 marks available. HINTS:
- First find MPW using the formula MPW = MPS + MPT + MPM. MPW = 0.3 + 0.4 + 0.1 = 0.8.
- Use the value of MPW to find the multiplier. Multiplier = 1 ÷ MPW = 1 ÷ 0.8 = 1.25
- Now you can use the definition of the multiplier to find the total rise in GDP.
  Total rise in national income = injection × multiplier
  = £100m × 1.25 = £125m

Page 89 — Aggregate Supply

1 Maximum of 1 mark available. HINTS:
- The correct answer is B.
- B is correct because the discovery of a new raw material would increase the factors of production that are available to an economy. If there are more factors of production available, in this case a new raw material, then the capacity of the economy will increase and the LRAS curve will shift to the right.
- Options A, C and D are more likely to affect the aggregate demand curve or the short run aggregate supply curve as they will change the costs of production. None of these options will increase the capacity of the economy.

Page 91 — Macroeconomic Equilibrium

1 Maximum of 8 marks available. HINTS:
- Draw a diagram to show a shift to the right of the short run aggregate supply curve.
- Your diagram should look like the one shown below.

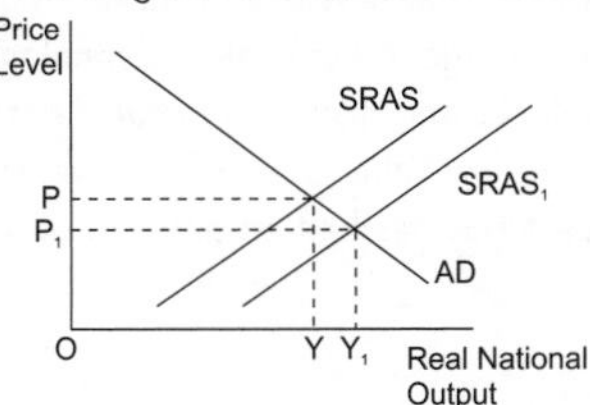

- Referring to your diagram, explain how a shift to the right of the aggregate supply curve (from SRAS to $SRAS_1$) means that output will increase (from Y to Y_1) and the price level will fall (from P to P_1). You should also point out that an increase in output will mean that unemployment will fall because labour is a derived demand. If more is being produced then the demand for labour will increase.
- You should also mention that a fall in the price level will make a country's exports cheaper, so exports will increase and there will be an increase in a balance of payments surplus or a reduction in a balance of payments deficit.

Section Eight — Government Economic Policy Objectives

Page 96 — Economic Growth

1 Maximum of 8 marks available. HINTS:
- You could start by explaining what's meant by an improvement in the standard of living, e.g. 'The standard of living in a country includes many things, such as the level of wealth and access to necessary goods and services. An improvement in the standard of living will occur when there's an improvement in people's economic welfare. This might be the result of increased wages, or improvements in the services that people use.'
- Then you should give at least two reasons why economic growth might improve standards of living, e.g. 'Economic growth means that output is rising, which will lead to an increase in jobs, causing a fall in unemployment, and a rise in wages. If more people are employed and have higher wages, then their standard of living will improve.' You could go on, for example, to mention how economic growth might lead to investment in cleaner, more efficient production processes — this will reduce pollution that harms the environment, and therefore improve living standards, e.g. if the air is cleaner, this may improve people's health.
- Balance your answer by considering how economic growth might not improve the standard of living, e.g. 'Short run economic growth can lead to inflation, and higher prices may mean that some people's standard of living will decrease, even when there's economic growth.'

Page 97 — Economic Stability

1 Maximum of 4 marks available. HINTS:
- Start by explaining what sustainable economic growth is, e.g. 'Sustainable economic growth means achieving economic growth now and in the future that won't cause problems for future generations.'
- Then describe two things a country must do to achieve this — for example, you could talk about the need to find a continuous supply of raw materials, such as land and labour, so that production can continue into the future. You might also mention that a country would need to reduce negative externalities, such as pollution, to a level where they don't hamper production or lead to problems in the future.

Page 99 — Unemployment

1 Maximum of 8 marks available. HINTS:
- First state what unemployment may mean for an economy, e.g. 'Unemployment means that an economy isn't operating at its full capacity, as there's wasted labour that isn't being used. As a result, there may also be other resources that are not being exploited, such as offices and machines.'
- Then explain how this will impact upon economic growth, e.g. 'A country's economic growth may be harmed if there's high unemployment because fewer people will have income to spend, which may mean that firms' profits and output will fall. However, a government might respond by increasing its spending on unemployment benefits, so spending might not decrease by a large amount.' You could go on to talk about how it's hard for people who are unemployed for long periods of time to get a job (because their skills become outdated), and how this might affect economic growth.

Answers

Page 101 — Inflation

1 Maximum of 12 marks available. HINTS:

- Start by giving a definition of inflation, e.g. 'Inflation is the sustained rise in the average price of goods and services over a period of time.'
- Give examples of the harm high inflation can cause, e.g. 'High inflation can reduce people's standards of living, especially those on fixed incomes. Prices are rising, but their incomes remain the same, so the real value of their money falls.'
- Discuss the potential advantages of keeping the rate of inflation low, e.g. 'If a country's inflation rate is below the inflation rate in its competitor countries, it's likely to become more price competitive.'
- Try to provide a thorough analysis of the positives and negatives, showing that you've considered the likely importance of each.
- You should also mention the difference between cost-push and demand-pull inflation. Demand-pull inflation tends to be less harmful, as it's caused by a rise in demand, whereas cost-push inflation is caused by an increase in the costs of production.
- Explain that deflation is a bad thing, and describe the effects it can have on the economy.
- Make a strong conclusion to your evaluation, explaining that a rate of 2% is considered desirable as some inflation is better than no (or negative) inflation, but that high inflation tends to be harmful.
- There are 12 marks for this question — make sure you provide enough examples and explanations.

Page 103 — The Balance of Payments

1 Maximum of 8 marks available. HINTS:

- Give a definition of the balance of payments, e.g. 'The balance of payments measures international flows of money. It measures flows of money out of a country, e.g. to pay for imports, and flows of money into a country, e.g. from the sale of exports.'
- Define the four sections of the current account, and state whether the UK has a deficit or a surplus in each (as well as their relative sizes — i.e. large or small).
- Discuss the likely reasons for the UK importing more visible goods than it exports, such as high levels of consumer spending, a lack of price competitiveness and, until more recent years, the high value of the pound.

Page 105 — The Balance of Payments

1 Maximum of 15 marks available. HINTS:

- You should start by explaining the possible negative effects of a rise in the value of the Chinese renminbi, e.g. 'A significant rise in the value of the Chinese renminbi is likely to cause a very large increase in the US's current account deficit on its balance of payments, at least in the short term, because it imports a lot of goods from China.' You could go on to mention how a rise in the value of the renminbi may also cause prices to rise in the US because it imports a lot of goods from China.
- You should then explain how the rise in the value of the Chinese renminbi might have a positive effect. For example, if demand was price elastic, then US consumers might stop buying so many Chinese imports and they may switch to buying domestic products. This would improve the US's current account deficit.
- Conclude your answer by stating what you think is most likely to happen — e.g. 'A rise in the value of the Chinese renminbi may not benefit the US balance of payments current account deficit if domestic products aren't suitable substitutes for Chinese imports or if domestic products are still more expensive than imports from China. Both of these factors would mean that the US current account deficit would worsen.'

Page 109 — Conflicts Between Economic Objectives

1 Maximum of 12 marks available. HINTS:

- Start by explaining what the four main macroeconomic objectives are, i.e. strong economic growth, reducing unemployment, low inflation and equilibrium in the balance of payments.
- Then describe how these four objectives can be achieved by an increase in a country's aggregate supply (or long run aggregate supply) — use a diagram to show this:

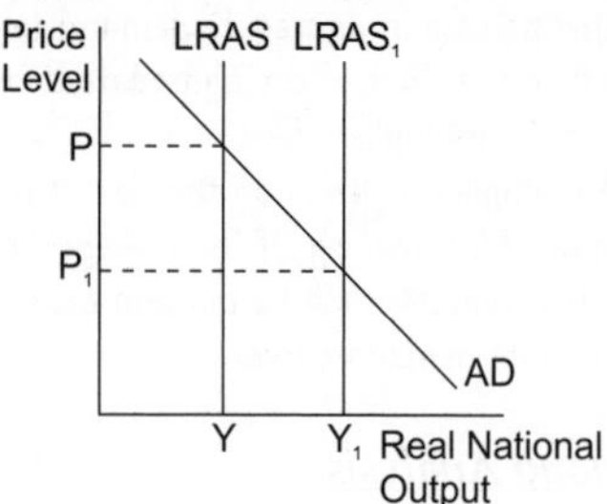

- You must explain what the diagram shows, e.g. 'If aggregate supply is increased so that the LRAS curve shifts to the right (from LRAS to $LRAS_1$)then this will achieve an increase in output (from Y to Y_1). This increase in output is economic growth, which will lead to a reduction in unemployment. In addition, the price level will fall (from P to P_1), so inflation will be controlled. This will also improve the country's competitiveness — so the balance of payments will improve.'
- You should give some examples of how a government could achieve this kind of increase in aggregate supply (i.e. long run economic growth), e.g. 'To shift the LRAS curve to the right a government would need to stimulate an increase in the quantity and quality of the factors of production. For example, it could encourage immigration in order to increase the country's workforce.'

Page 112 — Trade

1 Maximum of 6 marks available. HINTS:

- Define what is meant by comparative advantage, e.g. 'A country has a comparative advantage in the production of a good if the opportunity cost of it producing that good is lower than the opportunity cost for other countries.'
- Explain what effect this has had on the pattern of global trade — you can start off by talking about comparative advantage 100 years ago, e.g. 'A hundred years ago, developed countries, such as the UK and the USA, had a comparative advantage in manufactured goods, and developing countries, such as India, had a comparative advantage in primary goods, e.g. commodities. This meant that most trade took place between developing and developed countries.'
- You can then go on to explain how comparative advantage has changed over time — for example, that developed countries now tend to have a comparative advantage in high value, technologically advanced capital-intensive products, and developing countries tend to have a comparative advantage in low value, labour-intensive products. You'll need to explain the impact this has had on patterns of global trade.

Page 113 — Exchange Rates

1 Maximum of 1 mark available. HINTS:

- The correct answer is C — a managed floating exchange rate is mainly left to market forces, but occasionally a government will intervene to influence the exchange rate.
- A is incorrect because a pegged exchange rate system means the value of the currency is pegged to another currency or group of currencies — it isn't left to float freely.
- B is incorrect because a semi-fixed exchange rate is allowed to fluctuate within a certain band of exchange rates — so again, this type of exchange rate isn't left to float freely.

Answers

- D is incorrect because a fixed exchange rate is set at a target rate, so isn't allowed to float freely at all.

Page 115 — Exchange Rates

1 Maximum of 4 marks available. HINTS:
- Describe the likely effect on demand for a currency of a country hosting a major sporting event — e.g. 'A major sporting event, such as the Olympics, can attract tens, or even hundreds, of thousands of visitors to a country. These visitors will require the domestic currency, e.g. to pay for tickets, hotels and transport, so demand for the currency will increase.'
- Explain what effect this will have on the exchange rate — e.g. 'An increase in demand for a currency will cause its value to rise.' You can use a diagram like the one below to show how the value of the currency (e.g. the pound) rises as demand increases — make sure you refer to your diagram in your answer.

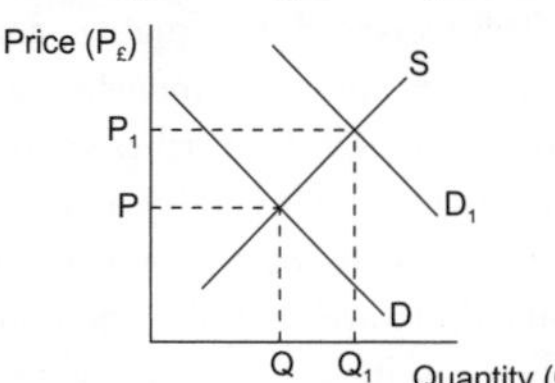

Page 117 — International Competitiveness

1 Maximum of 2 marks available. HINTS:
- The question asks for two factors, so you need to clearly state two different factors that will influence a country's competitiveness.
- There are a number of things you could mention — for example, productivity, real exchange rates, wage costs and non-wage costs, and research and development.

Section Nine — Macroeconomic Policy Instruments

Page 121 — Fiscal Policy

1 Maximum of 1 mark available. HINTS:
- The answer is C.
- A is unlikely because during a boom phase government is unlikely to stimulate the economy further with loose fiscal policy (i.e. by boosting aggregate demand).
- B is not particularly likely because in the long term a country is less likely to have loose fiscal policy, which involves running a budget deficit (with government spending exceeding revenue), when it has a large national debt.
- D can't be correct because loose fiscal policy means government is boosting aggregate demand, whereas a neutral budget position means government spending and taxation has no net effect on aggregate demand.
- C is the most likely because when there's a negative output gap government is more likely to use loose (expansionary) fiscal policy to boost the economy.

2 Maximum of 3 marks available. HINTS:
- Give a definition of progressive taxation, e.g. 'Progressive taxation follows the 'ability to pay' principle. Progressive taxation means that the amount of tax an individual pays, as a percentage of their income, rises as their income rises.
- You'll need to fully and precisely explain the term to get all 3 marks.

3 Maximum of 12 marks available. HINTS:
- Start by defining fiscal rules, e.g. 'rules a government makes to control its spending and borrowing'.
- Then explain how fiscal rules might create economic stability.
- You could start by talking about the effect they have on governments, e.g. 'Fiscal rules can help achieve economic stability because they should help to prevent a government from continuously borrowing and overspending to promote growth, which increases national debt and inflation. If these get too high government may need to take action (such as raising interest rates or cutting spending). This can lead to instability as it may result in confidence in the economy falling.'
- Then go on to explain how they might affect firms and consumers, e.g. 'Fiscal rules can also influence the behaviour of businesses and consumers, by increasing confidence in future economic stability. If confidence is high then consumers will be more willing to spend and firms are likely to increase investment.'
- The question says evaluate, so you need to discuss how effective they're actually likely to be. You could talk about whether governments actually follow them, e.g. 'Fiscal rules are only likely to contribute to economic stability if people and firms believe they will be kept to. For example, there isn't agreement on whether the 'golden rule' set by the UK government in 1997 was kept to, before being abandoned in 2008.'
- You could mention the role of the OBR in helping the UK government to keep to any fiscal rules it has set itself.

Page 124 — Monetary Policy

1 Maximum of 4 marks available. HINTS:
- First describe what the MPC's targets are when setting the interest rate. E.g. 'The MPC sets interest in order to meet the inflation target that's set by the government. This target is currently 2% inflation.'
- Then give a bit more detail about how interest rates are set to meet this target. E.g. 'If the MPC believed inflation was likely to go more than 1% above the target it would increase the official rate of interest to reduce aggregate demand.'
- Finally, mention that this isn't their only aim, e.g. 'Controlling inflation is the main aim of the MPC, but when setting interest rates it must also consider the aims of promoting economic growth and reducing unemployment.'

Answers

Page 127 — Supply-side Policies

1 Maximum of 25 marks available. HINTS:

- For this question you'll need to look at the advantages and disadvantages of supply-side policies, and also think about what role demand-side policies should play in an economy. You could start by briefly describing the role of demand-side and supply-side policies, e.g. 'Demand-side policies are most useful for managing an economy in the short run, as they can be used to make small adjustments to its performance. Supply-side policies will increase an economy's productive capacity and improve efficiency, which will lead to long run improvements in the economy.'
- You could then talk about the advantages of supply-side policies, e.g. 'Successful supply-side policies are crucial to an economy's long-term growth. For example, policies that improve efficiency, such as privatisation and deregulation, will help a country's firms to increase production. This will improve the country's international competitiveness and its balance of payments.' You could go on to talk about other supply-side policies and their importance to a country's economy, such as those aimed at increasing flexibility in the labour market.
- It's important to also talk about the drawbacks of supply-side policies. For example, too much deregulation can cause unintended negative effects, such as excessive financial risk-taking.
- You should then discuss when demand-side policies might be more appropriate than supply-side policies, e.g. 'Demand-side policies are more appropriate for short-term management of the economy. For example, sharp rises in inflation can be tackled more effectively by using monetary policies, like raising interest rates, than with long-term supply-side approaches to improve efficiency. Demand-side policies are especially important during a recession when aggregate demand needs to be stimulated quickly in order to create economic growth and jobs. It might cause too much harm to an economy, in the short run, if a government uses supply-side policies to tackle the effects of a recession.'
- To develop this further you could consider how supply-side policies and demand-side policies could be used together for the benefit of an economy, e.g. 'Supply-side policies will create more supply in an economy, but to bring the maximum benefits to an economy, demand will also need to be stimulated to match that supply. For example, if supply-side policies were introduced to make the labour market more efficient, then this might lead to lower real wages for workers, unless aggregate demand was also increased (e.g. by providing tax breaks for firms that employ more workers).'
- Make sure you conclude your answer with a judgement that sums up your arguments, e.g. 'Supply-side policies are very important for a country's economy and a government should try to increase aggregate supply in order to help it achieve its macroeconomic objectives. However, demand-side policies shouldn't be ignored as they're useful for managing an economy, e.g. controlling inflation, and are an important tool during a recession. In addition, for supply-side policies to be more successful they need to be combined with demand-side policies to create demand for the new supply that's produced.'
- You'll get marks for any relevant diagrams you include — as long as they're correctly drawn and explained.

Page 129 — Different Approaches to Macroeconomic Policy

1 Maximum of 6 marks available. HINTS:

- Mention at least two differences in the policy response to the two recessions. For example: fiscal policy was contractionary during the Great Depression, but expansionary in the recession after the 2008 financial crisis; banks were allowed to fail during the Great Depression, but not in 2008; expansionary monetary policy was used after the 2008 financial crisis, but this wasn't an option during the early part of the Great Depression.
- You're asked to 'discuss', so give some explanation of why the response was different in each case, and what the effect of this was. E.g. 'During the Great Depression there was a widely held belief that the most important economic goal of government was to balance the budget (i.e. not to run a budget deficit). This meant that when government revenue fell and spending increased as the recession hit, the government introduced contractionary fiscal policy in order to try and balance the budget. This worsened the situation, and the economy stayed in recession until expansionary monetary policy was brought in. In contrast, after the 2008 financial crisis the government brought in expansionary fiscal policy to try and limit the effect of the shock. This helped to stimulate the economy in the short term by boosting aggregate demand. However, it also contributed to budget deficits during the recession, resulting in rapidly rising national debt.'

Glossary

absolute advantage A country will have an absolute advantage when its output of a product is greater per unit of resource used than any other country.

accelerator process This is where any change in demand for goods/services beyond current capacity will lead to a greater percentage increase in the demand for the capital goods that firms need to produce those goods/services.

aggregate demand The total demand, or total spending, in an economy at a given price level over a given period of time. It's made up of consumption, investment, government spending and net exports.
Aggregate Demand = C + I + G + (X – M)

aggregate supply The total amount of goods and services which can be supplied in an economy at a given price level over a given period of time.

aid The transfer of resources from one country to another.

allocative efficiency This is when the price of a good is equal to the price that consumers are happy to pay for it. This will happen when all resources are allocated efficiently.

asymmetric information This is when buyers have more information than sellers (or the opposite) in a market.

average cost The cost of production per unit of output — i.e. a firm's total cost for a given period of time, divided by the quantity produced.

average revenue The revenue per unit sold — i.e. a firm's total revenue for a given period of time, divided by the quantity sold.

balance of payments A record of a country's international transactions,
i.e. flows of money into and out of a country.

bank rate The official rate of interest set by the Monetary Policy Committee of the Bank of England.

barriers to entry Barriers to entry are any potential difficulties that make it hard for a firm to enter a market.

barriers to exit Barriers to exit are any potential difficulties that make it hard for a firm to leave a market.

black market Economic activity that occurs without taxation and government regulation. Also called the informal market.

budget deficit When government spending is greater than its revenue.

budget surplus When government spending is less than its revenue.

capital account on the balance of payments A part of the record of a country's international flows of money. This includes transfers of non-monetary and fixed assets, such as through emigration and immigration.

central bank The institution responsible for issuing a country's banknotes, acting as a lender of last resort for other banks, and implementing monetary policy (e.g. setting interest rates).

circular flow of income The flow of national output, income and expenditure between households and firms.
national output = national income = national expenditure

command economy An economy where governments, not markets, determine how to allocate resources.

comparative advantage A country has a comparative advantage if the opportunity cost of it producing a good is lower than the opportunity cost for other countries.

concentration ratio This shows how dominant firms are in a market, e.g. if three firms in a market have 90% market share then the three-firm concentration ratio is 90%.

consumer surplus When a consumer pays less for a good than they were prepared to, this difference is the consumer surplus.

consumption The purchase/use of goods or services.

cost-push inflation Inflation caused by the rising cost of inputs to production.

cross elasticity of demand (XED) This is a measure of how the quantity demanded of one good/service responds to a change in the price of another good/service.

current account on the balance of payments A part of the record of a country's international flows of money. It consists of: trade in goods, trade in services, international flows of income (salaries, interest, profit and dividends), and transfers.

cyclical unemployment Unemployment caused by a shortage of demand in an economy, e.g. when there's a slump.

demand-pull inflation Inflation caused by excessive growth in aggregate demand compared to aggregate supply.

demand-side policy Government policy that aims to increase aggregate demand in an economy. For example, a policy to increase consumer spending in an economy.

demerit good A good or service which has greater social costs when it's consumed than private costs. Demerit goods tend to be overconsumed.

deregulation Removing rules imposed by a government that can restrict the level of competition in a market.

derived demand The demand for a good or factor of production due to its use in making another good or providing a service.

developed countries Relatively rich, industrialised countries with a high GDP per capita.

developing countries Countries that rely on labour-intensive industries.
They have a relatively low GDP per capita.

diseconomies of scale A firm is experiencing diseconomies of scale when the average cost of production is rising as output rises.

disposable income Income, including welfare benefits, that is available for households to spend after income tax has been paid.

Glossary

dividend A share in a firm's profits that is given to the firm's shareholders.

economic cycle The economic cycle (also known as the business or trade cycle) is the fluctuations in actual growth over a period of time (several years or decades).

economic growth An increase in an economy's productive potential. Usually measured as the rate of change of the gross domestic product (GDP), or the GDP per capita.

economies of scale A firm is experiencing economies of scale when the average cost of production is falling as output rises.

emerging countries Countries which are not yet developed, but which are growing quickly and are further along the development process than other developing countries.

equilibrium A market for a product is in equilibrium when the quantity supplied is equal to the quantity demanded.

equity This means fairness.

exchange rate The price at which one currency buys another.

externalities The external costs or benefits to a third party that is not involved in the making, buying/selling and consumption of a specific good/service.

factors of production These are the four inputs needed to make the things that people want. They are: land, labour, capital and enterprise.

financial account on the balance of payments A part of the record of a country's international flows of money. This involves the movement of financial assets (e.g. through foreign direct investment).

fiscal policy Government policy that determines the levels of government spending and taxation. Often used to increase or decrease aggregate demand in an economy.

fixed costs Costs that don't vary with the level of output of a firm in the short run.

free market A market where there is no government intervention. Competition between different suppliers affects supply and demand, and as a result determines prices.

free rider problem This means that once a public good is provided it's impossible to stop someone from benefiting from it, even if they haven't paid towards it.

frictional unemployment The unemployment experienced by workers between leaving one job and starting another.

full employment The situation when everyone of working age who wants a job at the current wage rates can get one.

government failure This occurs when government intervention into a market causes a misallocation of resources.

gross domestic product (GDP) The total value of all the goods and services produced in a country in a year.

horizontal equity This means that people in identical circumstances are treated fairly (i.e. equally).

human capital The economic value of a person's skills.

imperfect information A situation where buyers and/or sellers don't have full knowledge regarding price, costs, benefits and availability of a good or service.

income Money that a firm or person receives for providing a good or service.

income elasticity of demand (YED) This is a measure of how the demand for a good/service responds to a change in real income.

inequity Another word for unfairness.

inflation The sustained rise in the average price of goods and services over a period of time.

infrastructure The basic facilities and services needed for a country and its economy to function.

interest The money paid to the lender by someone who borrows capital. This will often be a fixed percentage rate — known as an interest rate.

investment The purchase of capital, such as new machinery, in the hope that this will help generate an increased level of output. Investment can also mean buying shares from the stock market — this is done in the hope of making a future profit or receiving dividend payments.

labour immobility This occurs when labour can't easily move around to find jobs (geographical immobility) or easily switch between different occupations (occupational immobility).

long run A time period in which all the factors of production are variable, so a firm can expand its capacity.

long run aggregate supply (LRAS) In the long run it is assumed that, because factors and costs of production can change, an economy will run at full capacity — so LRAS is the productive potential of an economy.

macroeconomics This is the part of economics that looks at the economy as a whole. For example, trends in unemployment and economic growth.

marginal cost The cost to a firm of producing the final unit of output.

marginal propensity to consume The proportion of an increase in income that people will spend (and not save).

marginal tax rate The rate of tax you pay on any 'extra' money you receive.

marginal utility The benefit of consuming one extra unit of a good.

market failure This is where the price mechanism fails to allocate resources efficiently.

merit good A good or service which provides greater social benefits when it's consumed than private benefits. Merit goods tend to be underconsumed.

microeconomics This is the part of economics concerned with individual people, individual firms and individual markets. For example, it covers things like how changes in demand affects the price of a good in a market.

Glossary

monetary policy Government policy that involves controlling the total amount of 'money' in an economy (the money supply), and how expensive it is to borrow that money. It involves manipulating interest rates, exchange rates and restrictions on the supply of money.

monopoly A pure monopoly is a market with only one supplier. Some markets will be referred to as a monopoly if there's more than one supplier, but one supplier dominates the market.

monopoly power The ability of a firm to be a 'price maker' and influence the price of a particular good in a market.

multiplier effect The process by which an injection into the circular flow of income creates a change in the size of national income that's greater than the injection's size.

national debt The total debt that a country has run up over time.

National Minimum Wage (NMW) A legal minimum hourly rate of pay, set for different age groups. There's a national minimum wage in the UK.

national output All the goods and services produced in a country in a year.

natural monopoly An industry where economies of scale are so great that the lowest long run average cost can only be achieved if the market is made up of a single provider.

non-pure public good See quasi-public good.

opportunity cost The benefit that's given up in order to do something else — it's the cost of the choice that's made.

output gap The gap between the trend rate of economic growth and actual economic growth. Output gaps can be positive or negative.

per capita Another way to say 'per person'.

perfect information This is when buyers and sellers have full knowledge of prices, costs, benefits and availability of products.

Phillips curve (short run) A curve that shows the relationship between inflation and unemployment in the short run — as the level of one falls, the level of the other rises.

price elasticity of demand (PED) This is a measure of how the quantity demanded of a good/service responds to a change in its price.

price elasticity of supply (PES) This is a measure of how the quantity supplied of a good/service responds to a change in its price.

price maker A firm that has some power to control the price it sells at.

price mechanism This is when changes in the demand or supply of a good/service lead to changes in its price and the quantity bought/sold.

price taker A firm that has no power to control the price it sells at — it has to accept the market price.

privatisation When a firm or a whole industry changes from being run by the public sector to the private sector.

producer surplus When a producer receives more for a good than they were prepared to accept, this difference is the producer surplus.

production possibility frontier (PPF) A curve which shows the maximum possible outputs of two goods or services using a fixed amount of inputs.

productive efficiency This occurs when products are produced at a level of output where the average cost is lowest.

productivity The average output produced per unit of a factor of production — for example, labour productivity would be the average output per worker (or per worker-hour).

profit A firm's total revenue minus its total costs.

progressive taxation A tax system where an individual's tax rises (as a percentage of their income) as their income rises.

proportional taxation A tax system where everyone pays the same proportion of tax regardless of their income level.

public good A good which people can't be stopped from consuming, even if they've not paid for it, and the consumption of which doesn't prevent others from benefiting from it (e.g. national defence).

public sector The part of the economy that is owned or run by the government.

purchasing power parity (PPP) An adjustment of an exchange rate to reflect the real purchasing power of the two currencies.

quantitative easing (QE) This involves a central bank (e.g. the Bank of England) 'creating new money' and using it to buy assets owned by financial institutions and other firms. It increases the money supply, which will enable individuals and firms to spend more, or lend it to other people to spend.

quasi-public good A good which appears to have the characteristics of a public good, but doesn't exhibit them fully.

quota A limit on the amount of a good that is allowed to be used, produced or imported.

real income A measure of the amount of goods/services that a consumer can afford to purchase with their income, adjusted for inflation.

real wage unemployment Unemployment caused by real wages being pushed above the equilibrium level of employment. It can be caused by trade unions negotiating for higher wages, or the introduction of a national minimum wage.

recession This occurs when there's negative economic growth for at least two consecutive quarters. Typically there's falling demand, low levels of investment and rising unemployment during a recession.

Glossary

regressive taxation A tax system where an individual's tax falls (as a percentage of their income) as their income rises.

revenue The total value of sales within a time period. It can be calculated using the formula: price per unit × quantity sold.

seasonal unemployment Unemployment due to uneven economic activity during the year.

share A share represents a portion of a company's value — giving the share's owner a right to a portion of the company's profits.

shareholders Individuals (or firms) that own shares in a company.

short run A time period in which at least one of a firm's factors of production is fixed.

short run aggregate supply (SRAS) This is aggregate supply when the factors of production are fixed.

short run Phillips curve See Phillips curve (short run).

specialisation Specialisation means people or countries doing only the things they're best or most efficient at.

speculation When things are bought (e.g. shares) in the hope that they will increase in value and can be sold for a profit at a later date.

structural unemployment Unemployment (usually) caused by the decline of a major industry, which is made worse by labour immobility (geographical or occupational).

subsidy An amount of money paid by a government to the producer of a good/service to lower the cost of production. This should increase supply, which will lower the price and increase demand for the good/service.

supply-side policy Government policy that aims to increase aggregate supply in an economy. For example, a policy to increase the productive capacity of the economy.

sustainability This is about meeting the needs of people now, without making it more difficult for people in the future to meet their own needs.

tariff A form of tax placed on certain imports to make them more expensive and discourage their consumption.

tax An amount of money paid to a government. It's paid directly, e.g. income tax, or indirectly, e.g. excise duty.

terms of trade A measure of the relative price of a country's exports compared to its imports.

total cost All the costs for a firm involved in producing a particular amount of output.

total revenue The total amount of money a firm receives from its sales, in a particular time period.

trade union An organisation of workers that acts to represent their interests, e.g. to improve their pay.

unemployment The level of unemployment is the number of people who are looking for a job but cannot find one. The rate of unemployment is the number of people out of work (but looking for a job) as a percentage of the labour force.

utility The 'benefit' or 'well-being' gained from an action.

variable costs Costs that vary with the level of output of a firm.

vertical equity This means people with different circumstances are treated differently, but fairly.

wage rate The price of labour, i.e. the rate of pay to employ a worker.

wealth The value of somebody's assets.

Index

Index